Praise for Colin MacCabe's *Godard*

"Jean-Luc Godard is the single most important individual in the history of cinema from 1960 to . . . the ascension of Steven Spielberg . . . [*Godard*] is filled with a wealth of illuminating, even surprising, material."   —J. Hoberman, *Film Comment*

"Deserves the highest praise . . . [MacCabe] does a superb job at tracing the evolution of Godard's ideas . . . Excellent."
—David Thomson, *The Nation*

"Godard's importance in film history is indisputable . . . [He] emerges from this biography . . . as a character of intense, single-minded devotion to personal vision."
—Dana Polan, *Los Angeles Times Book Review*

"MacCabe's book . . . provide[s] a wonderful history of a wonderful period in cinema."   —Nagle Jackson, *The Times* (Trenton, N.J.)

"Illuminating . . . Approached as a provisional take on an intellectual, political, and aesthetic life . . . *Godard* is very satisfying."
—Annie Wagner, *The Stranger*

"A solid, beautiful-mind-vs.-the-Establishment valentine . . . MacCabe's Godard is cast squarely in the prestigious intellectual-pioneer spirit of *Freud*."   —Howard Hampton, *The Village Voice*

Colin MacCabe

godard

Colin MacCabe is Distinguished Professor of English and Film at the University of Pittsburgh, where he has taught since 1985. In England, he teaches at the University of Exeter as a professor of English, and serves as the chairman of the London Consortium, which he helped to found in 1995. He is the author of numerous books, including *The Eloquence of the Vulgar* (1999), and his writing has been featured in *The Guardian*, *The Times* (London), *The Independent* (London), and the British edition of *Condé Nast Traveler*. A member of the European Film Academy and the British Academy of Film and Television Arts, MacCabe has produced several award-winning films, most recently *BaadAsssss Cinema* (2002) for the Independent Film Channel. He edits *Critical Quarterly*.

godard

godard

A PORTRAIT OF THE ARTIST
AT SEVENTY

Colin MacCabe

FILMOGRAPHY AND PICTURE RESEARCH BY Sally Shafto

Faber and Faber, Inc.
An affiliate of Farrar, Straus and Giroux
New York

Faber and Faber, Inc.
An affiliate of Farrar, Straus and Giroux
19 Union Square West, New York 10003

The Library of Congress has cataloged the hardcover edition as follows:
MacCabe, Colin.
    Godard : a portrait of the artist at 70 / Colin MacCabe ; filmography and research by
Sally Shafto.— 1st American ed.
        p.   cm.
Originally published: Great Britain : Bloomsbury Press, 2003.
Includes bibliographical references and index.
ISBN: 0-374-16378-2
    1. Godard, Jean-Luc, 1930–   2. Motion picture producers and
directors—France—Biography.   I. Shafto, Sally.   II. Title.

    PN1998.3.G63M33 2003
    791.4302'33'092—dc22
    [B]   2003061241

Paperback ISBN-13: 978-0-571-21105-0
Paperback ISBN-10: 0-571-21105-4

www.fsgbooks.com

1   3   5   7   9   10   8   6   4   2

For Minerva

Mæterlinck says: *If Socrates leave his house today he will find the sage seated on his doorstep. If Judas go forth tonight it is to Judas his steps will tend.* Every life is many days, day after day. We walk through ourselves, meeting robbers, ghosts, giants, old men, young men, wives, widows, brothers-in-love. But always meeting ourselves.

James Joyce, Ulysses

Contents

Preface

It was Peter Biskind, then editor of *American Film*, who urged me to write this biography in 1984 or 1985. I put the idea to Godard. He seemed to concur with my dislike of biography as a form and to share my doubts about the pleasure of the process. Two years later he asked me how the work was progressing and this encouraged me to bury my own doubts and to prepare a very detailed treatment. By the early nineties, however, it was clear that Godard no longer had any faith in the project.

In the nineties I was fortunate enough to bring two commissions to Godard and his partner Anne-Marie Miéville: *2 × 50 ans du cinéma français*[1] (*2 × 50 Years of French Cinema*) (1995) and *The Old Place* (1998), and I laid aside the biography indefinitely. Then in the summer of 1999 Godard wrote me a very generous letter about our past productions, which made clear that it was unlikely there would be any further collaborations.

It was in the aftermath of this letter that I thought seriously again about the biography. The initial problem of any biography was still there. Each life is infinite, its connections too complicated to allow of any representation which is not also a savage editing. But the fact that my subject was alive suddenly presented a solution. Any biography of a living person is necessarily incomplete, but a living subject allows the possibility of a portrait: a series of angles on Godard's life and work.

And it is the work that provides the real impetus for this biography, work that is the most astonishing, the most intriguing, the most illuminating of my time's art. The first moment of epiphany had been unattended – sitting in a Paris cinema in January 1967 watching a film in a language I did not understand, but which provided image after image of a beauty I had never before witnessed. In subsequent years Godard's engagement with both Maoism and feminism made him a constant point of reference, and then, as he began a re-examination of the canon of Western art and culture (which was to reach its culmination in the *Histoire(s) du cinéma*), our paths crossed directly.

In its range of reference – the history of cinema, the history of art, the history of Marxism – the work is as daunting as the life. It would be a fool who thought they had all the necessary competences to comment fully on this extraordinarily rich oeuvre which is constitutively allusive. But as with the life, the decision to choose a specific set of angles, to provide a particular portrait, was the enabling moment. Each chapter provides such an angle.

The first chapter is a family history. Godard's maternal family, the Monods, are one of the great Protestant families of France. The Godards, if less famous, are just as Protestant, and in both families there is a movement between France and Switzerland, which has been perhaps the most constant external feature of Godard's life.

Balzac would thus paint a man born from the very bluest of Swiss Calvinist/French Huguenot blood, up to his neck in the history of Europe, coming to Paris at a young age and, with his world collapsing as his parents divorce, discovering the cinema and America – a new promise and a new world. And this world had its prophets – fat Henri Langlois, the most charming of dealers, and thin André Bazin, a real saint. This chapter considers these figures from the point of view of intellectual history, to understand why it was in France that cinema reflected on its own past and produced not simply a magazine, *Cahiers du cinéma*, but an aesthetic that was to revolutionise world cinema, as the young *Cahiers* critics swapped pens for cameras and became the Nouvelle Vague, the New Wave.

To run in those years with Rohmer, Truffaut, Rivette, Chabrol, Gégauff, Bitsch, Schiffman – it is not hard to imagine how much fun that must have been. Crucial in the transformation from critics to filmmakers was an aesthetic which was also a new model of film-making, and it is this new model, with its lightweight technology and its small crews, which is one focus of the third chapter. The other is provided by

Anna Karina, the star of seven of the twelve films that Godard made between 1960 and 1966 and his first wife. Here the focus is film history proper as we track one of the greatest creative achievements in the history of the cinema.

But when Godard completes *Week-end* in 1967 he writes on the closing credits 'End of cinema', for the dream of the Nouvelle Vague had disintegrated at every level from the personal, with the breakdown of his marriage, to the political, where the American liberators of 1945 had become the imperialist oppressors in Vietnam. The fourth chapter takes the perspective of political history to understand Godard's abandonment of conventional cinema for a commitment to Maoist revolution, heralded in the prescient *La Chinoise*, a film that he made with his new student wife Anne Wiazemsky. It is this political perspective which illuminates the militant films of the post-1968 period, and explains the links between politics and aesthetics which underpinned the Dziga Vertov Group that Godard founded with a young Maoist, Jean-Pierre Gorin.

These first four chapters thus sketch four different kinds of history to provide the necessary angles on Godard: family history, intellectual history, film history, political history. The majority of the fifth chapter does not pretend to the status of history at all. It is a memoir; its determining angle is provided by my own contact with Godard through the eighties and nineties when I saw him once or twice a year, always in relation to specific projects and, almost always, very briefly. This period, which is impossible to understand outside of his enduring partnership with Anne-Marie Miéville, begins with a cycle of films from *Sauve qui peut* to '*Je vous salue, Marie*' which, while less well known than the films of the sixties, mark an aesthetic and intellectual achievement to rival the earlier decade. But from the mid-eighties onwards Godard's main focus of attention was his incredible *Histoire(s) du cinéma*, a history of his chosen art form which is also a history of his own life and a history of the century. It is difficult to find a comparison for this work, which certainly has no parallel within film or television, but perhaps the most apt is Dante's *Divine Comedy* which takes the elements of one life to provide a perspective on human history. Dante is also apt because it is the writing of the *Divine Comedy* in Italian which signals the beginning of a recognisable European culture; it is not an exaggeration to say that *Histoire(s) du cinéma* marks its end.

Although this work focuses on one individual, its major intellectual impetus is the attempt to understand an aspect of the history of European modernism. Modernism can be understood as the reaction by artists to the new forms of capitalist culture linked to mass audiences (starting with tabloid newspapers and culminating in our day with satellite television). The work of Godard is particularly interesting because, unusually, it takes place within those very forms. It poses the paradoxes of modernism at their most acute. There is an almost total rejection of the stereotypical and the generic which demands an extra-ordinary level of active engagement by the viewer within forms whose economic conditions of existence demand a mass audience.

I have been as careful as I am able to make sure that all the facts in this book are accurate, but I should not wish to hide that it is a partisan work. Its initial premiss is that Godard's film-making is amongst the most important European art of the second half of the twentieth century. The book's aim is to sketch the historical setting of that art, and its ambition is to find a larger audience both for the well-known work of the sixties and the lesser-known work of the seventies, eighties and nineties.

Colin MacCabe

9 January 2002, Paris – 9 January 2003, Pittsburgh

Abbreviations

My aim in referencing this book has been twofold. Firstly, I have been keen to obey the scholarly imperative which requires that sources and quotations are accurately identified. Without that imperative one's arguments cannot be properly examined by others. But I have not wished to burden the reader with sterile and prolix repetition. If it is clear from the text who is speaking then there is no footnote. Details of all interviews can be found in the bibliography. For Godard, all unreferenced quotations are from a two-day interview conducted in Rolle just before Christmas 1988.

The following abbreviations are used in the text:

Jean-Luc Godard par Jean-Luc Godard edited by Alain Bergala, 2 vols (Paris: Cahiers du cinéma, 1998) (G). There is an English translation of some of the first volume, *Godard on Godard*, edited and translated by Tom Milne (London: Secker and Warburg, 1972). Where an English translation exists it is referred to by the first of the two page numbers. Occasionally, I have altered a translation.

Cahiers du cinéma: Histoire d'une revue by Antoine de Baecque, 2 vols (Paris: Cahiers du cinéma, 1991) (C).

François Truffaut by Antoine de Baecque and Serge Toubiana, 2nd edition (Paris: Gallimard, 2001) (T).

1

Gods and Demi-Gods:
The Monods and the Godards

A Family of Foxes

In the autumn of 1963, Jean-Luc Godard had a rare meeting with his father Paul, whom he had barely seen for over a decade. At thirty-three, Jean-Luc was already an acclaimed film director, saluted by many as one of the greatest cinema talents of all time, even though his first feature, *Breathless*, had been released only three years earlier. Indeed, the occasion of their meeting was a festival of Godard's films in the French town of Annecy. Jean-Luc's younger sister, Véronique, had taken advantage of this event to bring her father from nearby Geneva, where he was living in retirement. Material for an episode of the television series *Cinéastes de notre temps*, was being recorded on 16 mm cameras, and there is footage of both Godard's father and sister. In the course of the programme Godard was asked about his relationship to his family. 'Il y a des Godards comme il y a des renards,' he replied: 'There are Godards like there are foxes.' The reply is typical. First of all the answer transforms the question by playing with language – Godard and renard rhyme in French. It is difficult to know why the interviewer, André S. Labarthe, posed the question: he was perhaps aware that Godard had been estranged from his family and hoped to produce one of those 'confessions' so suited to the televisual form. Instead, Godard asserted his family solidarity in the strangest and perhaps the strongest of terms. It is clear that his reply affiliates him with his family; there is no repudiation, but the terms of the affiliation are not in terms of a family, or even a race or a nation, but with a species, with a natural kind. There can be no question of repudiation because the basis of the question has been changed.

The play on words, the pun, the quibble (to use an old English term), is fundamental to Godard's attitude to language, be it written or spoken. Samuel Johnson thought that a similar attitude in Shakespeare was the English playwright's greatest weakness: 'A quibble, poor and barren as it is, gave him such delight, that he was content to purchase it, by the sacrifice of reason, propriety and truth. A quibble was to him the fatal Cleopatra for which he lost the world, and was content to lose it.'[1]

For Johnson's Age of Reason the relation between language and world must be single and simple; there can be no room for the multiplicity of angles introduced by the play on words as world and language shift in and out of different relationships in the same verbal form. But if the pun was anathema to the Enlightenment, it has been crucial to the twentieth century's understanding of language, most notably in Freud and Joyce. Indeed the principles of the pun, in which two conflicting meanings are held in suspension, can be understood as absolutely central to Godard's whole work. But this is not just an abstract aesthetic choice; the pun has been central to his manner of speaking from his very earliest youth. Indeed his eldest sister Rachel remembers it as a source of constant irritation to their father from Jean-Luc's earliest days.

While the pun holds patterns of meaning in suspension, it is in that moment that new emphases become apparent in reality. To answer a question about a proper name and a specific family as though it were a question about species is an amusing way to refuse the terms of the question. But it is also a way of drawing attention to the fact that while it is normal for siblings to share a family resemblance, it is very rare indeed to find four siblings so uncannily alike as Godard and his brother and sisters. The square face, the glasses, a particular smile – it is quite impossible not to recognise the Godards as a family. The physical resemblance is above all to the mother – Odile Godard. A photo from 1940 gives perhaps the clearest representation of the face shared by all of her children, and an earlier photograph from 1928, glasses and smile in place, almost makes her look like an imaginary fifth child, a sibling to Rachel, Jean-Luc, Claude and Véronique. But the similarities between the Godard children do not stop there. They all share the same soft voice

Clockwise from left: Rachel, Jean-Luc, Véronique and Claude, 16 October 1949.

Odile Monod, Jean-Luc's mother.

veined with a biting sarcasm which seems much more Anglo-Saxon than Gallic. And just as the mother can be discerned in the faces of the children, so the father can be heard in their voices, for descriptions of Dr Godard never fail to mention his soft voice nor his sarcastic wit.

It would be easy to depict Jean-Luc Godard as someone cut off and isolated from his family, and to date the film-maker from his violent break with his relations in the early fifties. But Godard, as in the 1963 television programme, has never failed to acknowledge his ties to his family. Indeed he remembers his childhood as a truly idyllic time, and understands the violent break as the only way he could separate himself from a too much loved and too seductive world.

Family History

One of the most striking features of Godard's childhood world (and indeed of his whole life) was that it was split between two countries: France and Switzerland. It would be hard to overemphasise the extent to which Godard is both French and Swiss, both a cultured and cosmopolitan member of elite Parisian society and a solid Swiss burgher, in many ways a typical representative of the canton of Vaud. It is in Vaud that one finds both Nyon, the town in which he grew up and went to school, and Rolle, the small village where he has lived and worked for the past twenty-five years. Both border Lac

Léman, the huge lake at the base of the Alps with Geneva at one end and Montreux at the other, the north shore Swiss and the southern shore French.

It is in the passage between Paris and Lac Léman that Godard has lived his life, and this pattern is deeply woven. It is there, long before he is born, when his two Swiss grandmothers marry his two French grandfathers. It is there when the tiny baby born in Paris moves with his father, mother and elder sister to a clinic outside Nyon. It is there in a childhood in which, astonishingly, to take the train for Paris or Geneva was no more remarkable than to take the local bus or subway.

Paul Godard, Jean-Luc's father.

It was in Geneva that Godard's maternal grandfather, Julien-Pierre Monod, met and married Cécile Naville. The Monods are one of the most illustrious families in France, counting amongst their members a Nobel prize winner, pastors and theologians, scientists, politicians, and financiers. They were also a fertile family. When in 1993 a gathering of the entire Monod clan was held in Paris's 5th arrondissement (Godard said that he would attend but failed to turn up) there were nearly 2,500 people present. It would be possible to describe the Monods in many ways, but any description would have to include the word Protestant, and if the family has followed many professions, that of pastor is perhaps the most significant and recurrent. Godard's brother Claude feels that Jean-Luc is indeed best understood as another in an ancient line of strict and severe Protestant pastors. William Monod, Godard's great grandfather, was such a Protestant priest and fathered eight children bought up in a household of great piety and modest means. Julien-Pierre was one of those children.

Born in 1876, Julien-Pierre may have intended to follow in his father's footsteps, first studying theology at the university. He soon switched to literature and law, subjects that were to be more significant for a man who made his living as a businessman and devoted himself to letters. From the beginning of his student career Julien-Pierre Monod had supplemented whatever modest support his father could provide by working as a tutor during the summer holidays. In the summer of 1901, he taught law to a Protestant friend from university, Arnold Naville.

The Naville family was rich and prosperous, and originally came from Neuchâtel, a French Protestant stronghold which had joined the Swiss confederation late. Arnold's father, Pyrame, was a wealthy business-man. His mother was from Lyons (thus demonstrating within the most Swiss of Godard's ancestry that the family was always connected to France) and had borne four children, Georges, Jean, Arnold and Cécile, before dying young. The summer of 1901, while Julien-Pierre was tutoring Arnold, was largely spent in the Navilles' summer house at Anthy, a tiny fishing village on the French shore of Lac Léman about twenty miles from Geneva. It was in these glorious surroundings that the young tutor and his friend's younger sister Cécile fell in love.

It seems unlikely that the father was overjoyed by his youngest child's desire to marry her brother's impoverished tutor, however brilliant and Protestant. The widower was, however, given little choice by the redoubtable Cécile, who according to family legend told her father very directly 'Moi, je veux épouser ce garçon' ('I'm determined to marry this young man'). Their marriage took place on 28 August 1903, and brought an alliance with the Navilles which made Julien-Pierre Monod a rich man. Perhaps the most significant aspect financially was that Arnold Naville, his friend, student, and now brother-in-law, took him into partnership in his ventures constructing railroads in Turkey. But there were also considerable interests in one of the major French banks – La Banque de Paris et Pays-Bas.

Perhaps more important than these financial opportunities, which a man as brilliant and as well connected within the Protestant bourgeoisie as Julien-Pierre Monod might have counted on, was Anthy. As part of her dowry Cécile brought with her the family's summer house. It appears in Godard's late film *For Ever Mozart* (1996) in a scene where Serbian tanks capture some young French actors in an abandoned chalet which has been daubed with slogans. The Monod grandchildren sold Anthy to the first of a series of absentee owners in the early seventies, and it has remained abandoned ever since. But for more than sixty years this square and imposing chalet, with its outlying buildings in which numerous guests could be housed, flourished as the Monod children's and grandchildren's emotional centre. Indeed its use in *For Ever Mozart* would seem to stand for a ruined European innocence, a personal symbol of what Europe lost in the breakup of the former Yugoslavia.

Anthy's grounds run down to the southern shore of Lac Léman. Lac Léman finds its western limit in the town of Geneva and for the first twenty miles the lake is relatively narrow. Locally this is known as the 'little lake'. But opposite Nyon the French shore widens, giving onto 'the great lake'. Anthy lies just at the beginning of the great lake facing the small Swiss town of Rolle, where Godard settled in the late seventies and has worked ever since. The chalet at Anthy has both a beach and a jetty where small boats can moor. It had been the site of their courtship, and it became for Julien and Cécile Monod the idyllic summer retreat where the whole family could holiday together. The large central chalet, with eight bedrooms, had been built at the end of the nineteenth century, but throughout the twenties and thirties Julien and Cécile added new buildings so that there were at least twenty bedrooms in which children and grandchildren could be distributed.

Each summer the Monods would entertain family and friends there, but the friends were probably not those of a typical banker. Julien-Pierre Monod was devoted to modern literature, and it was an enthusiasm which he shared with Arnold Naville, who was a friend of the novelist André Gide. (Arnold can be seen in Marc Allégret's 1950 documentary *Avec Gide* in a scene where Gide plays the piano as Arnold turns the pages of the score.) It is probably through Gide, a life-long friend and supporter of Paul Valéry, that Julien-Pierre Monod met the great French poet.

The publications of *La Jeune Parque* in 1917 and 'Le Cimetière marin' in 1920 had transformed Valéry from a man who had written some interesting verse in the 1890s to the defining voice of modern poetry, the French equivalent of Eliot and Yeats. He was to enjoy this position until his death in 1945, when de Gaulle ordered that he be buried with national honours. But Valéry's sudden fame had brought certain difficulties. As a young man he had become a great friend of Pierre Louÿs, who had introduced him to Mallarmé in Paris in the 1890s.

During the First World War, Valéry had written a series of long letters to Louÿs at the same time as he was writing his masterpiece, *La Jeune Parque*. Pierre Louÿs's last years were sunk in dissipation. His literary fame had waned and he was afflicted by blindness, sexual excess, and the promotion of one of the weirder theories of literary history: namely that the comedies of Molière had in fact been written by Corneille. When he died in 1925 his belongings were scattered, and amongst them the letters that Valéry had written to him which, given Valéry's fame, now had a certain commercial value. Valéry was horrified to find that they were being sold on the rare-book market in Paris. He felt that he was being treated as a dead man. Julien-Pierre Monod offered to take the matter in hand and, by one means or another, retrieved Valéry's letters. He then published them privately (as the French say, *hors commerce*) on 20 December 1925 with the title *Quinze lettres de Paul Valéry à Pierre Louÿs écrites entre 1915 et 1917 recueillies et publiées*.

The bond thus established between the two men was a strong one, and for the rest of Valéry's life, Julien-Pierre Monod was both Valéry's *homme d'affaires*, managing the poet's money, and his secretary, organising Valéry's extraordinarily busy schedule of international lectures and conferences. Valéry referred to him as his 'minister' and Julien-Pierre's study in the family home at the Boulevard Raspail was known as the Valérianum. The Pleiade collection of Valéry's work describes it thus: 'Under the name of Valérianum Julien Monod built up an important collection of rare editions and manuscripts and a very rare complete documentation.'[2] Amongst his most treasured possessions were the first editions, personally inscribed to him by Valéry.

It was in August 1926 that Valéry came to Anthy, by the waters of Lac

Léman. In a veritable congress of modernist poetry Rilke visited the French poet whom he so admired and whom he had translated into German, taking a boat on 13 September across the lake from the Valmont clinic above Montreux, where he was being treated. There are photographs of the two poets in the grounds at Anthy. Valéry wrote of their day together: 'Wandering amongst the trunks and the plants, tearing off a leaf here and there, we confronted, mixed and distinguished our feelings on poetry. What moments of liberty, of reciprocal gestures, those moments of the last September of his life.'[3] Rilke was to die in December of that year.

There is another photograph of Valéry, taken in that same summer, which shows the elderly poet standing slightly apart from a group of Monods and Navilles. One has the impression that Valéry has just pronounced some witticism, for the seventeen-year-old girl closest to the poet and standing next to her sister is exploding with laughter. The girl is Odile Monod, one of twins – her sister is named Aude – born to

From left to right: Paul Valéry, Odile, Aude, Guy, Cécile, her brother Georges Naville.

Julien-Pierre and Cécile in 1909. By then the couple, married in 1903, already had two boys (Olivier and Guy) and would go on to have three more (Didier, Dominique and Grégoire). Two years later, at nineteen, Odile would be married herself, and in 1930 she would give birth to two children: a girl, Rachel, born in January and a boy, Jean-Luc, born in December.

The man Odile married was Paul Godard. His family was not from the grande bourgeoisie, like the Monods, but just as Protestant and just as Franco–Suisse. The Godards came from the North of France, from a small town called Le Cateau, just south of the Belgian border, a hive of Protestantism whose most famous son was the painter Matisse. Like Julien-Pierre Monod, Paul Godard's father, Georges, grew up in relatively impoverished circumstances and also left poverty behind him. Georges' route lay not through the university and the world of finance, but through apprenticeship and trade. Born in the early 1870s, he came to Paris in the 1890s to apprentice himself in glassware. He worked in the rue du Paradis in the 10th arrondissement, which was then and still is the centre of glass in the city. The specific history which transformed him from a lowly apprentice in Paris to a well-off diamond trader based in Geneva became for the family an imprecise and shady legend. For if Julien-Pierre Monod 'took up the white man's burden' and voyaged east to bring railways and civilisation to Smyrna and beyond, Georges Godard was the figure who carried a revolver as part of his daily business,[4] a business which seemed, to his grandchildren, only a step away from criminality.

It was in Paris in the 1890s that he met and married Louise Baeschlin. Louise had French nationality but her father was Swiss-German. In the middle of the nineteenth century he had emigrated from the countryside around Schaffhausen, a textile town in the very north of Switzerland, to the Parisian suburb of Le Raincy, where he married a young woman from the Normand family. When the Protestant community built a church there, young Louise was chosen as one of the 'godmothers of the bell' and it was in this church that Georges and Louise were married.

Their first child, Paul, was born in Le Raincy on 1 June 1899. The Godards eventually had three more children, all daughters: Suzanne,

Madeleine and Hélène. Hélène was born in 1913, and three years later the family moved to Geneva in a further intensification of the Paris–Geneva pattern. Whether this move was motivated by business or by a desire to escape the First World War is no longer known. What is certain is that Georges Godard was anti-militarist, and the most immediately striking fact about his son Paul's life was the extent to which it was dominated by the desire to find peace and escape war. When Georges and Louise moved to Geneva, the younger sisters were sent to school there, but Paul, who was already at the Collège Chaptal in Paris, remained to finish his schooling, *en pension* with his maternal grandmother. In the summer of 1914 the young teenager was in England at Southampton, learning English. By 1 August it was clear that the war which was to destroy Europe was inevitable. Georges sent a postcard to his son:

> My dear Paul,
>   You must know from the English papers that the international situation is very serious; it's even possible that war will have been declared by the time you receive this postcard; in these conditions and given that it is too late to get you back safely, the best thing to do is to stay at Southampton and then we'll take stock in the light of how things develop. Tell Mrs Gaylon and Mr Wells this and let Mr Wells know that I'll send him money in good time; if, by chance, there is some delay because the post isn't functioning properly, say to Mrs Gaylon and Mr Wells that they should not worry at all and that whatever happens, they will lose nothing with me. Stay in Southampton. With God's grace. Let us pray to him if possible to spare us the horrors of war. I hope you're in good health and I send you all my love
>   Your father
>   G. Godard.
>   We're not leaving so continue to write here.

It would be the most facile of interpretations to ground Paul Godard's subsequent passion to avoid war in this dramatic moment. And to do so would be to ignore both the family tradition of anti-militarism and, probably more significant, the horrors of the First World War, 'horrors'

Postcard from Georges Godard to his son Paul on the eve of World War I.

which Georges Godard could hardly have imagined when he was
writing to Paul. In the annals of human conflict it is almost impossible
to find a parallel for the slaughter of young men on the Western Front in
the 1914–18 war. Perhaps only in the American Civil War before and
nowhere since has a ruling class been so willing to send its own children
to die in battle. In previous warfare, we see the terrible sacrifice of those
who have had no choice but to fight, but only in the First World War
does civilisation reach a stage where the powerful and the mighty have
no other desire than to imitate Abraham and offer up their own sons.
Nowhere was this sacrifice greater than in France – of the eight and a
half million men mobilised, over three quarters became casualties and
nearly one and a half million died. And nowhere was the disgust with
Western civilisation more pronounced than in France in the twenties and
thirties. A whole set of tiny political and aesthetic movements, of which
Surrealism and its offshoots were probably the most significant, sought
to break with what was seen as the fatal heritage of Western culture.

It is difficult to guess when Paul Godard developed his obsession with escaping war. It may have been formed in the years following 1914, as he watched his seniors at school go off to the slaughter. It may be that he was one of the few – John Maynard Keynes was another – who saw clearly that the terms of the Versailles Peace Treaty in 1919 were simply the terms for a new war. It may be that an anti-militarist father and a half-Swiss mother was enough. Certainly by the mid-twenties he had already formed the ambition to move to Switzerland, and above all to seek a refuge from European war where he could

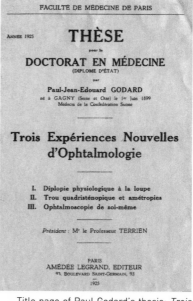

FACULTÉ DE MÉDECINE DE PARIS

Année 1925 THÈSE
pour le
DOCTORAT EN MÉDECINE
(DIPLOME D'ÉTAT)
par
Paul-Jean-Edouard GODARD
né à GAGNY (Seine et Oise) le 1er Juin 1899
Médecin de la Confédération Suisse

Trois Expériences Nouvelles
d'Ophtalmologie

I.   Diplopie physiologique à la loupe
II. Trou quadristénopique et amétropies
III. Ophtalmoscopie de soi-même

Président : M⁰ le Professeur TERRIEN

PARIS
AMÉDÉE LEGRAND, ÉDITEUR
93, BOULEVARD SAINT-GERMAIN, 93
1925

Title page of Paul Godard's thesis: *Trois expériences nouvelles d'ophtalmologie*, Paris, 1925.

practise his medicine in peace. His links with Switzerland were considerable: his family had moved there, his mother was of Swiss origin and part of his medical studies had been undertaken at Lausanne. His doctoral thesis itself, in ophthalmology, was deposited at the Faculty of Medicine in Paris in 1925. It was entitled 'Three New Ophthalmological Experiments', and its third section is fascinating in terms of his eldest son's later obsession with the reflexivity of vision, for it is on the topic of 'Ophthalmoscopy of oneself' or 'how to examine one's own eye'. Soon after he qualified as a doctor in 1925 he was splitting his professional time between Paris and the north shore of Lake Geneva, taking locums in the numerous private clinics which were built there in the late nineteenth century, in particular the Clinique Valmont at Glion-sur-Montreux. What is curious is that he was already perceived as Swiss, although it was to be over a decade before he obtained Swiss nationality and the right to set up his own practice in that country.

Julien-Pierre and Cécile Monod's eldest son, Olivier, had also chosen medicine as a profession. He was to become a very eminent surgeon and the father of Jérôme Monod, a well-known political and business figure on the Gaullist right who was to be the key strategist of Jacques Chirac's Presidential campaign in 2002. It was Olivier who invited his colleague Paul Godard to one of his parents' monthly gatherings at 16, Boulevard Raspail. These were worldly occasions where the Protestant grande bourgeoisie consolidated its social and economic networks. If the Great War had disenchanted a whole generation of artists and thinkers, it must be remembered that for the French ruling class it was perceived as a great victory over the Germans; a victory which had reversed the shame of Bismarck's lightning defeat of France in 1870. The Monods' gatherings were events brimming with social, economic and cultural confidence, and it was at such an evening that Paul was to meet Olivier's younger sister, Odile.

Odile had just passed her baccalauréat at the Lycée Victor Duruy and was preparing to go to university in Paris. Having completed her exams a year earlier than her twin sister Aude, Odile had decided to study medicine with her best friend, Jacqueline Morin. (This friendship endured throughout Odile's life and was so strong that Jacqueline was universally referred to by the Godard children as godmother (*marraine*), although technically it was only Rachel who was her godchild.) Women doctors were not unknown in the 1920s but they were undoubtedly rare, and it must have required considerable courage, as well as the support of a friendship like this one, to undertake such study.

That evening in the Boulevard Raspail, it was Jacqueline who introduced Paul Godard to Odile Monod as 'a Swiss doctor', an identity that was already a personal choice if not yet a bureaucratic reality. Odile Monod, still only a teenager, was obviously a considerable handful for her parents. The young woman with the courage to choose medicine as a career was not frightened to flirt with older men. No details of their courtship remain, but the flirtation seems to have progressed very quickly and, at least initially, to have been opposed by Odile's parents.

Their objection to a marriage with Paul Godard might have been on the grounds she was too young, because of the ten year difference in age, or perhaps the Godards were not held to be sufficiently HSP (*haute société protestante* – high Protestant society). In any case, Odile was despatched to London to begin her medical studies and to keep her out of the way of Paul Godard. She registered at Bedford College in October 1927 and, according to the College records, she initially planned to study chemistry and physics before returning to France to take the first year medical exams. But she was not the first student to discover that the sciences are taught differently in different countries, so she decided to drop these courses and concentrate on studying English. The records of Bedford College make clear that this was a temporary measure until she could get back to France.

The Monod parents' plan was not only unsuccessful on an academic level, but also a failure as a emotional stratagem. Paul knew London well. In addition to his studies at Lausanne and Paris he had followed medical courses in London and was affiliated to both the Royal College of Surgeons and the Royal College of Physicians (indeed contact with English medicine and English doctors was to continue throughout his life). If Odile was in London, then he would follow her. Bedford College records show Odile Monod applying for permission to let a Dr Godard visit her and she even introduced him to the principal. By March, her parents' objections had been overcome and Odile returned to Paris. When on 28 April 1928 Julien-Pierre Monod wrote to thank the principal for her help, he told her that Odile was going to take the first year of physics, chemistry and natural science in Paris in spite of her proposed marriage.

They must both have been at Anthy that year for together they produced by hand a booklet, dated 28 August 1928, entitled *Quelques essais* (Some Essays). The frontispiece also shows that the texts were the work of Odile and the drawings by Paul. The texts all bear a place (Paris, Anthy and London) and a date, from Paris in March 1927 to London in June 1928, which suggests that Odile stayed on in the city after she left Bedford College. They are adolescent prose poems of a recognisable type, and so abstract in their analysis of the evils of existence that it is difficult to take them as seriously as their author does. But they have moments of real talent – the last entry, a meditation on the notion of

Pages from *Quelques essais*, drawings by Paul and text by Odile.

being 'too late', has real force, as does an account of a visit to her old
school which recalls a moment when she got caught in a daydream
during an exam, with the result that she failed. In retrospect she judges
the daydream more valuable than the exam and the text ends with a
determination to go to the cinema. As with Paul Godard's thesis on
the examination of one's own eye, the prescience is uncanny. The
drawings are more adult and sophisticated; Paul Godard had a
genuine talent for drawing, a fact confirmed not only by his carica-
tures lampooning teachers in the medical faculty and, as a good
Protestant, the cardinals of the Roman curia, but also by the wonderful gastroscopic pictures that he produced long before photographic
imaging existed.

On 16 October 1928, at the age of nineteen and a half, Odile Monod
married Paul Godard, who had turned twenty-nine that June. Family
legend has her father blessing the marriage with the comment, 'Well, at
least I'll have got rid of her.'

Early Childhood 1930–39

The Godards began their married life at 1, rue Cognacq-Jay in the 7th arrondissement, a street which runs parallel to the Quai d'Orsay a few hundred metres from the Pont d'Alma.

Paul Godard divided his work between Paris and Switzerland, and the birth of two children, Rachel (born 4 January 1930) and Jean-Luc (born 3 December 1930), does not seem to have disturbed this pattern very much. For Rachel, the years between 1930 and 1933 were a constant train journey, and she claims to remember travelling in the luggage rack. Jean-Luc was not yet one when the family moved briefly to a clinic in Vevey and then back to Paris. In 1933 Paul Godard finally found the position that he wanted at a clinic called La Lignière, just outside the small village of Gland, in the canton of Vaud midway between Nyon and Rolle. This time the move was permanent. Odile, who was pregnant for a third time, Paul and the two young children moved into one of several small houses in the gardens of the clinic, where they were to live for five years.

Two more children were born in this period: Claude in 1933 at La Lignière itself and Véronique, the baby of the family, at Thonon-les-Bains in France in 1937. In 1938, the family moved to an apartment in 4, rue du Prieuré in Nyon, a beautiful eighteenth-century house with wonderful views down over the port and the little lake. The elder children had started their schooling at an *école maternelle* in Nyon on the route de Trelex but in 1937 they were separated by gender when they went into the primary school for the Collège de Nyon, a few minutes' walk from the rue du Prieuré. Rachel and Jean-Luc were practically twins and all attest to the closeness of their relationship. Rachel was to see each of Jean-Luc's films as direct messages to her, and she told me that she felt that she and her brother were two aspects of a single being. In his self-portrait *JLG/JLG: Autoportrait de décembre*, made just after Rachel's death in 1993, Godard comments, in one of those moments when one begins to hear the Protestant tones of his childhood clearly, 'Dieu la prend dans ses bras' ('God takes her in his arms'). But while Godard acknowledged the closeness of the relationship, he also acknowledged (a word repeatedly used when describing his immediate family) that she was 'independent'. Although for the last twelve years of her life they were no more than a short motorway or train ride apart, they saw each other on very few occasions. But this probably reveals something about the species of the Godards in general rather than Jean-Luc the individual.

Godard's own memories of his childhood are clear: 'Now I can look on it as paradise. I was very healthy and even if my own family was not that rich, we had access to all the resources or the wealth of my mother's family, as did all the grandchildren. It was one of those huge Protestant families that behave like a tribe with their own ritual, their own ceremonies . . . you were protected. It was like a Greek legend, my grandfather and grandmother were gods, my parents were demi-gods and we children were humans.' And Godard links this to one aspect of his adult life: 'I have a feeling that I'm not asking for power or riches or anything, because I had more than plenty until I was fifteen. More than anyone. It was very different from Truffaut, for example.'

This memory suggests what the other Godard children confirm, that family life was lived as easily with the extended Monod family in Paris as in Nyon. But the centre of all these rituals and ceremonies was Cécile Naville's dowry – the house and the grounds at Anthy. It was here that the Godard children would spend the summer holidays and much other time beside. Anthy is not much more than an hour's drive from Nyon through the centre of Geneva and even less by boat almost directly across the lake. As the Monods were a Protestant tribe, Anthy also had some religious functions. It was in the house there that all the Godard children were baptised, and their grandfather or uncles would often conduct Sunday services. When Rachel Godard died her ashes were scattered at the shore of the lake at Anthy, and their mother is buried in the local graveyard.

Protestants make up only two per cent of the French population but in the last two centuries they have had a disproportionate political and intellectual impact on French life. This may find some explanation in their terrible history, a history of blood and persecution. Protestantism is written deeply into Godard's life from his childhood on. If no simple correspondence between ideological structure and personal psychology can ever be more than tentative, it is notable how Godard's abiding belief in his own artistic choices reproduce the theological certainty of the Calvinist in his divine election, and it is also striking how the history of French Protestantism licences an individual and withdrawn practice of the faith.

When in 1517 Martin Luther nailed his ninety-five theses to the church door in Wittenberg, protesting at the abuses of the Papacy and affirming the primacy for a Christian of faith over works, he set in train a division of Europe into Protestant and Catholic. No country was spared what was to be two hundred years of religious warfare, but there is reason to think that France suffered both longer and more intensely than other major European countries.

The impact of Lutheran theology was immediate in France. The advent of the printing press meant that Luther's writings appeared in French editions almost contemporaneously, and nowhere were the reformers greeted more warmly than in the major self-governing cities on France's borders: Strasbourg, Neuchâtel and Geneva. Geneva was to become a model for Protestantism all over Europe when it summoned the leading French Protestant theologian Jean Calvin, then in exile in Strasbourg, to organise its civic and religious life. As Calvin constructed the rule of the elect, adding to Luther's emphasis on salvation by faith, the astonishing doctrine of predestination, France fell into half a century of civil war which centred on religious differences and saw the ruling aristocracy divided between Rome and the new faith of the reformers.

The massacre of St Bartholomew's Day in August 1572 – when more than two thousand Protestants were killed in Paris, a hotbed of militant Catholicism – set off a two-month killing spree all over the country that has come to symbolise two generations of venomously hostile conflict. This period came to an end when Henri, Prince of Navarre, the leader of the Protestant party and the heir to the French throne, converted to Catholicism with a historically atypical joke: 'Paris', he said on the day of his conversion 'is well worth a Mass.' His accession to the throne in 1589 inaugurated a religious settlement in France which had no parallel in Europe. In 1598 Henri IV issued his Edict of Nantes which, while paying lip service to a future reunion of all the faithful, recognised that there were two religious faiths in France and that both had rights. The Edict of Nantes was anything but a modern example of toleration. It was a severely practical document which attempted to grant the absolute minimum of legal rights to existing Protestant communities, while maintaining an overall dominance of the Church of Rome. Whatever its weaknesses, it did give Protestant churches a right to exist, and it was over the next hundred years under its protection that French Protestantism developed many of its specific characteristics.

If the aristocracy was now, once again, overwhelmingly Catholic, the Huguenots – as they came to call themselves, borrowing a term of abuse from their enemies (the name comes from the German *Eidgenossen*, meaning confederates) – were largely based in the towns. They were found in great numbers in those sections of the bourgeoisie and petit-bourgeoisie engaged in manufacture. There is perhaps no more famous sociological thesis than Max Weber's identification of the Protestant ethic and the spirit of capitalism, and no better example of it than the French Huguenots. In the Protestant idea of vocation and the certainty of spiritual salvation, Weber finds the necessary condition for the accumulation of surplus central to capitalism. The Huguenots were, however, completely dependent on the king. From the time of the Edict of Nantes they had lost any form of representation or influence at Court. They had no defence against the periodic waves of repression to which they were subject, and when an ageing Louis XIV, attempting to ingratiate himself both with God and his own image, revoked the Edict of Nantes in 1685, they were absolutely defenceless.

In his desire to be king of a totally Catholic country, Louis not only ordered the Protestants to cease practising their own religion or risk death or imprisonment but further required that they actively practise Catholicism. The difficulty and pain of the next hundred years of French Protestantism are captured in the name by which this period is known: 'The Time of the Desert'. France in the eighteenth century is famous for the Enlightenment and for the feudal despotism of the *ancien régime*, but it was also a country in which men and women were hanged, incarcerated for decades and turned into galley slaves for the very act of gathering together to pray according to the Protestant faith. The use of

Anthy as a church must have had many determinants, but it is also a reminder that the Protestants of the Time of the Desert were forced to carry out their religious duties in private. The first effect of the revocation of the Edict of Nantes was an enormous exodus from France, particularly from those areas of the country which adjoined the Protestant countries of England, the Netherlands and Switzerland. Some twenty-five per cent of the whole Protestant population is held to have fled, 250,000 people in all, and they had a considerable impact on the economies to which they brought their manufacturing skills.

Another effect of this massive emigration is that the movement from one country to another is written into the historical consciousness of those who descend from the Huguenots. When Paul Godard prepared his own obituary (in order, he ironically noted, that the devastated family should be spared this unwelcome chore) he observed that his studies in England and Switzerland had been undertaken because he 'preserved the tradition of certain French Protestants to leave their homeland'. The other tradition that the Time of the Desert bequeathed was an ethic of co-operation and trust within the Protestant community.

Two years before the Revolution of 1789, and after more than one hundred years of persecution, Protestants were accorded civil if not religious rights. But with the Revolution, Protestants entered fully into French public life for the first time. It is no surprise that a persecuted minority should be active in a movement whose political foundation was the declaration of the Rights of Man and in both the revolutionary period and the time of the Third Republic from 1870, Protestants were particularly prominent.

The Monod family entered visibly into the history of French Protestantism just after the Revolution. The newly enfranchised Huguenots had need of pastors and many came from the Swiss canton of Vaud. Jean Monod, who took up a post as pastor in Paris in 1808, came from Copenhagen, but he had been born in Geneva and his family was from Morges in the canton of Vaud. From then on it is impossible to read in the debates which animated French Protestatism without encountering a Monod. It would not be an exaggeration to say that in the nineteenth century they were the single most eminent family of the French Protestant faith.

Protestantism famously discards the Church as the necessary intermediary between man and God in favour of relation to God mediated
only by the Bible. Church government is derived not from a sacred
priesthood which finds its final authority in the Pope, but is based in a
priesthood of all the believers who join together to form a Church.
Despite a regular attendance at both Church and Sunday school,
Godard has little memory of God or the Bible, but the emphasis on
the individual was marked: 'I think we must have had the best upbringing possible. Very democratic. If for me there is a meaning of democracy
it's the way we were raised.' But over and above this spiritual democracy
was family ritual: 'It was one of those huge Protestant families that act
like tribes with their ritual and ceremony.' Calvin had encouraged each
family to be a little church unto itself,[5] and there is no doubt that the
ordered method of Calvinist practice within the home enabled the
Huguenots to survive for so many years when they could not publicly
practise their religion.

In one respect, however, the Protestantism of Anthy was not typical of
the Huguenot tradition. Historically, from 1789 onwards, there has
been a huge identification of French Protestants with the left. Two of the
most important French socialist prime ministers of recent times, Michel
Rocard and Lionel Jospin, are both Protestant. The identification is easy
to understand given the history of state persecution and Protestant
interest in toleration for minorities. But this aspect of French Protestantism was not part of Godard's heritage: Julien-Pierre Monod was,
relatively unusually for a French Protestant, of the right, and even more
unusually, anti-Semitic.[6]

If Anthy was the centre of the Monod tribe, the Godard family was
based on the other side of the lake, in Nyon. In 1938 Paul Godard was
finally able to realise his ambition and, as a Swiss national,
started his own private practice right in the centre of Nyon with his
surgery at 2, Place du Marché. He continued to work part time at La
Lignière but he now also became a familiar figure in Nyon going
about his daily rounds. He was obviously both talented and dedicated
as a doctor and was much appreciated in the town. Marcel Dreyfus,
Nyon's chronicler, records his painful devotion to duty, never hesitat-

ing to climb three or four floors to make his visits despite an ever more crippling arthritis.[7]

There has probably been human habitation on the fertile shores of Lac Léman for five or six millennia. Nyon itself, under the Roman name of Noviodunum, was founded around 50 BC by Julius Caesar after he had fought his Gallic wars against Vercingetorix. The first inhabitants were retired Roman soldiers and the colony was obviously designed to protect Roman Gaul's eastern flank. For three hundred years Noviodunum prospered and, in a period when Switzerland had no existence as a political or administrative entity, it was one of the most important towns of the region. Following the invasion of the German tribes in the third century, Nyon passed from the stage of world history and became a small town fought over by the counts of Savoy and the burghers of Berne, essentially of concern only to its own inhabitants and those of the immediately surrounding areas.

An extraordinarily fertile plain supporting a whole network of small farms stretches behind Nyon for two or three kilomentres to where the Jura mountains rise steeply. With the lake and the Alps in front of it and the farms and the Jura behind Nyon is surrounded by some of the most beautiful scenery in the world. It also offers almost every variety of sport, and the Godard children were sport fanatics; Rachel was devoted to tennis, Jean-Luc to football and skiing. In the summer the children and their mother would spend days at the beach about half a mile from the town, where the municipality had provided changing huts and diving boards. Jean Rosset, who courted Rachel from their schooldays and who was to be married to her for twenty years, still remembers his envy of the Godards' swimming ability and also Jean-Luc's skill as a goalkeeper, which earned him a place in the Nyon junior team. For Claude Godard, his elder brother's prowess as a skier was a constant reproach to his own more limited abilities.

The Godards' elegant second-floor apartment included a dining room, a salon, a huge kichen with a maid's room next to it, two small bedrooms for Rachel and Véronique and the parents' main bedroom with another bedroom leading off it used by Claude and Jean-Luc. The apartment was beautifully furnished with tables and chairs that the

Godards had bought in Paris after their wedding. The maid was mainly employed as a cook, for it was Odile Godard who concerned herself with the children and made culture as well as sport a major emphasis of their upbringing. The house was crammed with books and Odile would read aloud to her children, and she took them to concerts. Rachel was encouraged in her drawing, Claude in his playing of the piano, and Jean-Luc in his artistic ambitions. She also took them to the cinema, of which there were two in Nyon: the Rex and the Capitol. But cinema was by and large to be a French discovery for Jean-Luc. Perhaps most important of all, Odile was a dedicated and remarkably talented photographer, recording the life of her children in innumerable shots. Jean-Luc was to say later to his sister Véronique that he considered Odile a 'great photographer'. Paul too encouraged his children's interest in the arts, but his passions were painting and architecture.

It was also a strict upbringing. Children were not expected to speak at table unless spoken to, and if they were being punished they were made to eat alone in the kitchen. The parents often spoke English if they wished to discuss topics not suitable for children. Although this period of Jean-Luc's life is remembered by everybody as relatively tranquil and very happy, Rachel recalls her very small brother banging his head against the pavement in frustration and Jean-Luc irritating their father from a very early age, incessantly punning and balancing on chairs. But the most constant irritation was Jean-Luc's peering over his glasses, a gesture which is typical to this day. Rachel remembers her father complaining 'Don't look over the top of your glasses' and Jean-Luc regularly replying 'Who me?' before gazing down at his plate.

The blissful summers at Anthy included work as well as play. After the children had breakfasted in the kitchen, they would settle down to their 'devoirs de vacances'. Julien-Pierre Monod would resume his old role as tutor and take his grandchildren through a Latin prose or an exercise in French. Then, providing it was fine, they would go off to the beach or play a game of hide and seek in the grounds. A bell would alert the children to go and get changed for lunch and another bell, fifteen minutes later, would tell them lunch was ready. At lunch, as at dinner, children did not speak unless spoken to, although Rachel told me that if a child had a quotation which was relevant to the subject being discussed, that quotation would earn them the right to speak. The younger children have no memory of such a practice. After a brief siesta, the afternoons would be spent outdoors, swimming or going for walks. In the evening, or if it was raining, the family would play games. A particular favourite involved dividing into teams, and a letter of the alphabet would be selected along with a category such as rivers, mountains or authors. Each team would have to come up with the most rivers or mountains or authors beginning with the chosen letter. Jean-Luc was the acknowledged champion of this game. Above all there were books, and much of the time at Anthy was spent reading. Cinema was not a topic of conversation – apart from the huge impact of *Gone with the Wind*. The discussion about its immorality reigned for memorable days and, from then on, cinema was marked as the realm of the forbidden. Jean-Luc got his mother to promise him that he could read the book for his birthday.

War Years: 1939–45

If life around Lac Léman appeared eternally peaceful, the war which Dr Godard had feared was imminent. As Jean-Luc approached his ninth birthday, Hitler's Germany invaded Poland, and Britain and France declared war. For the first winter, the war was quiet and many wondered how long this 'phony war' could last. What no one imagined, except possibly the German General Staff, was that when Germany launched their offensive, they would defeat both the French army and the British Expeditionary Force within weeks, and France would capitulate. So quick was the collapse that Jean-Luc was trapped in Paris while visiting his grandparents, as a comfort to them on the death of the youngest Monod son, Grégoire. Unable to get back to Switzerland, Jean-Luc went with his mother's twin sister, Tante Aude, to Brittany. They probably stayed with her father-in-law, Dr Olgiati, at Quimper in Finistère, which the children knew from previous summer holidays at Beg-Meil. So difficult was it to return to Switzerland that Jean-Luc went to school in Brittany before he made his way back to Nyon via a prolonged stay in Vichy with the Doyen family:

'I remember during the war I spent about six months through family contacts in Vichy with a friend who was head of something there, and I remember that since I had nothing to do I went to the movies with the wife of this old friend every day. That was 1941. Small French comedies.'[8]

Swiss neutrality seems like one of the constants of European history, but it must be remembered that this neutrality has a history which is based on the force of Swiss arms and that in the summer of 1940 it was by no means certain that it would survive the Third Reich. By and large Jean-Luc Godard has made little of his Swiss heritage, and like many Swiss, if he mentions Switzerland it is often to complain about it, but it was because he was in Switzerland that he was able to pass his teenage years at peace and not at war.

Switzerland's early existence is the stuff of legends, with sturdy Alpine peasants like William Tell banding together to defeat their feudal Austrian overlords. If modern historians have left few of these myths in place, it is the case that the communal farming methods of the upper Alps were particularly resistant to feudalism, and that the diet and way of life of the Swiss mountain men made them the most feared soldiers in Europe. Indeed in 1477, when a Swiss army defeated Charles the Bold of Burgundy, it radically altered the history of Europe by removing one of the most important checks on the growing power of France. But Switzerland, with its heterogeneous cantons governed by different laws and regulations, was never likely to become a major European power, and after it lost the bloody and fatal battle of Marignano to the French in 1515, the Swiss withdrew within their own borders. What is striking is that despite a split between Catholic and Protestant as intense as anywhere within Europe in the sixteenth century, Switzerland held together as a confederation. This was perhaps due to the very looseness of the ties which bound together speakers of four languages (Swiss-German, French, Italian and Romansch) and two religions in a country with no natural borders.

The heterogeneity of the cantons – some democratic, some oligarchical – and the complexity of their forms of association was an affront to all the revolutionary and rational ambitions incarnated by Napoleon. At the end of the eighteenth century Napoleon occupied Berne and gave Switzerland a constitution which abolished all the complicated and overlapping relations between the cantons in favour of a democratic republic. Within five years Napoleon had abandoned this experiment and the new constitution, but he did retain Vaud as a new canton. The geo-political context of Godard's childhood was completed in 1815 when the Congress of Vienna redrew the map of Europe and not only granted Switzerland a narrow strip of land which linked Geneva to Vaud but also stated that the European powers recognised the perpetual neutrality of the Swiss state.

This neutrality was not seriously threatened until 1940. Switzerland's 1848 revolution was a relatively peaceful affair; it did not involve foreign powers and it produced an extremely durable constitution which balanced cantonal and federal interests. Even during the 1914–18 war, which split French and German Switzerland in their sympathies, there was never any question of Swiss involvement. The decision to base the League of Nations and associated international bodies in Geneva reaffirmed international commitment to the country's neutrality. But 1940 was different. As in 1798, Switzerland faced a conqueror who dominated all of Europe. Worse, the collapse of France had occurred so quickly that documents concerning a secret agreement to share information between French and Swiss military intelligence had fallen into German hands. There seemed to be a real possibility of invasion.

Historians now tell us that one way in which the Swiss averted this threat was to act as a reserve bank for Germany. And their record with regard to the persecution of the Jews is mixed – while they did take some Jewish refugees, many were turned back to their deaths. But at the time what clearly and immediately deterred any German invasion was the action of the Swiss army and its French speaking Vaudois commander Henri Guisan. On 25 July 1940, just a month after Paris had fallen, Guisan took the entire Swiss high command to the Rutli meadow, the legendary site of Switzerland's foundation, and speaking to them in German he pledged the equivalent of Churchill's 'We shall never surrender'. As important as this symbolic act was the military decision to withdraw most of the Swiss army from the frontiers and to base them in the high Alps, and to spend a fortune fortifying their new positions.[9] The message was clear. The army was prepared to see all of lowland Switzerland occupied, but any conqueror would face a long and bitter struggle in the high mountains.

When Jean-Luc finally returned to Switzerland from Brittany and Vichy in October 1940, he came back to a country which, although it was subject to rationing, knew none of the rigours of blackouts and bombings. At Easter 1941 he entered the Collège de Nyon after an entrance exam in French and Maths. The three elder Godard children were all to attend this school and it offered an excellent education of that time.

There had been a school in Nyon since the fourteenth century, but the Collège really traces its origins to the Reformation and in 1559 a building was purchased in the rue Saint Martin which was to become rue du Collège. This was demolished in 1784 and eight years later an impressive new building, partly constructed with material from the old, was opened which would house the pupils until the 1960s. But it is in the nineteenth century that the institution the Godards would attend began to take shape. An educational law of 1806 introduced a curriculum which included French, Latin, Greek and Geometry. Subsequently in 1834, German, Drawing, Maths and Natural Science were added.

In 1941 the school offered two sections – science and classics. Jean-Luc opted for classics, although throughout his time there he would be known as someone who was good at maths and won the top maths prize in his final year. Classes were segregated, the boys and girls being taught together only for music and Latin. All the pupils assembled on Wednesday mornings in winter, when they waited for the small train whose tracks start in the road outside the Lausanne–Geneva railway station and lead up through the small village of Trelex to the Jura mountains, and to the skiing at St Cergue. Jean-Luc was a noted skier but his athleticism led to more unorthodox exhibitions: Marcel Dreyfus records, with great disapproval, how Godard would hang on to the back of the last carriage with one hand, his body flying along in the train's wake.[10] Dreyfus was a life-long teacher at the Collège de Nyon but only a supply teacher[11] at the end of Jean-Luc's time as a pupil. His enduring memory of Godard is of someone who liked to 'play the fool'.

As well as drawing and singing, the Collège encouraged theatre, and 'les soirées du Collège' were real events in the small town. In 1945, in his final year, Jean Rosset inaugurated a revolution when he presented a Chekhov play with a mixed cast. Until then, all plays had been produced with an all-male or all-female cast. In 1946, his final year at the Collège, Jean-Luc was to play the sinister figure of Louis XI in Théodore de Bainville's *Gringoire*.

Throughout the war, Switzerland was unique in showing British as well as French, German and Italian films, and Godard remembers seeing *In Which We Serve* and both Italian and German comedies.[12] In Godard's memory Switzerland, like the rest of Europe, showed no American movies during the war; in fact, although they may not have reached as far as Nyon, American movies did play in Switzerland – both *Citizen Kane* and *Hellzapoppin'* screened in Geneva in 1942. Most striking of all, and a real Godardian education in sound and image, was that the Swiss had the privilege of seeing both German and English newsreels, in which the same images would often be accompanied by two completely different soundtracks. In Godard's own words, 'The same fight but different victors.'

The war was followed closely. Every evening at 7.15, Paul and Odile Godard would listen to the Swiss news, which had a deserved reputation for impartiality, and the children would observe their parents' reaction. Both were involved in Red Cross work and had carried out missions in France; Odile possessed a Red Cross passport. Separately, there was also some contact with the French resistance. Indeed one resistant fleeing over the Jura mountains, Yves Barthélémy, a brother of one of Odile's sisters-in-law, was to stay with the Godards for several months in 1944–45. Not all the Monods were on the side of the resistance; Julien-Pierre had a photo of Marshal Pétain by his bedside and was a firm supporter of the Vichy government. But the inhabitants of 4, rue du Prieuré, like most of Nyon, were firmly on the side of the Allies. Paul Godard had always been anti-German[13] (one of his obstetric textbooks written by a

German has anti-German slogans dotted in the margins) and was also extremely Anglophile. He kept in regular contact with many of the doctors with whom he had studied in England, and several were regular visitors to Switzerland both before and after the war. Both Jean-Luc and Claude were keen members of the Scouts[14] and Jean Rosset remembers that there were endless games which pitted the Free French against the 'Boches'.

The Black Sheep: 1946–50

In May 1945, the war came to the end, and the following year Jean-Luc graduated from the Collège de Nyon. Rachel had already gone to Geneva to take her 'matu', or *maturité*, the Swiss equivalent of the bac, but Jean-Luc did not follow her. He went instead to Paris to complete his studies at the Lycée Buffon. It may seen strange to send a sixteen-year-old boy to school hundreds of miles away but this is to forget how the passage between Geneva and Paris was now generations old, and also the size of the extended Monod family in Paris. For Godard, the move was unproblematic. It was, he told me, 'like you going to Charing Cross'. But there may have been more specific reasons for his departure from Nyon. Paul Godard and his eldest son were frequently at odds. In particular, family legend recounts a famous meal when the doctor so lost control that he hurled a bowl of mashed potatoes at his son's head.

This Oedipal dynamic may itself have been affected by the disintegrating marriage of the Godard parents. In a devout Protestant family, any talk of divorce was all but disallowed, and so it is difficult to give any clear chronology of the breakdown of the marriage until the final divorce in November 1952. The children have different memories of the split. For Claude, it occurs in 1949 when his mother moves to Geneva; for Véronique in 1951 when she returned from a skiing holiday to be told by her sister Rachel that their mother had left. Jean-Luc repeatedly told me that it came when he was fifteen, which would place it in 1945. What is certain is that Odile Godard had never reconciled herself to the move to Switzerland. Paul Godard may have been delighted to escape from being 'dragged around the worldly salons of Paris' (his daughter Véronique's guess), but Odile Godard missed those same salons dreadfully and made sure that both she and her children spent as much time in Paris as possible.

There are records indicating that as late as 1933, when she was pregnant with Claude in Switzerland, she was still trying to continue her studies in Paris. While she seems to have been a devoted and conscientious mother, involving herself and her children in a multitude of social and cultural activities, and while reading was obviously a passion, there is little doubt that the life of a Vaudois matron was not to her taste.

For Paul Godard, however, the life of a general practitioner in a small Swiss town seems to have been an ambition fulfilled. He played an active part in the more general medical world, producing occasional research papers with colleagues and entertaining visiting English doctors. But he took his holidays alone and did not normally join the family for the summers in Anthy, contenting himself with the occasional visit across the lake in his small boat with the intriguing name *Trait d'union* (French for hyphen). What the full back story of the marriage was can only be guessed at, but what is certain is that for Jean-Luc the marriage was finished with the war, and that by that time it was the subject of Nyon gossip.

In 1946, when Jean-Luc started at the Lycée Buffon, he was staying at a pension run by a Madame Melon in the rue d'Assas, opposite the Luxembourg Gardens. It was here that he took his breakfast and dinner. Lunch was taken not at school but with one of his Monod relatives, and it was such a large family that he had almost too many offers for each week. Godard remembers these meals as though they were Shakespeare plays, with very formal language and etiquette; many of his uncles and aunts he addressed with the formal 'vous' rather than the intimate 'tu'. But amongst the hosts of Monods, two households were particularly important: the grandparents, where he went on Sundays, and his mother's twin, Tante Aude, at 274, Boulevard Saint Germain, which became an alternative base to the pension. Perhaps even more significant was 'Marraine Jacko', his mother's best friend Jacqueline Morin, at 82, rue de Sèvres. At all three houses Godard felt himself to be a favourite, so much so at his godmother's that he said 'if I had been older, I would have almost been a lover'.

But the favourite of the family was about to turn himself into a black sheep. The first problem was school. In Nyon he had always been considered brilliant at maths and was much encouraged by a young teacher called Raymond Gaille, but his enthusiasm did not survive long at the Lycée Buffon: 'In the Collège I thought at one time I was good at mathematics but then I discovered in Paris that to be good at mathematics you have to work, and then it was over.' In fact in post-war Paris, Jean-Luc was beginning an incomparable education in the ciné-clubs of the capital. This, however, was invisible to his family. For them, Jean-Luc was failing at his studies. The only pressure that he could remember as a child was that he was expected to take a degree, and it soon looked as though he might not even get his baccalauréat.

But worse than that, he was a thief. For five years, until he finally landed in prison in Zurich in 1952, Jean-Luc was to steal repeatedly, and repeatedly to get caught. Godard's thefts were mainly petty affairs; the kind which Michel Poiccard inflicts on his friend Liliane at the beginning of *Breathless*, when he steals some notes from her purse as she is dressing. But not all were so petty. Godard claims that he financed his fellow student Jacques Rivette's first short, *Le Quadrille*, by stealing from an uncle, and even more significant was the theft of some of his grandfather's first editions of Valéry. As on other occasions, he seems to have taken little care to evade detection. The editions were sold to the nearest bookseller, where Julien-Pierre Monod, bibliophile that he was, would often browse. That he would immediately ask to see a new Valéry first edition was obvious; that he would recognise the dedication to himself certain. The result was predictable: Jean-Luc was expelled from the world of the gods of his childhood. The Monod family, with its huge all-enveloping support, was gone. For the next five years it was his parents alone who would concern themselves with Jean-Luc's future.

Godard produced a curious pamphlet at this time – it is dated 20 November 1947 and is addressed to the 'old ones of Nyon' (*vieux Nyonnais*), presumably his parents, for Christmas. It is a series of

Title page of *Le Cercle de famille: impressions d'ensemble.*

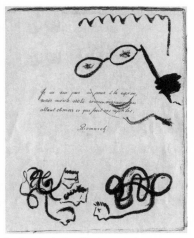

Le Cercle de famille: impressions d'ensemble. The quotation from Bismarck reads: 'I was not born to be a spy but I deserve some credit for going to look at what these reptiles do.'

sketches of various members of the family, with quotations attached – Godard's use of quotations starts early, with Bismarck, Pascal, Ecclesiastes, Prévost, Goethe, Aragon, Poquelin, Montesquieu, Camus, Montaigne, Cocteau and Sophocles all being summoned to give an accurate portrait of 'Le Cercle de famille: impressions d'ensemble' ('The Family Circle: Overall Impressions'). The pamphlet is nothing but pen and ink drawings, with carefully written commentaries and quotations, but it is produced with all the apparatus of a book; not simply a front and back cover but an elaborate page of publishing information which specifies that there is only one edition of this book on simple paper produced for 'les époux Godard' ('the Godard spouses'). The apparatus is exactly like one of those privately printed books that Valéry produced *hors commerce* for his close friends.

Behind an elaborate display of learning and an ironic use of language, one can read a rejection of the world of the Monods, be they 'grands' or 'petits bourgeois' (the work is divided into a 'concerto grand bourgeois' and a 'concerto petit bourgeois'). There is no direct identification of the family members, who are caricatured as snails or commented on by quotation and reflection, but there is a strong sense that bourgeois hypocrisy is being unmasked. Indeed, the back cover of this elaborately produced book shows the outline of a body from which two faces have fallen – a man's and a woman's – and the image is captioned 'Bas les masques' ('Off with the masks'). While the dedication to the 'vieux Nyonnais' is signed Jean-Luc Godard, the name on the title page in capital letters is IAM. Iam (pronounced 'yam') was Godard's nickname in his schooldays in Nyon, and was so well known in the town that Dr Godard himself was sometimes referred to as 'Iam's father' and his brother Claude as 'Little Iam'. There is yet a further author adorning the title page – 'Moi-même' (myself). Indeed the whole text is an elaborate play of self signification and ends with the declaration (this time signed by 'l'auteur'), 'And besides these Monods, I like them well enough and an impression is just an impression.'

It might be tempting to explain these thefts, in the vacuous terms of psychology, as an act of rebellion or a rejection of his family, but his brother sees them rather as a reaction to Protestant 'stinginess'. Godard himself places them within a comprehensive view of the desire to control his own world:

> I understood very quickly that the important thing in a film is to control the money; money, that is to say time, that is to say that to have money is to be able to spend money according to your own rhythm and your own pleasure. I will always remember that when I asked my father for money he would say 'Tell me what you want and I'll pay for it' . . . That wasn't any good at all. What I wanted was money and the power to spend it as I liked. And in the cinema, that has been my principal effort in the cinema . . . that's true power which I think very few people have enjoyed . . . except perhaps the very poor; they're left to their own devices because they've got so little money it isn't dangerous. But once there's a lot of money, real power isn't in the amount but in the time in which it is spent.[15]

The thefts made it impossible for Jean-Luc to continue to study in Paris and so he returned to Switzerland sometime in 1948. He did not go to school in Geneva, as Rachel had done, but in Lausanne. This was probably because in 1948 the Godards moved from Nyon. In 1945 Georges Godard, the gun-toting diamond dealer, died in La Lignière where his son had continued to work part-time. It may have been with money that his father had left him, and possibly with some that had been left to his sisters, that Paul Godard bought a clinic at the other end of Lac Léman. Montriant clinic is in a tiny village, Chamby-sur-Montreux, more than a hundred kilometres from Geneva but less than fifty from Lausanne, and very close to Valmont where Paul Godard had worked before his marriage.

One reason for starting this new venture was his own health. Since 1940 he had begun to suffer from progressive chronic arthritis, or Charcot's disease, and he was also affected by emphysema. The daily rounds of a general practitioner were becoming increasingly onerous. So Paul Godard gave up both La Lignière, where he had worked for fifteen years, and the private practice in Nyon that he had set up a decade before, in order to run his own clinic. The family moved with him, including Jean-Luc.

The new clinic was a large and imposing building in the foothills of the Alps which rise into the Valais, with beautiful views over the lake below. It is served by a tiny railway and on a summer day might seem idyllic. But it was very high up in the mountains and the winters were bitterly cold. It was this cold, above all, which was to render Montriant a financial failure. By 1950, it became clear that to keep the clinic open in the winter was uneconomic. But in 1948 the family moved into a small building attached to the main clinic and Jean-Luc shared a room once again with his brother Claude. He attended a college in Lausanne, Lémania, where he failed the crucial baccalauréat exam in the summer of 1948; he finally passed at Grenoble in 1949. For most of this period he seems to have been in Switzerland.

The importance of cinema was already evident. His future brother-in-law, Jean Rosset, remembers him writing a script in that summer of 1949. Rosset, who was to spend a life divided between teaching and amateur dramatics, was reading classics at the university in Lausanne, but he was also appearing in *Faust* with a young actress called Véronique Deschamps at the Château de Blonay. Godard gave both of them the script to read and talked of casting them in it. It was a modern adapation of *Aline*, an early novel by the Swiss writer Charles-Ferdinand Ramuz, which is the story of a young woman who becomes pregnant and is abandoned by her lover.

But the cinema was not yet Godard's chosen art; he was painting a great deal at that time and his mother organised an exhibition of his paintings in Montriant in the summer of 1949. His brother Claude remembers Jean-Luc being asked why blue was such a dominant colour in his painting. The reply was Godardian *avant la lettre*: 'I only had blue paint.' Jean-Luc was even then perfecting his interview technique, throwing an innocent and stereotypical question back at the questioner with its aesthetic assumptions exposed to ridicule. In the same period, Claude also remembers Jean-Luc telling him that he must read Balzac, and particularly *La Cousine Bette*.

Godard returned to Paris that autumn of 1949 and registered at the Sorbonne for a certificate in anthropology.[16] Once again, it seems to have been the Monod connection which was a determinant in this choice. Théodore Monod, a relation, was one of the leading anthropologists in France and had interested Jean-Luc in the subject. But by now cinema had begun to attract Godard, and he did not attend any classes, although his choice of anthropology is significant.

Anthropology was arguably the key subject of the twentieth century. It has its origins in the European desire to understand the 'primitive' peoples whom they were politically dominating and economically exploiting; indeed that understanding would facilitate more effective domination and more efficient exploitation. But by the twentieth century, anthropology had begun to demonstrate that 'primitive' peoples had social and symbolic structures just as sophisticated and complicated as supposedly 'civilised' ones. In any case, the horrors of the Western battlefield of the First World War and the death camps of the Nazi holocaust made any European claims to civilisation seem dubious at best and completely bogus at worst.

The man who was to demonstrate most effectively the claims of anthropology both to the other human sciences and to the more general

culture was the French anthropologist Claude Lévi-Strauss. It says something about Godard's phenomenal luck or judgment in spotting intellectual trends (luck or judgment that was to follow him throughout his life)
that he remembers hearing Lévi-Strauss lecture in 1949, the year in which
the anthropologist published *The Elementary Structures of Kinship*, a text
that some hold to be as significant for our general understanding of the
human as Freud's *The Interpretation of Dreams*. Over the next twenty
years Lévi-Strauss's thought was to affect fundamentally figures as diverse
as Lacan, Barthes and Derrida and to give birth in the mid-sixties to 'the
structuralist revolution'. However, its most important claim, and the
claim which generated such heat in the sixties and seventies was that
Western culture, both in its contemporary reality and in its canonical
works of art, needed to be analysed in just the same way and with just the
same distance as any other culture. This attitude is Godard's from the
beginning, and the encounter with anthropology may not have been as
inconsequential as the unattended courses at the Sorbonne might suggest.
It was in 1947 that the great film-maker Jean Rouch began his series of
African anthropological films, which Godard was one of the first to praise
in *Cahiers du cinéma*. And *Cahiers du cinéma* clearly made the connection
in an early review of *Breathless*, in which Luc Moullet astutely claimed
that the film could be best understood if one saw that Godard's ambition
was to be the Rouch of France.[17]

Godard was not a conventional anthropology student and the courses
he was following were, as we shall see in the next chapter, at the
Cinémathèque and at the ciné-clubs of Paris. It was also at this time that
the beginnings of a real group of cinephiles was forming, who were
writing their first magazines and making their first shorts (T:99).
However, Godard was still not completely settled on the cinema as
his artistic vocation. Suzanne Klochendler (shortly to become Suzanne
Schiffman, who was perhaps Truffaut's closest collaborator and also
worked on many Godard films) remembers Godard descending from a
bus at the Luxembourg Gardens in the autumn of 1949 and telling her
that he was going to be a great novelist. Godard, on remembering this
time when he was trying to be a novelist, said 'I think it was no good, or
too difficult, like mathematics.'

But if Godard wasn't writing novels, he was writing scripts. His brother Claude remembers reading a script in the summer of 1950 based on George Meredith's *The Fiancée* and entitled 'La trêve d'ironie, Claire' (Claire, Irony's Truce). On this occasion Godard had not only modernised but also localised it. The script ended with the heroine crashing and dying in her car as she descended the steep Jura bends towards Nyon.

Leaving Home: 1950–54

Whatever benefit Godard was deriving from his time in Paris, from his parents' point of view he was an absentee anthropology student, without purpose or drive. Their problem of what to do with Jean-Luc was temporarily solved towards the end of 1950 by his father's obsession with avoiding war. The victory of the Allies in 1945 was followed very quickly by the beginning of the Cold War, which threatened to bring to Europe the nuclear bombs which had destroyed Hiroshima and Nagasaki. Switzerland would offer very little protection. In 1946 Paul Godard had made a first trip to the Americas, travelling to Peru, Colombia, Jamaica and New York. The conjunction of Montriant's financial difficulties and the intensification of the Cold War (Communist seizure of power in Czechoslavakia in 1948, the Berlin airlift in 1949, the Korean War in 1950) seem to have combined to suggest to Paul Godard that he should set up a clinic in Jamaica, which would be both hot and, he hoped, at a reasonable distance from any nuclear fallout.

Having closed his freezing clinic, Paul Godard set out for the United States from Cherbourg in December 1950 with Jean-Luc and Véronique (who was delighted to be missing months of school). After five days on the boat, they arrived in New York where they stayed at the Beekman Hotel on First Avenue, opposite the United Nations. From there they took a train to Miami and then a plane which stopped in Cuba before arriving in Kingston. In Kingston, they stayed with Dr Wingate, an old friend of Paul Godard from medical school in England. Dr Godard quickly bought a house in Mandeville and, with his daughter, began to furnish it, while Jean-Luc set off on a long voyage to South America.

The first leg seems to have been a plane to Panama and then on to Lima where Godard stayed with his father's sister, Madeleine. In 1936 Madeleine had married Maxime Kuczynski who had been Professor of Tropical Medicine at Berlin before fleeing the Nazis on their accession to power. Godard was to stay at their house in Lima with their two children, Pierre-Paul and Michel, for several weeks. But he was apparently a rather morose visitor, unwilling to explore the area and preferring to stay in his room. He only appeared animated when talking to Kenneth Wasson, a visiting anthropologist with an interest in film. Wasson was the first to film a documentary on the Urus Indians in Titicaca lake. There is a glimpse of Jean-Luc in the memoirs of the *Le Monde Diplomatique* journalist Gunter Holzmann, when an emaciated stranger presents himself at his door and introduces himself as: 'Jean-Luc Godard, the relative of distant friends, originally Swiss and at that time living in Lima. His uncle Kuczinski [*sic*] – a doctor of great erudition . . . who was researching the health of the natives . . . had advised him to come and see me . . . Jean-Luc, then in his twenties, was rather quiet. After we had gotten to know each other better, he declared out of the blue he didn't understand how I could be content here, isolated from all culture.'[18]

His South American travels extended to Rio, and it was there that he ran out of funds. Without any money, or any means of getting some, he was forced to go to the French Embassy for help. He ended up with another of Paul Godard's sisters, Hélène, who lived in Santiago de Chile. He stayed for some time there and worked in the factory that her husband, Willy Gerig, had set up when he and Hélène had emigrated from Switzerland at the end of the war. He finally landed in France at Villefranche where his father, who had returned from Jamaica, and his brother Claude met him in April 1951.[19]

Truffaut was to tell Suzanne Schiffman on several occasions that he thought the South American journey had changed Jean-Luc radically – Truffaut dated his withdrawn manner and long silences from this trip. What had not changed was his parents' concern about his future. When

I asked Godard whether he had fought at this time with his father, he said 'One or two times in words, but no, not really. It was impossible when we had no way to fight with words. He was saying OK get away, if you don't want to do anything then just go away. But I was saying I want to make movies. But it's as if someone said they wanted to do music when nobody knows what music is. It was like an unknown territory for them, and even for me.'

Their first solution was for Godard to work for a company constructing dams in the Swiss Alps. This was followed by a job in the new audiovisual medium of television when Godard joined the Swiss television service in Zurich. Psychoanalysis would interpret Godard's adolescent criminality either as a desire to be found out or as a desire to be punished. He had already been found out, but when he stole from his new employers he was also punished. He spent three days in a Zurich jail before his father got him released and persuaded him to go into a mental hospital, La Grangette, which was an open medical clinic outside Lausanne specialising in psychotherapy. The exact length of time he was there is unclear. Godard estimates: 'Probably three months, two months, but not three days.' For Godard, his father's bafflement as to what to do with him is perfectly understandable: 'My father didn't know what to do, he was a general practitioner. He'd probably heard Freud's name but not much more. I think my father was very good and very human, very good as a generalist, but then he didn't understand what I wanted. With the other children it was clearer, but with me nobody knew and I didn't even know.' At La Grangette, Godard was treated by the head of the hospital, Dr Mueller, who was later to tell Claude that in his opinion his brother suffered from 'une forte névrose' (a serious neurosis).[20]

This episode seems to have occasioned a final break with his immediate family, for it it became clear at this time that he would have to earn his own money. He returned to the dam company in the Alps, but this time there were no parental offers to find him a better job. He saved his wages to such effect that in 1954 he was able to shoot and edit his first film, a documentary on the construction of the dam at La Grande Dixence entitled *Opération 'béton'*.

Godard now had effectively no contact with his family. But word did reach him, probably through Rachel, of his mother's death. The adventurous young woman who had wanted to be a doctor had remained just as adventurous in middle age. The new Italian scooter, the Vespa, was all the rage amongst the young. Odile Monod asked her father if he would buy her one. On 25 April 1954, at 9.30 in the evening, her Vespa came off the road in Lausanne and she died almost immediately from a fractured skull.[21] Godard went to the hospital from Geneva but he did not attend the funeral, which turned out to be an unusually painful affair. When Paul Godard accompanied his children to the station to meet the Monod grandparents, he was told by Cécile Monod (née Cécile Naville of Calvin's Geneva, the goddess of Anthy), 'Monsieur, on ne veut pas vous voir ici' ('We don't wish to see you here'). The body was buried at Anthy and the gravestone bears the name Odile Monod.

2

'The Cinema Is Not a Bad School':
André Bazin and the *Cahiers du cinéma*

Paris and the Cinema

Godard has often said that for him there is no real distinction between criticism and directing – both are ways of making movies. When in the autumn of 1946, Godard came to Paris to his pension in the rue d'Assas and to his lycée on the Boulevard Pasteur, he was coming to the world centre of writing and reflection on the cinema.

Above all, Paris was the best place in the world to see the entire range of world cinema both past and present. There were, as in other capitals, a huge number of cinemas showing a selection of current Hollywood and national productions. But in addition there were all kinds of specialist cinemas and ciné-clubs attempting to screen the greatest treasures from cinema's archives. In the West, this early interest in cinema as *the* art form of the twentieth century was specific to France. In the East, Lenin was to declare cinema the most important of the arts, and to throw the power of the new Soviet state behind its development.[1] However, for the majority of Western intellectuals, particularly those in England and America, cinema was merely the most pernicious example of modern culture: industrialised, crude and insensitive. As early as 1908, a mere thirteen years after the Lumière brothers had projected moving images for a paying audience, Anatole France, one of the great old men of French letters, had declared that he loved the cinema. But this slightly patronising affection, which was as much to do with cinema's ability to document as to fictionalise the world, was soon overtaken in the years just before the First World War by an avant-garde passion in which figures as various as Ricciotto Canudo, Abel Gance and Marcel

L'Herbier began to proclaim cinema as the art form of the twentieth century.[2] Even in this very early moment of reflection on the cinema, one can distinguish between those who praised cinema in terms of the sophisticated art it could become and those who praised it for the melodramas and comedies which were already produced. When the great modernist poet Apollinaire's magazine, *Les Soirées de Paris*, introduced a film column just before the First World War, there was little talk of the much vaunted 'cinematographic art' but a considerable appreciation of the incredibly popular hero of the long running serial, *Fantômas*. And Apollinaire's appeals to cinema as the art of the future did not conceive of it as the medium which would bring to a culmination all other arts, but rather that its popularity would allow for a complete reconceptualisation of art itself.[3]

In the years immediately after the First World War, ciné-clubs in Paris catered both to an intellectual avant-garde – the Surrealists' passion for cinema would culminate in Dali and Buñuel's shocking *L'Age d'or* – and to French high society. An account in the *Journal du ciné-club* of a matinée at the Colisée cinema on the Champs Élysées captures the aesthetic and social ambitions of French film culture: 'The room was filled with an elegant audience in which one could pick out a number of personalities from the world of cinema, theatre and music. M. Louis Delluc spoke of cinema in general, affirming that – although this art was scarcely at its beginnings, indeed one could even ask if it yet existed – that its current reality constituted the most important popular art since Greek theatre.'[4]

By the early twenties, Paris was clearly established as the world capital of film with the whole gamut of cinema, from Hollywood to the avant-garde, available to be seen and discussed. Although a partial explanation for this Parisian eminence can be found in the chauvinism which considered cinema a French invention, it owes much more to Paris's undisputed claim to cultural and intellectual supremacy in the Western world. How far back one cares to date the cultural supremacy of France and of Paris is almost a matter of choice.

From the very early Middle Ages and the founding of the Sorbonne, the time of Abélard and Héloise, Paris has been a centre of intellectual reference. But medieval Europe found its most important cultural models and debates in the Languedoc and the city states of Northern Italy, and as the struggle between Catholicism and Protestantism forged different national cultures all over Reformation Europe, it would be difficult to identify a single dominant city. But from the early seventeenth century on, as the absolutism of Richelieu and Louis XIV developed neoclassicism as its cultural arm through the Encyclopedists and the revolutionaries, Paris was the intellectual centre of Europe. If Romanticism was to stress the local and the national, and at least in its German form to pit these explicitly against French cultural supremacy, almost all the major developments in poetry and painting at the end of the nineteenth century, from Lautréamont to Mallarmé and from Manet to Cézanne, meant that Paris was the intellectual capital of the Western world at the turn of the century.

When T.S. Eliot graduated from Harvard in 1910 and chose, much to his mother's dismay, to spend a year in Paris following Henri Bergson's lectures at the Collège de France, he wrote, 'it is not an accident that led me to Paris. For several years France represented, above all in my eyes, poetry.'[5] Eliot is the pre-eminent twentieth-century thinker in English, for whom culture is still defined by the models of Greece and Rome and their development within Western Europe. But in his more radical poetry of the twenties – *The Waste Land* for example, which takes many of its images and themes from anthropology – he makes clear that Greece and Rome provide only one model amongst others, and in his most ambitious formal experiment 'Sweeney Agonistes' he tries to bring the classical tradition into juxtaposition with the new medium of jazz.

Paris in the post-First World War era combines the most serious reflection on the new medium of cinema with the most active investigation of other models of culture; Surrealism and anthropology come together to produce the milieu from which Bataille, Lacan and Lévi-Strauss will all, in the late twenties and thirties, begin the elaboration of their thought. From this perspective the Nouvelle Vague (the New Wave) and Structuralism are both part of the last wave of Parisian intellectual and cultural dominance of the West. What is strange, given

Antonin Artaud in Carl Dreyer's film *La Passion de Jeanne d'Arc*, 1927.

their geographical proximity, is how little these two worlds interact. There are the anecdotes which have Lévi-Strauss and Jakobson developing their theories in exile in New York in the early forties around repeated viewings of the Marx brothers. There is also the extraordinary figure of Artaud, his beautiful face captured on film and his whole life an attempt to live and dramatise anthropology – to reintroduce ritual into Western theatre.

From the point of view of intellectual history, Godard is at his most interesting as the figure who clearly participates both in the Parisian revolution in the humanities, which goes global in the sixties, and in the revolution in film which sweeps all before it as the New Wave. But the particular case of Godard should not obscure the fact that the ferment in the understanding of culture and the ferment around the most important, aesthetic change within the culture took place in montage rather than sequence shot.

Even if the luck of the historical draw had not made France the birthplace of cinema, it is likely that Paris would have given this new invention the most interest and attention. But the coming of sound in 1929 marked the end of this first wave of intellectual and critical interest in the cinema. The attractions of the universal art form disappeared as cinema fell back into the national languages which initially it appeared to have moved beyond. And the arrival of sound, with its vastly increased costs, also confirmed the dominance of Hollywood, marking this new art form, for many intellectuals, as irretrievably contaminated by commercial considerations. The speed with which the 'talkies' replaced silent movies was breathtaking. By 1932, the last great movie palace to show silent in Paris, la Salle des Agriculteurs had switched to talkies, and by 1934 even the cheap picture houses on the *grands boulevards*, which also functioned as unofficial brothels, had invested in the new projection equipment. There was now nowhere to see silent films and very soon companies started jettisoning the reels themselves. Not only were silent films now economically without value but the material from which they were made, silver nitrate, had a value of its own as the silver could be recovered from old film stock. Silent films were destroyed at a terrifying rate. The first movement to archive and save films began at this time in the different industrially developed countries. There is no doubt that the single most important figure in this movement, and a figure of continuous importance in Godard's life, was Henri Langlois.

Henri Langlois

Born in 1914, Langlois spent his early childhood in Smyrna in Turkey, where his father was a journalist. It was there that he saw his first films. After the occupation of Smyrna by the Turkish army in 1922, the family returned to Paris and Langlois was soon enjoying the full range of films available. By the time he started work at a printing press in 1934, he was already extraordinarily knowledgeable about the cinema. One of his co-workers, Jacques Franju, wrote about Langlois to his twin brother Georges, then on military service: 'He is completely mad but he adores the cinema: you'll like him a lot.'[6] The prediction proved correct and the

Langlois's bath, where he first started storing films.

two young men set about setting up a ciné-club. But they were not content with such an ambition. They wanted to set up a cinémathèque which would save the treasures of the silent era. In what reads almost like a fairy tale, they persuaded Paul-Auguste Harlé, the editor of the French trade journal *La Cinématographie Française*, to back them, and on 2 September 1936 they signed the papers setting up the Cinémathè-que. But they still needed somewhere to store the films. George Méliès, a figure from the earliest years of film history and the first to demonstrate film's ability to show impossible and fantastic worlds, was now old and ill in a home outside Paris. Franju knew him well and Méliès pointed out to them a ruined house in a park at Orly, near where he was living, which could serve them well as a base. Harlé bought and renovated the house, and put the keys in Méliès's charge, thus making one of the legends of early cinema the first curator of the Cinémathèque. Producer after producer was persuaded to store films there.

Right from the start Langlois distinguished himself from similar enterprises in other European countries. He was not simply interested in preservation but in showing the treasures he was collecting to an audience. In England, for example, archives were set up from which no film would be allowed to escape. Langlois, in contrast, was creating a cinémathèque, a library of cinema where spectators could come to view and consult the films of the past. Langlois had also adopted a comprehensive collection policy. If a film-maker was worth preserving, then it was worth preserving all of his work; Langlois refused to choose between films. His experience of discovering the genius of the early French film-maker Feuillade, whose *Les Vampires* and *Fantômas* were such favourites of the Surrealists even though for years they had been held up as examples of the banality of cinema, made him extremely wary of making collecting choices based on critical opinions which might later prove to be mistaken.

Langlois had left school after failing his baccalauréat, but his schooling had come from the cinemas of Paris and the bookshop José Corti, with its large collection of Surrealist writings, which was conveniently close to the Lycée Condorcet where he was nominally being educated. The variety of films shown on Parisian screens meant that Langlois really did have an extraordinary knowledge across an extraordinary range. There is no doubt that he felt that Surrealism and film had a particular affinity. Many years later in an interview he said: 'I am persuaded that Surrealism first existed in the cinema. You've only got to look at *Les Vampires* to understand that the cinema, because it was the expression of the twentieth century and the universal unconscious, carried Surrealism within it.'[7] One of Langlois's first acts of friendship to Franju was to take him to the cinema Studio 28 in Montmartre to see *Un chien andalou* and *L'Age d'or*.[8] However, if Langlois was open to the most avant-garde elements in film, he was also one of the first to appreciate the possibilities within Hollywood cinema, and particularly

Howard Hawks. In notes for a 1955 Cinémathèque screening of the 1928 classic *A Girl in Every Port*, starring Louise Brooks, Langlois stressed how the original release of the film was a moment at which one could see the future of cinema, rejecting the false aestheticism of Expressionism in favour of naturalness and simplicity of style. It is possible to imagine the young critics of *Cahiers du cinéma* developing their *politique des auteurs* without relying on Langlois's justification for collecting all the works of a great film-maker, but it is not possible to imagine them doing it without being able to see the majority of Hawks's works. The only place in the post-war world where you could appreciate Hawks across silent and sound cinema, across comedies, thrillers and Westerns, was at Langlois's Cinémathèque.

Before the Cinémathèque acquired its own screening rooms in the avenue de Messine in 1948, Langlois had shown his treasures through a ciné-club, the Cercle du Cinéma. As always with Langlois, it is difficult to distinguish between legend and reality when describing the Cercle du Cinéma. Did James Joyce and André Breton really attend its screenings in the late thirties? It is certain that Jean Rouch did, and it is also certain that unlike almost all other ciné-clubs, Langlois positively discouraged debates, contenting himself with the briefest of contextual introductions. At the same time the Cercle du Cinéma found its intellectual force (as the Cinémathèque was to do later), in the juxtapositions provided by the programming – a comedy by Chaplin would follow one from René Clair and then, to complete the evening, there would be one from the Soviet film-maker Protazanov, or an anti-Soviet German film would be followed by an anti-Nazi Russian film.

From its first year, 1896, when it travelled round the world at a speed which still astonishes, cinema has been the international medium, and Paris in the twenties was the best place to appreciate that internationalism. Perhaps it is therefore not surprising – but then almost everything about Langlois's career is surprising – that an unqualified twenty-four-year-old Frenchman was in 1938 the moving force behind the development of the International Federation of Film Archives, which brought together the French Cinémathèque, the British Film Institute in London and the Museum of Modern Art in New York. At the inaugural meeting in the Hotel Crillon, an uninvited guest arrived as an envoy from the German Reichsfilmarchiv: Frank Hensel.[9]

This meeting was to prove of the utmost significance for Langlois after the French defeat in June of 1940. Even at a distance of more than half a century it is difficult to comprehend the scale and nature of the French surrender in that fatal summer. That France was both outgunned and outmanoeuvred is obvious, but this does not explain the extraordinary loss of national nerve that is recorded so bleakly in Churchill's history of the Second World War. As the nine-year-old Jean-Luc was being hurried off to Brittany and then over a five-month period back through Vichy France, the generals whose whole raison d'être was to fight 'les Boches' capitulated to Hitler. It was left to a junior general, whose most notable achievement until then was to be Pétain's ghost-writer, to set up in open rebellion against his own constitutionally elected government, the government in exile, which despite Churchill's urging his political and military superiors had so signally failed to do.[10] Whether we explain the French behaviour as a collective shell shock of men who had spent their youth fighting in the trenches of the 1914–18 war, or as a political revenge of the upper classes against the ghost of the Popular Front, it is a determining feature in French political and intellectual history which resonates throughout Godard's life, and one which he will finally turn to address in the magisterial *Eloge de l'amour*, completed in his seventieth year.

For Langlois, arriving back in Paris after the military debacle, the situation offered an unparalleled opportunity to save more films. But this time it was not the glories of silent cinema which required rescuing from an industry which had abandoned them, but the huge array of films which had been pronounced anathema by Nazism. In large part due to his connection with Frank Hensel, he was able to save thousands of reels many of which he was to return to French-Jewish producers like Braunberger and to the American studios after the Liberation. It is impossible to understand Langlois's subsequent success without reckoning the huge amount of corporate goodwill earned by his wartime exploits. If other archives were frightened of showing films, it was not simply the poverty of imagination of anally retentive bureaucrats that was to blame; the national industries and particularly the Hollywood studios were deeply suspicious of the archives. Archives might hold films but they had to clear rights to show them, and the studios enforced their rights ruthlessly. Langlois's aristocratic disregard of such legal niceties (a disregard which Godard in his later career was both to emulate and, many would argue, to surpass) was not simply a reflection of his character but also the calling in of debts which had been well established.

Godard at the Cinema

In every account of both Godard and the Nouvelle Vague, Langlois's Cinémathèque is a clear point of reference, and there is no doubt that when it first opened its doors in the Avenue de Messine and later on the rue d'Ulm, it soon became the favoured meeting place for the young men – and they were almost all young men – who had found in the cinema a world in which they could recognise themselves. It was at Langlois's Cinémathèque, and only at Langlois's Cinémathèque, that they could see the whole history of this world which they wished to inhabit. But the Cinémathèque was merely a part of the incredibly rich world of ciné-clubs and specialist cinemas which made post-war Paris a continual feast of films. Langlois had an audience for his illuminating and provocative programming and that audience found friendship in the discussion of films. As they met again and again at the same locations – the Tuesday question-and-answer sessions at the Studio Parnasse, and above all at the rue d'Ulm – friendships of an intense and lasting nature were formed. Many of these cinéphiles were cripplingly shy, some such as Truffaut and Godard had been in trouble with the law, most were academic dropouts. These were friendships in which the cinema was not the incidental pretext but the very form and substance of human relationships. Godard himself talks of a family. The paradox is that the members of this family were unbelievably close, able to discuss any nuance of ethics or aesthetics by reference to films, but shared little of their personal lives. Even in this context Godard was considered particularly enigmatic and secretive. His double life in Geneva and Paris and his mysterious travels in South America no doubt contributed to this, but they do not completely explain it.

It is impossible to date precisely Godard's transformation from budding sixteen-year-old mathematician in the autumn of 1946 to twenty-year-old producer of Jacques Rivette's short, Le Quadrille, and film critic in 1950. Indeed the whole period from 1946, when he leaves the Collège de Nyon, until 1956, when Claude Chabrol secures a job for him as press officer at Fox, is full of unexplained absences and gaps. Godard's own memory of this time is very hazy – his answer to the question of where he lived was 'nowhere'. We could, however, have him leaving the Lycée Buffon after two years in the summer of 1948 and spending a year in Switzerland based at the clinic of Montriant, attending the Collège de Lémania.[11] He returns to Paris in the autumn of 1949 and if he was no longer in the good graces of the Monod family, he still seems to have had the wider support of the Protestant clan. In an interview given at the time of his second marriage, to Anne Wiazemsky in 1967, Godard said that he had spent this year lodging with the writer Jean Schlumberger at 78, rue d'Assas: 'Godard recounts that he stole many first editions that he then resold with some difficulty at the Pont Neuf to get money to see a Hitchcock or a Hawks. Sometimes in the evening old Gide would come and visit and the two of them would eat sandwiches in the kitchen.'[12]

While many of the interviews in the sixties contain erroneous information, there is always a kernel of truth in them. What is certain is that the pastor Wilfred Monod of the Louvre Oratory had been a close friend of another Protestant pastor, Elie Allégret. Elie Allégret was the father of the film-makers Marc and Yves Allégret, who were also part of the circle that included Gide and Schlumberger.

Later in the fifties Godard was to spend a great deal of time at Marc Allégret's house. Describing the shooting of Godard's first Parisian short, Charlotte et Véronique, in 1957, Jean-Claude Brialy says that Godard had met both of the women in the short, Anne Colette and Nicole Berger, at Marc Allégret's house, where he was living.[13] The producer of the short, Pierre Braunberger, says in his memoirs: 'My

meeting with Godard took place in 1955 when Marc Allégret introduced us. His parents were Protestant and owners of a huge clinic in
Switzerland. They were friends of Marc's father, the pastor Allégret.
They had sent Jean-Luc to Paris where he stayed with Marc.'[14] Allégret
was one of the film-makers 'of quality' whom the young critics of
Cahiers would deride, and Godard in particular wounded his former
patron with a review of his film *Un drôle de dimanche* in 1958 when he
wrote that it was 'of no interest whatsoever. The script is lamentable. As
are the actors' (G:99/1:150). Allégret's biographer confirms that his
subject felt this as a personal betrayal 'with all the more sadness because
he had housed or formed those who belong to this tendency. Jean-Luc
Godard, for example, who had really haunted the house at 11 bis, rue
Lord Byron. "Tu quoque, fili!" (You too, my son!)'.[15]

It is clear from these memoirs that Godard did not live quite as
marginal a life as some of his recollections suggest. But it is also certain
that he did spend a great deal of the fifties in small cheap hotels like the
one in the rue de Rennes. Another of his shorts, *Charlotte and son Jules*,
this time with Jean-Paul Belmondo and Anne Colette, was filmed in his
hotel room in the rue de Rennes in 1958. Sally Shafto's thesis emphasises
the nomadic quality of Godard's life at this time:

In our interviews together Charles Bitsch, Godard's assistant director on
many of his films from the 1960s and a former critic of *Cahiers du cinéma*
in the 1950s, emphasised Godard's aloofness during their communal time
in the 1950s. Godard hung out with the group, voraciously reading
books, firing off his own articles, while at the same time remaining the
loner . . .

'There were screenings at various theatres and at the Cinémathèque
that we attended and Jean-Luc would come along. But there were also
large chunks of time when Godard was absent. Where he was I have no
idea. We didn't have the reflex when we saw each other to inquire:
"Where were you this morning? What did you do last night?"'[16]

If throughout the fifties it is often difficult to give an exact address for
Godard in Paris or Geneva, where he begins a contemporary adult life in

the years 1953–56, it is certain that the year 1949–50 is the first to be
devoted entirely to cinema. It also marks his first real contact with what
would become the nucleus of his *Cahiers du cinéma* family: Eric Rohmer
and Jacques Rivette.

La Gazette du Cinéma

It is easy to believe the bad boy myths that have grown up around many
of the writers for *Cahiers du cinéma*, but it is crucial to remember that
those bad boys had been provided with an exceptional education by a
network of informal classes. Few could have been more impressive than
the Thursday afternoons when Maurice Schérer in the rue Danton would
comment on the film that he had selected that week for the Ciné-Club du
Quartier Latin. Maurice Schérer was then thirty years old and a literature
teacher in a lycée outside Paris. He had already published a novel in 1946
and wrote for *La Revue du cinéma*, the cinema magazine which Gallimard closed down in 1948, and *Les Temps Modernes*, the journal
founded by Jean-Paul Sartre in the immediate aftermath of the war,
which enjoyed an extraordinary level of contribution across the entire
breadth of society and arts. Schérer was soon to adopt the pseudonym of
Eric Rohmer because, as he has intimated in interviews, his mother would
have been shocked by his working in the cinema. Joël Magny, the author
of the most exact portrait of Rohmer, suggests that the reason was more a
professional one: serious teachers of literature didn't muck about in the
cinema.[17] Whichever explanation is true, they both testify to the extent to
which in the late forties and early fifties the cinema still had the whiff of
what William Burroughs calls 'carny'. It was somehow outside the law,
potentially sleazy and actually sexual.

It is crucial to remember this when considering Godard's desire to
work in the cinema; he himself stresses it, and Rohmer's 'nom de
caméra' is another index of this. Rohmer was much older than Godard,
thirty to his nineteen, and living the life of a successful teacher. It may
seem strange that this respectable figure, who was nicknamed 'Big
Momo' would forge close friendships with such delinquent students

as Godard and Rivette, who when confronted with the choice of watching a film or going to a lecture, inevitably chose the film. But the strangeness disappears when one realises how rich a film culture there was in Paris at that time and how the question of finding a way to think and write about this still unappreciated 'seventh art' provided a world in which there was no professional hierarchy, and where relationships could be forged across age and background. At the same time there is no doubt that Rohmer functioned for the young group of cinéphiles as a benevolent teacher. Paul Gégauff,[18] one of Rohmer's closest friends, describes Big Momo thus: 'Rohmer was dead straight, *un intègre*, a real prof. To us bums he constantly gave money but you always had to come up with your receipt, metro tickets as well as train tickets, even grocer's bills. He gave us exactly the sum necessary. An organisational question.' Godard, too, remembers Rohmer's salary as a means of sustenance. For Rohmer, Godard was another of those young men who shared his passion for the cinema, above all for the silent cinema that they were all discovering for the first time. Rohmer remembers Godard as distinguishing himself from his rather scruffy contemporaries by the smartness of his appearance. He also remembers that Godard always carried a book with him, often his beloved Balzac. But if Rohmer, unlike most responsible adults, applauded Godard and his friends' passion for the cinema, he was less enthusiastic about their other passion – playing pinball in Parisian cafés: 'If you love the cinema you cannot waste your time on games of chance.'[19]

Towards the end of 1949 Rohmer, with the help of his former pupil F.C. Froeschel, turned the regular *Bulletin du Ciné-Club du Quartier Latin* into a proper magazine, *La Gazette du cinéma* (C1:222). It was only to publish five issues before folding within a year, but to read it is to understand how at nineteen Godard, who contributed to almost every issue, was already deeply immersed in the mission to claim for cinema its status as the greatest of the contemporary arts. The range of films, from Ophuls and Kazan (both reviewed by Godard) to Jean Genet's recently finished clandestine masterpiece *Un Chant d'amour*, is impressive and the assured tone of the young critics is striking. But the magazine also makes clear that its aim is to draw on all the most vital strands of

Parisian intellectual life. As well as a short text by Valéry, the magazine
published across two issues a long lecture by Jean-Paul Sartre entitled
'Why the cinema is not a bad school'.

The dominance of the position occupied by Sartre in post-war Paris
cannot be overstated – you would have to go back to Bergson before the
First World War to find a comparison. In a possibly apocryphal story de
Gaulle compared him to Voltaire.[20] The pre-war publication of his
novel *Nausea* and his short stories *Le Mur* had already transformed
Sartre from an obscure philosophy teacher into a literary figure, but it
was the war that made him a national hero for a whole generation. This
was partly a function of the instant myths of the Liberation, when the
Resistance came to stand as a symbol for French refusal of the humiliation of June 1940 and the crimes of Vichy. In this sudden rewriting of
history, Sartre's own honest but inept attempts to resist lent him moral
stature. And in his major philosophical work, *Being and Nothingness*,
published in 1943, he had provided both a term, Existentialism, and a
philosophy which stressed the possibility for the individual to free
himself from the dead hand of tradition. Sartre's philosophy advocating
the supremacy of the autonomous individual subject has not worn very
well: from Lévi-Strauss to Lacan to Althusser, Sartre was under attack in
the fifties and sixties. If Lévi-Strauss stressed the culture into which one
is born, Lacan the unconscious that is formed in that birth, and
Althusser the economic conditions which render the individual possible,
all were agreed that these were not exterior constraints on the self but
written into the constitution of individual subjects.

But Sartre's importance was not simply as a philosopher and a
novelist, it was also as an example. Sartre's roots lay in the disillusionment of the First World War, and his philosophy was explicitly at the
service of a bohemian lifestyle which stressed the refusal of bourgeois
traditions. Nowhere was this more manifest than in his relationship with
Simone de Beauvoir, a relationship conceived as a non-exclusive sexual
partnership based on honesty and reason. If time has also sullied that
vision, both in terms of de Beauvoir's own reflections on the pain it
caused her, and in terms of the millions who have now found how
difficult, if not impossible, such partnerships are, the effort to find a new

way of life had immense appeal in a France still suffocating in a
bourgeois tradition which had, even in its own terms, failed, and failed
lamentably in June 1940. If that were not enough Sartre, while refusing
to abandon his individualistic philosophy, was persuaded by the experience of the war that intellectuals must engage themselves politically.
Indeed he was to devote much of his post-war life and writings to that
task.

Sartre's interest in the cinema was very considerable. *Les Temps
Modernes*, the magazine he founded, took its title from Chaplin's film;
he was on the editorial board of *L'Ecran français*, and he wrote both
about and for the cinema. Although it is still little known, the lecture
Rohmer published in *La Gazette du cinéma* is the best of Sartre's
writings on the cinema. It is not a text of the famous Existentialist
philosopher of 1950 but goes back twenty years to when Sartre took up
his first teaching post in the provincial town of Le Havre. In French
tradition the youngest teacher in the lycée gives the graduation address.
For the young Sartre, already secure in his rejection of the conventions
of bourgeois society, such an invitation must have posed innumerable
problems.[21] His solution is brilliant. He starts with a long quotation
from Anatole France on the importance and delight of the first visit to
the theatre – the anticipation for days ahead, the dressing up, the waiting
for the theatre to fill and then the magic as the curtain rises. Sartre
compares this dramatically with the delight of the first visit to the cinema
at five rather than twelve, with no dressing up, no anticipation, no
raising of the curtain. He enthuses on the ease with which one can go to
the cinema – the possibility of entering at any time and waiting for the
film to begin again. The genres are so familiar and physical access so
easy that the cinema is always and at every moment available. Sartre's
point, hammered home again and again in an elegant and formal style
suitable to the dignity of the occasion, is that the cinema is the modern
art. And this both because of its huge audiences and its particular
relation to time and space. It is this which enables the cinema to grasp a
simultaneity of events which is beyond the reach of any other medium.

Sartre's address is a good reminder of the extent to which the
revolution of *Cahiers* and the New Wave was based on an extremely

rich first wave of French cinephilia. The determination to claim cinema
as the 'seventh art', cinema's democratic potential in terms of its huge
audiences, cinema's specificity both in terms of medium and genres, even
the delight in the directness of action in American cinema: all these are
utilised as well-understood subjects by a newly graduated philosopher
of the Ecole Normale Supérieure who had used his four years at the rue
d'Ulm in Paris to train himself in the culture of the Parisian ciné-clubs,
just as he had trained himself in all the important cultural currents he
could identify, like the American novel and German phenomenology.
But if Sartre reminds us of the enormous fecundity of the culture which
produced Langlois, his article is also at a considerable distance from the
young critics of *La Gazette* – that distance has a name: André Bazin.

André Bazin

If Godard is unthinkable without the material that Langlois presented
at the Cinémathèque and if Langlois's method of demonstration by
juxtaposition was one he was to make his own, he is equally unthinkable without the philosophical and critical thinking of André Bazin.
Sartre and Rohmer both testify to the extent to which some of the finest
products of the French educational system were using their talents to
teach, in whatever unorthodox ways, the possibilities of the art of the
twentieth century. But Bazin is the only example of someone who,
having chosen with an extraordinary level of passion and commitment
the vocation of a teacher, then decided that his vocation would be
exercised entirely in relation to the cinema. For Bazin, like so many
others, the summer of 1940 was a crucial turning point. From a petit-
bourgeois background Bazin had proceeded brilliantly through the
French educational system. Significantly he did not go to the Ecole
Normale Supérieure on the rue d'Ulm but to its sister institution at
Saint Cloud. This was due at least in part to Saint Cloud's emphasis on
pedagogy – for Bazin teaching was not a chore to be endured but the
very purpose of intellectual inquiry: his conception of the teacher as
both the bearer and destroyer of his or her own community's traditions

is one of the most compelling arguments for a life devoted to education.[22] This faith was part of a larger belief in a Catholic activism which understood salvation in social terms. The thinker who most influenced Bazin was Emmanuel Mounier, the charismatic founder of the journal *Esprit*, the major forum for Catholic intellectuals. Mounier was himself a brilliant product of the French educational system who had decided to pursue his teaching vocation outside that system. *Esprit* was to serve as a crucial intellectual centre throughout Bazin's life. By the happiest of chances *Esprit* was the only journal of the thirties which took film seriously. Its main contributor was Roger Leenhardt, the 'godfather' of the *Cahiers du cinéma*.[23] Thirty years later, in 1964, Godard would use him as one of the few voices of hope in *Une Femme mariée*. As an old man Leenhardt speaks on behalf of the future, in favour of genuine inquiry and a real engagement, however difficult, with the new. Leenhardt can speak with authority in Godard's film because, as a young man, he had refused to acquiesce in the general denunciation of film that followed the introduction of sound. For many, sound spelt the death knell of what seemed so necessary after the fatal misunderstandings that had led to the First World War: a universal language. For others of a more aesthetic persuasion, sound mired cinema in a realism that the mute image had promised to transcend. For almost all, the incredible increase in budgets for even a low-cost sound film meant that cinema was inextricably tied to the rhythms and pressures of a capitalism doomed to destruction. The small fringe of intellectuals who had refused the simplicities that argued that film was the end of known civilisation now joined the almost universal chorus of contempt, misunderstanding and hatred which constituted the most general intellectual reaction to the cinema.

For Leenhardt, sound was the technological advance which would enable film to develop more fully its ability to engage with reality, to represent the very movement of social life. What was necessary, argued Leenhardt, was an audience educated enough about the cinema to demand better films from an industry which would otherwise always opt for the most stereotyped repetitions as the surest way of ensuring a financial return. This was a lesson that Bazin took to heart and it was the very raison d'être of the *Cahiers du cinéma*. Today, when film criticism has lost any kind of pressure on the industry, it may sound wildly optimistic. But right up until 1975 and the release of *Jaws*, even the biggest films were launched slowly in big towns and critical reaction was a small but significant factor within the industry. In the current marketing- and distribution-led industry, the politics advocated by Leenhardt have become apparently irrelevant but in an initial moment in France, that politics accomplished its aim of gaining control of a certain section of the French industry.

In *Esprit* Leenhardt published, across five issues, a little primer for spectators which explained how a grasp of the technology of cinema enabled one to understand and appreciate films more fully. This is the initial outline of the programme that Bazin was to develop magnificently in the popular organisations of the Liberation and later in the *Cahiers du cinéma*. But until the war, cinema was for Bazin merely one of the many intellectual and cultural activities in which any good teacher should be interested. The first step in his deepening engagement with the cinema came during the phony war when he was stationed near Bordeaux and became close friends with Guy Léger, whose parents owned a chain of theatres. Free tickets meant that the two young soldiers saw countless films together, and Léger shared his own considerable knowledge of the cinema with Bazin. The French defeat in the summer of 1940 was as important for Bazin as it was for so many others. Indeed it is no exaggeration to say that it is impossible to imagine Bazin devoting himself to the cinema without the intense disgust for existing state institutions which the establishment of the Vichy government caused among young men of his generation. Were it not for that disgust, Bazin's failure at the *agrégation* (the teacher's professional qualification) because of an acute attack of stammering in the oral in 1941 might have been but a momentary professional setback to be reversed in the following year's examination.[24] But in 1941 Bazin took his failure as a confirmation that he would not work within the rotten institutions of the state. The next year, however, he joined a youth organisation, the Maison des Lettres in the Sorbonne, and started a ciné-club. Within a year he had found his vocation. Alain Resnais, whose *Hiroshima mon amour* was to be a key film of the New Wave, was soon an enthusiastic member of the club, lending his 9.5 mm projector and German Expressionist films in order to hear Bazin's eloquent and impassioned analyses:

After the screening, a half-dozen enthusiasts would sit around a table and discuss the film; but it was Bazin who would talk most of all. Resnais marvelled at his ability to rethink an entire view of cinema on the basis of each new film. Bazin instantly leaped to ideas, not just about acting, editing, or lighting styles, as reasonable critics have always done, but about shot breakdown and the structuring of space. Every film seemed to give him new ideas; indeed, he couldn't see enough films.

Bazin had entered the Maison des Lettres with an interest in cinema scarcely greater than his interest in anything else: animals, literature, philosophy; but by the end of 1943, film had become a passion which never left him and which struck all those who met him thereafter.[25]

Bazin was now launched on his life's work; to improve the quality of cinema by the quality of criticism. From 1943, Bazin is clear that criticism is an essential element in a real improvement of the cinema. He has no doubt that, all other things being equal, an audience will prefer a good to a bad film, but the problem is that even film-makers have little understanding of the possibilities and traditions of their art. The collapse of the ciné-clubs and magazines, when intellectuals deserted the cinema after the arrival of sound, is a disaster which must be reversed and, almost single-handedly, Bazin sets out to do so. The scale of Bazin's activities in the post-Liberation years is awesome. He animates ciné-clubs from Germany to Morocco, he inspires intellectuals in the Latin Quarter and workers in the factories outside Paris. Above all, he writes regular columns for the mass circulation daily *Le Parisien libéré* and for the weekly *Observateur*, as well as major essays mainly for the magazine *Esprit*.

Bazin's writing is a marvel; rarely in the history of criticism, let alone film criticism, has there been a thinker who knows so well how to balance the particular and the specific – this film, this actor, this shot –

with the theoretical and the general, the history of cinema, the aesthetics of realism. Every article is part of a thoroughly understood and internalised strategy: to improve the aesthetic quality of French cinema. In the brief fifteen years that he wrote on the cinema, Bazin managed to produce what will appear as 17,000 pages of the greatest film criticism ever written when his collected works are finally published. If one required proof of how conscious Bazin was of his overall strategy and his individual audiences, it comes with the discovery that at his death there were no foul papers, no unpublished articles, no notes for a work unfinished – all his various knowledge had been continuously mobilised in the unswerving focus that took him from daily review to retrospective survey to general aesthetic reflection.[26]

Early in this trajectory Bazin produced his most important theoretical work, 'The Ontology of the Photographic Image'. This short essay, which places cinema in a cultural perspective that takes in the 4,000 years from Egyptian funeral art to the advent of sound in the cinema, is absolutely crucial to understanding Godard's œuvre. It is, to use Rohmer's term, the 'axiom'[27] from which all of Godard's theorems derive, from the documentary Opération 'béton' to the essay The Old Place, from the thriller Breathless to the abstract composition Eloge de l'amour.

Bazin locates the desire for realism in the struggle against death. The mummified bodies and the statues of the dead which inhabit Egyptian tombs are attempts to arrest time. But this desire for a realism which will preserve the body from corruption is at odds with the desire of the artist to use paint to investigate the reality of colour and shape. If medieval art combines both desires, the discovery of perspective sets painting on a realistic course which entails that painting's true vocation is subordinated to the vain representation of the world. The discovery of photography frees painting to resume its genuine vocation because photography, by its very technical mechanism, delivers a representation of the real which painting cannot challenge. There is in the process which leads from object photographed to photograph no intervention of a human subjectivity. While it is quite possible to produce photographs of a fantastic world, there must be, in front of the camera, the objects which will combine to look like a spaceship crashing into the moon.[28] In his defence of realism, Bazin is not arguing about film's ability to represent social reality; this is not an argument about whether Laurence Olivier's Henry V is realistic, rather it is an argument that cinema inevitably represents the reality of Laurence Olivier playing Henry V before the camera. The reason why Bazin's claim is so axiomatic is that it now becomes clear that the primary material with which the film-maker works is filmed reality. From this perspective, there is no difference between documentary and fiction. In all works of fiction, the primary material of the director is these actors in this place performing this text. It is impossible to understand the articles in *La Gazette du cinéma* or indeed the films of Rohmer, Rivette and Godard without understanding this axiom. There are of course huge differences. If we pursue Rohmer's metaphor, then he is indeed the geometrician of the three, most concerned with the articulation of bodies in space. Rivette is devoted to the algebra which moves between value and variable as he investigates the play of actor and role, and Godard is the arithmetician, or better, the number theorist, conjugating the prime numbers of social reality in an attempt to provide a comprehensible pattern.

One of the geniuses of Bazin's criticism is that it is continuously tied to developments within the cinema. The articulation of his realist aesthetic is unthinkable without the post-war experience of two directors: Orson Welles and Roberto Rossellini. There is no question that Rossellini, both in the initial moment of neo-realism (the trilogy *Rome, Open City*, *Paisà* and *Germany, Year Zero*) as well as in the films of the fifties, above all those with Ingrid Bergman (*Viaggio in Italia*, *Stromboli*), is more significant than Welles for both Bazin and Godard. But in the immediate aftermath of the war, it was around Welles and *Citizen Kane* that Bazin was to distinguish his view of cinema most clearly, in a debate with the great Sartre himself.

Citizen Kane was released in 1941, almost coincidentally with America's entry into the war. It was therefore one of the hundreds of American films which the French were unable to see before the Liberation, and was not premiered in Paris until 1946. Sartre saw the film on a visit to America in 1945 and devoted a short but incisive article to it in *L'Ecran français* in August of that year. Although Sarte recognised some of the merits of the film, he was passionately opposed to it. For him it was the work of an intellectual who has ignored the naive genius of American cinema to produce a work set in the past, while the whole point of the American cinema is to exist in the present. This weakness of the film is political – it shows how cut off from the masses American intellectuals are.[29] In short, for Sartre, the film is too arty and not committed enough.

Bazin replies a full two years later in the summer of 1947, at the same time as the young Godard was finishing his first year at the Lycée Buffon. Bazin never shirked confrontation – not with the Communist Party in 1950, and not with the French film industry in 1954 when he published Truffaut's savage polemic, 'A Certain Tendency in French Cinema', but, unlike most French intellectuals, he had little taste for aggressive posturing. It is very significant that he seems to have had no time for Nietzsche, the typical favourite of the enraged and powerless intellectual from Bataille to Foucault. Bazin writes two years after Sartre and a year after the film has opened, and attempts to sum up the debate on *Kane*. For some, it is the reinvention of the cinema, for others a huge intellectual bluff. The Communists, led by the historian George Sadoul and the Sartrean left, had condemned *Citizen Kane* as formal trickery. Bazin's article takes us luminously through two scenes to show how Welles has used the new lenses provided by his cinematographer Gregg Toland to compose a new kind of scene, one in which the lens's depth of field allows Welles to refuse to centre the action in the way that is obligatory with classical cross cutting or shot reverse shot. In *Kane*, reality is not presented to the spectator in a form which is already articulated; he or she must articulate it themselves. Here the ontological claim is historically developed: just as sound enabled a fuller representation of the reality before the camera, so too do the new lenses, which do not focus our attention on a limited part of the visual field. Welles's method, his technique, in fact his style allows us to enjoy a different and more profound relationship to the material filmed. Bazin's implicit argument is that it is useless to use a notion of political commitment

Bazin at his desk at Travail et Culture, 1947.

which ignores the specificity of the cinema. The task of the artist is to render reality in all its contradictions rather than to mould it to an externally determined model.

Such a position was extremely difficult to maintain as French politics developed after the jubilation of the Liberation. In the years just after the war, Bazin had found an enormous audience for his work through the organisation Travail et Culture, which sought to provide the best cultural entertainment for working-class audiences. So exciting was this project that Bazin gave up the opportunity to go back into the state educational system at the newly founded cinema school, the Institut des hautes études cinématographiques.[30] This decision must have been made easier by the fact that, since the Liberation, Bazin had earned a small but secure financial base as the film critic for *Le Parisien Libéré*, a mass circulation newspaper. For Bazin, the chances of educating through the popular organisations of the post-war era and through journalistic criticism were preferable to working within the formal educational systems of the state. But the great political hopes of that era died as the Cold War intensified. From the Marshall Plan and the withdrawal of the Communists from the government in 1947, through the Berlin airlift in 1949, to the outbreak of the Korean War in 1950, questions of left and right were mapped on to the struggle between Soviet Russia and the United States. Inevitably the French Communist Party began to organise an ever stricter control over the broadly based organisations that had been set up immediately after the Liberation. For many, this period is one of terrible political conflict, as deep allegiances on the left came into conflict with the demand for loyalty to Soviet Russia. The conflict was both more intense, and perhaps simpler, for anyone committed to the cinema. The party line was clear: American films were the product of a decadent capitalism, the real genius of film could be found in contemporary Soviet cinema, where the heirs of Eisenstein and Pudovkin were making films in praise of the great leader Stalin. In fact Hollywood was still enjoying its classic period, under-pinned by a vertically integrated industry and untroubled by television, while Soviet films were almost without exception vitiated by an adoring Stalinism.

The Founding of *Cahiers du cinéma*

Gradually deprived of the audience to which he had devoted himself from 1944 to 1948, Bazin responded by setting up a new ciné-club aimed not at the working class but at the literary and cinematic intelligentsia. Bazin's political position since 1943 had been sophisti-cated and consistent. He had always seen that critics would achieve the greatest effect by addressing those sections of the film industry belong-ing to the intelligentsia, the residents of the Café Flore in shorthand.[31] If the education of a mass audience was no longer possible, then Bazin would turn to the task of educating the elite, of creating a new and productive snobbery in which a love for films would be the motor of the production of better films.[32] Bazin's ciné-club was such a success that in 1949 it mounted a festival – the festival of cursed films at Biarritz. The idea of a cursed film, one which history has forgotten, is taken directly from Mallarmé, whose poem in praise of cursed poets was evoked by Cocteau, the president of the festival, in his introduction to the festival catalogue.

This festival marks the collision of the two worlds which were to make *Cahiers du cinéma* the most significant cultural journal of the twentieth century. On the one hand, there was the world of the avant-garde left, which was devoted to the cinema, and on the other the 'young Turks', as they would come to be called, the eighteen- and nineteen-year-olds who had been nourished by Langlois and the ciné-clubs, and whose love of film (and especially American film) was a genuine faith. According to Dudley Andrew, this first encounter was not without its problems:

Although an alternative film gathering, the Festival du Film Maudit still sported all the trappings of Cannes. Held in the ornate casino of this Atlantic resort it was presided over by Jean Cocteau and boasted a Committee of Honour consisting of the prefect of the department, the mayor of Biarritz, a Marquis d'Arcangues, Orson Welles and Cocteau. A doorman politely checked all guests and detained or turned away those who didn't belong or were improperly attired. Some of the people who clearly didn't belong were Rivette, Godard and Truffaut. All under twenty years old, "bohemian" and vociferous, they started a scene with the doorman until the timely arrival of Cocteau, dressed in tails. He shepherded his young friends in with a wave of his hand and, as president of the festival, succeeded in holding together, or at least at a safe distance, the aristocracy on the one hand and the young Turks on the other.[33]

One cannot be certain that this was the first time that Truffaut had met Godard and the rest of the 'Schérer gang'.[34] It seems likely that their paths had crossed at the Tuesday nights of Studio Parnasse or at the Cinémathèque. It is certain, however, that this is where Truffaut, Rivette and Charles Bitsch, who was to be Godard's assistant for most of the films in the sixties, became firm friends.[35]

François Truffaut is a key, perhaps *the* key figure in the decade that took these bohemian rejects of 1949 to the dominating position that they

François Truffaut with Godard, Festival du Biarritz, 1949.

occupied in French cinema at the beginning of the sixties.[36] His was the polemic pen which was to outline the manifesto of the New Wave with his famous article 'Une certaine tendance du cinéma français'; his was the film, *Les Quatre cents coups*, which in 1959 was to be the great success of the Cannes festival; it was his name which was to assure for Godard his first chance of directing a feature.

A year younger than Godard, Truffaut had a desperately unhappy childhood, which furnished much of the material for *Les Quatre cents coups*. It was not until he was twelve that he was to discover that his legal father was not his biological father (T:19–35 and 481–487), but from the first it was clear he was an unwanted child. Unhappy at school and unhappy at home, he was constantly in trouble with almost every kind of authority. From an incredibly early age, cinema became his passion, and a passion which embraced information about the cinema as well as the cinema itself. Despite being a truant for most of his adolescence, he became the real scholar and archivist of the *Cahiers* critics. He seems to have attended every ciné-club in Paris in the immediate post-war years, and he started his own when still only sixteen: Le Cercle des cinémanes (The circle of ciné-maniacs). When he discovered that Travail et Culture was running a ciné-club at the same time as he had chosen for the Cercle des cinémanes, he went there to persuade Bazin to switch to another day. The meeting was to prove momentous. Bazin was much taken with this young and troubled cinephile, and was effectively to adopt him.

At Travail et Culture, Truffaut was also to meet Chris Marker, who in July 1951 was perhaps to alter the whole history of French cinema when, passing between Les Deux Magots and Saint-Germain des Prés, the very epicentre of French intellectual life, he bumped into Truffaut. Marker, a real bohemian, was not someone to remark upon a person's dress, but he did notice that Truffaut wasn't wearing any socks inside his shoes. He asked him what was up, and Truffaut said that he had deserted from the army and was now going to seek out Jean Genet to whom he had written in the South of France. 'What about André?' said Marker. Truffaut confessed that he was frightened to contact Bazin and that he was taking the train south that night. Marker made Truffaut promise to wait until morning, while he contacted Bazin. Once he told Bazin the news, 'André, despite being a good Christian, began to curse God in a very extravagant fashion, but he told me to get François in touch with him immediately.' Marker met Truffaut the next morning and after an extraordinary series of adventures which had Bazin searching military prisons for the young cinephile, Truffaut and Bazin were finally reunited and Truffaut was to live with Bazin for much of the fifties. (T:126–128).

Two years earlier Biarritz was to link Truffaut to his peers from the Latin Quarter – to Rohmer, Rivette and Godard, to Bitsch and Chabrol. Godard's nostalgic memory of passing by his godmother's with Truffaut to steal money to go to the cinema, recounted in his introduction to Truffaut's letters, must be placed in the autumn after Biarritz.[37] From then on they were a group, sharing ideas, enthusiasms and passions.[38]

The conditions which gave birth to *Cahiers du cinéma* were then also ripening fast. From the outset, Bazin's position had implied the need for a specialised journal addressing those for whom cinema was a passion. Just after the war, Jean-Georges Auriol had persuaded Gallimard to start the cinema magazine, *La Revue du cinéma*, which took up many of the themes and attitudes of a magazine of the same title that he had edited as a very young man at the end of the twenties. *La Revue du cinéma* published both Bazin and Rohmer, and Godard says that he submitted articles to the review which were rejected (G1:9).[39] His contact was Jacques Doniol-Valcroze, Auriol's right-hand man, because Doniol-Valcroze's mother and Odile Godard were old friends. Gallimard closed *La Revue du cinéma* in 1948, and from then on Doniol-Valcroze was concerned to try and find another backer for a film magazine. Rohmer's own effort with *La Gazette du cinéma* must be put in the context of the closing of *La Revue du cinéma*, and when *La Gazette* (albeit a much more modest project) in turn failed, the pressure to find a forum for a serious discussion of film intensified.

The political and intellectual conditions for *Cahiers du cinéma* were finally put in place when in the summer of 1950, Bazin published a long article in *Esprit* entitled 'The Myth of Stalin in Soviet Cinema'. Bazin refused to accept that contemporary Soviet cinema was continuing the great tradition of the early years of the revolution. Whereas the major films of Eisenstein and Pudovkin had shown individuals caught up in the process of social transformation, the Soviet films of the post-war years showed an all-powerful individual, Stalin, controlling the processes of history. For Bazin this was simply myth, and myth which didn't even enjoy the real box-office support of a Hollywood myth like Tarzan. Bazin could not have been suprised at the result of this sacrilegious act. The comparison of Stalin to Tarzan was a particularly acute and unforgivable blasphemy. He was anathematised in the Communist press, and his final links with Travail et Culture were severed.

Having rejected the state educational system, Bazin was now cut off from the Communist left. But he and Doniol-Valcroze were determined to found a new journal. Interestingly they were unable to persuade the major intellectual publishers, Gallimard and Le Seuil, to back such a venture. It finally got off the ground when a Parisian cinema owner, whose son had been involved in the Objectif ciné-club, offered to help. It is worth emphasising that *Cahiers du cinéma* found both its economic and its intellectual basis in a love of cinema far removed from the all-powerful publishing and intellectual circles of the time. Doniol-Valcroze and Bazin were both men of the left, but they were giving cinema a primacy which was admitted neither by the dominant literary culture nor by the anti-American left. *Cahiers du cinéma* was thus conceived as a project which rejected both the culture of the state and the culture of the Communist left. There is an account of *Cahiers* in the fifties which sees the leftism of the founding generation replaced by the rightism of the young Turks, who under the leadership of Truffaut won the journal over to a defence of American cinema (and above all of Hitchcock and Hawks) and the *politique des auteurs*, and placed it securely on the right. There is no doubt about the victories won for American cinema and for the conception of an 'auteur', but to characterise these as 'of the right' is simplistic at best.

While it is true that Truffaut flirted with right-wing positions, it is also the case that he repudiated them, as well as the characterisation of *Cahiers* as right wing. But it misses the whole point of *Cahiers*, and the almost messianic hopes invested in it, if one measures it against the very

Godard's article 'Pour un cinéma politique' in *La Gazette du cinéma*.

limited options of the Cold War. Doniol-Valcroze, the most urbane and ironic of men, confided to his diary that he felt that his dead friend Auriol, killed in a car crash in 1950, lived again in him as he prepared to launch the magazine (C1:51). Such a sentiment makes clear the scale of what he and Bazin thought they were accomplishing. They were taking the most popular and the greatest art of the twentieth century and they were going to improve that art by producing an educated taste. This is a political programme in itself. Something that was clear to the nineteen-year-old critic Jean-Luc Godard.

Godard's Early Criticism

Godard's first long article, published in the third number of *La Gazette du cinéma*, is called 'Towards a Political Cinema'. He sets out from the most unlikely of moments – a newsreel which shows East German youth parading in the celebrations of the First of May. Godard sees in this an image of life in the Eastern bloc. But what might at first read like the most alarming and slavish celebration of Stalinism is something much more complicated, for Godard then goes on to read the history of Soviet film in relation to two contrasting images of the individual's relationship to history. What Godard emphasises – a point that Bazin makes in his almost exactly contemporaneous article on Stalin – is that the cinema is not just a representation of reality, but becomes part of the reality itself. The young bodies wheeling in unison in Berlin are wheeling to create the cinema image, the image in which the regime finds its truth and justification.

If we are to combat this politics then we must first admit the force of these images, as Rossellini does in *Germany, Year Zero*, the third film of his famous post-war trilogy. This film ends with the suicide of a twelve-year-old boy, a scene so shocking because it faces up to the reality of Nazi rule and attempts to confront its power, a confrontation which must start with an admission of the power of even the most virulently anti-Semitic films.

Godard's 1950 article cannot be read in terms of the politics of 1950, because it starts from the assumption that film is, in fact, a crucial part of politics. However, only when one understands the position that cinema and reality are one does it become possible to comprehend the incredible Utopianism which is the foundation of *Cahiers du cinéma*. It also makes clear that any simple reading of *Cahiers* in political terms ignores the fact that cinephilia was a politics in itself – to improve the cinema was to improve the world. An appreciation of the scale of this ambition makes it possible to under-stand the force of the New Wave, and however successful it was at the level of the cinema, it was only when that success transformed reality that the programme would really be complete. Godard ended this first essay with a flourish, calling on French film-makers to make films from the history of collaboration and resistance, but he made clear how different those films would need to be from conventional notions of a political film by linking them to efforts to represent the tax system (G:17/1:74) – the bourgeois equivalent of the wheeling youths in Red Square. If Soviet Communism found its most intense reality in huge state-organized demonstrations and marches, bourgeois society was most evident in its systems of taxation. If you wish to transform reality, you must first film it.

La Gazette du cinéma closed at the end of 1950, just as Godard left Europe for South America, and by the time he had returned *Cahiers du cinéma* had produced its first number in April 1951. The importance and success of *Cahiers du cinéma* in its first decade can scarcely be overestimated; those ten years made *Cahiers du cinéma* the most successful cultural magazine of the twentieth century. In 1959 Godard was able to write: 'We won the day in having it acknowledged in

principle that a film by Hitchcock, for example, is as important as a
book by Aragon. Film *auteurs* thanks to us have finally entered the
history of art' (G:147/1:194).

Godard here makes explicit that the real achievement of *Cahiers* is to
have elevated film to the rank of an art. In 1923 Ricciotto Canudo had
written a manifesto entitled 'The Seventh Art', which claimed a place for
film alongside the classical arts. *Cahiers* achieved this ambition by
emphasising that film is an art because the director can be an artist.
But it is important that Godard cites Hitchcock in this context and not
Welles, Rossellini or Renoir, who Bazin considered to be the three key
film-makers. For what the young Turks had accomplished, thanks more
to Langlois's programming than to Bazin's criticism, was to use the
concept of the author as the key to organising and evaluating the
cinematic riches of Hollywood. The concept of the author is all but
articulated by the end of the forties: by Bazin himself and by Alexandre
Astruc, who was the closest link between the world of Sartre and the
Cahiers and who, in a famous article of 1948 in *L'Ecran français*
entitled 'La Caméra-stylo', likened the camera to a pen. For both Bazin
and Astruc, the grammar of film is now established and is available to be
used by a director as a means to express his vision of the world. In his
diary for 11 February 1948, three years before the launching of *Cahiers*
and long before *la politique des auteurs*, Doniol-Valcroze wrote: 'It is
necessary to have a doctrine at *La Revue du cinéma*, doctrine for which
the starting point would be the theory of the caméra-stylo of Astruc and
which would result from an alliance and a similar viewpoint between
Astruc, Bazin, Kast and me' (C1:33).

Five years later when Truffaut began to elaborate his *politique des
auteurs*, with Rohmer and Rivette acting as his theoretical outriders, his
central figures were not simply American film-makers, but American
film-makers who were universally derided by intellectuals as mere
technicians working at the service of big business, men like Alfred
Hitchcock and Howard Hawks who were held to have sold their
talented souls for a mess of capitalist pottage. It is a major paradox,
and one that reflects on the curious double life of film as both central
and marginal in the history of the twentieth century, that exactly as

Barthes, Lacan and Althusser are beginning their critique of the autonomous subject (which underpins the very notion of the author), the
writers of *Cahiers* are using the concept of the author as a method of
validating the language of cinema in its claim to be the major art of the
twentieth century.

In fact the paradox is not quite as acute as it might appear. Barthes
objected to the notion of the author since it occluded all the historical
conditions of writing, the genres and idioms which are in no way the
creation of an individual. But the first curiosity of *Cahiers*'s theory of the
author is that it exactly emphasised these specific features of the cinema.
One locates one's author not by ignoring the specificity of his artistic
medium, but by emphasising it. Hawks becomes an author only when
you have understood how the genres of comedy and the Western
function and how, across these genres and conventions, Hawks's use
of lighting, actors, design and camera reveals a genuine author at work.
In this sense, the *Cahiers* theory is not a Romantic hangover, but rather
another of those twentieth-century modernisms which locates the deepest ethical and aesthetic level of a work in its form. As, if not more
important, *Cahiers*'s author theory is the only theory of the author
which is formulated from the point of view of the audience, and indeed
explicitly formulated as a method to move from the position of the
audience to that of the artist. Leenhardt's 'Little School for the Film
Spectator' and all of Bazin's work are dedicated to turning an audience
into creators.

It is easy to fall into a chronology which has the *Cahiers*'s critics
moving from criticism to direction, but Rohmer and Rivette had made
short films before *Cahiers* started; and the older generation of Leenhardt, Kast and Doniol-Valcroze were already film-makers. Only Bazin
had decided, after an initial experiment which he would never let anyone
see, that direction was not for him.[40] While one should not underestimate the importance of a specifically French avant-garde tradition
which encouraged intellectuals to pick up a camera, nor the fact that
anyone who ran a ciné-club was inevitably caught up in the mechanics
of distribution, it is crucial to recognise that the making of films was an
integral part of the whole project. From as early as 1943 Bazin had

sketched out very clearly the programme which would produce an educated audience who would develop their taste in terms of a snobbery about particular directors' styles. This snobbery would allow the poor to become cinema's real patrons. The eight years of experience in Travail et Culture and Objectif 49 allowed Bazin and Doniol-Valcroze to produce a magazine which, while deeply committed to the theoretical and the historical, was above all devoted to what could be loved in contemporary cinema. From the very early numbers, *Cahiers* placed itself squarely within the contemporary: its covers were chosen from current releases, it reviewed, and it published all kinds of information about current film projects.

1952 Criticism

On more than one occasion Godard has said that he came late to *Cahiers*, and it is true that the majority of his articles date from after 1956. But in fact he was the first of the very young critics to write in the magazine, before Rivette, Truffaut or Chabrol, and he contributed two substantial articles in 1952, which together with 'Towards a Political Cinema' sketch out an extraordinarily complex and complete aesthetic. The articles are not signed Jean-Luc Godard but Hans Lucas, a German rendering of Jean-Luc which he had also used for some of his contributions to *La Gazette du cinéma*.[41] These are not much commented upon and the English translator's notes deem them 'impenetrable' (G:245).[42] It must be agreed that they are not written in the usual pompous French intellectual style of, say, a Foucault, never writing three pages when thirty will do. They are violently compressed, and the argument is constantly carried by allusions to and examples from particular films. They do, however, constitute a continuous discursive argument, a form that Godard will all but abandon in later criticism and writing, and they also sketch out a clear aesthetic strategy which illuminates the rest of his work, from his first shorts to his most recent feature.

The 'Défense et illustration de découpage classique' is the most programmatic of them all. The ambition of the piece can be judged by the allusion in the title. Four centuries earlier, in 1549, the young French poet Joachim du Bellay wrote a manifesto for the group of young poets who would come to be known as La Pléiade, in which he argued for the cultural value of the French language. This manifesto was entitled the 'Defense and Illustration of the French Language'. Du Bellay's text is part of that European-wide movement, starting with Dante's *Divine Comedy*, to assert the value of the vernacular languages of Europe as cultural rivals of Latin, which had been the European language of culture and learning for over a millennium. The arguments for the vernacular tongues were nationalistic, often Protestant, and always at the service of an ideology which sought to find an audience for writing outside the priestly caste. But if there was a radical impulse in them, it stopped far short of a democratic inclusion of the whole nation. If these poets sought an audience in the new urban bourgeoisies, they had no thought for the huge number of illiterates in the population. And when the universal schooling of the late nineteenth century had introduced quasi-universal literacy, it still left literature as the preserve of an educational elite. The promise of film, a promise that Godard underlines with his title, is of a new language of art available to all. Just as du Bellay's text can be taken as signalling the beginning of French literature, Godard's piece inaugurates the next great democratic development of art. His homage to du Bellay makes clear the radical and democratic claims of film, claims that Bazin had emphasised repeatedly in his work. However, Godard is not concerned simply to repeat Bazin's claims, but to develop them.

In articulating his aesthetic of realism, particularly in relation to Welles's use of deep focus, Bazin had promoted an aesthetic in favour of the sequence shot, in which action developed within one continuous shot, rather than the classical montage of American cinema, where narrative development or the direction of a character's gaze made invisible the cuts which propelled the action, or the radical montage of Eisenstein which emphasised the juxtaposition of images but found cinema's justification in that very juxtaposition.

Bazin's position can be understood in the historical context of those cinematic movements such as German Expressionism and early Soviet cinema that favoured the manipulation of the image. For those who wished to argue for the cinema as an art of the image, the advent of sound was a disaster. In his desire to assert the primacy of the real, and thus the huge advance marked by sound, Bazin was driven to adopt a position in which logically there should be no editing at all. But this position, as Godard argues brilliantly, is nonsensical, for all positioning of a camera is already editing. Godard is as fiercely realist as Bazin – for Godard the strength of film is in its capturing of the real. But this strength is always the result of a particular angle, whether the angle is provided by the camera or by the editing. The real does not simply present itself to us, it is grasped by the specific articulation of the film. The task of the film-maker is to find that articulation which is the most appropriate. Godard is not arguing for a separation between editing and shooting, or proposing what he calls in a later article on montage a producer's axiom: 'We'll save it in the cutting room' (G:39/1:92). His point is that in capturing reality the juxtaposition of images is sometimes as important as the *mise-en-scène* within the image. The argument is there in the 1952 article but finds its clearest expression in the complementary piece, 'Montage my fine care', written four years later:

> If direction is a look, montage is a heartbeat. To foresee is the characteristic of both: but what one seeks to foresee in space, the other seeks in time. Suppose you notice a young girl in the street who attracts you. You hesitate to follow her. A quarter of a second. How to convey this hesitation? *Mise-en-scène* will answer the question 'How shall I approach her?' But in order to render explicit the other question 'Am I going to love her?' you are forced to bestow importance on the quarter of a second during which the two questions are born. It may be, therefore, that it will be for the montage rather than the *mise-en-scène* to express both exactly and clearly the life of an idea or its sudden emergence in the course of the story. (G:39/1:92–93)

One of the absolute premisses of Bazin's criticism, a premiss shared by Astruc's article on the 'caméra-stylo', was that cinema had, after a decade of sound, developed a fully articulate language utilisable by any director. Godard dissents in the strongest terms: 'Nothing can be more wrong than to talk of classical construction as a language which had reached its peak of perfection before the Second World War, with Lubitsch in America and Marcel Carné in France, and which would therefore be tantamount to an autonomous thought process, applicable with equal success to any subject whatsoever' (G:28/1:82).

For Godard there is no cinematic language which can represent reality. This would suggest two separate registers of being. What cinema, or the camera, does is to allow the possibility of representing reality, of seizing it in a language which is continuously variable. For Godard, there is not reality and then the camera – there is reality seized at this moment and in this way by the camera. Here we might indicate the theoretical problem around which all Godard's work turns. In 1952 Godard writes in the defence of cinema as the classical art of the twentieth century. He starts his manifesto by considering the problems of modern literature, and then dismisses the latter as irredeemably sullied by the need for the author to draw attention to his activities: 'I have no use for a writer who directs my attention to himself and to his wit instead of the people he is interpreting. I want, to quote Fénelon, "a sublime so familiar that each will be tempted to believe he would have discovered it easily himself, although few are capable of discovering it." Too much brilliance dazzles and embarrasses me: I prefer the pleasant and the true to the astonishing and the marvellous' (G28/1:81).

Here Godard is following Rohmer in what will throughout the fifties be the *Cahiers* line. Cinema, by virtue of its popular appeal and its well-understood genres, is a classical art. Historically, neoclassicism was developed in the seventeenth century in France as a project to make explicit the rules of art based on the models of Greece and Rome. We now understand the neoclassical project above all as an attempt to provide a cultural arm for the absolutism of the French monarchy, and we know that it was based on real misunderstandings of the classical texts that it took as models. Nonetheless, the vision of an art in which creators and audiences both fully understood the rules of the game has been a captivating one for many. For Rohmer, Godard and the *Cahiers* critics, the classicism of film makes it the art which really can capture modernity. Godard insists on this point again and again. It is worth noting, however, that the modernity it captures is understood in Bazinian terms. What interests in Hitchcock is not the tedious detective story, but the perfect seizing of a cityscape or an object: 'In fact, if the cinema were no more than the art of narration which some would make its proud boast, then instead of being bored, one would take pleasure in those interminable efforts which are concerned above all with exposing in meticulous detail the secret motivations of a murderer or a coquette. But there is a look posed so afresh on things at each instant that it pierces rather than solicits them, that it seizes in them what abstraction lies in wait for' (G:27/1:81).

As for Hawks, there the interest is in action: 'If the emergence of American comedy is as important as the advent of sound, it is because it brought back swiftness of action, and allowed the moment to be savoured to the full' (G:27/1:81).

If we consider Godard in 1952 we notice two things. First, at a theoretical level, the claim for cinema as a classical art is weakened by fusing representation and reality. If each director has to find again and for himself the correct relation between the camera and reality, then the risk of the cinema becoming a host of competing modernisms is already there: the worm is in the bud. Literary modernism can be understood at its deepest historical level as a crisis of the audience, as the reaction by writers to educational and social changes which produce a universally literate audience with no interest in literature. The pressure then comes to write for an ideal future audience – 'I write for those who are far off' says Nietzsche. Joyce's formulation is 'an ideal reader suffering from an ideal insomnia'.

For many other writers in the first half of the twentieth century, this future is political. It is the future revolutionary society which will provide the ideal audience. *Cahiers*'s classicism is in tune with many of the great names of literary modernism: Nietzsche or Joyce, Pound or Broch. The common enemy is Romanticism's focus on the extraordinary individual sensibility: 'I have no use for a writer who directs my attention to himself.' But whereas the literary modernists must find their audience in the future, at some vanishing point when a new classicism will render their experiments conventional, cinema – and this is the joy of the *Cahiers* critics at escaping the conflicts of modernism – provides that audience now, in the present.

The deep irony is that the conditions which allowed this current classicism were vanishing as Godard and the other *Cahiers* critics wrote. One might argue from examples as diverse as the Shakespearean stage or post-war British broadcasting that periods of great art are dependent on economic monopolies, allowing the producer rather than the audience to dominate taste. What is certain is that from the end of the First World War till the end of the Second, Hollywood enjoyed an extraordinary economic monopoly. It was almost without other competitors as a mass medium; radio and a popular press did exist, but television, recorded music, video technology and digital technology did not.[43] Internally the studios, best understood economically as huge distribution systems dominating both production and exhibition, were all-powerful. The result was that very little turned on the fate of an individual film pushed through a system which offered the spectator little choice. Variants in box-office takings might affect a star's next contract or the choice of acceptable subjects, but it was unthinkable that an entire studio might be bankrupted by one film as Fox nearly was by *Cleopatra* in the sixties and as United Artists was by *Heaven's Gate* in the eighties. The studios made what they wanted to make and the taste of the studio heads was all-determining.

Thus the conventional *Cahiers* wisdom, which made the director the key figure in this classical art, has not survived more recent excavations of studio history. The painfully slow and cliched explanatory scenes which Jack Warner insisted Hawks cut from *The Big Sleep* show that, in Godard's terms, Warner had just as good if not a better grasp of what mattered in the cinema as the movie's 'author' Howard Hawks.[44] But however one allocates creative responsibility in what we can genuinely call the classical period of Hollywood, it is certain that the economic conditions which had made that period possible were now fast passing away. The anti-trust suits of 1948, which obliged the studios to divest themselves of their cinema chains, and the advent of television, were to set in train processes which rendered *Cahiers*'s analyses obsolete at the very moment they were being formulated. But that, as Godard would say, is another story.

Geneva and First Shorts

Godard chose to leave Paris in late 1952 or early 1953, to base himself in Switzerland. As always in this back and forth between Paris and Switzerland, it is unwise to be too definitive about place, but it is certain that he does not appear again in the pages of *Cahiers* until the summer of 1956. Pierre Rissient, who was four years younger than Godard and later worked as his assistant on *Breathless*, remembers that when he first started going to the Cinémathèque and the Studio Parnasse in 1955, he asked after Hans Lucas, the author of 'Defense et Illustration du découpage classique', and was told he was in South America. The initial reason for his disappearance from Paris to Switzerland was that Godard stole money from *Cahiers*'s petty cash.[45] *Cahiers* was a tiny magazine which lived from hand to mouth, and the incident was serious enough to make him *persona non grata* for a considerable time. But he also determined that the time had come for him to live on his own resources, and Switzerland offered more opportunities in this regard than Paris (G:13–14).

From the time of his return from South America in the late spring of 1951, if not before, he had a group of friends who were largely based in Geneva around a café called the Parador, and from 1953 until the beginning of 1956 Godard seems to have lived between Geneva and Lausanne where, as Jean-Paul Belmondo loudly proclaims in *Breathless*, the most beautiful girls in the world are to be found. Belmondo's claim is borrowed from Godard's friend Roland Tolmatchoff, as are his gestures at the beginning of his car journey to Paris, with which the film opens.

A larger-than-life figure, a womaniser and a teller of tall tales, Tolmatchoff was to be Godard's witness at both of his Swiss weddings and worked for him intermittently throughout the period up to *Contempt*, after which he devoted himself to travelling, visiting, he claims, all but three of the countries that make up the globe. The child of a

Ukrainian father and a Swiss mother, Tolmatchoff was another early
cinephile, determined in Truffaut-like fashion to gather together as
much information about the cinema as was possible. He describes
himself at the time as a 'walking encyclopaedia of film' and adds that
he was 'a completely useless one'.

Determining exactly where Godard lived at this time is made particularly difficult by the fact that he should not have been in Switzerland
at all. In 1952, his father had persuaded him to take Swiss nationality to
avoid having to fight in Indo-China. It is worth stressing that the end of
the Second World War did not mean for France the end of military
conflict. In both Indo-China and in Algeria the French army was to be
involved in military operations on such a massive scale that a conscrip-
tion period of three years was enforced. The signing of peace accords
with the Algerian FLN in March 1962 marked the first time that France
had not been engaged in a major conflict since before the Second World
War, which had ended seventeen years earlier. But Swiss nationals also
had considerable military obligations: a long initial training period was
followed by annual tours of duty. Godard availed himself of a provision
which allowed Swiss citizens living abroad to avoid this military service
but to enjoy that provision he must have avoided having a legal domicile
in Switzerland. Indeed while making *Le Petit soldat*, Godard ran afoul
of the Swiss authorities on more than one occasion.[46]

Godard's most important base was neither in Geneva or Lausanne but
a huge construction site high in the Swiss Alps called La Grand Dixence
where for more than a decade a huge dam had been under construction.
The network of family relations seems to have worked in Godard's
favour in getting the job,[47] but by the time he was working there Godard
seems to have had no direct contact with his family. Tolmatchoff says
that the watchword of the young men who met in the Parador was
Gide's 'Famille – je vous hais' ('Family – I hate you'). Because of the
extreme weather conditions the construction site could operate fully
only in the summer, but a twenty-four-hour telephone exchange oper-
ated all year round and Godard was taken on as one of three telephonists. Tolmatchoff claims that it was he who had suggested to
Godard that instead of working three eight-hour shifts, the telephonists

should pool their labour and each spend ten days on twenty-four-hour duty and take the other twenty days off. Godard was thus able to earn a full wage while enjoying twenty days a month between Lausanne and Geneva. While in Geneva he often stayed at the studio of another friend, Hugues Fontanet, in the rue Winkelried. His stealing had now become an in-joke amongst his friends, and Tolmatchoff claims to have joined with Hugues in spying on Godard at the studio, watching him carefully calculate how much money he needed to take – for Godard's thefts seem to have been carefully calculated in relation to his immediate needs.[48]

The attraction of the work at the dam was that it would enable Godard to put aside money towards a short film, but once he was there he had the idea to make the film about the construction itself: 'Not to go to Paris to make films but make them there where I was' (G:14). Godard engaged a camera operator whom he had met in Lausanne, Adrien Porchet, and in the summer of 1954 he shot and edited a twenty-minute documentary entitled *Opération 'béton'* (Operation Concrete). The film clearly places itself in a long tradition of documentaries following industrial processes, which were a staple of cinema from its first decade. The tone of the film is a relentlessly upbeat celebration of man's ability to dominate nature and while the film is extraordinarily well shot and constructed, well enough to earn it a cinema release in 1958 as an accompaniment to Minnelli's *Tea and Sympathy*, unlike Godard's other shorts it gives little hint of the work to come. But Godard did succeed in selling the film to the dam construction company for a sufficiently large sum to bankroll himself for the next two years.[49]

He remained in Switzerland for this time, and in November 1955 he shot another short called *Une Femme coquette* with a camera borrowed from Actua Films, the distributors of *Opération 'béton'*. Based on Maupassant's *Le Signe* (which was also one of the inspirations ten years later for *Masculin Féminin*), the story is an account written by a married woman to a friend of how she imitated a prostitute in order to pick up a man. Starring Tolmatchoff as the man and Maria Lysandre as the woman, it also features Jean-Luc Godard as the first possible client. The themes of prostitution and of feminine betrayal will return again and again in Godard's work but this silent 16 mm short does little more than rehearse them.

Une Certaine Tendance du Cinéma Français

When Godard left Paris, *Cahiers du cinéma* was a new and little-known magazine, but by the time he returned in 1956 it had become a significant player within the French industry, vigorously calling for a renovation in French cinema. The single most important article that it published, and arguably the single most important article in the history of French cinema, was François Truffaut's 'Une certaine tendance du cinéma français' (A Certain Tendency in French Cinema) in January 1954. In fact, Truffaut had written a version of the article almost a year before, but Bazin and Doniol-Valcroze had demanded revision after revision before they published it. As Doniol-Valcroze wrote afterwards: 'Neither Bazin nor I, and we'd both spent a lot of time thinking before we published the article, had the slightest idea that the "bang" would be so big.'[50]

The article was a vicious and cutting attack on what Truffaut called 'the tradition of quality'. For Truffaut this French tradition, the tradition which was held to be the glory of the French cinema, the tradition which won international acclaim and large domestic audiences, was marked not simply by a reliance on literature but by an aesthetic of adaptation which simply ignored the resources of film. The great adaptors of French cinema, Jean Aurenche and Pierre Bost (and part of the savage genius of the article is that it is relentlessly personal and relentlessly specific), never thought about how to produce effects through light-

François Truffaut, 'Une certaine tendance du cinéma français' in *Cahiers du cinéma* 31 (January 1954).

ing or camera position – they simply went through a book selecting what could be set out in a dramatic scene and then inventing scenes for those aspects of the text which resisted such treatment.

Truffaut is not against adaptation as such; his article gains much of its force by comparing how a film-maker like Robert Bresson adapted Georges Bernanos's *Journal d'un curé de campagne* to Aurenche's attempts with the same novel. What he is resolutely opposed to, what he hates, is an aesthetic position which refuses to understand the particular resources of cinema. The director should not be deciding how to frame a completed screenplay; he should be thinking with the camera in the very process of adaptation.

There can hardly be an *enfant terrible* in all history who would not have been gratified with the response that 'A Certain Tendency' provoked. The entire French film establishment united in condemning the miscreant, and Truffaut found himself a star at twenty-two. From then on he was the leader of the 'Schérer gang', and continued his campaign against the French film establishment in the monthly *Cahiers* but also, and as importantly, in the right-wing weekly *Arts*. Doniol-Valcroze was a little alarmed by the way in which the young critics were taking a line both less political and more pro-Hollywood than he and Bazin had envisaged. But Bazin was unruffled: *Cahiers* needed a new generation, and one might comment on their excesses[51] or even mock them a little under the great coinage of 'the Hitchcocko-Hawksiens', but their energy and love of the cinema excused their political and aesthetic lapses. As *Cahiers* came to stand more and more for a complete renovation of French cinema, so the young critics penetrated further and further into that cinema.

Initially this was through the magazine itself. The early fifties saw the first portable tape recorders, and *Cahiers* critics used this new technology to encounter their favourite directors and subject them to the most intense of cinephile grillings (C1:127–131). Their grasp of cinematic processes was very considerable, thanks to Leenhardt and Bazin, and director after director was astonished by their knowledge and enthusiasm. By 1956, *Cahiers du cinéma* was making a small name for itself in Hollywood. Back in Europe, Truffaut was working as Rossellini's assistant and if the experience produced little in the way of films, it taught Truffaut, and thus his friends, the extraordinary world of film finance where one juggles stars, stories and money.

Fox

Most significant for Godard was the fact that Claude Chabrol was taken on in the press office at Fox in the autumn of 1955. Chabrol is perhaps the odd man out of the famous five of *Cahiers*. While Truffaut and Godard were having brushes with the law, Chabrol's rebellion took the more conventional line of winding up his professors.[52] And if he shared an enthusiasm for Hollywood in general and Hitchcock in particular, writing an influential book on that director with Rohmer, Bazin was never the deep personal influence for Chabrol that he was for Truffaut, nor the theoretical master that he was for Godard, Rohmer and Rivette. Chabrol was also unlike the others in that he was a great bon vivant, devoted to the pleasures of the table. Under his jovial influence, the press office at Fox became a salon which, amongst other things, provided *Cahiers* with the latest and most reliable Hollywood gossip. Chabrol took his duties at the press office very seriously. He claims the greatest achievement of his life was increasing the number of secretaries in the office from one to three. He was also inordinately fond of the tall tales that he promulgated in the service of getting more coverage for Fox films in the press – his favourite was an invented story about Jayne Mansfield, reproduced across France, in which by the age of eleven she had astonished herself with the size of her breasts.[53]

The first of the gang recruited to Fox by Chabrol was Paul Gégauff. Gégauff was a key figure in the circle and was to become a very successful scriptwriter (for Chabrol and Rohmer amongst many others). He was also, unlike most of the other cinephiles, a noted womaniser, and he met his death in 1984, stabbed by a wife forty years younger than him. Rohmer describes him thus: 'Gégauff was a seducer . . . But he was more a man who was loved by women than a man who loved women. What attracted us in the man and in the characters that we based on him, was his nonchalance and his calm, a certain insolence, whereas we were much more uptight.'[54]

It was Gégauff who introduced Godard to Chabrol. When Chabrol left Fox to begin making his own films, he managed to get Godard taken on in his stead, and for two years Godard handled publicity and press for a Hollywood major. It is an important element in Godard's formation, reflected in the hugely successful press campaign for *Breathless* and in all his subsequent management of the press. Fox was his entry to the world of commercial film-making and led directly to one crucial encounter: with his future producer, Georges de Beauregard, at the beginning of 1958.

[Beauregard] who was seeking a distributor for *La Passe du diable*, presented the film at Fox, in front of Zanuck and some fifty other people. At the end of the screening, only one person stood up, a bearded gentleman, in fact more unshaven than bearded, his eyes hidden behind dark glasses who said to Beauregard very directly 'Your film is a load of shit' ('Votre film est dégueulasse'). It was Jean-Luc Godard who was working then in the Fox press office. He said it without any nastiness because Jean-Luc was intelligent and nice, but he had a rather brusque way of explaining himself. [Beauregard] who had a nose for both people and things . . . was not annoyed by this interchange. On the contrary that was the birth of a long and enduring friendship.[55]

But it was another famous producer, Pierre Braunberger, who was to give Godard his first chance to work professionally in film. He employed him to write the commentary for a series of short animal films and Godard took the opportunity to work in the editing room as well:

I did some editing work on documentaries for Braunberger. That was the real beginning of my professional film career. I also edited travel films for Arthaud which were shown in the Pleyel cinema. My idea was to try to find in the documents the means to organise them according to the classical rules of editing. Wherever possible I employed classical construction. If there was someone who looked to the right, I looked for the image of another who could cross that look. (G:14)

Parisian Shorts

Braunberger provided the camera and material for Godard's first 35 mm fictional short, *Charlotte et Véronique, ou Tous les garçons s'appellent Patrick*, shot in the summer of 1957. The script was by Rohmer, and although Godard was to work with other scriptwriters the film is interesting as the only example of Godard working with a script entirely written by someone else. The film tells the story of two girls who are picked up by the same boy in the Luxembourg Gardens, and who tell each other the story of their day without realising they are talking of the same flirt. It is a typical Rohmerien satire – gentle and symmetrical.

The editing shows the fruits of Godard's experiments in classical construction, but there are several features which are much less orthodox. The cameraman, Michel Latouche, remembers being surprised that Godard constantly asked him to reframe his shots, cutting out most of the sky over the Luxembourg Gardens and often having the action happen at the edge of the frame. Even more striking is the constant attention to the presence of the media: radio, records, books, posters, paintings and newspapers – all emphasise the complicated circuits of information in which the characters live. And there is a constant reference to the cinema, most striking in the huge poster of James Dean which decorates the girls' apartment with the arresting slogan 'This film explains the drama and the fury of living of the unforgettable James Dean' ('Ce film explique le drame et la fureur de vivre de l'inoubliable James Dean').[56] The girls are played by Anne Colette and by Nicole Berger, the boy by Jean-Claude Brialy.

Brialy became friends with the *Cahiers* critics when he found himself in the same car as Bitsch and Chabrol on a visit to see Renoir's production of *Julius Caesar* at Arles, and he was to star in many of their first films. In his memoirs he gives a fascinating account of what appeared to him to be a revolutionary cell, its members plotting to storm French cinema.[57] He also stars in Godard's second short, *Une Histoire d'eau*. At the beginning of 1958, Braunberger suggested to Truffaut that he make a short on a subject of his choice. Paris and the surrounding countryside had just suffered spectacular floods, and Truffaut took off

The poster for *Rebel Without a Cause* in *Tous les garçons s'appellent Patrick*, 1957.

with Jean-Claude Brialy and Caroline Dim and shot some remarkable footage of the young couple in a drowned world. But Truffaut's whole attention was on making his first feature, and it was Godard who took the footage and turned it into a film (T:251–252). Godard chose to unify this very disparate material by using a continuous voice-over punctuated by drums to produce a stream of consciousness as the young girl makes her way to Paris having hitched a lift with Brialy. The stream of consciousness digresses over an enormous range of subjects unified by a famous story of the French poet Aragon.

Lecturing at the Sorbonne on the great Italian love poet whose sonnets to Laura were to dominate European love poetry for centuries, Aragon spoke for forty-five minutes in praise of Matisse. When a voice from the audience yelled 'Get to the point', Aragon concluded his sentence by emphasising that digression was the key to the art of Petrarch. One can in retrospect discern much of Godard's ambition in this voice-over: to find a way of uniting the classics of Europe's past with the great modernists of the twentieth century through a cinema which will allow any and every subject. It is also an object lesson in how the most fragmented set of images can be turned into a film.

Godard's final short, shot early in 1958, was again financed by Braunberger, starred Anne Colette and was shot for a third time by Michel Latouche. But the male lead was Jean-Paul Belmondo, a young actor whom Godard had noticed in the Allégret film that he had so much disliked. The same review had noted that in the right hands Belmondo would be 'the Michel Simon and the Jules Berry of tomorrow' (G:99/ 1:150). If the first two shorts had their basic material provided by Rohmer and Truffaut, *Charlotte et son Jules* is entirely Godard's work. Its very simple premiss is the return of Charlotte (Anne Colette) to the flat of her boyfriend ('son Jules' is Jean-Paul Belmondo) whom she has just left. He, thinking that she has come back to him, harangues her for twenty minutes in a misogynistic tour de force which leaves no aspect of her personality unvilified. The wind is, however, taken out of his sails when she reveals that she has returned not to eat humble pie but to pick up her toothbrush before departing with her new boyfriend (Gérard Blain), who has promised her a future in films.

Michel Marie sees in this conversation, and above all in the camera movements in a small hotel room, a first sketch of the famous central scene in *Breathless* between Belmondo and Jean Seberg.[58] If that may be slightly overstating the case, its enthusiastic dramatisation and ruthless dissection of misogyny announces one of the major emphases of Godard's work throughout the sixties. Belmondo's voice is provided by Godard as the actor's departure for military service prevented him from dubbing himself. Godard's rasping delivery could hardly have been improved by the actor, and the entire film gains a real edge from the grain of the voice. This film, even more than the first two, is saturated by cinematic references.

The situation is a gender reversal of Cocteau's famous sketch *Le Bel indifférent* which was written for Edith Piaf and has an older woman pleading with a younger, and indifferent, male lover. In Godard's version the cinema is taken severely to task by the jealous Belmondo:

You really want to get into the cinema. There's twelve thousand other blokes you're going to have to sleep with. And anyway, why the cinema. I think that's dishonourable, dishonourable and completely out of date. It's true. What's the cinema? A big head making grimaces in a small room. You've got to be an idiot to like that. But I know what I'm talking about. The cinema is an illusory art. The novel, painting, OK. But not the cinema. Everybody will tell you you're nuts. But you're never willing to listen. Result: you're the only girl in Paris who anybody can have for free.

However one looks at these shorts, it would be foolish to pretend that they have much more than historical interest. Godard himself seems to have been very dissatisfied with the form of the short. In a long article that he contributed to *Cahiers* in February 1959 on the short film festival at Tours, he made clear how limited he found the short film. Unlike the novel and the short story, there are not two forms, there is only one and the result is that the short is just that – too short: 'A short film is not long enough to allow one to study the character in sufficient depth or to round out the action . . . a short film does not have the time to think' (G: 110/1:158–9).

Ray, Tashlin, Rouch

While he had begun to make films, Godard's most powerful statements in this period are still in the form of criticism. From August 1956 onwards, he is a regular contributor to *Cahiers*, and from July 1958, thanks to Truffaut, to the weekly *Arts*. These articles include considerable assessments of Mizoguchi and Bergman, a continuing commitment to Hitchcock, and an absolute devotion to Nicholas Ray:

> If the cinema no longer existed, Nicholas Ray alone gives the impression of being capable of reinventing it, and what is more, of wanting to. While it is easy to imagine John Ford as an admiral, Robert Aldrich on Wall Street, Anthony Mann on the trail of Belliou la Fumée or Raoul Walsh as a latter day Henry Morgan under Caribbean skies, it is difficult to see the

director of *Run for Cover* doing anything but making films. A Logan or a Tashlin, for instance might make good in the theatre or music hall, Preminger as a novelist, Brooks as a school teacher, Fuller as a politician, Cukor as a press agent – but not Nicholas Ray. Were the cinema suddenly to cease to exist, most directors would be in no way at a loss; Nicholas Ray would. After seeing *Johnny Guitar* or *Rebel without a Cause*, one cannot feel that here is something which exists only in the cinema, which would be nothing in a novel, the stage or anywhere else, but which becomes fantastically beautiful on the screen. Nicholas Ray is morally a director, first and foremost. (G:43/1:96)

What differentiates Godard most from the other critics, however, and what is perhaps most significant for his own cinema, are his liking for the screwball comedies of Frank Tashlin, and the central place he awards to the anthropological films of Jean Rouch. What Godard loves in Tashlin is the uncomfortableness of the grotesque and the way in which that discomfort reveals the acme of stupidity of the bourgeois world – his comparison is to Flaubert's *Bouvard et Pécuchet* (G:36/ 1:88). The speed and ease of Tashlin's cartoon style enables him to avoid the boredom that would soon descend on Jerry Lewis's and Dean Martin's clowning and enables that clowning to become instructive. The importance of Tashlin for Godard's films is considerable. Perhaps even more important is Jean Rouch.

Moi, un noir was released in 1959 and completed a trilogy of films set in West Africa. For Godard, the hand-held camera and the closeness to the action, the possibility of constructing *mise-en-scène* which reveals reality in a documentary setting, comes close to realising cinema's full potential. Rouch's visiting card says 'Research Assistant to the Museum of Man' and Godard comments, 'Is there a better definition of the film-maker?' (G:132/1:180). Nowhere is Godard's enormous debt to Bazin more evident than in these articles on Rouch, in which he argues that documentary and fiction cross and re-cross one another so that when they are properly done they become the same thing.

Moi, un Noir de Jean Rouch.

L'AFRIQUE VOUS PARLE
DE LA FIN ET DES MOYENS

par Jean-Luc Godard

Nos lecteurs le savent déjà par les extraits du commentaire que nous avons publié dans notre numéro 93, avec *Moi, un Noir* (ex-Treichville), Jean Rouch ajoute un troisième volet à son immense triptyque nigérien. Les deux autres étant constitués par *Jaguar* (on l'oit, le premier long-métrage de Rouch, non enti encore à ce jour), et *Les Fils de l'eau*, composé d'une série de courts métrages ethnologiques, allant de *La Circoncision aux Maîtres Fous*.

Comme *Les Cousins* sont le contraire du *Beau Serge*, dans *Moi, un Noir*, Jean Rouch raconte une histoire inverse de celle de *Jaguar*. Tel un reporter d'actualité filmant Jayne Mansfield à la descente du Los Angeles-Paris, ou François Mitterrand sortant de l'Elysée, Rouch filme les mésaventures d'une petite bande de Nigériens.

19

Godard's review of Jean Rouch's *Moi, un noir* for *Cahiers du cinéma*.

The Death of Bazin

It is strange in some ways that Bazin never answered Godard's articles on montage, for he certainly engaged with other young critics, correcting the excesses of auteurism as they appeared. But there was no question of him commenting on Godard's reviews of *Moi, un noir*. Four months earlier, on 11 November 1958, André Bazin died at the age of forty. Bazin had exhausted himself in the years from 1943 to 1948 when he animated film cultures from Morocco to Germany almost single-handed, pouring all of his energy into writing, organising, and speaking. From the late forties on, he had been an ill man, first with tuberculosis and then with the leukaemia that eventually killed him. In the intellectual history of the twentieth century, it would be difficult to find a more sympathetic or engaging character, or one who accomplished so much and whose ideas had such lasting effects. By a coincidence which seems close to the mystical, the night he died was the first night of the shooting of François Truffaut's first feature *Les Quatre cents coups*. Truffaut rushed from the set to be with his adoptive father, the man who had led him out of truancy and saved him from military prison, the man who had encouraged him in his writing, even when he was critical of it. It is vain to consider what Bazin would have made of the future that he himself unleashed: it is difficult to imagine that he would have been surprised by the Nouvelle Vague, but as one moves down the years it becomes less easy to speculate. What would he have made of his much-loved Truffaut making films in the tradition of quality that he had so bitterly attacked? But then it is worth remarking that Bazin always refused Truffaut's blanket condemnation of that tradition. And what of a Maoist Godard? Though the questions become senseless, it is a mark of the importance of Bazin as a thinker that one is tempted to ask them. What is certain is that no critic or theorist since his death has come close to his ability to hold together the formal and social analysis of film. In December 1977, Truffaut wrote a foreword to Dudley Andrew's excellent biography of Bazin and ended with these words:

> Bazin was forty when he died; he would have been nearly sixty today and his presence would have helped to dissipate the thick fog in which cinematographic reflection finds itself. To be a critic in 1978 is much more difficult than it was in 1958, first of all because production has become enormously diversified at the same time as the ambitions of filmmakers have grown . . .
>
> In the era in which Bazin wrote, the average production lacked artistic ambition to such an extent that the role of the critic frequently was to point out to one or another workaday filmmaker the talent which he had never noticed in himself. Today it is quite the contrary. More often it happens that although the ambitions of filmmakers are very high their execution can't keep up with them. Bazin, if he were still alive, would have helped us to understand ourselves well enough to establish a better harmony amongst our projects, our aptitudes, our goals and our style.
>
> Yes, we miss André Bazin.

Twenty-five years later the thick fog has become thicker. In the cinema the critic is dead, no longer even the tiniest cog in the economic circuits of value. The death occurred on 20 June 1975 when Universal opened *Jaws* in that massive release pattern underpinned by television advertisements which has become a model for all blockbusters. This first summer release was to set a new pattern which rendered all specialist newspaper critics redundant as an element in any film's success. Seven years later, in 1982, not only Bazinian criticism but Bazinian cinema was dead. Of course the projection of images is still with us but the guarantee that the image on the screen is the image of a reality before the camera, the fundamental Bazinian ontology, evaporated in 1982 with the release of *Tron* and the successful use of computer-generated imagery. The story since then is very complicated. CGI has not swept all before it as was first predicted. If it is used in many films, it is rarely used centre stage. Those who envisaged films with virtual actors now look totally foolish. One might even suspect that there is an audience resistance to this new form of spectacle, that there is an audience demand for that realism that Bazin found so significant. But there is no denying that the cinema of truth and criticism, the cinema that began with the Lumière brothers and Méliès ended with *Jaws* and *Tron*. Death robbed us of the figure who in his sixties and seventies (he would be eighty-five if he were alive today) might have helped us to make more sense of recent developments, who would have helped us to avoid the easy pessimisms of the intellectual while retaining the genuine standards of the critic. It is a mark of Bazin's stature that it is not ridiculous to echo Truffaut's words from three decades ago: we still miss André Bazin.

3

A Certain Tendency of French Film Production: The New Wave of Karina and Coutard

The Political Economy of the New Wave

'To make a film all you need is a girl and a gun' – like all great aphorisms, Godard's dictum condenses multiple meanings.[1] The most immediate is the emphasis on film's direct appeal to sex and the simplicity of its easily predictable genres – in this case the gangster movie. But perhaps even more important is the sense – vital to the *Cahiers* critics – that films must be made cheaply. If one wants to be an author then control must be retained, and the only way to control a medium so intrinsically expensive is to ensure that one makes cheap films. One can find this argument again and again in Godard interviews right up to the present, and it is scattered vigorously through the pages of *Cahiers*. One of its clearest statements comes in an interview that Godard did with Pierre Kast in February 1959 for the weekly paper *Arts* about Kast's film *Le Bel âge*. Truffaut's columns in *Arts* had become so popular that they were often the front-page lead. In 1958 when the festival of Cannes, infuriated by yet another wounding article, refused to give him press accreditation for the festival, he even became a minor news story himself. There is a reference to *Arts* in *Charlotte et Véronique, ou Tous les garçons s'appellent Patrick* where one of the customers is reading an issue of the paper with the headline 'French cinema is collapsing under false legends' – the title of one of Truffaut's most stinging attacks on the French film establishment. By February 1959, Truffaut was deeply engaged in editing *Les Quatre cents coups* and had all but given up criticism. But Godard, whom Truffaut had

Pierre Kast in Brittany.

François Truffaut and Roberto Rossellini at Cannes, May 1959.

introduced to the pages of *Arts* along with many others of the *Cahiers* gang, was still writing reviews and conducting interviews.[2] Pierre Kast, who was one of the older generation of *Cahiers* – those who had lived through the war as adults – is an astonishingly attractive figure. A Marxist dandy, he obviously found some of the more aesthetic of the young Turks a little difficult to tolerate when they had the vapours. There is a hilarious moment in one of the discussions in which he self-deprecatingly refers to himself as 'the house Marxist' when he once again enunciates two or three home truths about the economics of film-making.[3] Godard's interview with him is so illuminating, both in its lapidary opening and in its content, that it is worth quoting in full:

> The good fairy chance has twice leaned on Pierre Kast's shoulder. Firstly in 1940, arrested by the Germans, he had to postpone his agrégation.[4] He read and discovered Raymond Queneau. Secondly just after the war, happening to meet Henri Langlois – and by the same token cinema – he began to frequent Murnau, Griffith, Vigo, Stroheim and Eisenstein at the Cinémathèque. Pierre Kast then met Jean Grémillon, and became his assistant. With him, he made a documentary about the conventions of

Jacques Rivette, with Jean Herman, unknown man, Charles Bitsch (in profile) and André Mrugalski, on the roof of the Sarah Bernhardt Theatre, during the shoot of *Paris nous appartient*, 1958.

'Salon' art of the Belle Epoque, Les Charmes de l'existence. *He then became assistant in turn to Preston Sturges, Rene Clément and Jean Renoir, while at the same time making a good many short films including* Les Femmes du Louvre, Goya, L'Arithmétique *(written and performed by Queneau),* M. Robida, l'explorateur du temps, Ledoux, l'architecte maudit. *In 1957 Pierre Kast made his first feature,* Un Amour de poche, *with the collaboration of France Roche. And with Claude Bernard-Aubert, he has recently set up the Association des cinéastes indépendants (Association of Independent Film-makers).*

JEAN-LUC GODARD: *Le Bel âge* is a project set up entirely independently of the industry?

PIERRE KAST: Entirely. The shooting of *Un Amour de poche* was a pretty discouraging experience. Luckily I came across a short story by Moravia, 'An Old Fool'. I decided to make a half-hour film based on this story, shot with my own money in districts of Paris which I love. Some producer friends helped me to finish it. Once the final print was ready I noticed something: which was that as it turned out I had made the film exclusively with old friends. Counting up, I found there were twenty-five of them. So then I thought: why not go on filming my friends and see what happens? Why not make a feature with and about them, and about myself too? So I made another half-hour film which is the sequel to the first. Other producer friends again helped me with it. Once the final print was ready, I thought: why not go on? I therefore introduced my producer friends of the first film to my producer friends of the second, and they agreed to make the third episode of *Le Bel âge*.

In effect the subtitle of *Le Bel âge* could well be: Pierre Kast and his friends Boris Vian, Jacques Doniol-Valcroze, Marcello Pagliero, Gianni Esposito, etc. I shot the second episode in summer. At that time all my friends were in St Tropez. So I set up my cameras.

Now I'm off to Switzerland, to La Valais, because that is where the three actresses happen to be whose exploits will shape my third and last episode. That is what interests me, this Pirandellian aspect of reality: the fact that I know a lot of people who have very amusing or very sad adventures, and no one is there to bring them back alive. But that, to a large extent, is what cinema is for.

One thing I dislike about current French film-making is that when you go on set you are usually assisting at a very mournful operation: you laugh after the takes, never during, as it were. This is very serious. Because in the days of Sennett and Griffith when everything was being invented, cinema was created by very jolly people. They had enormous fun. They worked in an atmosphere of wonderful spontaneity. But not today. I think it is this verve and simplicity in film-making we must try to recapture.

GODARD: Financially, your system has a great many advantages.

KAST: Yes, it's fantastic. *Le Bel âge* will cost less than 250,000 FF. But it isn't so much that which is fantastic. What I wanted to prove to French producers was that it is possible to finance a ninety-minute feature film by tripling the cost of a half-hour short.

GODARD: As *Le Bel âge* is the story of a real-life group of friends, will it therefore also be the story of their women?

KAST: Yes, of course. That is just what *Le Bel âge* will be: I mean, my friends and their girls, or my girlfriends and their friends. The important thing is to stick to a personal world in order to gain a relative if not an absolute freedom. Thus as I make the film I am also writing the novel. The even chapters tell the story of the people making the film, the odd ones their story at the moment when they intervene in the film itself. In the last two chapters, both odd and even, you will find the ringmaster – the director, in other words – writing a science-fiction short story which will give point to everything which has gone before, which will in a sense be the parable of *Le Bel âge*.

GODARD: In other words, you are running systematically counter to the usual attitudes?

KAST: More or less. Even on the level of production, as I told you. I think so. It's an attitude which is important. At the moment, moreover, we are witnessing an extraordinary phenomenon, unthinkable five years ago even. A whole galaxy of young people are in the process of taking the old Bastille of French cinema by assault. The same thing is happening in the cinema as happened after the First World War with the Cartel in the theatre, Les Six in music, the School of Paris in painting, the pioneers of airmail in aviation. The young French cinema of today – of Resnais, Franju, Chabrol, Malle, Astruc, Rivette, Bernard-Aubert, Truffaut, Rouch and all the rest of the best – is like the front-wheel drive when Citroën launched it: it is adventure, sincerity, courage, lucidity. Giraudoux and his gardener will tell you that all this boasts a glorious name, which it so happens is also that of the greatest film in all cinema: *Sunrise*. (G:122–123/1:169–171)

In the introduction to this interview, which effectively sketches out many of the most important emphases of the Nouvelle Vague and which signals the new dawn as it is breaking, there is a surprising absence. Godard underplays Kast's role in the Resistance, limiting the reference to 1940. In fact Kast ended the war as the president of the Communist student union. After 1941 and the German invasion of the Soviet Union, the Communist Party became arguably the most important force in the French Resistance, and much of its prestige and attraction in the post-war years was due (as was the case in Italy) to the commitment and the heroism of its members in the struggle against Nazism. But then Godard was hardly likely to mention Kast's Communist history in the pages of *Arts*, which was a right-wing magazine and ferociously hostile to the Communist Party.

A lot of ink has been spilled on the right-wing nature of the *Cahiers* critics, not least by its great rival *Positif*, which wrote about film from an avowedly left-wing and avant-garde perspective. There is no doubt that the most simple intellectual history of France in the late fifties would make some identification between *Cahiers* and the 'hussards' (hussars).[5]

The hussars, a group of writers who, like the young Turks of *Cahiers*, identified themselves as post-Resistance and -Liberation, also defined themselves as right-wing anarchists. This group, whose most important members were Roger Nimier and Jacques Laurent, wanted to reclaim much of the literature which had been buried in the settling of debts following 1944. Most importantly, they celebrated the works of Céline, then completely taboo because of the overt Fascist and anti-Semitic opinions they contained. The hussars openly mocked the doctrinaire Stalinism of the Communist Party and the ponderous political engage-ment promoted by Sartre. Their name was one applied by their enemies in December 1952 when Bernard Franck published in no less an authority than Sartre's magazine, *Les Temps Modernes*, an article entitled 'Hussards et Grognards' ('Hussars and Groaners').[6]

It is all too easy to understand why anyone like Truffaut, with a commitment to the importance of the aesthetic, and above all the aesthetic of American film, would be only too happy to find another political position, particularly if it had the added advantage, for a young man on the Balzacian make, of getting up the nose of everybody in a position of cultural authority. Truffaut's scrupulous biographers pro-duce all the evidence that Truffaut's initial flirtation with this position led him to some statements of complete stupidity, where he openly drew not just on the hussars' oppositional stance, but also on the ferociously nationalistic and anti-democratic positions of Charles Maurras[7] and L'Action Française.[8] Such stupidity was all the easier because one of the great cinema critics of the pre-war era was the anti-Semitic Lucien Rebatet, and the most famous literary name amongst those shot for collaboration in 1945 was Robert Brasillach, whose works include the first serious history of the cinema in French.[9]

A fuller understanding of why the extreme right engaged so seriously with the cinema is beyond the scope of this biography, and perhaps would make sense only within a more general history of European Fascism. Over half a century ago, in 'Towards a Political Cinema', Godard identified Rossellini's *Germany, Year Zero* as the first step in such a history. Despite the wealth of valuable historical material since then, it is exactly the allure of Fascism which remains unanalysed; historians, like literary critics, tend to forget that cinema is the crucial political art of the twentieth century.

If Truffaut flirted briefly with the right, it was a flirtation that came to a definitive end when he read Roland Barthes's *Mythologies* on its publication in 1957. *Mythologies* analysed the culture of contemporary France in a way which conforms with a fundamental Marxist view of history, but which also looks specifically at how the bourgeois culture of contemporary France transformed that history into nature. Indeed, had Truffaut wished, *Mythologies* would have given him a whole new set of sticks with which to trash 'le cinéma de qualité'. But Truffaut was more interested in refusing the right-wing tag with which both he and *Cahiers* were increasingly labelled. In the issue of January 1958, he wrote a coruscating Barthesian analysis of the prose of the articles in *Positif*, which claimed to be of the left but which refused all terms such as intellectual, aesthetic or ethical. *Cahiers* stood above all for the importance of looking at the specificity of cultural forms and it was this, from a left perspective, that was the theme of Barthes's book. Indeed Barthes showed, and Truffaut repeated the lesson with glee, that those who simply treated culture as a symptom of social malaise were in fact taking up Fascist positions.[10]

From the point of view of intellectual history, this is one of the great missed encounters. Had Truffaut continued with his criticism, then the conjunction of the new wave of French thought might have broken simultaneously with that of the Bazinian criticism of *Cahiers*. But Truffaut, faithful to that Bazinian criticism, was now almost entirely focused on making films. *Les Quatre cents coups*, which he had started shooting on the day of Bazin's death, was finished by the beginning of April 1959 and was selected for the festival of Cannes. In the pages of *Arts*, Jean-Luc Godard expressed his joy that Truffaut, the critic who had been banned from the festival in 1958, was to represent France in 1959 as a director. Godard identified the change with the new Gaullist regime:

> As soon as the screening was over, the lights came up in the tiny auditorium. There was silence for a few moments. Then Philip Erlanger, representing the Quai d'Orsay, leaned over to André Malraux. 'Is this film really to represent France at the Cannes Festival?' 'Certainly, certainly.' And so the Minister for Cultural Affairs ratified the Selection Committee's decision to send to Cannes, as France's sole official entry, François Truffaut's *Les Quatre cents coups*. (G:146/193)

For Godard, Malraux's decision was that of a great artist, the author of *La Condition humaine* and the director of *L'Espoir*. Godard's article follows the current political line of *Arts*, which saw in de Gaulle's return to power in May 1958 the beginning of a new political era. From the perspective of the state, however, it is easy to imagine the new Minister of Culture simply following the advice of his state bureaucrats. In fact, the selection of Truffaut can be seen as the development of a policy which had already been clearly signalled in the pages of *Cahiers* itself. Exactly a year before de Gaulle came to power, *Cahiers* devoted a special number to the situation of French cinema. The interview format had become one of the trademarks of *Cahiers* and this issue carried one with Jacques Flaud, the head of state funding for cinema, the Centre National du Cinématographie. The importance accorded to it can be gauged by the fact that this time it was not the young Turks who carried the tape recorder but, unusually, André Bazin and Jacques Doniol-Valcroze.

The Centre National du Cinématographie had been created at
the end of 1946, while France
was still riding the wave of the
Liberation, but in a paradox
which runs deep into the surrender of 1940, it did little more
than confirm the reorganisation
of the cinema that had been set
up by Pétain's Vichy government.
Before 1940 there had been little
state interference in the film industry, which was thus subject to
the most brutal fluctuations of
the economy. Fascist ideology
was corporatist – the state inter-
vened in the functioning of the
economy by creating industrial
structures which linked the state,

Cover of *Cahiers du cinéma* showing a still
from Jules Dassin's *Celui qui doit mourir.*

capital and labour. Within a month of Pétain being installed, there were
organising committees for each industry, and by 26 October 1940 there
was a detailed law in place which in its essentials has governed French
cinema from that day to this. It would be tempting to say that the speed
of this legislation proved the Fascist tendencies of the state that had
surrendered itself to the Germans. In fact, however, the laws put in place
had been formulated in 1936, even before the election of the Popular
Front.[11]

From a longer historical perspective it may be that the corporatism of
French cinema owes little to Fascist ideology, and a great deal to an
older corporatist model: the state capitalism developed by Colbert,
Louis XIV's great minister of finance, whose influence is still omnipresent within the current French state. Whatever its historical provenance,
this legislation put into place two key elements. The first was a state
subsidy system which allowed a producer to draw down money against
future receipts, and the second was a rigorous professionalisation,

which meant that nobody could work in the industry without the appropriate 'ticket'. For any producer who works independently of banks or large corporations, the most difficult problems are first of all to find the initial slice of money which will attract the rest, and secondly to earn anything from a film after the sales agents, the distributors and the exhibitors all have had their bite of the cake (a bite which in the case of the sales agents' and distributors' expenses is always massive and often fraudulent). The post-Liberation governments did not really alter any of the fundamentals of the Pétainist settlement. By 1948 the French system of *avance sur recettes*, with a hypothecated tax directly on ticket sales which came back to the producers, meant that the métier of producer was a genuine one. Provided you could bring some initial money to the table for your first film, there would always be money in the CNC bank – money which could only be used to make another film. At the same time the unionised apprenticeship system ensured a very high level of professionalisation.

The economic story of French cinema in the fifties was one of success.[12] The 'cinéma de qualité' that Truffaut and his gang so loathed was a very good business. But these same structures ensured conservatism. Once you were in you were in, but getting in as a producer, a director or technician took forever. The number of first-time directors was low, and producers had no incentive to be inventive or innovative. The political situation of the Fourth Republic, in constant governmental chaos and fighting two major colonial wars (Indo-China and Algeria), added a fear of government censorship which means that if you look at the films of that period for any sign of contemporary France, you look in vain. In fact the CNC was as worried by the situation as anybody else and before de Gaulle arrived in power it was looking for ways to stimulate innovation. This is made clear by Flaud when he tells Bazin and Doniol-Valcroze at the beginning of the interview:

> It is normal from my point of view to speak about the situation of French cinema from the perspective of economics. That will allow me to correct certain errors on the subject of the current economic health of French cinema and to pose the problem: What constitutes this apparent health?

We will talk of the subsidy to the cinema, which is the principal source of this prosperity, but also of failures on other levels, banal repetition, lack of imagination, lack of heart . . . the fact is there: an economic reality which is good for the economic situation but bad for the artistic situation.[13]

Godard may have imagined that Malraux had in mind *La Condition humaine* and *L'Espoir* when he gave the thumbs up to *Les Quatre cents coups*, but it is as likely that he was thinking of the aristocratic disdain of the much-quoted last sentence of his *Esquisse*: 'Apart from that, the cinema is an industry,' and an industry which his civil servants were telling him was desperately in need of regeneration.[14]

The young Turks were in fact pushing at an open door and in the spring of 1959 it swung open. First through was Chabrol. Using money from his wife's family he had shot two films, *Le Beau Serge* between December 1957 and January 1958 and *Les Cousins*, both painfully direct accounts of life in contemporary France.[15] After the exhausting process of regularisation through the French bureaucracy Chabrol found distributors, and on 11 February and 11 March 1959 respectively they opened to good notices and fairly full houses. But even that triumph (saluted by Godard in terms which Chabrol today finds comically excessive [G:98–99/149–50, 128–9/1:176–177[16]]) was as nothing to the reception that greeted *Les Quatre cents coups* at Cannes, where Truffaut was awarded the prize of best director.

The Nouvelle Vague, the New Wave, as it came to be known in the spring of 1959, was perhaps the first time that a moment in film history was front-page headlines, but that was mainly because it was a front-page headline which gave the moment in film history a name. The term 'Nouvelle Vague' came from *L'Express*, a magazine modelled on *Time* and *Newsweek* which was itself a sign of the new consumer capitalism that was coming late but quickly to France. In 1957 *L'Express* commissioned a series of polls to determine a difference between generational attitudes, and Françoise Giroud wrote a series of articles based on their findings. The theme of a difference between generations was not new – it went back to the First World War if not earlier – nor was it confined to

France: in America the arrival of Elvis Presley and James Dean in 1955 had revealed that teenage pathology now had real spending power.[17] But it was only in France, after Giroud's initial articles, that this difference became identified with the cinema. In 1959, following Cannes, that identification went global.

The immediate economic success of the Nouvelle Vague and the international dimensions of that success was real. Ignace Morgenstern, one of the most senior of French distributors and the financier of Truffaut's film, must have been a little surprised to find the entire budget of *Les Quatre cents coups* (tiny, as *Cahiers*'s thinking and economic reality demanded) recouped by a single foreign sale to the United States before Cannes (T:265). Suddenly everybody wanted a piece of the action, and as the New Wave surged, it was Godard who surfed it. The films of both Chabrol and Truffaut had been financed by family money.[18] Rivette's *Paris nous appartient* and Rohmer's *Le Signe du lion* were being made hand-to-mouth and would take two (1958–60) and three (1959–62) years respectively to complete. Godard may have been coming late to the party (a familiar Godardian complaint), but he came in style.

Breathless

For a film all you need is a girl and a gun but you need someone to pay the girl and buy the gun. You need a producer. The depth of Godard's debt to the producer that he found can be judged by the pages that he faxed to the trade paper *Le Film français* on 21 September 1984, the occasion of Georges de Beauregard's death:

> . . . So there . . . the phrase-makers have made phrases . . . the weepers have wept . . . the forgetters have forgotten . . . already . . . as they have forgotten Romy . . . Roberto . . . André . . . Jany . . . Henri . . . Nicole . . . the credits-list is long of the stars whose light they have have put out . . . instead of boosting the voltage . . . after all the testimonies rich in cheap sentiments . . . here is a poor false testimony . . . since

Godard's homage to Georges de Beauregard in *Le Film Français*, no. 2003, 21 September 1984.

it is no more than true . . . that Georges de B has only made a false departure . . . in giving us the slip . . . like poor Vincent . . . without yellow in his eyes . . . but at the tips of his fingers gnawed by Players . . . Georges de B has only taken death in order to go to another <u>star</u> . . . he has finally climbed to the deep summit . . . of that curve of feeling . . . from which the good Raoul had nevertheless told him . . . that the harder would be the fall . . . but Georges de B had . . . the soul of a Faust under the appearance of a shopkeeper . . . and French cinema . . . being so low . . . he had to go and see higher . . . if there wasn't something to project . . . for the pleasant screens of our still beautiful country . . . project something other than sad revolvers . . . or botched sex . . . so he needed . . . to gain height . . . Georges de B . . . and it's difficult . . . he was no saint . . . Georges de B . . . just a Tom Thumb . . . from 10 in the morning . . . things zigzagged . . . because of bank charges in the stomach . . . so a little glass of champagne . . . it was his breakfast . . . a real production worker . . . this Georges de B . . . and he went off to fight . . . the ogre at the bank . . . the dragon at the CNC . . . more often KO than victorious . . . but it produced Belmondo's first smile and Bardot's last . . . I salute you, Gorges de B. J-L.

This tribute is one of the very rare occasions on which Godard acknowledges his two most famous films: *Breathless* (the first smile of Belmondo) and *Contempt* (the last smile of Bardot). Beauregard, a lover of wine, women,[19] and cinema, was a man who lived on the edge. By the summer of 1959 it was getting edgier by the minute. On 19 May 1959, Beauregard's film *Pêcheur d'Islande* opened in Paris and was a total flop. He was 600,000 FF in debt and the 'ogre of the bank' was at his door. Ever since their first memorable meeting, Beauregard had been talking to Godard about a possible first feature. Indeed, Godard had worked on the script of *Pêcheur d'Islande* and turned down the opportunity of directing it. Now Godard proposed to Beauregard four alternative projects.[20] For one he wrote to Truffaut: 'If you've got the time to finish in three lines the idea of the film begun in the metro Richelieu-Drouot (those were the days), even though I haven't got Françoise Sagan I can do the dialogues.'[21]

Truffaut, who had already unsuccessfully tried to persuade his father-in-law to finance a Godard project which would later become *Une Femme est une femme*, dashed off four pages. The pages were based on a story that had fascinated tabloid France in 1952, when a man named Michel Portail, having spent a summer living the high life on the Côte d'Azur with an American girlfriend, shot a motorcycle policeman while driving to Brittany to see his dying mother. He was turned in to the police by the girlfriend.

The four pages were enough to convince Beauregard. With the hot name of Truffaut attached, the penniless producer persuaded a major distributor, René Pignières, who like everyone else after Cannes was looking for a New Wave film, and another producer with money in the CNC bank, Gérard Beytout, to provide the extraordinarily modest budget of 510,000 FF (a third of the average cost of a French film at that time). By a correspondence that would have delighted Baudelaire or Joyce, the money waiting to be drawn from the CNC bank had been earned by two of Fritz Lang's last films, *The Tiger of Eschnapur* and *Journey to the Lost City*.

Any producer backing a first-time director is taking an enormous risk. From an economic point of view, an independent production can be likened to an industrial process in which one builds a small factory, manufactures one product and then dismantles the factory.[22] Whatever view one takes of the auteur theory, the basic form of the product made is grasped by one person and one person only, the director. Beauregard had a high opinion of Godard, but to provide an extra safety belt and to give the film even more of a New Wave brand he persuaded Chabrol to act as its technical director. Both Truffaut and Chabrol, already wise in the ways of contracts, made their participation provisional on Godard being the director.

It has been well said that casting is seventy-five per cent of direction. Certainly Godard has almost always had superb casts. For *Breathless*, he had what none of the gang had enjoyed so far: a star. The good fairy on Godard's shoulder was waving her wand when a young lawyer called François Moreuil heard that the film was casting. Moreuil, who himself had ambitions in the cinema, was married to the 21-year-old actress Jean Seberg. Seberg is one of the rare examples in the whole history of cinema of someone who was a world star before she had shot a foot of film.

In 1956, and on a Hollywood roll, Otto Preminger announced that he was going to audition unknowns for the role of Joan of Arc in his film adaptation of Shaw's play. Not since the casting of *Gone with the Wind* had there been so much publicity before a film, and Hollywood cynics awaited the production of an already-chosen starlet at the end of the process. But it was, in fact, an unknown from Marshalltown, Iowa, who was presented to the world's press at the end of the long media event, and a star was born.

The irony was that the two films that she made with Preminger, *Saint Joan* and the adaptation of Sagan's famous novel *Bonjour tristesse*, were more or less total flops. Yet they ranked amongst *Cahiers du cinéma*'s favourite movies and the *Cahiers* critics declared Seberg 'the new Divinity of the cinema'.[23] Seberg's lack of commercial success along with Moreuil's combination of legal skill and chutzpah,[24] and a twelve-page telegram from Godard which offered Columbia (who had Seberg under contract) $12,000 or 50 per cent of the film's back end, combined to give Godard a major star for what was, in Hollywood terms, a derisory sum.

CAHIERS
DU CINÉMA

80 ★ REVUE MENSUELLE DE CINÉMA ● FÉVRIER 1958 ★ **80**

Jean Seberg in Otto Preminger's *Bonjour tristesse*.

In the film's terms, however, her fee amounted to a quarter of the total budget. (Needless to say the lawyers at Columbia had pre-ferred the money up front to the promise of jam tomorrow.)

There have been few directors who have quite had Godard's genius at rendering female beauty, and Seberg was no ex-ception. The combination of toughness and fragility, the con-tradiction of a Midwest maiden well aware of her sexuality and, most importantly, a woman des-perate to make a success of a profession for which she lacked most of the requisite skills, are forever captured in this movie. In

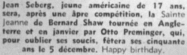

Jean Seberg, jeune américaine de 17 ans, sera, après une âpre compétition, la Sainte Jeanne de Bernard Shaw tournée en Angle-terre et en janvier par Otto Preminger, qui, pour oublier ses soucis, fêtera ses cinquante ans le 5 décembre. Happy birthday.

Jean Seberg in Otto Preminger's *Saint Joan*. *Cahiers du cinéma, no 65 December 1956.*

a life full of unhappiness which ended in madness and tragedy,[25] *Breathless* is a moment of hope and joy.

If Godard had one star when he started the movie, he had two when he finished. His initial meeting with Jean-Paul Belmondo was less than auspicious. Belmondo, the much-loved son of a famous sculptor, and an actor with almost certain success before him, was less than impressed when they first met in the Latin Quarter. Godard's dark glasses and Vaudois accent left him cold, and when three weeks later Jean-Luc sidled up to Belmondo at the Brasserie Lipp and asked him if he'd shoot a short in his hotel room, Belmondo thought he was dealing with a homosexual pass. Belmondo's wife thought differently when he related the encoun-ter, and Belmondo soon changed his opinion after a day's shooting at the hotel, where Godard's casual style entranced him. Belmondo was even more impressed by the long and tender letter Godard sent him as he did his military service in Algeria asking his permission to let Godard dub him in *Charlotte et son Jules*. The letter ended 'The day that I make my first feature it will be with you.'[26] Godard held true to his promise, and a new star exploded as the cameras rolled: 'In *Breathless* I was looking for the subject of the film all through the shoot, finally I became interested in Belmondo. I saw him as a kind of block that it was necessary to film to discover what lay behind'(G:175–176/1:219).

With his cast in place, Godard set about assembling his crew. In the summer of 1959, he bumped into Pierre Rissient on the Champs Élysées. Rissient, today an *éminence grise* of French cinema, was then a young Turk of the young Turks. A crucial few years younger (b. 1936) than the 'Schérer gang', Rissient had started attending the Cinémathèque and the Tuesday evenings at the Studio Parnasse (from which Chabrol would give him a lift home) when Godard was still in Geneva. Rissient's passion was contemporary American cinema and he used his knowledge to programme a cinema called the MacMahon, which catered to American soldiers. So sure was his taste that the cinema soon picked up a cinephile audience as well, and 'MacMahonian' became an adjective signifying total loyalty to contemporary American cinema and particularly thrillers. Godard asked Rissient if he would be his assistant on the film he was about to shoot with Seberg and Belmondo. Rissient reminded Godard that Rohmer had wanted him to be the assistant on *Le Signe du lion*, but that his lack of a union ticket had been an impossible hurdle. Godard reassured him that this time it would happen.[27]

But if Godard was to overcome the union problem with his assistant, he was less successful with his cameraman. Michel Latouche had shot all three of his Parisian shorts and Godard was very keen to use him on the new film. But Beauregard had another candidate: Raoul Coutard. The importance of Coutard to Godard is impossible to estimate accurately but 'cher Raoul' shot all but three (*Masculin Féminin*, *Sauve qui peut*, *Détective*) of Godard's conventionally crewed films.[28]

Coutard (b. 1924) was older than Godard, and he likes to emphasise that while the rest of the New Wave boasted of their 'bad boy' status, he himself had been a hardworking and brilliant student who wanted to study chemistry until a lack of money had forced him in 1943 to take up the trade of photography. But his passion was for the army. He volunteered for a French force that was being prepared to fight the Japanese. When Hiroshima and Nagasaki ended the Second World War before the new army could be deployed, he opted to go to Indo-China, where the first of the major anti-colonial wars was being fought.[29] Coutard stayed for over a decade, five years as a soldier and then six more as a photographer recording the conflict which was to end in the defeat and humiliation of Dien Bien Phu, where Ho Chi Minh's armies under the brilliant generalship of Giap inflicted a crushing defeat on the French, for whom 1940 was still an open wound. Even in his eighties Coutard has the bearing and appearance of a soldier, and he was to bring all his courage, determination and honesty to his new profession when Pierrre Schoendoerffer, with whom he'd worked on stories in Vietnam, asked him to be the cameraman[30] for his feature. The film, *La Passe du diable*, was shot in Afghanistan in 1956 in difficult conditions, including a four-month hiatus caused by Suez when Britain and France tried to turn back the colonial clock in a desperately foolish and inglorious adventure.

The conditions of film production forge strong alliances and enmities. The necessity to capture a particular moment from a particular angle imposes the most rigorous working conditions. Nowhere are these conditions more rigorous than around the camera. If the light is wrong, if a shot is misframed, if the focus is out, if the film is damaged in any way, then all the time and money spent on the shot has been wasted. Beauregard had formed a high opinion of Coutard during the shooting of *La Passe du diable* and imposed him on Godard. Coutard was unhappy with the situation and went to Godard to assure him that, if Godard really didn't want him then he would withdraw. When Godard realised that Coutard was absolutely willing to shoot the film as a reportage, he agreed that Latouche would step down to work as an assistant.[31]

It is crucial to realise that the reason Godard could make a film for a third of the normal cost was because he was working with an extremely reduced crew. This was partly due to developments in the technology, but also to a definite easing of the union restrictions, possibly to encourage innovation. It is also important to understand that for

Godard, good Bazinian that he was, a reduced crew increased the possibility of capturing reality on the run.

The crew for *Breathless* was so small and worked so fast that the passers-by on the Champs Élysées didn't know they were there. They often finished the day's work in a time which was almost unbelievable for anybody used to the pompous hesitancies of normal filming. Certainly they stretched Beauregard's credulity. Finding the whole crew ensconced at Fouquet's, one of the most expensive restaurants on the Champs Élysées, for lunch with the day's work finished, he threw one of the fits for which he was famous and launched a scorching memo telling his team that they had better shape up.[32] This memo is at the root of hundreds of stories of a chaotic and disorganised shoot. But Rissient, a man of meticulous accuracy, is adamant that the shoot was conducted with great precision, and that Godard never showed the slightest sign of not knowing what to do. Chabrol, the technical advisor on the film, is equally adamant that there was no chaos. For him, Beauregard's memo was just a wind-up ('il rigolait').

Godard, Raoul Coutard and Jean Seberg during the shoot of *Breathless*.

Belmondo, Godard and Georges de Beauregard at Saint-Germain des Prés.

Raoul Coutard filming *Breathless*.

The other reason for the speed of the shoot was that almost no artificial lighting was used. Godard was determined to use as little artificial light as possible, because the lighting of a set both takes the most time and makes filming most conspicuous, thus destroying the environment that is being filmed.[33] Anybody who has seen a film crew in action can testify to the ostentation of their activity and the destruction that they leave in their wake. As a war cameraman having to seize images in a split second, Coutard was familiar with the fastest, that is to say the most light sensitive, of stocks. For the night shoots on *Breathless* they used a stock (Ilford HPS) which only existed for still photography. The crew had to stick together as many rolls of 17.5 metres as would make up a magazine of film.[34]

Godard's apprenticeship in the cinema had been very thorough; most directors are more technically literate than an outsider might expect, but Godard's devotion to the science and technology of his art is without obvious comparison. His apprenticeship had also included, as well as editing, the writing of dialogues which he had done for Beauregard and others.[35] Jean Seberg was initially amazed when she discovered that she would get her lines on pieces of paper given to her on the morning of the shoot or even shouted at her in the middle of the scene. But after the horror of working with Preminger (who had bullied her unmercifully) anything seemed bearable, and her husband was constantly on set to reassure her.

Godard could shout because *Breathless* was shot mute, and the sound and dialogue were dubbed on later in a mixing studio. Shooting with sync sound on locations like the Champs Élysées would have thrown up major problems with the editing because of the changing level of background noise. Later in his career Godard would shoot in sync, and in keeping with Bazinian precepts, he often sourced his sound within the image, but in the summer of 1959 there was no money and no time, and the shoot had to be completed in an extraordinarily short four weeks. The conditions were designed to allow Godard to work like Jean Rouch, but instead of a veteran back in Africa after his disgrace at the defeat in Dien Bien Phu, it is Seberg and Belmondo on the run in Paris.

If Godard took a very short time to shoot, he spent a very long time,

relatively speaking, composing the soundtrack.[36] Tolmatchoff was
summoned from Geneva, and Godard devoted what was in contemporary industrial terms an inordinate amount of time to the recording
and mixing of sound. His perfectionism did have some limits. One day
Tolmatchoff turned up for a briefing on the exact number of different
cars' engines needed (*Breathless* is, amongst other things, a petrol-head's
dream) but Godard was nowhere to be found. The next day he turned
up announcing that he had been to Rome to see Rossellini's *Generale
della Rovere*, and the sound was so terrible that he'd decided he didn't
need to record a different sound for every car.

Breathless is unique in Godard's work in that it is from beginning to
end faithful to one genre. If the interview scene with Parvulesco and the
famous twenty-minute long love scene in the Hôtel de Suède mark
genuine breaks with convention, and if the editing inaugurated a
revolution which still continues, *Breathless* is, to use the French term,
a 'polar' (a cop story). Its huge success both in France and abroad is in
large measure due to the classicism of this first film, a film that could
have been made with 'Défense et Illustration du découpage classique'
pasted to the camera. This may seem paradoxical given the reputation of
Breathless as the film that completely revolutionised editing and which
broke with the classical construction that had, according to Bazin, been
fully developed by the late thirties. But Godard's argument with Bazin is
that classical construction could still be developed and no less an
authority than Pierre Rissient hazards his opinion that when Godard
was shooting *Breathless*, he was thinking in terms of a much more
conventional edit.

There is an old Hollywood saying that each picture is made up of five
different pictures. There is the picture you write, the picture you cast, the
picture you shoot, the picture you edit, and the picture you release. To
make a hit all five have to be perfect. By September 1959, three of the
five elements were in place. The first rough edit, however, posed a real
problem – it was forty-five minutes too long.

'My film was more that 2 hours 15 minutes long. We took each shot
and we systematically cut what could be cut while keeping the rhythm of
the scene. For example there was a sequence of Belmondo and Seberg in

the car and it was one shot on him then one shot on her in a question and response sequence. There, rather than shorten a little each shot, we played double or quits by entirely cutting one or the other.'[37]

Breathless was notorious for its 'faux raccords' (false matching shots) before it had even played in the cinema. Classic Hollywood film constantly works by effacing all signs of its activity either before the camera, where the actors must preserve an identity of appearance from one take to the next, or by a style of cutting, in which each cut is 'motivated' either by an actor's look or a narrative development. Above all, the camera must obey a set of rules which renders the text seamless (the camera's angle of vision must never approach an actor's eyeline by less than 30 degrees lest the audience becomes aware of the camera, and no two shots cut in sequence must be more than 180 degrees from each other). Godard broke all the rules.

If there is a representative of the rules on the set it is the continuity girl (la scripte) – it is she who reminds the director and the actors that they have changed their appearance, it is she who provides the notes from which a production coordinator or manager writes up their reports. Not surprisingly Godard disliked the function intensely – it is 'un métier de con' ('a job for a complete nerd') he told Isabelle Pons when she asked his advice about work in 1966, and on the set of *Breathless* he sought to exclude la scripte, Suzanne Faye, from the hotel room in which the central scene was shot. The result was inevitable: in the middle of the bedroom scene where Patricia goes into the bathroom she is shown wearing a short-sleeved striped top which bears no correspondence to the long-sleeved sailor top that she wears both before and after.

But much more radical were the jump cuts, where Godard simply advanced the action without any regard to narrative logic or to a motivated look. These innovations showed that Godard had learnt his lessons at the Cinémathèque well – if audiences had once enjoyed the jump cuts of Méliès and Eisenstein, why could they not do so again? His use of editing was, as is often said, as revolutionary as Welles's use of deep focus in *Citizen Kane*, and in fact its developments were longer lasting. In England a group of young commercial advertising directors, of whom the only really abiding name is Ridley Scott, used Godard's aesthetic to create a real transformation in the language of cinema, a transformation which went hand in glove with the increasingly rapid development of consumer capitalism in the West. It should be noted, however, that Godard's experiments took place in the context of a film which is largely edited according to the most classic of codes. Michel Marie's brilliant and painstaking shot-by-shot analyses prove this beyond the shadow of a doubt.[38]

The editing also provided the music. For the first and last time to date, Godard used jazz, a genre then not yet eclipsed by pop music as the hip sound of Paris. And it wasn't just any jazz but that of Martial Solal which riffed on the soundtrack, providing in its repetitions and emphases a sure thread through the narrative for any spectator alarmed at being invited to see anew.

The film edited, there remained the film to be released. Never can a film that cost so little have had such a huge launch.[39] The distribution company that had financed it gave it the classic opening for 'big films' in four of the best cinemas in Paris. There were three posters, a novelisation, a soundtrack record. But Godard, using his training at Fox, had also ensured that the shoot had been covered extensively both for still photographs and for on-set reports. It is also possible that the debate convulsing the world of French film in the weeks before it opened on 16 March 1960, which can be summarised as either 'It's a mess done by a critic who doesn't know how to edit' or 'It's another Orson Welles – the revolution has arrived', was in fact spun by Godard himself and the brilliant press attaché Richard Balducci employed by Beauregard, whose bankruptcy had been averted by the cheque he received on the last day of shooting.[40]

The great French film historian Jean-Pierre Jeancolas has well said that, with Godard more than any other film-maker, the commentary can never be a substitute for the film.[41] In addition, the commentary on any Godard film is a more complex matter than that of any other film-maker of whom I am aware. The young Peter Sellars, who was to play William Shakespeare the Fifth in Godard's *King Lear*, remembers taking Alfred Guzzetti's Godard class in his freshman year at Harvard. For fourteen weeks they analysed *Vivre sa vie* frame by frame and Sellars located forty-five different literary references in this one film. Michel Marie has compiled eighteen different sequences, from Ray and Fuller to Rouch and Godard's own shorts, on which sequences in *Breathless* play complicated riffs. Jean-Pierre Gorin summarises Godard's entire career as 'an assault on the notion of intellectual property'. That assault includes both music[42] and painting as well as literature and cinema.

At the same time Godard's work is also of an extreme simplicity. Raoul Coutard emphasises, 'There are only two subjects in Jean-Luc's films: death and the impossibility of love.' The four pages that Truffaut dashed off for his friend stressed the perfidy of women – Godard added death. The conclusion of Truffaut's treatment focused on the media fame that descended on Michel Portail/Poiccard in his final days. Godard's fifteen-page development emphasised the physical reality of Poiccard's death and led to the only creative disagreement between the two: 'He had chosen a violent end because he was sadder than me. He was really without hope when he made that film. He needed to film death. He needed the end he had chosen. All I asked him was to cut one terrible sentence. At the end when the police shoot, one of them says "Quick in the spinal column!" I told him "You can't put that in." I was very insistent. He took the line out. I like the end as it is.'[43]

The only other creative disagreement came with Jean Seberg. She wasn't overjoyed that she was going to turn her lover in to the police, and when she learnt that she was also meant to steal money from him, she drew the line.[44]

Anna's Story

It is a truth universally acknowledged that the history of the cinema is the history of a plot by shy unprepossessing and sex-obsessed men to surround themselves with heartrendingly beautiful women. From this point of view *Breathless* had been an astounding failure. The relationship between directors and actors takes us deep into the realm of what Lacan, in his re-reading of Freud, calls the imaginary, the complicated process by which each human interaction models itself on and possibly transforms the picture that we have of ourselves. That picture has its lines drawn by the most fundamental relationship: that to the parents who take us from dependent to independent being. The fundamental infantile question for Freud is that of origins: Where do I come from, why do my parents love me, why did their love create me?[45] Freud's great discovery was that the psychoanalyst/analysand relationship was one which allowed the analysand to work out and work through their fundamental self-image. The name he gave this process was transference. Psychoanalyst and analysand are not the only couple who form a transferential relationship. Where there is a clear asymmetry of power and authority, there is transference: doctor/patient, teacher/pupil are the most obvious. The relationship between director and actor is perhaps as powerful an example of a transferential relationship as we have in our Western culture. It should also be noted that in these transferential relationships, the opposite of love is not hate but contempt.

For the avid film historians of *Cahiers*, one deeply learned history lesson was the love that could blossom between a director and his actress. From Griffith and Lillian Gish to Orson Welles and Rita Hayworth to Roberto Rossellini and Ingrid Bergman, the young Turks dreamed not of a harem but of their star – the woman who would come alive before their camera and fall in love not with money or worldly power, but with the genius of their art. One only has to look at the covers of *Cahiers* or read the lascivious descriptions of favourite actresses to realise how deep this went.[46] Much of this was adolescent fantasy of the most banal kind, the belief that the cinema would provide the beautiful girls so sadly lacking in life, but it also responded to one of the deepest levels of cinema. In the year before his death, Bazin's acuity of vision and thought burned ever brighter in a series of astonishing articles. One directly addresses the question of eroticism in the cinema in a review of Lo Duca's *L'Erotisme au cinéma*.[47] Using his usual comparatist methods, Bazin argues that while the theatre is without erotic charge and erotic literature is a particular genre within a wider medium, cinema is fundamentally an erotic medium because of its relationship to dreaming.

Godard's dream appeared on the screen in the summer of 1959. He was in the middle of casting *Breathless* when he saw a couple of soap ads for Palmolive and Monsavon which featured an extraordinarily beautiful young girl in a bath, up to her neck in soapsuds. He asked Pierre Rissient to track her down. The ad agencies provided the girl's address and Godard sent her a telegram: 'Would you please come to Georges de Beauregard's office for a small role – Jean-Luc Godard'. When the girl appeared at Beauregard's offices on the Champs Élysées, she found the director in dark glasses who immediately informed her that she had the small role he'd advertised.[48] 'Mind you', he said 'you'll have to take your clothes off.' The girl took immediate offence: 'I don't take my clothes off.' Godard replied 'But I saw you in the soap ads.' At this point the girl lost her temper. 'Are you mad? I was fully clothed in those ads – the soapsuds went up to my neck. It was in your mind I was undressed.' And with that she left, slamming the door.

The girl was Anna Karina, or to give her the name she had been given at birth, Hanne Karin Bayer. She was Danish, eighteen, and had arrived in Paris the year before. She had spent a miserable childhood with a mother with whom she not felt the slightest understanding and who, as far as Anna can remember, never cooked a meal for her.[49] She had never seen her father. He was a ship's captain who had left her mother before Anna was a year old and she was to meet him only twice in her life. As an infant, Anna was sent to her maternal grandparents where she stayed until the age of four, when her grandmother died. For four years she was in and out of foster homes before her mother married a man called Benny Blarke. No sooner had Anna established a good relationship with him than her mother took up with his best friend, Holger, who detested the little girl. Forbidden from seeing Benny and miserable at home, Anna became a serial runaway, trying to find boats to take her to America, Sweden, anywhere far away from Copenhagen. She felt herself unloved and, in her own words, 'terribly wanting love'.

Her one dream was to become an actress, but drama school in Denmark started at twenty-one – an eternity away. Anna was rarely at school, and when she did turn up to take her certificate exams, the school refused to believe that she could have achieved such good marks without cheating. This final injustice was too much for her, and at fourteen she left. Her first job as a lift operator in a department store lasted about three days. Bored by the monotony and outraged by the number of customers who groped her, she ceased to turn up. When her mother found out three weeks later, this earned her a clip round the ear and a catastrophic exit interview with the manager of the store. She then found a job working with an illustrator, Bent Nordberg, and he suggested to her that she could find work as an extra.

Anna had in fact already appeared in a short film. The director Ib Schedes had approached her in the street and cast her as the lead in his forty-minute film *The Girl with Shoes*. For a couple of years she got work as an extra but the situation at home did not improve. One evening, in the course of a huge row during which Holger had beaten her badly, she told her mother that she was going. 'You haven't the right to go,' her mother crowed. 'You haven't the right to live with this bloke,' replied Anna, daring to remind her mother that she was still married to Benny. 'Either he goes or I do.' She set out with about £10 in her pocket, a parting gift from her grandfather, and headed this time for Paris, where some of the actors and film people she had met as an extra now were.

When Anna got to Paris in the summer of 1958, mainly by hitchhiking, she found her way to the Maison Danoise on the Champs Élysées where a young priest found her a tiny room on the rue Pavée, just behind the Bastille. For weeks she eked out an existence from what she could literally pick up from the streets. She was practically starving and could speak no French; English had been her foreign language at school. One day she went into the elegant Café de la Paix by the Opéra and scrutinised the menu to see if there was anything she could afford. She was pleased to see that a 'couvert' cost only twenty centîmes, which was within her very limited means, and she ordered one. A kindly waiter explained that a 'couvert' was a cover charge.

She had better luck on a sunny August day when her wanderings around Paris took her for the first time to the Left Bank and Saint-Germain des Prés. At that time Saint-Germain was still mainly bookstores and students rather than boutiques and tourists, and Anna sat for a moment at Les Deux Magots, the café that Sartre had made famous. A woman called Catherine Harlé approached her and asked her whether she would be willing to do some photos. Anna was suspicious of any such request and asked how many people would be involved. When Harlé said ten, her caution disappeared. Two would have sounded dangerous, ten sounded safe. She did the shoot for *Jours de France* at the end of which Catherine Harlé, who worked for the ad agency Publicis, told her that she wasn't very talented but nevertheless gave her some other addresses.

She was an instant hit, overwhelmed with advertising offers. One of them was from *Elle*, and on that shoot she noticed an extraordinary looking woman with her hair cut in the severest of bobs. It was the legendary Coco Chanel. Chanel approached her and asked her what she wanted to do. When Anna explained that she wanted to be an actress, Coco asked her name. 'Hanne Karin Bayer,' she replied. 'You can't possibly become an actress with a name like that.' By the time she left the shoot they had agreed that she would be credited as Anna Karina, although that issue of *Elle* featured a certain Anna Carina, much to Anna's chagrin. But Anna Karina she was from then on.

Karina's minority status (this was still a time where parents effectively controlled children's lives until they were twenty-one) was a constant problem – she couldn't even have her own cheque book even though she was now earning considerable sums of money and was able to move into a small apartment just off the Champs Élysées on the rue de Bassano, where Marlon Brando was a neighbour. Her dream was still that of her childhood: to earn enough money to go to drama school. Now, however, she wished to add French lessons to her future education. In the meantime she learned French by sitting all day in the cinema, watching films again and again until the dialogue made sense.

It was at the end of the summer of 1959, a year after she had arrived in Paris, that she received a second telegram: 'Mademoiselle, this time it's for the principal role, J-L Godard'. Godard had no sooner finished shooting *Breathless* than he agreed to make a second film with Beauregard. He was sure that if they went to Geneva, where he was really on home turf, then they could bring in a film for under $30,000. And this time they would not waste a quarter of the budget on an already established star whose husband was on the set from morning to night. He would make a star. Karina had only a vague memory of their first encounter (the one thing she remembered about the director was his rather odd dark glasses), but both her boyfriend, the photographer Ghislain Dussart, with whom she was living, and Claude Brasseur, who had become a friend, told her that Godard was the hot name in town. The private screenings of *Breathless* were a knockout, and although the film hadn't yet been released, when it was everybody would know the name Godard. With some hesitation, Karina presented herself again to the director. He looked her up and down. 'You're right for the part. We'll sign the contract tomorrow.' Anna was so shocked that she could only stammer out a question asking him what the project was.

'A political film,' he replied.

'But I don't know anything about politics,' she said.

'All you need to do is what I tell you.'

'But will I have to undress?'

'Not at all.'

At this point Anna remembered that as a minor she could not sign a contract, her constant problem.

'Well then, your mother can sign.'

'But she's angry with me and in Copenhagen.'

'Get her on a plane.'

Godard handed her the phone. Anna spoke to her mother for the first time in over a year. 'I've got the lead role in a political film – will you come and sign the contract?' Her mother put the phone down. But another phone call persuaded her, and the next day she arrived by plane in Paris to sign.

But there was another hiccup before Karina took the part. *France Soir*, the most popular broadsheet of the time – the newspaper Michel Poiccard buys throughout *Breathless* – published a piece of gossip which said that Jean-Luc Godard had found his 'amie' for his next film. Anna read this as a clear indication that she was the director's girlfriend and telephoned the production's press officer, Richard Balducci, in a fury. Through tears she said, 'I'm not going to do this film. I'm not a whore.' Within hours there was a knock on the door, and there stood Godard

with fifty red roses and a telegram. The telegram explained
that he and Truffaut had come
up with the idea of advertising for
the part in the trade paper, *La
Cinématographie Française*. The
ad, in Godard's beautiful handwriting, read 'Jean-Luc Godard
who has just finished "Breathless" and who is in pre-production of "Le Petit Soldat" is
looking for a young woman between 18 and 27 who will be
both his actress [interprète] and
his friend [amie]'[50]

Whatever the telegram said,
Anna's boyfriend determined that
he would join the shoot as the unit
photographer, and at the beginning of 1960 they set out for

Godard's advertisement for the lead actress
in *Le Petit soldat* in *La Cinématographie
Française, no.1847, 19 December 1959.*

Geneva and a small studio flat while the rest of the crew stayed in a hotel.
Tolmatchoff worked as Godard's assistant. Tolmatchoff knew everybody
in Geneva and could help to make the small budget go a very long way.

In Anna's memory, the shoot was much slower and much more drawn
out than those of subsequent films on which she was to work with
Godard. Tolmatchoff confirmed that day after day he would be rung by
Godard at 6 o'clock in the morning to be told that he had no ideas and
the crew should be stood down.[51] The cry 'I have no ideas' is perhaps
Godard's most constant catch phrase, but it is a phrase which needs
much interpretation. Usually it seems to function as a way of increasing
the pressure on the creative moment until something live appears. On
this occasion, however, Godard's focus seems to have been off-camera,
and Karina certainly felt he was taking his time so that he could spend
longer with her. Coutard: 'Jean-Luc dragging out the shoot of *Le Petit
soldat* so that he could court Anna? Possible.'

Anna Karina in *Le Petit soldat*, 1960.

Karina remembers a great deal of eye contact on the shoot but nothing more. Tolmatchoff remembers Godard taking Anna to the cinema and later showing him the cinema tickets on the back of which he had written 'Anna I love you'. But the message seems never to have been delivered. In the middle of the shoot, Tolmatchoff invited the whole crew to dinner in Lausanne. Anna's boyfriend was at the head of the table with Godard on his left and Anna on his right, facing each other. Halfway through dinner and with a great deal of eye contact, Anna felt a hand grasp hers under the table and put something in it. With her boyfriend beside her, she could not look at what it was, and before long Godard stood up and said he was leaving. No sooner had Godard gone than Anna rushed into the next room, desperate to see what he had given her. The piece of paper said, 'I love you. Rendez-vous at the Café de la Paix at midnight.' But her boyfriend had rushed after her and grabbed the paper out of her hand:

'You're not going.'
'Yes I am.'
'You don't know the guy.'
'But I love him.'

They returned to the studio together, and Anna packed all her belongings into the little cardboard suitcase that had accompanied her from Copenhagen. The boyfriend, in tears, continued to try to dissuade her, but Anna was more than smitten. At the café, Godard was reading the paper, Anna sat down in front of him and waited an eternity for the paper to lower.

'So here you are.' A beat. 'Let's go.'

As they walked to the hotel Godard discussed Mozart.

In the morning Anna awoke to find herself alone, but Jean-Luc soon returned with roses and the white dress that she was to wear in the film. As Karina says: 'Roses and a white dress – it was a bit like a wedding.'

They were inseparable for the rest of the shoot. When it finished, Godard drove her, Laszlo Szabo and Michel Subor back to Paris. They were all wearing dark glasses and were stopped at the border. As they reached Paris, Godard said: 'Where should I leave you?' Anna replied, 'You can't leave me. I've only got you in the world.'

Of the woe that is in marriage it is impossible to speak truly. All sexual relationships are ultimately private affairs, and any public representation is both inaccurate and impolite. For Godard, the story is of crippling jealousy; for Karina, of desperate solitude. Karina, as beautiful as the dawn and 'desperately seeking love', would smile at everybody. Godard, obsessed with cinema, would spend his time at *Cahiers* or say he was going out for some cigarettes and return three weeks later. For Anna, the image is of waiting alone in an apartment by a telephone in a time before answering machines soothed the anxiety of missing the crucial call. The only way she knew where he was – New York: 'I went to see Faulkner', Rome: 'I went to see Rossellini' – was by the wrapping on the presents that he brought back for her. For Jean-Luc, the image is probably *Contempt* – a beautiful woman falls out of love with a man who sacrifices her to his work. Coutard is rumoured to have described the film as the most expensive postcard a man has ever sent to his wife.

After they returned to Paris, they spent their first weeks together in his hotel, the Alesia, on the rue Chateaubriand, before Godard asked her to find them an apartment, and she rented one in rue Pasquier behind the Madeleine. There were great pleasures: driving around Paris the night

one of their films opened watching the queues form; running from
cinema to cinema to catch fifteen minutes of this and half an hour of
that; Godard in a restaurant overhearing a man denouncing *Vivre sa vie*
and going up to offer him the price of a cinema ticket 'so you can go and
see an Autant-Lara' (Truffaut's *bête noire*). They bought a couple of
dogs. Godard wanted to name them 'Viens ici' ('Come here') to save
time calling them, but Anna prevailed and they were called Pousse
Pousse Blanc and Pousse Pousse Noir. It was with Pousse Pousse Blanc
that she fled to the Bois de Boulogne for the night when they had their
first row.

The film they had made together, *Le Petit soldat*, must certainly be
ranked with the 'cursed films' so beloved of *Cahiers*. It is one of the
extraordinary features of the history of the magazine that throughout
the fifties there is not a single reference to Algeria, and yet it was Algeria
which completely and totally dominated French life in the late fifties.
Every young man faced three years of military service which brought not
only the danger of death, but also the horror of torture. It was in Algeria
that modern torture was perfected by the French army and modern
terrorism by the Front de Libération Nationale. The prospect of a third
defeat, and this time on soil which was genuinely believed by many to be
French, led the army ever closer to mutiny. De Gaulle's return to power
in May 1958 had many of the characteristics of an army coup, but the
'man of 18 June 1940' was no military dictator. The army was faced
down and in March 1962 Algeria gained independence. For the first
time since 1939, France was genuinely at peace, but the quasi civil war
which had opposed the supporters of the FLN and the OAS had
produced levels of violence and bitterness which had no parallel in
Europe at that time.

Le Petit soldat was shot in the spring of 1960, when it was not yet
clear which way the General or the army would jump, and violence in
France was at a dangerous level. It tells the story of Bruno Forestier, an
OAS supporter on the run from France and engaged in a surrogate war
in and around Geneva. But it is a war in which he has no real belief. The
image of political engagement comes from the left and Malraux's
engagement in Spain. As with *Breathless*, the armature of the story,

a relatively well worked out spy movie of deception and betrayal, is of little concern. The subject is death (this time dealt out by assassination) and torture (planned and executed by men living in apartments of stunning ordinariness), and, yet again, the impossibility of love (Karina, in all the wonder of her young beauty, caught up in the sordid duplicities of politics). In its focus on torture and terrorism, *Le Petit soldat* is an astonishingly prescient work; Claude Godard believes that it is still the most current of his brother's films. But no one except the censor was to see it for three years. Any film about France's quasi civil war, whatever the opacity of its politics, or perhaps particularly because of the opacity of its politics, was potential dynamite. The film rested in its cans until 1963. This was a disaster for Beauregard; once again the ogre of the bank was at the door. But it was also a tragedy for Karina – she was the star of a film which didn't exist.

According to Karina, Godard wanted her to give up acting completely, and when she was cast in Michel Deville's *Ce Soir ou jamais*, Godard, already prey to the jealousy that was to be a constant factor of their relationship, insisted on accompanying her to the set each day. He was already casting for his next film, *Une Femme est une femme*, and was thinking about 'every actress in Paris', but when he saw Deville's film he immediately decided that Karina was going to be his heroine once again.

After a thriller and a spy film, Godard's project this time was in a completely different genre: musical comedy. But it was musical comedy à la Rouch and Bazin – the most unrealistic of genres was to be shot in the most realistic of settings. Godard had his heart set on the apartment of an old couple in Strasbourg Saint Denis, one of the less fashionable quarters of Paris. It was in this unlikely environment that he would play out the story of Angela, the stripper with a heart of gold and a determination to have a baby. The old couple were to be lodged in a luxury hotel during the shoot, but at the last moment they took fright at all these unlikely people from the crazy world of cinema – Beauregard and Godard must have made a truly striking combination – and said they wouldn't move. When the film was already in pre-production Godard and Beauregard decided to shoot in a studio.

By and large crews prefer working in a studio rather than on location. Sets are constructed so that walls and ceiling can be moved to accommodate the camera, and ambient sound can be completely controlled. Nothing could be further from a Bazinian aesthetic, and Godard set to work to reproduce the conditions of location shooting in a studio. He had the apartment he had wished to film meticulously reconstructed with immovable walls and ceiling, and with a real front door which he locked every night at the end of the shoot. As there was no other sound but the sound of the crew working, Godard recorded them and put that distracting noise on the soundtrack. There could be no clearer lesson of Godard's determination to capture the real on the run, in which camera and object are caught in a mutually illuminating relationship, rather than to shoot a fabricated reality, in which the camera can record only lies.

Une Femme est une femme is the most joyful of Godard's films, indeed perhaps his only joyful film. Karina – starring this time with Brialy and Belmondo, the two male stars of the Nouvelle Vague – produces a performance of guileful innocence as she blackmails Brialy into agreeing to a child by cultivating Belmondo's interest in her. Karina's memories of the shoot are happy ones; she now felt accepted by the crew, and particularly by Coutard. Coutard's own memories are not as rosy as one might wish. Belmondo, now the star of French cinema, was not overjoyed to be playing what was in effect a supporting role, but his original contract with Beauregard left him no choice. And while Godard and Karina were obviously madly in

Anna Karina and Jean-Paul Belmondo in
Une Femme est une femme, 1961.

Godard and Raoul Coutard during the filming of *Une Femme est une femme*, 1960-61.

love, it was a love which was always, according to Karina, tempestuous – 'on the moon or in hell'. The astonishing loyalty and dedication that Godard could inspire in his crews, and his disregard for the standardised working practices that had dominated French cinema, was evident when, on Christmas Eve 1960, he asked the crew to work on Christmas Day.

By now Godard and Karina had moved to 13, rue Nicolo in the smart 16th arrondissement, just around the corner from Brigitte Bardot. For Godard, more than for any other figure in the cinema, film and reality are one and the same thing. So it was hardly surprising that when shooting a film about a woman desperate to have a child, Karina became pregnant. Godard immediately decided that they would marry both in the French church and the Swiss state. Karina says she was unhappy about marrying in a church when pregnant but that Godard insisted 'Tu te maries avec moi devant Dieu' ('You will marry me in the sight of God'). The wedding in Paris in March 1961 was captured in magnificent

Godard and Anna Karina during the filming of *Une Femme est une femme*, 1960–61.

photos taken by Agnès Varda, who was to cast the couple in the silent movie extract in her film *Cléo de 5 à 7* that summer. But Godard also insisted on a Swiss wedding in Begnins with Tolmatchoff as witness which, amongst other things, meant Karina could get Swiss citizenship. Karina remembers meeting Godard's father at the wedding, and being put off by the fact that he only shook her hand and did not meet her eye.

Varda's key presence at the Paris wedding is an indication both of how Godard's social

Anna Karina and Godard's wedding on the cover of *Paris Match*, 25 March 1961.

world had widened beyond *Cahiers*, but also of how the New Wave was a phenomenon which reached far beyond the *Cahiers*'s directors. There was a group of film-makers, including Alain Resnais, Chris Marker, Jacques Demy and Agnès Varda, who inhabited a wider artistic world in which cinema was less of an all-consuming obsession and rather just one of a variety of modes of expression. Resnais and Marker were older and they had experienced the war and liberation as adults – Marker had worked at Travail et Culture with Bazin, and Resnais had been crucial to Bazin's film education during the war. Like Bazin, they were all men and women of the left. Although they had been making films throughout the fifties – Michel Marie chooses Varda's 1954 film *La pointe courte* as an example of the new kind of production that came with the Nouvelle Vague[52] – it was Alain Resnais's *Hiroshima mon amour* in 1959 that showed the Nouvelle Vague had a historical significance and an aesthetic range that made *Breathless* look like a teen-flick. Godard witnessed the shock felt by the gang at the realisation that there was more to the world of French cinema than the 'cinéma de qualité' and the Hitchcocko-Hawksiens.[53]

Anna Karina in *Marie-Claire*, no.97, November 1962.

Quand la nouvelle vague se parodie

Derrière un visage d'ange un peu sophistiqué qu'elle est en train de rendre célèbre (elle vient de tourner « Schéhérazade »), Anna Karina cache une malice d'écolière. A ses moments perdus, elle s'amuse à imiter ses non moins illustres partenaires de la nouvelle vague. Les reconnaissez-vous?

Alain Delon.

Jean-Paul Belmondo.

Jean-Luc Godard.

Jean-Pierre Cassel.

Anna Karina parodies her peers in *Marie-Claire*, no.97, November 1962.

Godard and Anna Karina in *Cléo de 5 à 7*, 1961.

Throughout his most productive period between 1960 and 1966 (when he makes an average of two films and a short per year), Godard is not much influenced by the *Cahiers* gang's films. Both Truffaut and Chabrol took routes through the cinema which took them far from Godard's rigorous application of a Bazinian aesthetic. If Rivette's and Rohmer's films remain points of comparison, those films belong to the late sixties. Rivette took over the editorship of *Cahiers* at the beginning of the sixties, and Rohmer took a long time to recover from the failure of *Le Signe du lion*; it wasn't until 1969 and the international hit of *Ma nuit chez Maud* that Rohmer began to shoot films regularly. But Resnais's *Last Year at Marienbad* (1961), Varda's *Cléo de 5 à 7* (1962), Demy's *Lola* (1960) and Chris Marker's magnificent *La Jetée* (1962) all in their different ways opened up new vistas for the cinema and for Godard.[54]

But first of all there was failure. At the same time as Godard was becoming a worldwide name in cinema, his films were failing in France.

After the censor's ban on *Le Petit soldat* came the commercial failure of *Une Femme est une femme*.[55] For his next film, *Vivre sa vie*, Godard switched producers to work with Pierre Braunberger, one of the doyens of French cinema and the man who had produced Godard's three Parisian shorts. The genre this time was tragedy, the remorseless tale of the prostitute Nana's death and destruction. Karina's performance, already more than impressive in *Le Petit soldat* and *Une Femme est une femme*, is both stunning and moving. If the sign of *Une Femme est une femme* is joy and birth, that of *Vivre sa vie* is sorrow and death. And death there had been. Karina's

Anna Karina as Nana in *Vivre sa vie*, 1962.

Frame still of Anna Karina as Nana, watching Carl Dreyer's *La Passion de Jeanne d'Arc* in *Vivre sa vie*, 1962.

pregnancy had ended with a very late miscarriage which not only delivered a stillborn child but also left her infertile.

Karina has the memory of a nightmare trip after the miscarriage, when Godard suggested a holiday on the Côte d'Azur. A hundred kilometres outside Paris he said, 'I don't have the time for this. There's work to do with François, with *Cahiers*,' and he turned the car around. Twenty-five kilometres outside Paris he changed his mind and set out again for the South. Halfway there, he exploded, 'It's incredible that you won't let me work.' 'It was your idea,' Karina shot back, and they turned again for Paris. As they approached the capital he said, 'Are you sure you don't want to go?' At this point Karina flew into a rage, hitting and kicking the car. In the same year Godard sent an undated postcard to Truffaut:

> We never see each other any more, it's completely stupid. Yesterday I went to
> see Claude [Chabrol] shoot, it was terrible we had nothing to say to each
> other. Like in the song: in the pale light of dawn there isn't even any friendship.
> We've each taken off for our own planet and we no longer see each other in
> close up but only in long shot. The girls that we sleep with separate us more
> each day instead of bringing us together. It's not normal. (T:371)

Whatever problems the couple had faced before, they now became
worse, at least for Karina. There were suicide attempts and a constant
strain of horrific sorrow.

At the same time Godard encouraged Karina to realise her ambition of
acting in the theatre. The first step was taken with Jacques Rivette. Rivette,
the son of a chemist from Rouen, was in many ways the spiritual leader of
the *Cahiers* gang. If Big Momo was the godfather and Truffaut the general
who led the journalistic battles, it was Rivette who defined an idea of
cinema so pure that it compelled belief. Godard acknowledges his extraordinary influence: 'I might like a film very much but if Rivette said "It's no
good" then I would agree with him. There was something Stalinist in these
relationships. With Rivette, it was as though he had a privileged access to
cinematographic truth and for a time I accepted that' (G:10).

Rivette was also perhaps the most determined to make films without
any money at all. Even before he arrived in Paris in late 1949, he had
shot a short in his home town of Rouen and for many his 1956 short *Le
Coup du berger* is really the first film of the gang. Rivette's early work
might also be considered the most collaborative of this era. The script
for *Le Coup du berger* is credited to Bitsch, Truffaut, Chabrol and
Rivette and *Paris nous appartient*, which took three years to make,
contains the familiar names on the credits: Bitsch, Schiffman, Truffaut,
Chabrol. When the editing of *Paris nous appartient* was finally finished,
Rivette began to explore the possibilities for his next film with Georges
de Beauregard. They soon settled on the idea of Diderot's eighteenth-
century satire *La Religieuse* and discussed the idea of putting it on first
as a play, to avoid problems of censorship.

Rivette started writing the adaptation in the spring of 1961 with Jean
Gruault. He had not yet fixed upon a particular actress, but a dinner

with Anna and Jean-Luc helped him to reach a decision. He saw in Karina someone who could bring the grace of Griffith's heroines to the role.[56] Beauregard wasn't convinced, mainly because of the problems of Anna's Danish accent. But Anna persevered, taking lessons to improve her pronunciation, and by the end of 1962, with Georges de Beauregard in tow, Godard sought out Antoine Bourseiller, who was then running the Studio des Champs Élysées, to see if he would put on the production which Godard would underwrite himself. The meeting was to lead to a long and close friendship: Bourseiller's children were to act in Godard's films, Godard was to shoot *La Chinoise* in Bourseiller's flat and Godard was to buy Bourseiller a theatre. In immediate terms, it led to a staging of *La Religieuse* which played from 6 February to 5 March 1963. Anna's performance was a triumph, winning prizes and the greatest compliment of all from Lotte Eisner: 'It is the most beautiful theatre that I have seen since Bertolt Brecht.'[57]

By the time Anna was performing in *La Religieuse*, Godard had already shot another film, *Les Carabiniers*. This film, which was of course his father's favourite, was about the horror and pointlessness of war. Rossellini had drawn Godard's attention to a play by Joppolo, and Godard made of it a dull and grey picture of all wars. The story of two peasants, Michel-Ange and Ulysse, who enlist in the army of the king to pillage the world, *Les Carabiniers* ignores the ideological justifications of different wars in order to emphasise the similarity of the use of violence. The postcards the soldiers send home, which

Godard and Geneviève Galéa, with Charles Bitsch and Catherine Ribiero (behind), looking for costumes for *Les Carabiniers*, 1962.

What do soldiers do before battle?

Before battle soldiers are frightened.

Sequence of images and writing from *Les Carabiniers*, 1963.

On a débarqué en Italie et jalonné notre passage de mille cadavres.

We landed in Italy and littered our route with a thousand corpses.

On voyait mourir sans un cri des grenadiers, des généraux, le ventre ouvert, les uniformes sanglants, les yeux troués.

We saw die without a cry soldiers and generals, guts open, uniforms covered in blood, holes for eyes.

Un bel été quand même.

A great summer all the same.

punctuate the action as the episodes of Nana's life had punctuated *Vivre sa vie*, are drawn from a variety of sources – German soldiers encircled at Stalingrad, or a cavalry officer in Napoleon's Spanish campaign[58] – but their message is single and univocal: 'We leave behind us blood and dead men, much love'.

Perhaps the single most striking formal feature of Godard's cinema is the use that he makes of writing – unparalleled in the history of the cinema. Christian Metz (perhaps the most important theorist of the cinema since Bazin, and the thinker who tried most rigorously to follow through the thought that cinema was a language) identifies five separate matters of expression – there is the image itself; there are three different forms of sound (dialogue, music and recorded sound); and there is writing. Most film-makers use writing only for credits or for occasional information (e.g. 'Five years later'). For Godard, and this becomes more and more clear from *Vivre sa vie* and *Les Carabiniers*, writing is the privileged element which breaks the classical unity of the cinema – the unity of narrative and vision which defines Hollywood cinema. Writing is used to comment on the action and to distance the viewer from the immediacy of the image. There is a sequence in *Les Carabiniers*, as the soldiers prepare for battle, in which instead of images of the psychological condition of the soldiers, we have generalised written comments about the feelings of soldiers as they prepare for combat. The effect is humorously distancing but also emphasises the theme of the film – all wars are the same: nasty, brutish and long.

Contempt

The *Cahiers* aesthetic had been classicist instead of modernist. Indeed, the great virtue of the cinema was that it rescued the artist from the dead ends of modernism by providing an audience secure in its knowledge of genres and of stars, who allowed the artist to demonstrate his art within a popular and established medium. But this classicist aesthetic was to buckle and break as the New Wave encountered the problem of the audience in its most direct form – failure at the box office – and as

Hollywood, which the gang had idolised, was destroyed before their eyes. The challenge of television and the cumulative effects of the studios' loss of a monopoly in exhibition led to a real collapse in the late fifties, with a slump in the number of films released and an increasingly desperate investment in 'epics' to lure viewers from their televisions. And as Hollywood slumped at home, it sought more and more investment abroad, above all in Europe.

This situation provided both context and text for what is, for many, Godard's greatest film, *LeMépris* (*Contempt*). Godard himself is insistent that *Contempt* was not a big studio film, and that when one took away the actors' fees, in particular Brigitte Bardot's, he had no more than twice his usual tiny budget. But whatever the truth of the figures, this was a film which saw a radical break in production methods, a break which Godard neither enjoyed nor repeated. Godard is explicit in his *Cahiers* interviews of the early sixties that his desire to benefit from the resources of a big production was more than outweighed by his conviction, shared by many of the *Cahiers* directors, that a big budget gave the producer a whip hand over the director, because a big budget always entailed that the producers had final cut. Hehadin fact pulled out of the brothers Hakim's movie, *Eva*, at a late stage for exactly this reason (G: 183/1:224).[59] With *Contempt* Godard changed tack, and amongst other things, found himself for the first and only time in his life with an American producer. The key to the changed production relations was Brigitte Bardot.

Brigitte Bardot was not simply the biggest actress in France, she was the biggest in Europe, quite possibly the biggest star that European cinema has ever known. Her first film made with her husband Roger Vadim, *Et Dieu créa la femme* (1956), is for many the first film of the Nouvelle Vague, not because of any formal originality but because of its presentation of contemporary France, and a contemporary France defined by an acknowledged female sexuality. Bardot embodied this moment and she became, for more than a decade, *the* image of both the film star and the modern woman. For the partisans of the 'cinéma de qualité', Bardot was not an actress, but for *Cahiers* her manner of speaking and acting signalled a truth which escaped the over-sophisticated style of classic French film acting.[60]

Brigitte Bardot on the cover of five issues of *Paris Match*, three issues of *Jours de France* and one issue of *Cine-Révélation*, 1955–64.

Godard had become friendly with her through her boyfriend at the time, Sami Frey; Frey and Bardot lived around the corner from the bungalow at 13, rue Nicolo. Once Bardot had signalled her willingness to work with Godard, the financing became easy. Beauregard had produced both *Une Femme est une femme* and *Les Carabiniers* with the Italian producer Carlo Ponti. Ever since an agreement signed in 1949, Italian-French co-productions had been an important element in the economic ecology of French film-making,[61] and following the two films shot in France, Godard

Brigitte Bardot.

was contracted with Ponti to make a film in Italy.

It had been difficult to agree on the casting until Bardot said that she wanted to make a film with Godard. At that point, Ponti was able to get the backing of an American producer, Joe Levine. But the price of a big budget film was working within the constraints of normal production. There was a script, of which there are four versions, a schedule which demanded a fixed number of minutes shot each day, and an Italian film crew wedded to highly unionised working hours. Coutard remembers Godard, frustrated by a fixed break for the crew, urging them to eat their *panini* faster. But Godard also brought with him what was now becoming his regular team. In addition to Coutard there was Charles Bitsch, who as the assistant director took much of the strain of Godard's relations with cast and crew.

Bitsch was one of the oldest of *Cahiers*'s hands. He had first met Truffaut and Rivette when they shared a dormitory at Biarritz in 1949. Born in Mulhouse in Alsace, Bitsch had moved with his parents to Paris, where they had a café which in the mid-fifties became one of the favourite hang-outs of the young critics. He remembers being very shocked the first time he asked Godard to come and have a meal with his parents, after Rivette warned him that Godard was famous for stealing. He was even more shocked when one day Godard opened his wallet and showed him a razor blade which he kept 'in case he wanted to commit suicide'. He also paints a picture of Godard as a very special member of the gang. If they were all gathered in the *Cahiers* offices, Jean-Luc would sit apart and stay silent for long periods as the others talked. Although they would see him at the Cinémathèque, he did not join them in their daily visits to the cinema, which were orchestrated above all by Truffaut. After Biarritz, Bitsch studied at the film school in the rue de Vaugirard and met up again with Truffaut and Rivette at the famous evenings in the Studio Parnasse, where Rivette always won the quizzes.

In the mid-fifties Bitsch was a major contributor to *Cahiers*, and some of his happiest memories are of visits with Truffaut to see Bazin at Joinville. Because of his technical knowledge, he was much in demand as the young critics began to make their films, and he worked on both *Le Coup du berger* and *Paris nous appartient*. He had been unable to work as assistant on *Breathless* because *Paris nous appartient* was an incredibly prolonged production. He then suffered two years of ill health, but when he recovered he went first to the offices at 146, avenue des Champs Élysées where Godard was crewing up for *Vivre sa vie*. Godard immediately took him on to be camera assistant to Coutard.

When Coutard had to leave for another film with four days of shooting to go, Bitsch really appreciated how challenging it was to be Godard's cameraman. Quite apart from questions of lighting, Godard's desired framing always broke classical norms. On static shots this was a problem that could be dealt with, but it was extremely difficult to hold the framing required when the camera was tracking or panning.

But Bitsch understood early that crisis was Godard's method of invention, that the unforeseen and the accidental were crucial to his aesthetic, and he asked for only a minimal amount of information when he became his assistant director on a regular basis. Like the other members of the crew, he took Godard's genius as a given and did not dispute the principle that 'Jean-Luc makes the rules'. At the same time, he found the position of interface between Godard and his cast and crew – particularly the actresses – difficult, and as Karina's relationship with Godard deteriorated from its early complicity, the atmosphere on set was sometimes 'very sad'.

On *Contempt*, one of Bitsch's major problems was dealing with the arrangements with Bardot. Although it's not entirely true that Bardot invented the modern phenomenon of paparazzi, it is certain that she was the first figure of whom any photograph in any situation was of journalistic value; her image on the cover of a magazine was a guarantee of extra sales, and perhaps only Princess Diana has rivalled her since. A documentary of the shooting of *Contempt* shows how Bardot could not step into the street without cameras flashing, and when the shoot moved to Capri, the Villa Malaparte was under siege from dawn to dusk.[62] Bitsch's first tactic was to take a beautiful villa outside Rome which would offer some protection from the Roman photographers. But as soon as Bardot saw it, she pronounced it absolutely unacceptable – she had to be in the centre of Rome. The villa thus became Bitsch's own quarters during the shoot, and it can also be seen in the film as belonging to the producer Prokosch (Jack Palance).

Bardot meanwhile was installed in an apartment in the middle of Rome and had to be provided with a phalanx of bodyguards so that she could set foot outside the apartment. When the shoot moved to Capri, the situation became even more chaotic – the paparazzi hired boats and scaled mountains for a glimpse of BB (as she was universally known). When Bitsch finally foiled all their attempts by increasing the number of bodyguards, ensuring that the final week of the shoot was free of unwanted intruders, Bardot complained about the unaccustomed peace.

Bardot also brought with her an entourage (make-up artist, hairdresser, confidants) and the demands of a star, which dictated that it was impossible for her to shoot first thing in the morning. Godard praised her professionalism both at the time and in subsequent interviews, but there is no doubt that this 'star behaviour' was difficult for him to tolerate.

Godard demonstrating for Jacques Doniol-Valcroze the handstand he performed
for Brigitte Bardot during the filming of *Contempt*, from Doniol-Valcroze's
documentary on Godard, 1965.

Any problems with Bardot, which Godard used to ameliorate by doing
handstands to amuse her, paled into insignificance beside his problems
with the film's producers, both real and fictional. Palance arrived with
very definite ideas about how he was going to settle scores with various
producers he had encountered in his career, and he took great exception
to Godard's direction. Godard's sets were unusual for their silence; both
Coutard and Bitsch are men who keep their own counsel and both think
that one of the main reasons Godard worked so often with them was that
they did not pester him with questions. Palance, from a particular school
of film-making, demanded that Godard explain every gesture he was
asked to perform. The situation deteriorated so quickly that within a
week Palance would speak to neither Godard nor Bitsch, who were both
fluent in English, but insisted on addressing all his remarks to the Italian
grip, who knew no English at all.

Jack Palance, Brigitte Bardot and Michel Piccoli in *Contempt*, 1963.

The tensions of the story between the American producer Prokosch and the German director Lang, with the French writer Paul Javal (Michel Piccoli) and his wife Camille (Brigitte Bardot) caught in the middle, were reproduced not only on set but also in the relationships between Godard and his producers. Godard says that when he showed the completed film to Ponti before sending it to the Venice Film Festival, Ponti was happy enough, but then Joe Levine saw the Bardot vehicle in which he had invested and discovered to his complete consternation that, despite the fact that this was a film of adultery and sexual betrayal, there was no shot of Bardot nude. But Bardot *was* nudity – that was what Levine had paid for and that was what he was going to get.

The subsequent rows were exceptionally violent and although no guns were brandished, as ill-informed rumour still claims, Gorin says that Godard did hire a squad of ruffians who would surprise Ponti as he went about his daily business and kick him in the shins when he least expected it. Godard at first wanted to take his name off the film, but he finally agreed to shoot three extra scenes, one long opening scene of Bardot nude in bed talking with Piccoli, one of her and Palance getting dressed after making love (which was never used) and a set of inserts of

Five frame stills from *Contempt*, 1963:
Brigitte Bardot; Raoul Coutard; Michel
Piccoli and Fritz Lang; Jack Palance;
Brigitte Bardot, Michel Piccoli and Fritz Lang.

Bardot. Bitsch, who ran the finances of the re-shoot, asked Godard what each crew member should be paid and remembers Godard telling him to pay them all double what they asked: 'If the producers want a supplement then they'll get it.'

The re-shoots demonstrate clearly the difficulty of any aesthetic which would simply oppose creativity and money, for there can be little doubt that *Contempt* would be a much less beautiful and moving film without the long opening scene of Bardot naked on a bed.[63] This highly stylised scene, both in the repetitive naming of the parts of the body and in the use of very strong primary colour filters, delivers neither the pornographic charge nor the psychological explanation which Levine wanted. It does, however, provide perhaps the most beautiful portrait of Europe's most photographed woman and a hint of the married bliss which will turn to catastrophe in the course of the film.

The inserts represent one of the most curious moments in all of Godard's cinema. There are whole chapters of the classic grammar of cinema that Godard never or rarely uses. The most evident of these is the shot/countershot, the standard way of shooting a conversation so the spectator grasps the space from both sides, and in the same moment understands the subjectivities which occupy that space. Godard's films can all perhaps be analysed as a refusal of that 'mastered space', whether that mastery is understood visually or psychologically. It is the ability of the camera to explore fully the visual space of a conversation that convinces the spectator that they have also understood the psychology of the characters. The spectator of a Godard film, on the other hand, is always aware of a shot as a shot, as a particular angle on reality, and of the characters as characters, that is to say as patterns of behaviour which cannot be unified under some notion of a subjective psychology.

Levine's rage at Godard's first cut was partly due to the absence of Bardot's naked body for which he had paid so much. But it was also caused by his confusion over the fact that Bardot's contempt for her husband, the very title of the film, is never explicitly explained or understood. Godard shot a set of inserts which represented the earlier stages of the marriage. Although technically they work as 'flashbacks' in a long scene in which Godard provides an anatomy of the marriage, they do not function in the explanatory fashion of the classical grammar of cinema. In fact, Godard had already used flashback in the scene at the producer's villa, where Camille has been sent ahead by her husband against her will. For the only time in his career, Godard adopts a classic subjective sequence in which we 'enter' into a character's imagination to find out what they are thinking. Without parallel in all of Godard's movies, this sequence frustrates more than it illuminates, for the subjective shots which 'give' us Camille's thoughts are in fact nothing other than a further series of shots of Camille. They no more explain her contempt for her husband, nor her decision to have an affair with Prokosch, than anything else in the film.

Contempt is unusual amongst Godard's films not only in its conventional production relations and its full script, but also in the fact that the script is a genuine adaptation of a novel. There are other films, for example both *Bande à part* and *Pierrot le fou*, where the film acknowledges its inspiration in a novel, but the novels are pulp fiction and the links between them and the final film are certainly not obvious. With

Contempt, on the other hand, the novel chosen, *Il disprezzo*, is by one of the most famous Italian novelists of the twentieth century, Alberto Moravia, and Godard's adaptation, while never 'faithful' in the tradition of the much loathed 'cinéma de qualité', is a genuine reworking of Moravia's fiction.

The story is a story of the cinema, of the battle between a producer who represents the claims of commerce and a director who is struggling for his art. The battle is over the interpretation of the *Odyssey*, and the reference is to the 'sword and sandals' epics which were a favourite of Italian cinema in the fifties. Apart from elegantly compressing a novel which covers more than a year of a production into a day at Cinecittà and a day on the island of Capri, together with the extraordinarily long scene in which Piccoli and Bardot dramatise the state of their marriage, Godard's major change is to alter the aesthetic stakes in the battle between producer and director. In the novel, it is the director who wishes to follow his artistic intuition in a 'modern' adaptation of the Odyssey and the commercial producer who is wedded to the classical version.

Brigitte Bardot and Michel Piccoli in *Contempt*, 1963.

But Godard does not merely invert the original terms of the novel. It would be a mistake to imagine, as almost all commentators do, that the film is simply a defence of classicism. It is true that this position is maintained by the tragic and heroic figure of Fritz Lang, one of the great directors of the silent era in Germany and the man who, when the newly installed Goebbels offered him control of the German film industry, immediately fled the country.[64] But one of the central planks of *Cahiers*'s position of the fifties was that Lang's Hollywood films (*The Big Heat*, *Rancho Notorious*) were every bit as much great art as the acknowledged classics (*Metropolis* and *M*).

The Lang of the film dismisses his own American movies in favour of a rigorous classicism, but the film undercuts this by emphasising that in returning to Greece one must pass by way of Rome. The film talks not of Odysseus, Athena and Poseidon but of their Latinised equivalents: Ulysses, Minerva and Neptune. The very transmission of culture ensures that there is no simple origin, no homeland to which we can return – the final shot of the film shows Ulysses gazing on an Ithaca which is off-camera. If the cinema had seemed to promise 'a world which accords with our desires' (as Bazin's epigraph to the film states) we must now, Godard adds, begin to understand the history of that world. Bazin died at exactly the same moment as the Hollywood which Paul Javal evokes at the beginning of the film, and we have now entered into a history in which any simple return to a classical origin is impossible.

Quite how impossible had been made clear at the beginning of the production of *Contempt* when *Les Carabiniers* opened in Paris to some of the worst release figures ever recorded (fewer than 3,000 ticket sales in the first two weeks). The problem of the audience, which had agonised the traditional arts in the twentieth century and had been solved for the cinema by stable genres and a monopolised industry, was now a central problem for Godard, perhaps *the* central problem. Indeed, it is possible to understand his entire career since the early films as an attempt to find an audience on his own terms, and this, in fact, might serve as the very definition of modernism.

As the production team leaves the cinema where they have been trying to cast Nausicaa, Lang quotes to Piccoli Brecht's famous 'The ballad of poor BB'. Brecht's poem, written during his Hollywood exile, talks of the writer going down each morning to the market where one sells dreams. From *Vivre sa vie* to *Tout va bien*, Brecht becomes an ever more important reference for Godard – in a key scene in *La Chinoise* in which the study group considers the contemporary *maîtres à penser*, Brecht is the only name which survives the group's intense questioning.

It is of course possible to understand this turn to Brecht in terms of politics. Brecht was the only major Western artist who engaged fully with the Stalinist regimes of the post-war era, and his plays are arguably the most thorough attempt to make sense of the wreckage of global history in terms of an optimistic future. But it is probably more illuminating to think of Godard's engagement with Brecht in terms of modernism.

From the thirties onwards Zhadnov, Stalin's cultural commissar, had imposed an aesthetic of 'socialist realism' through the Comintern. The committed artist was called to represent the current state of the class struggle, in which the work of art becomes nothing more than the reflection of a reality understood entirely in terms of economics. Nothing could be further from Bazin's realism, which emphasised the real objects in front of the camera, nor from Godard's, which adds to Bazin's the reality of the position of the camera. But both of these emphases can be found in Brecht, with his determination that the raw material of any fiction must be drawn from the historical record, and that the transformations of that material must form part of the subject matter of the work of art. In the thirties, under the twin pressure of Stalinist dogmatism and his own commitment to the practice of the theatre, Brecht sketched out one of the most powerful of modernist aesthetics.

It is usual to talk of modernism in terms of the 'laying bare of the device' (to use the language of the Russian formalists), to talk of that moment when traditional art, be it in literature (Mallarmé and Joyce), painting (Picasso and Matisse) or music (Stravinsky and Webern), begins to foreground its own processes and practices. But this moment of foregrounding takes place in a specific context – the advent of universal education in the democratic societies of the West. This development negates any simple neoclassicism, where the artist finds his audience through the rules and conventions of an understood art, or Romanticism, where the artist finds his audience through the singularity of his genius. Now the artist is aware that the audience is multiple, and multiply uninterested in the traditions from which the arts of the West derive.

The response to this situation is varied, but one can indicate two influential reactions. The first and dominant one can be labelled the aesthetic. Here the audience is projected into a virtual future – Nietzsche's reader who will be 'far off' or Joyce's 'ideal reader suffering from an ideal insomnia'. The second is a conservative position, most powerfully articulated in English by T.S. Eliot, in which the minority nature of art is acknowledged within a hierarchically organised society, where art contributes to all through its particular and allocated minority audience. This conservative position could also be developed into the fully corporate Fascism of Ezra Pound.

Bazin and *Cahiers* had articulated their theories in a conscious rejection of both of these possibilities and, most immediately, of a third solution, in which artists merely used their art at the service of an agreed political objective. The cinema, the great democratic art, with its genres and its audiences, solved all these problems at a stroke. But as the cinema began to reveal its own historicity, as the problem of the audience erupted on both sides of the Atlantic, Brecht provided an alternative perspective.

For Brecht, the audience was provided by the political situation, and that meant that any artist must calculate his art in relation to politics. But Brecht also argued for the genuine autonomy of art – for the necessity to take seriously its forms and techniques. How far Brecht ever solved these contradictions is more than moot. His most accomplished theoretical work, the *Little Organon of the Theatre*, which explicitly attempts to provide an alternative to Aristotle's articulation of science, art and politics, is in constant contradiction between two discourses.

The first (and it is worth remembering that the text was, amongst other things, Brecht's job application to the East German politburo to run the Berliner Ensemble) places theatre totally at the service of the new science of Marxism, charged with simply representing the knowledge that Marxism generates through the party. But there is a second discourse which weaves its way through the whole text, in which the theatre provides a space where representation and audience can connect to produce a new knowledge.[65]

The Berliner Ensemble's tours of the mid-fifties, in which Brecht's theories were realised in stunning theatrical practice, were of crucial importance in the revivifying of left discourses on art. There is no doubt that they were crucial in Barthes's elaboration of an aesthetic which took seriously both the claims of politics and the claims of the specific languages of art. For over a decade, and a decade in which more and more of his writings became available in translation, Brecht is the most important thinker through which Godard tries to theorise his relationship to the audience.

But in *Contempt* when Lang speaks to Piccoli, cocooned in the homosociality of the Western cultural tradition, of 'our dear BB', the reference is much more complicated than it might at first appear, because for the viewers of the film, for the European cinema-going audience, 'our dear BB' is not Bertolt Brecht but Brigitte Bardot, and the explicit focus of the film is the inability of Paul Javal to retain the love and admiration of Bardot. Bardot's beauty and life is what escapes all the Western discourses on art. Chris Marker remembers a young Communist friend who became tremendously excited by this scene when the film was first released. In the superimposition of the two meanings of BB he saw a symbol of the possible reconciliation of the old revolution (the struggles) with the new revolution (the mores).

Contempt is one of the few real examples of European cinema: four of the great European languages – English, French, German and Italian – circulate freely on the set of this production of a Greek story transposed with Roman names.[66] This crucial change from Moravia's novel (in which although the director is German, the story is entirely in Italian) was Godard's. Godard told Giorgia Moll, the actress who took the role of the translator and a favourite of *Cahiers*, that he had the idea for her part when he saw Mankiewiez's *The Quiet American* where Moll plays a Vietnamese girl to whom Audie Murphy proposes via the interpretation of Michael Redgrave. Moll, the daughter of a German father and an Italian-German mother, was bilingual from birth and had an obsession with languages, which meant she was also fluent in English and French. She was already a successful actress in the Italian cinema and knew Ponti, who had first suggested to her that she take screen tests when she was an eighteen-year-old model. She remembers how little direction Godard would give ('You come down the stairs and you cry' 'Why do I cry?' 'I don't know') and how few takes there were. Her overwhelming impression was of someone who knew exactly what he was doing. The refusal of psychological interpretation, constant in all accounts of Godard is, of course, shared by Brecht.

However significant the reference to Brecht, there is a much more important presence within *Contempt*, and one indeed which survives every twist and turn of Godard's career: Roberto Rossellini. It is impossible to overstate the Rossellini's importance for both Godard and the Nouvelle Vague. Bazin's theories are unthinkable outside a continuous dialogue with Rossellini's brilliant war trilogy, but he was also *the* director for the young critics in the fifties. There were no limits to their admiration for Welles and Renoir, Hitchcock and Hawks, but Roberto was *sans pareil*. He was the man who had not only provided a totally new language and film-making practice for Europe in the post-war years (and it would be possible to make an argument that the Nouvelle Vague's aesthetic is little more than a development of Rossellini's practice) but who had also gone to Hollywood and won the most beautiful of Hitchcock's actresses, Ingrid Bergman. The series of films he made with her were panned by the press and ignored by the public, but for *Cahiers* they were the very definition of modern cinema.[67]

Of all the films, *Viaggio in Italia* was perhaps the most loved and admired. This film which had nothing of the cinema, which was simply a couple (George Sanders and Ingrid Bergman) nervously destroying each other as they travel through Italy visiting the ancient sites of the Mediterranean, from the sybil at Cumæ[68] to the ruins of Pompeii, was for Godard, for Rivette and for Truffaut the greatest of modern films.[69] In fact it would not be inaccurate to read *Contempt* as a remake of *Viaggio in Italia*. But there is a difference. *Viaggio in Italia* ends on a note of incredible optimism as the camera pulls away in an astonishing crane shot (all the more astonishing because Rossellini, of all the great directors, is normally the most uninterested in the possibilities of the camera), leaving the couple united in the midst of a popular religious ceremony. In *Contempt*, the couple end in a separation sealed by Bardot's death, and the final shot is a Utopian vision of a film that Fritz Lang will never make.

The End of the Affair

In the extraordinary central scene of the movie, Bardot and Piccoli perform a complicated dance for more than twenty minutes through a half-finished modern apartment. As we see their marriage fall apart before our eyes it might be tempting to interpret this as a representation of Godard's relationship with Karina.[70] It is true that some of the dialogue is taken from Karina,[71] it is true that Bardot wears the Louise Brooks wig that Karina had worn in *Vivre sa vie*, it is true that Piccoli wears the same hat as Godard throughout the film.[72] But we are not seeing Godard and Karina together; we are seeing Bardot and Piccoli working through the dilemmas of an instinctual woman and an intellectual man caught up in the professional and financial toils of the cinema. It is not a question here of a representation of another reality but the reality of this representation in demonstrating the reality of the modern couple. The 'catastrophe' of which Piccoli talks so movingly was already upon them. Karina would fly in from Spain where she was shooting at the weekends, but the tension was palpable. Karina herself tells of a visit to a nightclub where, when she accepted an offer to dance with someone else, Godard hit her. Perhaps even more chillingly, she recalls how glad she was of the attention.

In the late summer of 1963, and with the first edit of *Contempt* completed, there was a happy interlude. Karina took the lead role in Bourseiller's production of Giraudoux's *Pour Lucrèce*[73] which was performed at a summer festival in Normandy. Godard was not working at the time, and Bourseiller suggested that he take a small part as the notary. Karina remembers this time as one of great happiness. But the return to Paris in the autumn was grim. The couple had left the rue Niccolo with its unhappy memories and bought an apartment in the Latin Quarter at 9, rue Toullier.

That winter in the rue Toullier, still crazy with grief for her lost child, Karina tried to commit suicide for the third time. Her first two attempts had been prevented by Jean-Luc, but this time she was alone in the house for a full weekend. She would have died if the Italian painter who was decorating the house had not forgotten his keys and come back to retrieve them. At this point Jean-Luc had her committed to a mental hospital. After a nightmare incarceration, Karina found herself talking with a doctor about why she wanted to die, and for the first time came to some kind of acceptance of her baby boy's death. When Jean-Luc came to pick her up at the end of February, he told her that they were to begin shooting in three days. When they got back to the rue Toullier, Karina remembers the roar of the traffic from Boulevard Saint Germain as the loudest and most terrifying sound she had ever heard.

The film they were going to shoot was *Bande à part*, for which the original working title had been 'Arthur, Sammy, Anouchka'. Anouchka was Godard's pet name for Karina, but in the film the name is changed to Odile. Karina remembers talking with Godard about this woman he had named after his mother – naive, fragile, 'à part' – and decided to give her speech a very particular intonation. For many Godard lovers including, one imagines, Quentin Tarantino, who named his production company after it, *Bande à part* is the quintessential Godard film. A film made from nothing, following the lives of a girl and two boys living on the margins of society doomed to failure and caught in the toils of a culture they barely understand, who nevertheless find moments of incandescent life in the grey suburbs of their existence. The film marks another step in the Rouchian observation of Paris and yet another revelation of what Karina was capable of as an actress.

Anna Karina in *Bande à part*, 1964.

But the film that Godard had been trying to get off the ground from early 1964 onwards was *Pierrot le fou*. Originally entitled *The Demon at 11 o'clock* after a pulp novel by Lionel White, it was a much more expensive project than the minimal *Bande à part*. *Contempt* had sold 220,000 tickets on its Parisian opening, and while this was a very good result for a Godard film, it was not a good result for a Bardot movie. According to Belmondo's biographer, Godard came to Belmondo about *Pierrot le fou* because he couldn't raise the money for the film. Belmondo was now a huge star both in France and internationally, and his agreement was sufficient to raise the money.[74] But Belmondo had a busy schedule, and in the end Godard had shot two more films before Belmondo was finally available.

The first was *Une Femme mariée*, the result of one of those 'challenges' which Coutard understands as crucial to Godard's film-making. The Venice Film Festival had rung Godard at the beginning of the summer of 1964 to see if he was finishing a film. Godard told them that he was very sorry but he had nothing available, although, as always, there were many projects. The conversation developed and concluded with the agreement that if Godard could get a film ready on time then it would screen at the festival.

According to Coutard, Godard then filmed and edited *Une Femme mariée*, from first day of pre-production to final answer print in a month, an awe-inspiring feat. Even the least ambitious of low budget movies requires a month each for pre-production, shooting and editing, and Godard's schedule would be considered impossible by many producers and directors. To reduce this to a single month and then to produce a masterpiece of the cinema is a demonstration, if demonstration were needed, of the extent to which Godard was now a complete master of his chosen medium. But the formal virtuosity of this film (or 'these fragments of a film' as the credits describe it) may in the end owe something to the extraordinarily compressed production time.

The film is without a strong narrative. We follow Macha Méril (Karina, who was shooting, was unavailable) through a day which takes in lover, husband, son and, most importantly, the new consumer world of the sixties. The characters are constantly caught in formal or informal interview and are as likely to come out with advertising slogans or a particularly raw chunk of Céline as with anything approaching believable dialogue. Perhaps the most important element of speech is Méril's interior monologue which accompanies her travels around Paris, a stream of associations which provides no interior subjectivity.

While Godard has used both the interview and the contemporary iconography of consumer capitalism from *Breathless*, this is the first film in which they become the major structuring principles fracturing both the narrative and the image. Brecht, in his call for an epic theatre which would engage as well as delight the audience, had insisted that for this to happen the dramatist must achieve a radical separation of the elements: music, dialogue, staging. The fiction must not be unified by its form but present its elements to the audience to be analysed and recombined. In *Une Femme mariée* one finds the real beginning of the Brechtian aesthetic which will dominate Godard's work until *Tout va bien*. Macha Méril, whose blankness of expression is such a key part of the film, remembers Godard's hatred of perfection in its shooting, knocking the camera sideways when everything had been done to make a perfectly organised shot.[75]

One of Brecht's greatest supporters in France was Roland Barthes, who saw in the great German playwright a man of the left who was nonetheless interested in the problems of form and language. Godard asked Barthes to be in *Alphaville* but Barthes, an extremely shy and reserved man, refused. Barthes's thinking still makes a useful counterpoint to *Une Femme mariée*. In *Mythologies*, which had so affected

Truffaut on its publication in 1957, Barthes takes as his text the new consumer society, analysing the ways in which the bourgeois presentation of the world is constantly denying history in favour of a totally fake appeal to nature. And it is this fake appeal to a Paris created from nothing which runs through the advertising texts of *Une Femme mariée*. The banished history of the Second World War is not, however, so easily denied, as is evident in the subtext of the Auschwitz trials (amplified by references to Céline, a great writer who was both anti-Semitic and pro-German) and the references to Resnais's *Nuit et Brouillard*, which is playing in the cinema where the lovers have their adulterous assignment.

Une Femme mariée, as *Bande à part* before it, is also particularly interested in questions of theatre and theatricality. It was at this time that Godard became the principal backer of Bourseiller in his acquisition of a little theatre in Montparnasse, Le Théâtre de Poche. When Bourseiller asked what he wanted in return, Godard said, 'My dream is to be able to come to a theatre any night I like and sleep in the last rank of the stalls', a dream which he realised on numerous occasions.

Godard on the set of Jacques Doniol-Valcroze's documentary about him, 1965.

Une Femme mariée (*A Married Woman*) had as its original title 'La Femme mariée' ('The Married Woman'), but the Gaullist censor with whom Godard had already clashed over *Breathless*, *Le Petit soldat* and *Vivre sa vie* was more than offended by this portrait of French married women. It was only after much argument and a change of title that the film could be shown in France. Meanwhile *The Demon at 11 o'clock*, the film that he had pitched to Belmondo as the history of 'the last romantic couple', was delayed once more as

Godard accepted a suggestion to make an Eddie Constantine film. Constantine was an American actor who had made a career in France as a hard-boiled private eye, Lemmy Caution. By 1964, his career was somewhat in decline, but Godard accepted the 'challenge' of making a film with a figure who was widely considered to be a truly terrible actor. In fact Godard has already shown what it was possible to do with Constantine in a brilliant 1961 sketch entitled 'Sloth', his contribution to the multiply-directed *Les Sept péchés capitaux* (Seven Deadly Sins). Constantine's unchanging expression had worked wonderfully in a story about a

Anna Karina and Eddie Constantine in *Alphaville*, 1965.

seducer so lazy that he can't be bothered to get undressed to sleep with a girl who has taken him back to her flat.

Alphaville is subtitled 'A Strange Adventure of Lemmy Caution' and offers itself as another in a series of B movies. But the setting this time is the future – the city of Alphaville in which people's lives are dominated by the huge computer Alpha 60 and where all emotions and words to express them have been eliminated. It is typical of Godard's aesthetic that the future capital of Alphaville was constructed without sets or dressing from the new suburbs that had begun to burgeon around Paris, which also provided the subject matter both for *Une Femme mariée* and *Deux ou trois choses que je sais d'elle* (Two or Three Things I Know about Her). The voice of Alpha 60, which controls this totalitarian world of the future, was not produced mechanically but by someone who had lost their vocal cords and had relearnt how to speak using a mechanical voicebox.

The use of Lemmy Caution allows Godard a final homage to the genres which had seemed so crucial to the young *Cahiers* critics. Eddie Constantine was a star of 'polars' (cop stories), and the film in which Lemmy comes to Alphaville to discover what has happened to the secret agents who were his predecessors would probably be best characterised as a 'spy movie', a popular genre during the Cold War. But Godard also talks of Constantine in terms of a Western hero,[76] and the dominant genre is science fiction. It is as though Godard has brought together all the popular genres of the century, in a style which mixes comic strip and high modernism, Eddie Constantine and Paul Eluard, whose collection of poems entitled *Capital of Pain* punctuates the film.

Much of *Alphaville* is derivative of other dystopian futures (the obvious reference, which Godard never makes, is to George Orwell's *1984*).[77] But it is difficult to think of any parallel work which so successfully shows the future in the present, and which can sustain

Anna Karina and Laszlo Szabo in
Alphaville, 1965.

viewings forty years after it was made. It is also the last of Godard's films of this period and it ends on an explicit note of optimism – Anna Karina mouths 'I love you' as Misraki's music swells to a sentimental climax. Karina once again succeeds in giving an incredibly moving and brilliant performance – it is difficult to think of any other actress of that time who could have carried off the ending. Godard himself recognised this in the lectures he gave in Montreal in the late seventies: 'Anna Karina, who was really a Nordic actress, had a great deal in common with the actors of the silent period. She acted with her whole body and not at all in a psychological manner.'[78]

It is difficult to date the end of a relationship. Karina says, 'With Jean-Luc it was never over. Go away. Come back. Wonderful letters of love.' For Godard, at least talking to Michel Vianey, it was after *Contempt*.[79] But perhaps the most reliable account comes from Jackie Reynal, the make-up artist. Godard famously disliked the false appearance of make-up, and the fact that Reynal did eight Godard features between *Une Femme est une femme* and *Made in USA* testifies to the fact that she was a significant member of the regular Godard team. She did Karina's make-up on all the films from *Une Femme est une femme* onwards, and she is certain that their great love was still alive during *Alphaville*. But that was the end.[80]

Pierrot le fou

Pierrot le fou clearly and consciously marks itself as a culmination of all that had gone before. Part of the publicity campaign advertised *Pierrot le fou* as 'A little soldier who discovers with contempt that one must live one's life, that a woman is a woman and that in a new world one must live as an outsider in order not to find oneself breathless.' Gilles Jacob, at this time probably Godard's most attentive French critic,[81] described *Pierrot le fou* as a 'striking retrospective':

> We find again love which leads to death, tenderness and awkwardness, taste, sometimes annoying, quotations (here Elie Faure on Velasquez), the need to inconvenience the spectator in his comfortable position (the reflection of the street lights on the windscreen recall the headlights in the eyes of *Alphaville*), the love of cinema (allusions to *Johnny Guitar*, Laurel and Hardy, *La Chienne*, Michel Simon, *Pépé le Moko*) and those tranquil references to his own work: the final presence of the sea, as in *Contempt*, the ballet of motor cars from *Bande à part* and *Alphaville*, the car theft and the reversal of Belmondo's journey in *Breathless*, a film often present as a counterpoint in our memory as we watch *Pierrot*.
>
> We recognise the search for freedom, the unfinished nature of things for

characters in transit: from this point of view, the bathroom with raw bricks not even covered with plaster rhymes with the unfinished apartment of *Contempt* and the unfurnished villa in *Bande à part*. The same modern tableaux, the same slaloms in sequence shot of a prying camera. One could go on . . .

To summarise, after ten films, feeling that with *Alphaville* a culminating point had been reached, Godard felt the need to take his bearings, to put his ideas and his work in order. He runs through his repertory, he recapitulates. There will be those who are disappointed and finding that he doesn't take a step forward or sideways will not hesitate to assert – isn't it an obsession of Godard to extract the roots of words – that in recapitulate, there is capitulate, that the film-maker is repeating himself, going back to the same old story, marking time, that having read all the serious articles devoted to him, he has ended up by taking himself for Jean-Luc Godard . . .

For myself I do not see self-pastiche . . . nor wearisome reiteration of an author abandoned by inspiration (Dreyer) nor a crisis of creative impotence in a jaded forty-year-old (Fellini). Many of the greatest artists have only shot a single film, always the same, and it doesn't displease me that Godard has thought it a good idea to offer us this table of contents which allows us to move through his work more easily.[82]

If *Pierrot le fou* does mark a sort of *summum*, a reworking of all the themes to date, and if Karina and Belmondo together themselves seem to anthologise Godard's early cinema, there are new features in this story of doomed romantic love on the run. *Pierrot* is the first film in which the old political theme of Algeria is in counterpoint with a much stronger reference to Vietnam and American imperialism. The violence is also much more brutal and death more omnipresent than in the previous films. Karina's death and Belmondo's suicide end the film on a note of total pessimism. When Godard's sister, Rachel, saw the film at a private screening in Geneva, she was terrified. She always saw each film as a personal message from the brother who was her twin spirit, and for her the clear message of *Pierrot* was suicide.[83]

Anna Karina in *Pierrot le fou*, 1965

Jean-Paul Belmondo and Anna Karina in *Pierrot le fou*, 1965

Jean-Paul Belmondo in *Pierrot le fou*, 1965.

Pierrot undoubtedly marks a break of sorts. Godard's next film found him with a new producer (Anatole Dauman), new stars (Jean-Pierre Léaud and Chantal Goya), and, perhaps most significantly of all, with an almost completely new production team. Gone was the hitherto inevitable Coutard, gone was Bitsch, gone was Reynal, and gone too was Suzanne Schiffman, a member of the Truffaut gang from the very earliest days, indeed Truffaut's closest collaborator on his films, and the person who had the difficult and delicate position of continuity on most of Godard's movies. The one collaborator remaining on *Masculin Féminin* was Agnès Guillemot, who had edited all the films since *Le Petit soldat.*

With de Beauregard and Braunberger, Dauman made up the great trio of New Wave producers – he had produced both Resnais and Marker and he suggested that Godard should film a couple of Maupassant short stories. One was 'The Sign', the story of a woman who imitates a prostitute, which Godard had used for his second short. The second was entitled 'Paul's Mistress' and is a much longer and more consequential work which details the agony of the sensitive romantic Paul as he loses his mistress Madeleine to a lesbian lover. There is a detailed treatment of more than twenty pages which does indeed marry these stories.[84] The narrative of Paul's mistress forms the framing device, but over half of the film is taken up with a visit to the cinema where Paul and his lover see 'The Sign'. The final film retains very few of these elements. The hero is called Paul (Jean-Pierre Léaud) and the girl Madeleine (Chantal Goya) but the theme of lesbianism is replaced by a more conventional ménage-à-quatre in which Catherine-Isabelle (Catherine-Isabelle Duport) and Elisabeth (Marlène Jobert) are the rather irritating best friends sharing Madeleine's flat when Paul moves into it early on in the film.

In some ways *Masculin Féminin* can be read as developing themes from *Contempt*. Paul inhabits the world of classical music and literature while Madelaine is completely caught up in the new culture of pop music and youth magazines – the sounds and images of the present. But there is a new element. In *Contempt*, Bardot finds a membership card for the Italian Communist Party in Piccoli's trousers. This throwaway reference is expanded to become a major character in *Masculin Féminin*: Paul's friend Robert (Michel Debord). To the feminine world of pop culture, Robert opposes not the classical art of Europe but the masculine world of politics. Robert is a member of the French Communist Party concerned with petitions, strikes, and demonstrations against the war in Vietnam. Paul is caught between the masculine world of politics and the feminine world of pop culture. His most direct statement of his beliefs and his love, an elegiac reworking of advertising jingles in the form of a modernist poem, is addressed to a non-existent audience in a record-your-own-voice booth.

Chantal Goya in *Masculin Féminin*, 1966.

Jean-Pierre Léaud in *Masculin Féminin*, 1966.

The film marks a step even further away from the world of the classical fiction film. When Paul and the girls go to the cinema, not only is the projection faulty (a favourite Godard theme) but the cinema is portrayed as fundamentally inadequate: 'We often went to the movies. The screen lit up and we trembled. But more often than not Madeleine and I were disappointed. The pictures were dated, they flickered. And Marilyn Monroe had aged terribly. It made us sad. This wasn't the film we dreamed of. This wasn't the total film that each of us had carried within himself . . . the film that we wanted to make, or, more secretly no doubt . . . that we wanted to live.'

In the interviews he gave around this movie Godard emphasised two things. The first was his concern with a new generation – the protagonists of the film were a good ten years younger than his own generation. No longer obsessed by Bogart and Hawks, they use the film's most famous and most prescient intertitle 'The children of Marx and Coca Cola – understand who will'. The second is Godard's role as a

Intertitles from *Masculin Féminin*, 1966.

researcher, as a scientist. If in the early films the documentary style of Rouch or Marker is balanced against the fictional models of Hollywood, the emphasis now is entirely on the investigation of daily reality. At the time he often said to his friend Antoine Bourseiller – who has a cameo role with Brigitte Bardot in *Masculin Féminin* – that he thought of himself as a scientist. And it was this comparison that he used in an interview with *Les Lettres Françaises* shortly after the release of the film:

A chemist doesn't succeed every single time. One day the experiment goes along very nicely, and another day it doesn't; there are even experiments made in a vacuum . . . Since I'm an experimenter, without meaning to speak well or ill of myself – it's just a way to make a living like any other – obviously you can't go to a bank and say: 'Subsidise me.' I still haven't found what I'd like to do. I'd like to be paid by the Ford Foundation to make films. I'd be paid by the year and we'd settle accounts later.[85]

Pauline Kael, writing in the *New Republic*, underscored the difference from the earlier films:

> Godard has liberated his feeling for modern youth from the American gangster movie framework which limited his expressiveness and his relevance to the non-movie centred world. He has made up the strands of what was most original in his best films – the life of the uncomprehending heroine, the blank-eyed career-happy little opportunist betrayer from *Breathless*, and the hully-gully, the dance of sexual isolation, from *Band of Outsiders*. Using neither crime nor the romance of crime but a simple kind of romance for a kind of interwoven story line, Godard has, at last, created the form he needed. It is a combination of essay, journalistic sketches, news and portraiture, love lyric and satire.[86]

Immediately after *Masculin Féminin*, Godard made a further film for Dauman which took this new form of movie-making a stage further. The starting point of *Deux ou trois choses que je sais d'elle* is not a nineteenth-century fiction but a contemporary news story. Housewives in the new Parisian suburbs were resorting to prostitution, not to feed their families but to keep them in the consumer durables which were now, if one believed the advertisements, a necessity of modern life. Prostitution had been one of Godard's favourite themes since his very earliest fiction, the prostitute functioning both as the most direct form of sexual exchange and as a metaphor for all forms of modern work where labour is not expended for love but for money.

Deux ou trois choses is referred to by Godard in later interviews as the first film which was not totally dominated by the previous history of the cinema. But the break between, for example, *Une Femme mariée* and *Deux ou trois choses* does not seem as sharp as this comment would suggest. It is true that *Deux ou trois choses* does dispense almost entirely with narrative – there is not even the lure of an adulterous affair – but its form is very much that of *Une Femme mariée*: twenty-four hours in the life of a contemporary French woman. The real innovation comes on the soundtrack where Godard's voice provides the male lead to Marina Vlady's Juliette Jeanson. Godard had appeared in his own films before –

most notably in a cameo role as the informer in *Breathless* – and he had taken the lead in one of Rohmer's early shorts, *Charlotte et son steak*. But this is the first time that he is really an integral part of the film: the sound which plays against the image to make the very matter of the film. In the late seventies Godard was to describe his film-making practice as 'to show and to show myself showing',[87] and if we take that as an accurate account then *Deux ou trois choses* is indeed a new departure.

Astonishingly, and in perhaps the most spectacular of his 'challenges', Godard shot *Deux ou trois choses* not back to back but at the same time as *Made in USA*. After shooting *Made in USA* in the morning, he would then turn his attention to *Deux ou trois choses* in the afternoon. If aesthetically and politically *Deux ou trois choses* looked forward – the Vietnam war and the contemporary remodelling of Paris are the dominant political themes – then *Made in USA* looked back. Dedicated to Sam (Fuller) and Nick (Ray) who 'educated me in the use of sound and image', *Made in USA* has some of the trappings of a genre movie.

Laszlo Szabo as Richard Widmark shows his police card while Paula Nelson (Anna Karina) looks on in *Made in USA*, 1966.

Clad in a Bogart trenchcoat, Karina plays Paula Nelson investigating the death of a former lover mixed up in murky French post-colonial politics, most notably the Ben Barka affair when the French state apparently colluded in the murder of a Moroccan opposition politician. Towards the end of the film the commentary remarks, 'We were certainly in a film about politics: Walt Disney plus blood.' But what the film actually demonstrates is the complete inability of the form to deal with the reality of a politics which eludes the easy solutions of the thriller genre. In some ways, the simple and sombre message of the film is the inability of the left to

Widmark's police card in *Made in USA*, 1966.

cope with the developments of consumer capitalism: 'Left Year Zero' is a repeated slogan as the film builds to its anticlimax.

Made in USA is perhaps more easily understood as a re-run of *Le Petit soldat* and an almost conscious farewell to Karina. Karina no longer plays the innocent and fragile girl who ends up tortured and dead — she is a character in charge of her own destiny who drives away at the end of the film into her own future. Karina constantly speaks of Godard as Pygmalion to her Galatea, Professor Higgins to her Eliza, but in this

Anna Karina in a bar in *Made in USA*, 1966.

Donald Siegal (Jean-Pierre Léaud) dies in *Made in USA*, 1966.

version Pygmalion gives up his creation and acquiesces in his own demise. In one of the most shocking moments of the film, Karina asks the character Donald (played by Jean-Pierre Léaud), 'If you had to die, would you prefer to know beforehand or would you rather it was sudden?' 'I'd rather it was sudden,' he replies. She shoots him, and all we hear from him as he dies are his cries for his mother.

If Karina achieved a fictional release within the film, the shoot was less easy for her. In setting up two films at once, Godard had created an almost unparalleled situation. If the dialectic of master and slave between director and actor changes dramatically in shooting (in casting and editing the director is absolute master, on the set it is finally the actor who calls the shots), Godard had created a situation in which he had another film and another lead actress (Marina Vlady), with whom he was to have some sort of affair.[88] Indeed Karina remembers Godard being so unpleasant to her on set that even Coutard was moved to comment that he shouldn't treat her so badly. Many bitter and unspeakable things were said. It was really over.

Last words go to Karina: 'He was and will remain the greatest love of my life.'

4

Student Revolution: Wiazemsky and Gorin

May 1968

When Chou En Lai, the Chinese Communist leader, was asked his
opinion of the French Revolution of 1789, he said that it was 'a bit soon
to tell'.[1] We are now more than three decades away from 1968, but the
events of that year still elude definitive historical judgment. Few would
dispute that 1968 is a key year in charting the latter half of the twentieth
century.

In February the Vietcong, backed by the North Vietnamese army,
launched their Tet offensive against the South Vietnamese government and their American backers. While the Americans and their
clients repulsed these attacks, the losses were so heavy and the initial
success of the offensive so startling, that it would not be absurd to
suggest that the Tet offensive was the key element in redefining
American foreign policy for the next four decades. America's withdrawal from Vietnam and its entire military strategy for the rest of
the century was dominated by the fact that a lightly armed guerrilla
army was able to inflict an unacceptable level of casualties on the
world's greatest military power.

In August of the same year, Soviet tanks at the head of a Warsaw Pact
alliance invaded Czechoslovakia and brought to an end the experiment
of 'Socialism with a human face'. It also brought to an end what had
been one of the most important ideological crusades of European
history. When Lenin had split the Russian Social Democratic Party
in 1903 and promulgated the idea of a social revolution led by a

vanguard party, he was a marginal figure within European socialism. When the Bolsheviks dissolved the Constituent Assembly and seized power in October 1917, Lenin and Leninism became the dominant political force of the century. Partly through direct imitation, following the founding of the Third International in 1920, Communist parties were established across the world. But Leninism was also a key term in defining Fascism, where the idea of a totalitarian vanguard party was appropriated for anti-Communist politics.

Czechoslovakia in 1968 seemed to allow the possibility that within the terrible history of Soviet Russia and its satellites, there was still political life in the idea of a just society ushered in by a Communist party. For all except the most dedicated of sectarians, August 1968 marked the definitive end of the idea that there was any life in the Soviet model. It was to be another twenty-one years before a date as significant, 1989, would mark the absolute end of Leninist rule in Europe, but the corpse was visibly rotting from August 1968 on. Perhaps even more important were the assassinations in America of Martin Luther King and Robert Kennedy. If there had ever been a real possibility of articulating the anti-Vietnam-war movement and mainstream progressive politics, it died in that year.

And yet 1968's talismanic power, its ability to define a generation, does not derive from any of these events, but from a month of student protest in Paris. May '68 had no tangible political results whatsoever, nor did it lead to a change of regime, and yet it was to become the shorthand for a whole series of political and cultural ambitions and aspirations, ambitions and aspirations which still animate much of the opposition to the global dominance of neo-liberalism. There is no major artist who is more closely linked to May '68 than Godard. His film *La Chinoise*, pilloried on its release in the autumn of 1967 as wildly unrealistic, has come in retrospect to foreshadow the events of the following year. Even more significantly, 1968 marked Godard's definitive break with his previous methods of production, and ushered in four years of political experimentation with film.

Vietnam

From the moment that American marines landed in Da Nang in March 1965, opposition to the war in Vietnam became the most important international movement of the post-war era. This is immediately reflected in Godard's films; from *Pierrot le fou* on, the Vietnam war, or to be more precise the French attitude to the war in Vietnam, is a major emphasis. America, the liberator of Europe in 1945, had turned into the imperialist oppressor, and Vietnam was the most visible sign of this oppression. It was certainly the most obvious element in Godard's radicalisation. Its presence in *Pierrot le fou* was offensive enough to the American Academy for the screening to be halted when it was projected there. Godard began to appear more and more as an intellectual of the left, signing petitions and taking part in platforms such as the 'Six Hours for Vietnam' meeting at the Mutualité in May 1966. Perhaps the high point of this type of engagement was his contribution to the collective film *Loin du Viêt-Nam (Far From Vietnam)*.

Even while making two films a year Godard had invariably found time to contribute sketches to multi-authored films, which enjoyed a certain vogue in the fifties and sixties. But this was different. Instead of bringing together a group of well-known film-makers around a 'sexy' title such as *The Seven Deadly Sins*, *Loin du Viêt-Nam* found its subject matter in politics. Largely an initiative of the Left Bank group of film-makers (Godard in his film mentions Agnès Varda and Chris Marker as the people who had asked him to participate), *Loin du Viêt-Nam* had contributions from a broad political and aesthetic range, from the politically committed documentary maker Joris Ivens to Claude Lelouch, who had just won the Foreign Language Oscar for the box-office hit, *A Man and a Woman*.

The spirit of collective endeavour ran through the production, with material and labour being donated for 'the cause'. If Godard was late with his offering, with the familiar complaint that he didn't have any ideas, his contribution to the film made clear how for him Vietnam was a subject very close to home as well as very distant. Godard talks about how the struggle against the aesthetic imperialism of America isolates him from the working class in France. Addressing a huge Mitchell camera, he reflects on how the cinema is caught up in the systems of oppression, of which the struggle in Vietnam is only one aspect. The point is made very clearly in the handwritten introduction to the press book for *La Chinoise*: 'Fifty years after the October Revolution, American cinema dominates world cinema. There's not much to add to this state of affairs. Only that at our modest level, we must also create two or three Vietnams at the heart of the immense empire, Hollywood-Cinecittà-Mosfilms-Pinewood, etc, as much economic as aesthetic, that's to say struggling on two fronts, to create national cinemas, free, brotherly, comrades and friends' (G:243/1:303).

In the many interviews that he is to give to underground leftist journals in the late sixties and early seventies, the linking of his own oppression to the struggle in Vietnam is a constant theme. His solidarity with the Vietnamese is not born from a liberal sympathy for their predicament, but from his own experience of the very same predicament. Godard is careful to note that the oppression of a 35-year-old successful film-maker in the West is not as grievous as the Vietnamese direct experience of imperialist aggression, but he is nonetheless insistent that the oppression is the same. And that oppression is understood both as economic and aesthetic. The problem is not simply that American money dominates the cinema as Joe Levine had dominated *Contempt*, but rather that the forms of cinema themselves are dominating; that they insist on a way of understanding the world which is fundamentally false, promising a knowledge in the coincidence of sound and image which is simply illusory.

The Life of a Student

Politics was never absent from Godard's work. His initial essay, 'Towards a Political Cinema', demonstrated an interest in the relationship between society and its representation which is not evident in his fellow critics. Indeed, politics is always there in the films, from de Gaulle and Eisenhower driving up the Champs Élysées – an ironic counterpoint to the Franco-American alliance of Michel and Patricia in *Breathless* – to the Communist Party card that Camille finds in her husband's pockets in *Contempt*. But it is from the time of *Pierrot le fou* that Vietnam and politics become a major theme. In a long interview with *Cahiers* called 'Let's talk about Pierrot', the editors ask him if he would be interested in making a political film: 'What would interest me would be the life of a student, for example, the story of *Clarté*, for instance' (G:225/1:269).

Clarté was the magazine of the Communist student movement and, in the early sixties, this movement began to show that there was life within the Communist tradition. Stalin had consolidated his power both in Russia and in the international Communist movement around a series of calamitous decisions. Internally, in Russia, it was the economic programme of 'socialism in one country', a nonsense in classic Marxist theory which is above all a theory of globalisation. In political terms it was the left turn in the Comintern and the disastrous slogan of 'class against class' which identified European social democracy as the principal enemy in a situation where revolution was imminent. The Nazi victory in Germany in 1933 was a direct result of this policy. Ideologically, it involved the codification of Marxist-Leninism in Stalin's own *Principles of Marxist-Leninism*, a reduction of Marxism to a theory of economic determinism and Lenin to an apostle of bureaucratic organisation. Under this new dispensation, all matters of culture belonged to the superstructure and all questions of art could be solved by appeal to the notion of 'socialist realism', in which the job of the artist is no more than the representation of the truths of society revealed by Marxism and interpreted by the Party.

In the global struggle against Fascism which was to dominate the entire decade from 1935 to 1945, these positions became absolutely dominant. Alternative Marxist traditions both of the right (Kautsky, Bernstein) and of the left (Lukàcs, Luxembourg) were simply forgotten. Bazin broke with this paralysing orthodoxy in 1950 and specifically, with great acuity, over the question of the representation of history. This was the founding intellectual moment of *Cahiers*, but it was a moment in which alternative Marxisms such as the Brecht–Lukacs debate over realism in the thirties, or the mystical and elliptical writings of Walter Benjamin, were not available.

Two years before Bazin died, Khrushchev delivered his famous 'secret speech' to the twentieth congress of the Soviet Communist Party in which he denounced the crimes of Stalinism and condemned 'the cult of personality'. It is very difficult to overestimate the effect of this speech. The figure who for nearly thirty years had been the imaginary father of every Communist was revealed as a megalomaniac tyrant. The shock was so great that many Communist parties simply refused to believe it, and continued as though Khrushchev's speech had never happened.[2] Perhaps the most significant of these was the French Communist Party.

Above all a product of the Second World War and the Resistance, when the ties to Russia were not simply those of a brother party but also of an indispensable military ally, the French Party could be described as more Stalinist than the Stalinists. If in the early sixties it had to bend itself to the notions of 'peaceful co-existence' and follow the Khrushchevite thaw, the French Party had no doubt that it would continue to organise itself, with total discipline, around the narrowest of ideological agendas. But there was another model of Western Communism available just across the Alps.

The Italian Communist Party had a very different history from the French; it had been an underground organisation for nearly twenty years after Mussolini's March on Rome in 1922, and it had been even more central in the organisation of the partisans who helped the allies to drive Germany from Italy after the Italian government surrendered in 1943. Perhaps as important as this institutional history is its first leader, Antonio Gramsci, who was an original and inventive thinker. Mussolini had argued for Gramsci's imprisonment in 1924 with the frank acknowledgement that 'we must stop this man's mind working for a decade'. In fact prison gave Gramsci the time to reflect on both the Italian and Soviet experience before he died in Mussolini's jails in 1937. His martyr's death and his place within the Italian Party's pantheon gave real weight to his *Prison Notebooks* when they were finally published in the fifties.

Gramsci undoubtedly accepted Marx's analysis of class struggle as the fundamental social process and he did not dissent from the key role that Lenin allocated to the party, but his thinking was at complete variance with Stalinist orthodoxy. His theory of social change, while acknowledging the importance of both economic development and political organisation, stressed the centrality of ideological struggle – of developing ways of understanding the world which could bind together disparate class forces. The bourgeoisie did not take power simply because of the new money relations of capitalism, or because of the representative state that they invented, but primarily because their account of economics and politics, the naturalness of wage labour and representative politics, became hegemonic for all classes. Given the importance of ideological hegemony, it was crucial that Communists should engage with all the important cultural and political developments in a society in order to provide an equally convincing and hegemonic account of social solidarity, and a more directly popular politics.

Throughout the early sixties, and taking their cue largely from developments within the Italian Communist Party, the French organisation of Communist students and their journal *Clarté* attempted to open out the Communist tradition to a real engagement with the politics and culture of the present; they quickly became known as 'the Italians'. In March 1965, in a brutal organisational coup of a classic Stalinist kind, the 'Italians' within the Communist student movement were purged. In the 'Let's talk about Pierrot' interview published in October 1965, Godard acknowledges the importance of this institutional putsch by saying that it was not the right moment to make his film about *Clarté* which should have been made two years before, in other words when the 'Italians' and their ideas were coming to prominence. But Godard is sure in the interview that there would be another moment in the future when Communist students would provide the subject for a film. In fact it would be only two years before Godard did make his political film about students, not about the 'Italians' but about the 'Chinese'. And when the film was released at the end of August 1967, the student who would play the lead role in *La Chinoise*, Anne Wiazemsky, would not only be associated with obscure anarchist groups at the new university of Nanterre, she would also be his new wife.

Anne Wiazemsky

Godard had first seen Karina in a cinema advertisement in the Champs Élysées in 1959. It was also through the cinema that he met his second

Article announcing Anne Wiazemsky as the lead in Bresson's new film *Au hasard, Balthazar* in the 'Loisir' section of *Arts*, 3–9 November 1965.

wife Anne Wiazemsky, but she was not in an advertisement – she was the lead in Robert Bresson's *Au hasard, Balthazar*. For the *Cahiers* critics in the fifties, Bresson was one of the few directors who redeemed French cinema. The purity of his aesthetic vision might have repelled those who went to the cinema for entertainment, but for those who loved the cinema his mesmerising films – in which the precise order and juxtaposition of image and sound are everything – were masterpieces. And such was the power of that cinephiliac audience that Bresson slowly continued to produce his beautifully crafted films.

In 1975 Bresson published a statement of aesthetic faith in the form of a series of epigrams with the title *Notes sur le cinématographe*. Godard is to quote this text again and again in his later films, particularly in

Eloge de l'amour. In fact many of Bresson's epigrams read as perfect summaries of Godard's own aesthetic concerns. Bresson's insights link a Bazinian vision of the centrality of the camera's relation to the real with Godard's own obsession with the precise moment of the image, the precise moment of the relation of the camera to the real (the moment when the angle of the camera captures the real), and then in the articulation of the image with other image and sounds. For Bresson, as for Godard, images only find their meaning in their juxtaposition; for Bresson, as for Godard, the sound is as important as the image; for Bresson, as for Godard, cinema as an art of the real is hostile to fabrication, particularly in relation to actors — what the camera records is not a performance but a performer. Yet Bresson's aesthetic is more rigorous and precise (as well as more limited) than Godard's. His dislike of acting, an art which he associates with theatre, the domain of the fabricated, meant that from very early on he refused to use actors and instead took non-professionals to whom he gave the title of 'models'. With these models he felt it was easier to produce a genuine art of cinema, an art of the real.

Anne Wiazemsky had been brought to Bresson's attention by a family friend who knew he was casting for his next film. She was seventeen years old and had been born on 14 May 1947 into the world of cultured and educated Paris. She was the daughter of a White Russian aristocrat and the granddaughter of François Mauriac. Mauriac was the conservative equivalent of Sartre, a Nobel-prize-winning novelist who had been at the centre of every political and ideological conflict of the century. He had seen the danger of Hitler early, had supported the Republicans in the Spanish Civil War, and had resisted the German Occupation. But he was a convinced Gaullist and had the courage to defend many of those on the right who were executed in the savage settling of debts at the Liberation.

Anne had never thought of a career in the cinema, although her uncle, Claude Mauriac, was a well-known film critic, but she had thought of applying to the Conservatoire to become an actress. Bresson offered her the main role in his next film, *Au hasard, Balthazar,* and she accepted. Godard and Wiazemsky met briefly during the shooting of *Au hasard, Balthazar.*

Anne Wiazemsky as Marie in *Au hasard, Balthazar*, 1966.

By the summer of 1965, Godard was a central topic of cultural conversation. Were you for or against this film-maker who either broke all the rules, or made them up as he went along? Was he a genius or a charlatan? One way or another, it was essential to have an opinion. For the very reason that the 'pressure of opinion was too strong', and because 'you were obliged to have an opinion on Godard', the young Wiazemsky had refused to see any of his films. But in January 1966, long after *Au hasard, Balthazar* had finished shooting, she went to see *Pierrot le fou* and, in June, *Masculin Féminin*, which had just been released. She was completely overwhelmed by them. She sat down and wrote a letter to Godard telling him that she loved the films so much that she loved the man who made them. Not having Godard's address, she sent the letter to the *Cahiers du cinéma*. Godard rarely picked up his mail from *Cahiers* and when he did he often left it unopened, but a secretary had opened Wiazemsky's letter and thus he saw her signature and read the letter. By that time she was in the south of France picking peaches and difficult to contact, but contact was made.

The Student Movement

When Wiazemsky returned to Paris in the autumn of 1966, she attended university by day and studied cinema by night. Every evening she and Godard would go to the cinema at six, eat at eight, and go back to another film at ten. Godard liked his 'role of professor of cinema', and she was delighted to be instructed. In return she provided lessons in philosophy. If she had not thought much about film before working with Bresson, the experience had convinced her that she had found her home in the cinema. She was much less comfortable in the university. Because she lived in the bourgeois neighbourhood of the 16th arrondissement, she was allocated not to the Sorbonne but to one of the new universities on the city's periphery. Paris was being remade as Gaullist modernisation constructed new suburbs to serve the city, and amongst these suburbs were the new universities that a modern economy demanded.

Godard has taken these new suburbs as his theme for *Deux ou trois choses que je sais d'elle*, in which building sites with their attendant sounds punctuate the film. Nanterre was one of these half-completed sites – indeed the rector was to advise his students to come to class in wellington boots. But Nanterre also harboured a minority of students deeply dissatisfied both with the society in which they lived and the university in which they studied; they produced endless tracts outlining their analyses. Jean-Luc was a regular visitor to the campus, coming to pick up Anne in his sports car, and he too was soon reading these strange denunciations of capitalist society and the universities which served it.

In the present day, when the permanent threat of unemployment has produced docile student bodies desperate to equip themselves with the skills and diplomas which will help them face the insecurities of the job market, it is difficult to imagine a time when large numbers of students were willing to refuse the authority of their teachers and argue with them in public. But students in the late sixties were in a very unusual historical moment. When the Western powers had mobilised the huge armies that would defeat Nazi Germany, the promise of full employment when the war ended was part and parcel of that mobilisation. The bitter lessons of the First World War had been learnt by the industrialised working classes: there was no question of repeating the First World War formula of mass sacrifice followed by mass unemployment. And the deal had been honoured; the students going up to university in 1967 were the first generation in the history of capitalism to have lived in a fully employed society. Indeed, so secure was employment that students' anxieties and worries were not whether they would find a job but whether the jobs on offer – secure and boring as they were – would not be too alienating.

Alienation was a key term of this time. In its everyday sense it was a description of the psychological state of young students contemplating the pre-allocated roles envisaged for them; in its philosophical sense, it was an attempt to understand how Man found his labour used against him, how the immense resources of the modern economy were not utilised for the good of the many. The events of 1956, both Khrushchev's anti-Stalin speech and his Stalinist crushing of revolt in Hungary, had shattered the monolithic control that the Communist Party exercised over Marxism. In the late fifties and early sixties the works of Lukàcs, Korsch, Luxembourg, and the whole history of the Second and Third International once again became matter for debate. But this long and erudite tradition was more or less completely outside the university – it provided an alternative authority for students keen to analyse their society and the university's role within it.

In the early sixties, the richness of the Marxist tradition had been emphasised by a focus on the newly discovered texts of the young Marx, the *Economic and Philosophical Manuscripts* and *The German Ideology*. The Marx who had dominated much of working-class politics of the nineteenth and twentieth century was the Marx of *Capital*, the Marx who had argued for socialism not on moral grounds but as the ineluctable result of capitalism, where unplanned development led to inevitable overproduction. For Marx, the trade cycle would finally become so destructive that socialism would be a welcome alternative. This Marx seemed less persuasive in the climate of full employment, when Keynesianism and demand management seemed in those halcyon days to have solved the endemic problems of the trade cycle. The young Marx had been a far more messianic figure, who concentrated on the alienation involved in capitalist production and looked to Communism as the historical moment at which individual subjectivity and the social whole could be brought into a transparent and productive relationship. The young Marx came to stand for a whole eruption of socialist theory which stressed both economic and psychic liberation.

The interest in the psyche went hand in hand with a whole wave of new theories of neurosis and madness. Psychiatry was increasingly identified with the most callous of drug and electro-shock treatments. Psychoanalysis had been developed in the United States as a treatment to produce an ego which identified with prevailing social and moral norms. But from very different theoretical perspectives, writers such as Laing, Foucault and Lacan were beginning to question notions of 'normal' and 'mad' behaviour as related less to individual pathology and more to social expectation. One feature of this work was to open up the whole history of psychoanalysis, most emblematically with the figure of Wilhelm Reich. Again a whole tradition of scholarship and inquiry which had been scarcely engaged within the university suddenly became available to students.

But if both psychoanalysis and Marxism offered alternative intellectual traditions to students, it was in their everyday life that the contrast between them and their elders was most evident. In 1967 the pill first became freely available in France, but Godard had already acknowledged its centrality to the life of the young in *Masculin Féminin*. For the first time in human history, women could control their own reproduction with ease and without abstinence.

Almost forty years on it still seems very early to divine the long-term consequences of this extraordinary transformation; at the time, it marked an absolute divide between the generations. The sexual wisdom of the ages seemed, at least in that moment, to be discounted. The 'generation gap' has probably been with us since the dawn of time and has been a recognised phenomenon since the early part of the twentieth century. But there is perhaps no equivalent for that moment in the sixties when daughters had to make decisions about their conduct in conditions very different from those of their mothers. In an era when sex has become the most fundamental form of commodification, it may seem strange to recall its subversive power and its force as a symbol of the division between generations. It was a divide that was to be manifested in an iconic confrontation at Nanterre. Amongst the student groups operating on the campus was an anarchist grouping called, simply, the Anarchists. One of its more charismatic members was a young sociology student named Daniel Cohn-Bendit. Wiazemsky already knew him well. She'd first encountered him when he tried to pick her up, using the unorthodox political slogan 'Solidarity amongst redheads'. It was just such an unorthodox approach which was to make him a hero of the campus.

On 8 January 1968, Nanterre was visited by François Missoffe, the Gaullist minister of sport and youth who had just produced a three-hundred-page volume on the current state of French youth. Cohn-Bendit, or Dany as he would soon be known across the campus, had the temerity to beard the minister and ask him why there wasn't one word about sex in the three hundred pages. Sex was a hot topic at Nanterre because of the strict rules which segregated the student residences by gender. The minister suggested that the overheated student take a cold bath. Cohn-Bendit's riposte gained him instant fame: 'That's a reply worthy of the Hitler youth.'[3]

Sex was the most evident divide between this new generation and their parents, and it was no longer automatically understood within the norm of the heterosexual couple, but there were two further elements: drugs, and rock and roll. Drugs came in a variety of forms: cannabis, amphetamines, LSD. As with developments around the pill, it is extraordinarily difficult to calculate the long-term effects of the introduction of a whole variety of psychotropic drugs into a society which had for centuries limited itself to alcohol and nicotine. What is certain is that it introduced another element into the lives of young people about which conventional wisdom had nothing to say. Finally, there was a new musical form born of the developments of electronic technology which simply escaped previous aesthetic categories, but which occupied a privileged position in the emotional lives of young adolescents.

These developments, with all that they promised of a life determined by relations other than financial, of futures which escaped the routine of a nine-to-five job, found a compelling focus in the war in Vietnam. The struggle of the Vietnamese against the imperialist aggressor built on and developed the heroic image of Castro's Cuba; here were Third World societies trying to build a world in which life was not determined by Mammon and the United States.

Maoism

And then from the East came China. In the summer of 1966, bands of very young students, called Red Guards, began a Cultural Revolution in Communist China which was to find the most curious of echoes in Paris. Mao Tse Tung was already a name to be conjured with in Marxist circles even before, at the advanced age of sixty-six, he incited his country's youth to attack their own government. He had always been an original political thinker – the idea that a Marxist revolution could be launched from a peasant countryside was even more unorthodox than Lenin's belief that the tiny Russian proletariat could incubate socialism. But in reflecting on the Cultural Revolution, it is worth remembering that Mao was a genuine Marxist-Leninist, a political leader whose thinking for nearly fifty years had developed within the analyses of Marx and Lenin.

The awful excesses of the Cultural Revolution are now well documented and take their place amongst the other Red terrors authorised by Lenin's Jacobinism. But what is now little mentioned is that Mao's belief that the party and state leaders were taking the 'capitalist road' has been triumphantly vindicated by China's embrace of modernisation. The excesses of the Cultural Revolution undoubtedly owe much to the idiosyncrasies of one man, but it is impossible to understand the impact they had in Paris in 1966 unless one considers them within the overall history of Marxism.

One of the odd features of Marx's writings is how little attention is devoted to the future organisation of society. In the three volumes of

Capital there are fewer than ten paragraphs about how production will be arranged, and those paragraphs suggest a touching faith in the ability of a disinterested rationality to organise economic life.[4] This faith was probably the result of a life spent as a nineteenth-century revolutionary agitator, which would have shielded Marx from having to confront almost any of the realities of institutional life. Thus his horrifyingly acute analysis of capitalism and its endemic crises was not accompanied by any equivalent political insight – British politics, for example, baffled him throughout his thirty-year sojourn in London. Marx was ferociously hostile to the form of the bourgeois state and its politics. He understood it as little more than a guarantor of exploitation. Although he insisted on the necessity of the dictatorship of the proletariat during the transition to communism and the withering away of the state, there was very little sense when he died of what a Marxist politics would be. There were gestures to the Paris Commune, when for a few brief weeks in 1870 Paris had known a popular democracy. But the short life of the Commune, before the communards were suppressed and slaughtered in their thousands, was hardly a detailed blueprint for the future.

In the decades after Marx's death, the German Social Democratic Party, relying very heavily on his economic analysis, took a line which stressed the necessity for socialism to wait for the moment at which the contradictions of capitalism would inevitably summon forth a new world to replace the old. Lenin broke decisively with this tradition, arguing for the need of a new kind of vanguard party which, informed by the science of Marxism and its position at the heart of the working-class movement, would be equipped to direct both a revolution and a new kind of workers' state. Such a party was necessary because the European social democratic parties, with their attachment to the legal forms of the bourgeois state, would be completely unable to stop the coming imperialist war in which the nations of Europe would take the competition for world resources to the battlefield.[5] This war was to bring Lenin's party into power, but the backwardness of the country and the failure of revolution to spread through Europe in the immediate post-war years meant the reintroduction, after the period of War Communism, of forms of capitalism in the New Economic Policy.

It was at this moment that Lenin, literally on his deathbed, put forward the notion of 'cultural revolution'. If the party was unable to immediately usher in changed economic relations, then it was necessary to inaugurate a cultural revolution which would prepare the ground for socialism. Lenin's ideas, which would challenge both traditional Marxist arguments about the ideological superstructure as a product of the economic base, and his own ideas about the primacy of the party, did not survive his death. But more than forty years later, when Mao Tse Tung saw his own revolution succumbing to a party bureaucracy, it was Lenin's term which he used to justify 'the bombardment of headquarters'.

Like Lenin, Mao never followed through the theoretical consequences of the term; in the end he never challenged the primacy of the party. To have done so would have been to unravel his own revolution which, like Lenin's, relied on a belief that the party was the tool which allowed the revolutionary to ignore the economic backwardness of Russia and China.

The Cultural Revolution soon collapsed into the fiasco of the Lin Biao coup, and Deng Xiao Ping returned from disgrace to lead China on a capitalist road, which even in his worst nightmares the Great Helmsman Mao could scarcely have imagined. But in 1966, those still wedded to the Leninist tradition could see the Cultural Revolution as a longed-for moment of renewal.

The Cultural Revolution had an impact in France as nowhere else in the West. But this impact was very localised and, in many respects, it was due to one individual, the philosopher Louis Althusser, and one institution, the Ecole Normale Supérieure on the rue d'Ulm.

The Ecole is an elite institution which prepares teachers for the university and secondary school system. Students enter the Ecole by taking a ferociously competitive exam which requires at least two years of special preparation. Once within its walls, students receive a very generous salary and, apart from the year when they prepare the *agrégation* (the next stage of competition which qualifies them for a teaching post), they have the freedom to follow their own intellectual interests to an extent that is unparalleled in any other national educa-

tional system. This is partly a function of its origins in the French
Revolution, when it was founded in conscious opposition to a university
system seen as irretrievably reactionary and medieval. The roll-call of its
alumni, from Sartre to Foucault, from Aron to Bourdieu, is staggering
given its small size.

There are no teachers as such in the Ecole but each subject has an
organiser, a 'caïman' in the jargon of the Ecole, who acts in a pastoral
role for his pupils and arranges the classes for the *agrégation*. These
caïmans are very young, picked from the Ecole's own ranks, and usually
remain in their position for only a relatively short time before moving on
to a post in the university system. Louis Althusser, who became caïman
for philosophy after the war, was unusual in that he moved into an
administrative position within the Ecole and thus by the mid-sixties had
been there for nearly twenty years.

Althusser was above all a philosopher of science, in the tradition of
Canguilhelm and Bachelard, and a member of the Communist Party,
which he joined in 1948.[6] He was fiercely opposed to the new humanist
and historicist versions of Marxism which rested on readings of the texts
of the young Marx. Between those texts and the *Communist Manifesto*
of 1848, Althusser wanted to argue that there was a epistemological
break, a break which involved dropping the ideological concepts of the
individual and society in favour of the scientific concepts of class
struggle and surplus value.

Politically, Althusser was unusual in being violently anti-Stalinist but
insisting on a rigid distinction between Lenin and Stalin; he thus
challenged the French Communist Party as it was, but in the name
of Lenin. Above all, Althusser's philosophical emphasis was on Marxism as a science and on a strict divorce between science and ideology. If
the French Communist Party could rid itself of the errors of Stalinism
and return to the science of Marxism, it would once again become a
revolutionary party.

Althusser's philosophy of science was rigorously anti-empiricist. If
you simply believed the evidence of your senses, then the sun obviously
did go round the earth; it was only as a consequence of theoretical
abstraction that it became possible to grasp reality. If an abstract science

was the only realm of truth and reality, ideology was always a matter of representation rather than truth; there was no possibility, as the humanists and the historicists claimed, of passing from false to true consciousness. Instead, ideology was to be judged by its politics, whether they be progressive or reactionary, proletarian or bourgeois. But – and here Althusser reversed Stalinism most decisively – neither economics nor politics would tell you in advance how to distinguish 'progressive' and 'reactionary' in ideology. Ideology was not a state of consciousness but a discrete series of practices, all of which had their 'relative autonomy' and in which the class struggle was fought out according to the specific forms of those practices.

For Althusser, philosophy was always to be understood as the working out of the class struggle in theory, where the class struggle was defined by the Communist Party. Of all the great theoretical names of the sixties – Lévi-Strauss, Barthes, Foucault, Derrida, Deleuze – it is Althusser's name that has faded the fastest.[7] But for a brief moment in the sixties, it was his thinking that galvanised the most intellectually talented students, and it was largely due to his influence that the Ecole (and its feeder lycées of Louis le Grand and Henri IV) were the focus of French Maoism.[8] Althusser made it possible for a new generation to engage with the Communist tradition and retain its separate intellectual and artistic interests. The relative autonomy of the ideological does not stand up to much intellectual examination – either a practice is autonomous or it is dependent – but its force as a slogan should not be underestimated. It is certainly difficult, if not impossible, to imagine Godard's engagement with Maoism without Althusser, and it is clear that Althusser is one of the dominant intellectual influences of *La Chinoise*. The preface to his first book, *Pour Marx*, is quoted extensively and his essay on Brecht is referred to by Jean-Pierre Léaud, as is the *Cahiers Marxises-Léninistes*, a journal produced out of the Ecole Normale Supérieure by Althusser's students.

But *La Chinoise* is not an orthodox Marxist-Leninist film.[9] Its narrative focus is on violence and on an attempt to assassinate the Soviet Minister of Culture when he makes an official visit to France. The Aden Arabie cell[10] have spent the summer in an apartment debating the

Anne Wiazemsky. *Paris Match,*
5 August 1967.

correct line, and terrorist violence is the conclusion of their debates. Violence also forms the subject of the discussion between Wiazemsky and the philosopher Francis Jeanson, with which the film ends. Jeanson had been Wiazemsky's philosophy teacher and, more significantly, the head of a network that supported Algerian terrorists; his trial in September 1960 was the major domestic event of the Algerian war. Jeanson's arguments against the terrorism rather hesitantly espoused by Wiazemsky (who was being fed her lines by Godard through an earpiece) seem to be conclusive but Godard himself said that while it was for viewers to make up their own mind, he himself favoured Wiazemsky's arguments (G1:303).[11]

Terrorism is indeed part of the Leninist heritage; its use at any particular time is determined by tactical, not moral, considerations. In fact within a long-term perspective Godard's emphasis on the link between student revolutionaries and violence seems an essential ingredient of *La Chinoise*'s strange prescience; the Weathermen in America, the Angry Brigades in Britain, the Baader-Meinhof gang in Germany, and the Red Brigades in Italy all testify to the potential for terrorism within the student movement. In France, however, no significant terrorist group developed, and Godard's focus on violence appears to be the most personal part of the film.

In between the shooting of *La Chinoise* in March 1967 and its screening at the Venice festival in August, Wiazemsky and Godard were married. Godard had proposed in January, but it was not until 21 July that the wedding took place. Once again Begnins was the place chosen and again the trusty Tolmatchoff acted as witness. The Swiss official who had conducted the wedding with Karina toasted the couple with the words, 'Here's to the next time', covering himself in embarrassment but amusing Godard and Wiazemsky considerably. At the end of the summer, the couple went first to Venice and then on to the theatre festival in Avignon for the premiere of *La Chinoise*. Unfortunately, Wiazemsky's mother had announced the wedding in *Le Figaro*, which even thirty-five years later her affectionate daughter qualifies as an 'unbelievably stupid' decision. The 36-year-old *enfant*

Article on the Godard-Wiazemsky wedding in *Paris Match*, 5 August 1967.

terrible of French cinema, lately revealed as an extreme leftist, marries the teenage granddaughter of that pillar of Gaullism, François Mauriac. When they arrived at Avignon for the premiere, they were the front-page. Wiazemsky seems to this day to have been traumatised by the experience of being hounded by photographers at every turn – one even got into their bedroom. Mauriac publicly blessed the union with the observation that Godard 'did not belong to the race of seducers'.[12]

Wiazemsky did not return to Nanterre in the autumn of 1967 – she had become disillusioned with philosophy and ever more enamoured of acting. Pier Paolo Pasolini had offered her a role in his parable of bourgeois repression, *Theorem*, and she decided to drop her studies. Meanwhile, Godard made his last film within the conventional relations of French commercial cinema: *Week-end*. *Week-end* begins with a psychoanalytic session of the utmost sleaziness and ends with a woman eating her husband in a communal feast. The final credits read 'End of story. End of cinema.' In between the viewer has been presented with an orgy of violence as the carnage of weekend traffic is juxtaposed with the tale of a bourgeois couple desperate to ensure their inheritance through murder.

Two frame stills from *Week-end*, 1967.

Godard has always claimed that he was absolutely prepared for the revolutionary break of 1968, and *Week-end* confirms this to be true. It is clearly made by someone who has reached a position of total disgust and rejection of his own society. The revolutionary leader announces at the end of the film, 'Our guts throb long after making love. Because of man's immense horror of his fellows.' The individual pessimism of *Pierrot le fou* was leavened by the beauty of Karina and the charm of Belmondo; in *Week-end*, they are replaced by Mireille Darc and Jean Yanne, conventional stars who incarnate brilliantly their bourgeois personae. In *Pierrot* there is still the beauty of nature; in *Week-end* the countryside is the scene of nothing but murder – by man or by machine. Here Godard demonstrates his total formal control of cinema; the film includes a tracking shot of 7–8 minutes along the most deadly of traffic jams and a 360-degree pan around a farmyard which is the scene of a piano recital, but this formal control seems merely to emphasise the fundamental problem: 'What is it ultimately that makes one run a shot on or change to another?' (G:233/1:269)

La Religieuse and the Cinémathèque

With *Week-end* Godard demonstrated that he was ready for revolution. He even told the crew he had worked with for almost a decade that they should seek other employment. But if we are to understand why it was France that erupted into near revolution in May 1968, and not any of the other Western countries, then we will have to look not at what was common to all these societies – not the new revolutionary thinking on politics and the psyche; not the sex and drugs and rock and roll; not the rejection of consumerism; nor even the Vietnam war. What was specific to France was an authoritarian Gaullist state which treated its citizens with a level of contempt that was unparalleled in any other Western democracy. Students experienced this in the cavalier manner in which the government reformed the universities; film-makers felt it in an extraordinarily repressive censorship system.

De Gaulle had signalled early on his determination to gain firm state control over the question of which films the French public were able to see. He altered the status of the Fourth Republic Censorship Commission so that it became merely an advisory body. From 1960, censorship decisions became the minister's responsibility, a responsibility he exercised repeatedly on Godard's films.[13] The most egregious example was *Le Petit soldat*, which wasn't released until three years after it was finished. However, from *Breathless* (where he'd had to cut footage of de Gaulle and Eisenhower) to *Une Femme mariée* (whose original title he had been forced to change), Godard's encounters with the censor give a real edge to his feeling of oppression.[14]

These constant problems were intensified in April 1966 with the banning of Rivette's film of Diderot's *La Religieuse*, and again two years later, in February 1968, when Henri Langlois was sacked from the Cinémathèque, which he had founded. In the first of a series of ferocious outbursts on the subject of *La Religieuse* in the pages of *Le Monde* (3–4 April 1966) Godard thanked the Minister of the Interior who had banned the film, for he now saw clearly 'the true face of the current intolerance'. But his open letter to André Malraux, then Minister of Culture, published two days later in *Le Nouvel Observateur*, was even more extreme. He addressed one of the great heroes of the Resistance as a collaborator whom he would refuse to shake by the hand. Paradoxically, Malraux gave permission for *La Religieuse* to be selected at Cannes, and thus created the extraordinary situation of a French film which would be shown to the world but not to France.[15]

There are those who would argue that the scandal of the banning of *La Religieuse*, which would rumble on throughout 1966, marked an important moment in the decline of Gaullist power. There are many more who would claim that when, on 9 February 1968, Henri Langlois was dismissed from his post as director of the Cinémathèque, the Gaullist regime instigated its own endgame. Later that month, de Gaulle himself was famously to ask 'Who is this Henri Langlois?' But Malraux, who took the decision to fire him, should have been in no doubt. In January 1966, on the occasion of the opening of a season of Lumière films, Godard had addressed to the Minister of Culture an extraordinary speech entitled, 'Thanks to Henri Langlois'. The speech, published in *Le Nouvel Observateur* on 12 January 1966, can be read as a first draft of the ideas which a generation later would become the *Histoire(s) du cinéma*. More immediately, it is a public declaration of the debt owed by film-makers all over the world to the man who had recognised the importance of their art. Godard is not a man to confer praise lightly, but for him Langlois's Cinémathèque was not simply the place where one learnt the art of cinema but is also where one could revivify one's faith in that art: 'If I have taken the liberty of speaking at greater length than is usual, that is because I wished to make public acknowledgement of my debt to Henri Langlois and his faithful staff . . . It is both sad and comforting to imagine that if the Cinémathèque had existed thirty or forty years ago perhaps Jean Vigo would have consoled himself here after his difficulties with Gaumont and restored his strength' (G: 237/ 1:283).

Within a day of Langlois's sacking, film-makers from France and from all over the world began bombarding the Cinémathèque with telegrams forbidding the use of their films. The list speaks for itself: Gance, Resnais, Franju, Marker, Astruc, Bresson, Mocky, Richard Lester, Lindsay Anderson, Henri Cartier-Bresson, Michel Simon, Busby Berkeley, Dreyer, Kurosawa, Oshima, Jerry Lewis, Chaplin, Rossellini, Lang. Organising this boycott was the *Cahiers* gang: the new editors Comolli and Narboni, but also the old guard – Truffaut, Godard, Chabrol, Rivette – reunited in a common cause which seems to have rejuvenated them all.

Malraux's decision was not simply an act of folly. Even though the Cinémathèque owed its very existence to Langlois, it had been run as a personal fief in which the orderly cataloguing and conservation of films according to bureaucratic norms was unthinkable.[16] Any state might have considered that it had a problem, but it was typical of de Gaulle's France that the solution should be a state coup – in the morning a packed committee ratified a minister's secret decision, and in the afternoon the newly appointed head of the Cinémathèque inaugurated his tenure by sacking the staff and changing all the locks.

Still more typical was the state's instant recourse to police repression and media manipulation when the size and strength of the opposition became apparent. In a rare display of unanimity, every paper in France, from the right to the left, condemned the decision, with *Le Monde* and *Combat* leading the charge, but there was absolutely no mention of the affair on state-controlled television. The French television news also failed to report a major demonstration called for 14 February, even though the state engaged more than thirty coaches of riot police and five other countries sent television crews – extraordinarily there was no crew present from the French state broadcasters.

If there had been, they could have recorded the trailer for the main film that history had programmed for May, three months later. The three thousand demonstrators, led by Godard and Truffaut, were prevented by police lines from gaining access to the Cinémathèque. Wiazemsky actually did get through, following a charge by Rivette, but finding themselves isolated they had to retreat through the police lines to rejoin the main body of the demonstration. The police then charged, and fierce street battles broke out. Godard was slightly injured, breaking his glasses in the scuffle (a problem that was to recur during the May demonstrations). At that point, having taken charge of the demonstration, Godard gave the signal to disperse, but not before Jean Rouch had delivered a speech to an audience which included the young Nanterre student Daniel Cohn-Bendit. Rouch declared that they were witnessing the start of a cultural revolution, one in which a new generation was refusing the oppressive power of the state.[17]

The Language of Cinema

This prelude to revolution was successful, although it was not until 22 April that an extraordinary general assembly of the Cinémathèque reinstated Langlois (a delay which simply enabled the government to save face). By a curious irony, as the Langlois affair broke Godard had just finished shooting his first commission for the ORTF, the French television station. Entitled *Le Gai savoir* (Joyful Knowledge), the film had been commissioned as an adaptation of Jean-Jacques Rousseau's *Émile*.

Émile is one of the few classics of educational theory, a fictional account of how a child is educated by being allowed to develop his own interests and thoughts rather than having to follow a rigid and pre-ordained pattern. Needless to say, Godard's adaptation bears no resemblance to Rousseau's ponderous and well-meaning bible of progressive education. His presentation of education is audiovisual and takes the form of a discussion between two representatives of modernity: Émile Rousseau, played by Jean-Pierre Léaud, and Patricia Lumumba, played by Juliet Berto.

The aim is to understand the working of sounds and images, of film and television, not to start from zero but to return to zero. In its concern to understand the language of cinema by taking it back to its component parts, and in its funding and subsequent rejection by television, *Le Gai savoir* can be taken as a model for all the subsequent Dziga Vertov group films. It signals not only an intensification of an engagement with revolutionary politics, but the interrogation of the Bazinian aesthetic that had sustained all of Godard's previous film-making.

At the end of his famous article on the ontology of the film image, Bazin had announced in a single pregnant sentence, 'And besides, cinema is a language.' The *Cahiers* of the fifties had let the sentence lie, but the *Cahiers* of the sixties explored its possibilities in depth. In 1962 Rohmer had been replaced by Rivette as the editor of *Cahiers* in a coup which had Godard's backing. The immediate reason for the change of editor was that the New Wave directors, all undergoing a slump in their box-office fortunes, felt that Rohmer was not working hard enough to support them (C2:13–26/70–86).

Rivette used his new responsibility to engage with the new thinking which had developed alongside the old *Cahiers*. The anthropology of Lévi-Strauss and the literary criticism of Barthes offered a very different view of art and the individual. Fundamental to Structuralism in all its various forms was its insistence that individual subjectivity and social meaning were simply a consequence of structures or systems. Be it the anthropologist's myth, the Marxist's class, or the literary critic's genre, meaning becomes a mere effect of processes and systems which escape the individual's control. Sartre's existential hero making his determining choices becomes a bad joke; the 'hero' is an idiot who mistakes the real determinations of his existence. The overriding emphasis in this new intellectual dispensation was language. Functioning both as model and metaphor, language provided the perfect example of a system which no individual had created and yet in which each individual had the illusion of creating meaning.

From figures as diverse as the film-maker Pasolini to the academic Christian Metz, the sixties saw a variety of attempts to use this linguistic model to produce a semiology of the cinema. Godard was more than sceptical of efforts to develop a grammar of cinema. To *Cahiers du cinéma*, he talked of such efforts as 'completely useless' (G1:312), to Bernardo Bertolucci at the festival of Pesaro in 1965 he was even more direct: 'Pasolini and Barthes are cops (flics).'[18] However, the moment of classic Structuralism, when the imposition of a linguistic grid on every activity from fashion to film-making would have them yield up their grammar, did not last long. Structuralism in its classic form presupposed an object of analysis – in this case, film – and a method – the categories used in the analysis of language. But a powerful argument developed which asserted that the choice of the object was not neutral – it always involved the active subjective position of the investigator – and that the categories used in the analysis of language did not enjoy the unquestioned objectivity necessary. They too were products of wider systems of meaning and interpretation. The Structuralists held up the model of the neutral observer establishing the grammar of a signifying activity.

Against this position Jacques Derrida, drawing on powerful modernist traditions, from Mallarmé and Joyce to Bataille and Artaud, argued in favour of a much more active investigation of the symbolic structures of matter and meaning. There was no question of going back to a pure subjectivity outside language, still less to the historically prior phenomenology of a Husserl which attempted to produce the pure objects of consciousness. But there was equally no question of reading subject and object as effects of constant structures waiting to be neutrally discovered. The new model was of writing – the subject working on the structures that constituted him and the world, the aim being to produce a more fluid subject open to the most basic processes of signification. Derrida himself never proposed a Manichaean model which opposed a bad subject bathing in transparent meaning to a good subject fully open to the processes of signification; nor did he propose a bourgeois subject stuck in an eternal unchanging world of nature and a revolutionary subject constantly open to change and actively participating in history.

But it was possible to offer such an interpretation and even to link it to a version of Maoism. One of the features of Maoism was that the opposition revolutionary/bourgeois or revolutionary/revisionist became almost entirely ethical. Mao did not tamper with the fundamentals of Marxism or Leninism; the distinction between a capitalist roader and a revolutionary was not a question of property relations or bureaucratic structures. Such an analysis would have undermined the very basis of the People's Republic of China. Instead, the decision to choose the revolutionary line became a pure act of will. If that suddenly risked reintroducing the autonomous subject choosing his fate, one could attempt to finesse that by emphasising that the choice was not an individual one but that of a whole class. The most serious attempt to synthesise the new thinking of Derrida with Maoism and avant-garde artistic practice was made by Phillippe Sollers and his magazine *Tel Quel*. Indeed at the time of *La Chinoise*, Godard said to Wiazemsky after a dinner with Sollers, 'Why do I think that Sollers is so clever?' and then answered his own question, 'I suppose it's because he thinks the same as I do.' Godard was so impressed with Sollers that he wanted to use him in the final long discussion of *La Chinoise*.[19]

From right to left: Godard, Alain Jouffroy, Jacques Roubaud, and Eugène Guillevic (third from left) marching with members of the Syndicat des acteurs, 29 May 1968.

Certainly the strategies and composition of *Le Gai savoir* are best understood in terms of the revolutionary modernism proposed by Sollers. The cover of Derrida's 1967 classic, *De la grammatologie*, appears in the film, and while it would always be a mistake to assume that Godard had read a particular book,[20] it is clear that *Le Gai savoir* is an attempt to deconstruct the conventional relations between sound and image.

In intellectual terms, what is striking about Godard in 1968 is that within a decade he had travelled from a position of pure classicism (using established genres and an accepted language to address an established audience) to one of pure modernism (deconstructing established genres and grammars to address an ideal audience). It is possible to give a variety of accounts of this trajectory, ranging from the collapse of classic Hollywood to the failure of his marriage with Karina, but it is probably worth stressing the failure of the New Wave. To talk about failure in relation to the New Wave sounds perverse: there is no more

Images of Daniel Cohn-Bendit, including the celebrated slogans 'We are all German Jews' and 'We are all undesirable', from silk-screen posters.

famous movement in the history of the cinema. Throughout the sixties and across the world, from Italy to Brazil, from Japan to the United States, young film-makers were identifying themselves in relation to Godard and Truffaut and the rest. Two points are worth making, however. The first, banal though it is, is that the New Wave was never a major success at the box office. The second is much less tangible. The Bazinian faith, which believed that a real criticism of film would lead to better films and that better films would contribute to a better world, was much more difficult to sustain at the end of the sixties than it had been a decade earlier. And this, not least, because the young critics had taken different paths, and the intense collaboration and conversations of the *Cahiers* days were a thing of the past.[21]

May

There would seem little doubt that part of the excitement and enthusiasm of the Langlois affair was the feeling of rediscovering a common faith. No sooner was the Langlois affair resolved than the events of May, of which Daniel Cohn-Bendit was to become the iconic figure, gave France a month in which revolution was more than in the air. For a brief moment, as Truffaut and Godard led the efforts to close down the Cannes Film Festival in solidarity with the striking workers and the students occupying their universities, it might have seemed as if the New Wave was still breaking.[22]

During May, Godard demonstrated and filmed at the same time, contributing to the anonymous *Film-tracts*,[23] short three-minute films made up of stills and intended to contribute directly to the struggle. He also shot a film entitled *Un Film comme les autres* (A Film Like Any Other) which recorded students and workers discussing the political situation. This film is as far from conventional agitprop as one could imagine. The students sit in the middle of a field and the camera makes no attempt to follow the dialogue, which is merely a banal resumé of May 1968.[24] In retrospect, one should not underestimate how many people were convinced that a revolution was in the making, as students and police clashed on the streets of Paris and as the entire work force came out in a general strike which paralysed the country. Charles de Gaulle, when he

Godard, Paris, May 1968.

fled Paris on 29 May and flew to confer secretly with the army on the Rhine, seemed in little doubt. And when the young Jacques Chirac, then working for the prime minister, Pompidou, began negotiations with the unions at the rue de Grenelle, he made sure that he was carrying a gun. But on the other hand, the huge right-wing demonstration of 30 May and the crushing right-wing victory in the June elections marked the end of any genuine prospect of dramatic change. For the vast majority of the French, 'May' ended with the calendar month, but there was a small yet significant number of the politicised young for whom 'May' was to dominate the coming years.

Godard, then nearing forty, threw in his lot with the young, and in so doing broke his oldest alliances. Wiazemsky recalls a very violent argument that summer when Godard tried to persuade Truffaut to lend his backing to the campaign to close the Avignon festival. Truffaut refused, not only citing his friendship for Jean Vilar, the director of the festival, but also making clear that if there had to be a choice between supporting the proletarian riot police and rich kids intoxicated by revolution, then he was on the side of the police.[25] Godard broke not only with Truffaut, but also with Antoine Bourseiller. He had

Godard, Paris, May 1968.

enjoyed the closest of friendships with Bourseiller's family but Bourseiller was now informed that he was a 'mandarin' and that Godard
would not be able to see him again.[26]

Travelling with the Revolution

Despite choosing youth over age Godard was not choosing promiscuous
sex or illegal drugs. Although in Isabelle Pons's phrase the period was
one when 'nobody slept in their own bed', Wiazemsky insists that she
and Godard shared a 'puritan' sexual ethic. And there are no accounts of
Godard taking drugs: he told Gorin that they had too strong an effect on
him. But rock and roll did interest Godard, and for him it was to
dominate the rest of 1968.

Godard's initial idea was to make a film about Trotsky, with John
Lennon playing the part of the Russian revolutionary. Yet after two
meetings with the Beatles at Apple the project had got nowhere, as
Lennon was extremely suspicious of Godard. The Rolling Stones proved
more amenable. During the summer of 1968 Godard shot a film in

Godard and Mick Jagger during the filming of *One Plus One*, 1968.

London, the basis of which was five days in a recording studio filming the Stones as they laid down the track 'Sympathy for the Devil' for their *Beggars Banquet* album. The film, which Godard entitled *One Plus One*, juxtaposed this material with a series of other elements ranging from Black Power revolutionaries in a car junkyard, to readings from *Mein Kampf* in a pornographic bookstore, to a series of interviews with Eve Democracy (Anne Wiazemsky). While the footage of the Stones is extraordinary, and while the film often intrigues, there is no doubt that the montage has too much work to do. Heterogeneous ideas are yoked together, but the links between Black Power and the Stones' music or Fascism and pornography are asserted rather than explored.

The shoot was marked by constant rows between the producer, Iain Quarrier, and Godard.[27] In Godard's film we never see a full and final version of 'Sympathy for the Devil', which leaves the film intentionally incomplete, inviting the audience to add *One Plus One* for themselves. This was a step too far for the producer, who edited his own version with a complete take of the song and, for good measure, gave the film the title *Sympathy for the Devil*. At the opening night of the London Film Festival, Godard disowned the producer's cut and invited the audience to see his own version of the film being projected outside. As he was leaving the cinema, he punched his producer.[28]

In Godard's letter of 1966 to Malraux, he had announced himself as 'submerged in hate' (G: 238/1:286), and many of Godard's words of this time are extremely violent. Godard had recently tried to acquire the rights to Robert Merle's *Un Animal doué de raison* but Roman Polanski had outbid him. When Godard heard the news of the murder of Polanski's wife, Sharon Tate, he said to Wiazemsky, 'Good – he just stole those rights from me.'[29] Two years later, on a tour of America, he repeatedly expressed his wish that three endangered astronauts aboard Apollo 13 would not return to earth but would die in space.[30] But Wiazemsky also insists on Godard's amazing capacity for the most extreme tenderness and affection and, from a very different perspective, Mike Dibb remembers how pleasant it was to interview Godard when he made a short magazine piece for the BBC on the shooting of *One Plus One*.

One Plus One is a transitional film still vestigially governed by conventional production relations. It was also the last film that Godard was to make with his editor, Agnès Guillemot, whose name had appeared on all of his features since *Le Petit soldat*. Like his other close collaborators, she emphasises the silent nature of Godard's direction: 'We hardly ever talked in the editing room, the real communication went beyond words. I was at the editing machine. He was beside me. It was a question of breathing with the same rhythm. Collusion. Complicity.'[31] With the departure of

Godard and Agnès Guillemot in editing room, 3, rue Washington.

Guillemot, the last collusion with his past productions, the last complicity with the old order was gone. Godard also sees these films as transitional: 'After the events of '68 everything was more or less broken. I had to take a break and I left Paris. I went to Cuba, to Canada, to the States, trying to make pictures. I knew the pictures were not successful but it sort of broke the routine. '68 helped that, to break the routine.'

In a year which had already included a visit to Cuba with Wiazemsky, the Langlois affair, riots in Paris and the Rolling Stones in Britain, the next step was the Jefferson Airplane and America. But before arriving in the United States, Godard made a detour via Canada for one of the weirdest episodes in this year of new beginnings. Godard had met Claude Nedjar at the Cinémathèque in the mid-sixties, and they had spent many hours discussing subjects such as who was the actual maker of any film and where one could isolate the decisive choices. Nedjar was a producer and later produced for the Dziga Vertov group. He had contacts in Canada and had obtained control of a radio station in the far

north of the country for a month. Nedjar had already arranged one trip
to Canada for Godard, and Godard was keen to return. Nedjar now
persuaded Godard and Wiazemsky to join him in a trip to the frozen
north where they broadcast selections from Mao's Little Red Book and
invited the local population to come and make their revolutionary
demands known. But after only three days, when no members of the
town had come forward to seize the microphone and Wiazemsky was
ubable to cope with the temperature of 25 below zero, their attempt at
Canadian revolution was abandoned. On the drive south, Nedjar and
Godard planned a book on the links between Maoism and climate.[32]

Godard had visited the United States on many occasions in the sixties,
and of the many projects mooted, the most important had been *Bonnie
and Clyde*.[33] But when he finally started shooting a film in the United
States in November 1968, it was with the documentary film-makers
Leacock and Pennebaker. Both these Americans had scientific back-
grounds, and their ability to work with and develop the latest technology was a crucial part of their observational style of film-making. They
made their name with films on Kennedy's primary campaign in 1960,
entitled *Primary*, and *Crisis*, on the battle over integrating the University
of Alabama in 1963.

Until that time, Godard's relationship to their work had been extraordinarily ambivalent. In late 1963, he had contributed various entries
to a *Cahiers* dictionary of American film-makers, and his entry on
Leacock was savage. For Godard, an aesthetic which promoted the idea
of capturing reality raw, without reflecting on the position of the
camera, was anathema. 'Cinéma vérité'[34] films did not think aesthetically; they did not consider questions of lens or angle of shot. But
without these questions, without thinking of the camera as a relationship between director and spectator, there was, for Godard, no chance
of grasping reality. He advised *Cahiers* readers to buy a book on
Kennedy's primary campaign rather than watch Leacock's film
(G:202–203/I:250–51). Earlier in the same year he had shot a short
(*Le Grand escroc*) in Morocco in which the lead was a television
reporter called Patricia Leacock (played by Jean Seberg) who was
completely unable to understand the world in which she finds herself.

At the same time, Godard was interested enough in Leacock's films to want to use his cameraman, Albert Maysles, for a sketch on Paris that he shot in 1964 (*Montparnasse-Levallois*). Although the film was a fiction, Godard asked Maysles to shoot 'as a newsreel cameraman, as if he were faced by real events over which he had no control. I tried to organise the happening in the best way possible, but not to direct it like a theatrical production' (G:212/1:259).

In 1967, Pennebaker shot a rock concert in California. The film, *Monterey Pop*, had originally been shot for television, but Pennebaker thought it could be shown in cinemas. His instinct proved accurate and the film became one of the most commercially successful documentaries of all time. As a result, Leacock and Pennebaker found that their company could grow a distribution arm. They acquired *La Chinoise* for the United States and sent Godard on a tour of the country to accompany its opening in March 1968.

This visit to the United States led to him shooting a film funded by Leacock and Pennebaker's company in the autumn of that year. The project was a portrait of America, ranging from Eldridge Cleaver, one of the leaders of the Black Panthers, to a young Wall Street banker, and it was to culminate with the Jefferson Airplane, then the rock icons of the counter culture. Both Leacock and Pennebaker acted as cameramen on the shoot, and Godard was later to complain that he never knew which camera was shooting what.[35] But this dissatisfaction did not manifest itself during the shoot. It was only when he was in the editing room that Godard found himself unable to finish the film, which had the working title *One A.M.* (*One American Movie*). Pennebaker himself went on to make a film from the abandoned footage[36] called *One P.M.* (*One Parallel Movie*). There is a fascinating sequence at the beginning of *One P.M.* where Godard explains to the crew what he wishes to do in the film: every interviewee's words will appear twice, but on the second appearance the words will be spoken by an actor. This determination to 'decompose and recompose',[37] to take both himself and the audience back to a zero where everything is constructed and nothing is available for direct inspection, is a constant of the period. However, in both *One Plus One* and in the abandoned *One A.M.* the image, whichever way it is repeated or juxtaposed, has a force which hampers the investigation. Godard's next step was to go back to *Le Gai savoir* and to use a much more minimal image and a much more dominant soundtrack.

The Dziga Vertov Group

Both *One Plus One* and *One A.M.* were financed for cinema release and, despite their formal experimentation and wearying political content, it is possible to imagine them as theatrical films. It is impossible, however, to imagine the next five films that Godard was to make outside the classroom or the political meeting, and yet they were, with one exception, made for a television audience.

The production story in each case was similar. A European television station commissions the great film-maker to make a documentary on some current aspect of politics and then refuses to show the subsequent film for technical reasons. All the films are in some simple sense unwatchable – the premiss of each is that the image is unable to provide the knowledge that it claims; that the camera is not a neutral recorder of reality but an essential element in the reality that is being represented. They constantly demonstrate the reality of the camera, most importantly through an emphasis on the sound, which does not work merely as the invisible complement to the image but as an autonomous element.

The films have been classified by Jean-Pierre Gorin as UVOs, Unidentified Visual Objects, and this description is not a bad one. It is difficult to think of a parallel in film history. No other mainstream director has chosen to use five commercial budgets to make experiments in sound and image, and no experimental director has made five films which are still recognisably within the genre of 'current affairs' documentary. Godard himself says that they are not 'movies' but admits that they have 'some interesting moves in them'. Considered as conventional documentaries they are unwatchable; considered as experiments in sound and image they contain lessons even more relevant today than when they were made.

The first of the films was made in Britain and its aesthetic programme was announced on the title card where after the word 'British', the word 'Images' is crossed out to be replaced by 'Sounds'. The film is composed of six long sequences: a car production line, a naked woman walking around a house, a right-wing denunciation of immigration, workers discussing capitalism, Essex students trying to produce radical lyrics for a Beatles song, and a bloody hand reaching for a red flag. Sound and image are never held in conventional relations.

As we track interminably down the car production line, we hear sequences from *The Communist Manifesto*, but they are almost drowned out by the wall of sound produced by the production line as it grinds away. The naked woman walks around the house in total silence, while one of the earliest British feminist texts by Sheila Rowbotham is read out on the soundtrack. Unlike the first sequence, there is a moment where the text can be understood as describing the image, but then the woman picks up a phone and starts repeating some of Rowbotham's words in strange counterpoint to the voice-over. The neo-fascist speaker addresses the camera in television's classic form of direct address, but it is impossible to read sound and image together, partly because of the shock of hearing racism being articulated from a position of liberal authority and partly because the images of Britain which punctuate his speech in the classic form of the news report do not 'illustrate' what he is saying. The political conversation of workers from the Cowley car plant at Oxford never marries sound and image; the camera does not focus on who is speaking, only on the listeners. While the sequence with Essex students does contain shots of individuals speaking, the camera records the group searching for the right sounds that will turn a Beatles track into a revolutionary song. But still the film does not provide the beginning or end that would place the students' efforts in a 'comprehensible' context. It is only the final sequence which suggests sound and image in concert, as a bleeding arm inches across the snow to grasp a red flag while a medley of revolutionary songs make up the soundtrack.

British Sounds was produced by Kestrel Productions, a company set up by Tony Garnett and other left-wing film-makers to take advantage of the franchise round which British television had just transformed. Mo Teitelbaum, the wife of one of the partners, Irving Teitelbaum, had come up with the idea that Kestrel should get six European directors to make documentaries on Britain. She knew Godard from May '68, when Gérard Fromanger had introduced them, and Godard saw her in London when he was making *One Plus One*. When she put the idea to him, Godard agreed on the proviso that she would be his assistant, and also that the film would be made in a different way from a conventional production.

The Teitelbaums thus found their small St John's Wood house functioning as production office and as location for two of the sequences, and they found themselves running a hotel for the revolution.[38] Godard had brought with him a young Maoist student called Jean-Henri Roger in order, as he explained to his hosts, that the film could be made 'democratically'. Mo Teitelbaum was amazed at how much Godard seemed to want to impress his revolutionary credentials on this young man. Roger had all but adopted Godard and Wiazemsky since the May events, which had not been to Anne Wiazemsky's taste – she was not overjoyed to be treated as an adoptive mother by someone of her own age, nor to have Roger constantly living in their apartment.[39] But for her all this was part and parcel of Godard's great need to kowtow to the young.

Relations on the production were difficult. The cameraman, Charles Stewart, had a handlebar moustache and wore tweed jackets and the Teitelbaums believe that Godard felt almost obliged to provoke arguments with someone of such bourgeois appearance. In addition, there was the usual problem that Godard was very unwilling to explain what he wanted. In Irving Teitelbaum's words, 'It was all in his head but if you weren't in his head then that was your fault.' Some of the discussions were more amusing. The Teitelbaums were members of a Trotskyite grouping and when Godard met its leading figure, Gerry Healey, Healey informed him that he was 'in the business of crushing business'. 'Oh,' said Godard, 'so you're in business too.' This brought the Maoist/Trotskyite *rapprochement* to a very swift conclusion.

For Mo Teitelbaum the shoot was dominated by 'frustration and despair that 1968 had fizzled out in France, and a desperate desire to re-create and refind it'. When they went up to Essex, then held to be one of the revolutionary universities, Godard was 'horrified at how well-behaved the students were'. Some politically active students were quickly rustled up but Godard's disappointment was so great and so visible that Mo Teitelbaum even wonders if the fact that some of those filmed subsequently set up the Angry Brigade, Britain's only terrorist grouping, can be traced to the emotions of that day.

The film got its fifteen minutes in the media sun because of the long sequence where a naked woman walks through a house. Although there is absolutely no erotic or pornographic context, London Weekend Television, for whom Kestrel were making the programme, refused to show it. Godard's idea for the sequence came when Mo Teitelbaum pointed out to him an article by Rowbotham in the leftist journal *Black Dwarf*. It was one of the first texts of Women's Liberation in England, and Godard immediately decided to include it in his film. Sheila Rowbotham records her meeting with Godard in her memoir of the sixties:

> His idea was to film me with nothing on reciting words of emancipation as I walked up and down a flight of stairs – the supposition being that eventually the voice would override the images of the body. This made me uneasy for two reasons. I was a 36C and considered my breasts too floppy for the sixties fashion. Being photographed lying down with nothing on was fine, but walking downstairs could be embarrassing. Moreover, while I didn't think nudity was a problem in itself, the early women's groups were against what we called 'objectification' . . . Why on earth did the pesky male mind jump so quickly from talk of liberation to nudity, I wondered . . .
>
> Godard came out to Hackney to convince me. He sat on the sanded floor of my bedroom, a slight dark man, his body coiled in persuasive knots. Neither Godard the man nor Godard the mythical creator of *Breathless* were easy to contend with. I perched in discomfort on the end of my bed and announced 'I think if there's a woman with nothing on appearing on the screen no one's going to listen to any words', suggesting perhaps he could film our 'This Exploits Women' stickers on the tube. Godard gave me a baleful look, his lip curled. 'Don't you think I am able to make a cunt boring?', he exclaimed.[40] We were locked in a conflict over a fleeting ethnographic moment.

In the end a compromise was settled. The Electric Cinema had recently
opened in Notting Hill and needed money. A young woman (with small
breasts) from there agreed to walk up and down the stairs and I did the
voice over. When *British Sounds* was shown in France . . . the audience
cheered as I declared 'They tell us what we are . . . One is simply not
conscious of "men" writers, of "men" film-makers. They are just "writers", just "film-makers". The reflected image for women they create will
be taken straight by women themselves. These characters "are" women.'
As for Godard's intention for making a cunt boring, I cannot say except
that a friend in International Socialism told me that his first thought had
been 'crumpet' – until the shot went on and on and on, and he started to
listen.[41]

The film's ending, in which the will to revolution triumphs as a
bleeding arm struggles across snowy ground to reach a red flag, was
shot in the Teitelbaums' garden. When it was suggested that the arm
should be bleeding, Teitelbaum said he would pop down to the Kestrel
offices where there was a bottle of fake blood. Godard told him not to
bother and cut his own arm to provide the colour for the final scene.

Godard shot his next film in Czechoslovakia, almost immediately
after leaving Britain. The commission came from West German television who asked for a documentary on Czechoslovakia six months on
from the Russian invasion of August 1968. Once again Godard was
accompanied by Jean-Henri Roger, but this time they were joined by
Paul Bourron, the cameraman Godard had wanted to shoot *British
Sounds*. The film is called *Pravda*, both the Russian for truth and the
title of the official Soviet newspaper. It is even more explicit than *British
Sounds* in its refusal of standard documentary conventions and in its
scepticism of finding any truth in the image. Its attack on all ideologies
of vision is much more explicit than in Godard's previous film, where
the long sequences do carry a considerable truth content. (Indeed it
would be possible to see *British Sounds* as a more successful remake of
One Plus One.) *Pravda* refuses any such luxuries.

The opening shots of Czechoslovakia are accompanied by a semi-
sarcastic commentary which emphasises the 'revisionism' of Czech

society. The 'direct cinema' of *British Sounds* has been replaced by a conventional television documentary form with a relation between sound and image, even if that sound – 'Many workers would rather wash their cars than fuck their wives' – falls outside television norms. But this opening section is then dismissed as a mere 'travelogue'. The film then begins to develop its rational analysis of the political situation, while at the same time tearing apart the normal relations between sound and image which inform television documentaries.

As the camera moves in on a conversation between Czech workers, instead of the inevitable voice-over translation we are told, 'If you don't know Czech then you'd better learn it fast.' Similarly, a discussion of the peasantry is accompanied by an image of peasants loading hay as the camera zooms in and out. The zoom signifies conventionally that we are getting closer to reality but there is a complete dislocation between the commentary and the zoom so that we become aware of the zoom merely as an alteration of distance to the object being filmed, and the alteration provides us with no real knowledge.

At one level, the problems of the film are the problems of the contorted Maoist line on Czechoslovakia, which was against the Russian invasion but even more against the Czech liberalisation that had preceded it, both being examples of the deadly sin of 'revisionism'. But it is those problems which allow a hilarious deconstruction of the conventions of television documentary, a savage attack on the tenet 'seeing is believing'.

While Godard was editing these films, he spent a considerable amount of time discussing them with another young Maoist, Jean-Pierre Gorin. Gorin did not go on the shoots or to the editing rooms because he was laid up in hospital after a serious motorbike accident. But he had been talking to Godard about the cinema for more than two years. They had first met at a dinner party given by Yvonne Baby, the film critic of *Le Monde*, while Godard was making *La Chinoise*. Gorin had just started work on the book pages of *Le Monde*. He was twenty-three, and by every account both brilliant and charming. Although he had failed to get into the Ecole Normale Supérieure, his time attending the preparatory classes at Louis le Grand meant that he was deeply engaged in the new thinking, be it Althusserian Marxism or literary Structuralism.

The preparatory class of Lycée Louis-le-Grand 1960/61. Jean-Pierre Gorin is seated third from the left in the front row. Robert Linhart is in the second row (standing) third from the right. Raphaël Sorin is to his right, Jacques-Alain Miller to his left.

For Godard he appeared to be someone 'better than me in thinking and philosophy'. At the end of the evening at Baby's, Godard said to Gorin that they should meet and talk again. They did, and on one of those occasions Godard astonished Gorin by showing him not only *Deux ou trois choses que je sais d'elle* but also a trailer that he had cut for Bresson's film *Mouchette*, a trailer that was, says Gorin, both 'pure Godard and pure Bresson'.

Gorin, like many of the young leftists of that time, was absolutely passionate about the cinema. The cinephilia of the post-war years was still a reality; the Latin Quarter housed a huge number of repertory cinemas and in addition there was the new *Cahiers* of Rivette's editorship. For Gorin, *Cahiers* linked high and low culture together in an innovative conjunction – it was the 'new paradigm'. Gorin's association with Godard became much closer when he was fired from *Le Monde* at the beginning of 1968 because he was unable to write up an assignment on Cuba, and asked Godard for a job. At that time Godard was working on a project to make twenty-four hours of films, two of which he planned to do himself, with the rest to be farmed out. Godard suggested that Gorin could make one of the films: 'I'll pay you by the week.' Gorin was terrified by the sums of money involved and lost his nerve. Rather than be paid by the week he went off to write a whole script, but when he returned with it, he found that the project had collapsed in a welter of recriminations.

Despite this their conversations continued, and by the time Godard was to go Italy to shoot his next film, *Vent d'est* (Wind from the East), starring Anne Wiazemsky and Gian Maria Volonté, he was insistent that Gorin should accompany him. The doctors were adamant that Gorin should stay. Gorin's solution was to send Raphaël Sorin in his stead. Sorin was one of Gorin's closest friends; they had attended Louis le Grand together, where the fact that they both had Jewish mothers was a very strong bond, and they had talked of setting up a film-making collective. Sorin's memories of the shoot of *Vent d'est* make it sound like a comic nightmare in which the collective delusions of '68 were distilled into their purest form.

Raphaël Sorin and Jean-Pierre Gorin (left) with unknown friend, 1973.

The money was provided by a radical Italian millionaire and seems to have been of dubious provenance – certainly Sorin remembers ferrying huge quantities of cash from France to Italy. There were many rumours about where the *Vent d'est* money was finally distributed in this radical fashion – perhaps the most charming is that it was used to set up a transsexual bar in Milan. But more disastrously, the film was to be run 'democratically', in other words, by mass meeting (*assemblée générale*). If there was one unifying theme of the student movement of the late sixties, it was the distrust of any representative bodies. Lenin's slogan, 'All power to the Soviets' had been little more than a strategy to destroy the institutions of representative democracy, but in the student movements after 1968, a belief in direct democracy determined that all decisions had to be made in vast unwieldy mass meetings. In the initial moment of 'free speech' in Berkeley or in the days of the barricades in Paris, the mass meeting may have been an exciting and liberating innovation, but it very quickly turned into a repetitive and unmanageable forum open to all kinds of opportunism and to a perpetual 'more leftist than thou' form of moral blackmail.

Anne Wiazemsky, who remained constantly sceptical of the wilder revolutionary rhetoric, had little faith that the film could be made in this fashion. Meeting after meeting opposed the anarchists, led by Cohn-Bendit, the media 'face' of '68, to the Maoists. Whatever their disbelief in institutions of representative democracy, the anarchists did not have a problem with representation as such; they wanted a left-wing Western which would be able to represent the class struggle in the most popular of genres. The Maoists, schooled in Althusser and Brecht, wanted none of this. In words from *British Sounds*, 'If you make a million prints of a Marxist-Leninist film then you get *Gone with the Wind*.' There could be no question of using the standard form of narrative, of allowing sound and image to become comprehensible for an unknown audience. They could only make a militant film which would act as a blackboard for a militant audience – a starting point for thought.

The impasse was resolved when Godard summoned Gorin. He telephoned the Paris hospital and told Gorin, 'Either you come and do the film with me or I stop the film. There's a prepaid ticket waiting for you at Alitalia.' Gorin's doctors tried to stop him from leaving, but he made it to

Rome. In Rome, he stayed in the same hotel as Godard and was thus in a privileged position during the last chaotic weeks of shooting. It was at this point that the relationship between Godard and Gorin entered its most productive and intense phase, which would last until 1973 and would see them produce five movies together: *Vent d'est, Lotte in Italia (Struggles in Italy)*, *Vladimir et Rosa*, *Tout va bien* and *Letter to Jane*.

On *Vent d'est* they were to prevail together in what Wiazemsky calls a 'putsch',[42] after which Wiazemsky's initial scepticism became even more pronounced. All that is left of Cohn-Bendit's Western, which was to have had a mining strike as its narrative focus, are some fragments of narrative on the soundtrack in the opening section. Instead of representing a particular strike in particular images, the film asks what it would be to represent any strike. Perhaps the key sequence in the film is a mass meeting, not of striking miners but of the film crew lying around discussing whether an image of Stalin should be used in the film. The second voice of the soundtrack (and *Vent d'est* makes the sound even more dominant than *British Sounds* or *Pravda*) states that just as mass meetings must be analysed in terms of their specific circumstances – who are they for and who are they against – images must be analysed in similar fashion. The image of Stalin is used by capitalists to represent repression, but from a revolutionary point of view it is a repressive image in so far as it prevents a proper analysis of Stalin as a political phenomenon. *Vent d'est* is the most experimental of the series of Maoist films; it is also the most coherent in its application of Althusserian politics.

The six or seven months which followed, first in Rome and then in Paris, were an intense period of discussion and experimentation. For Gorin, Godard was someone who had acted as a seismograph; he had predicted the earthquake of 1968, but now the earthquake had happened and he had to reinvent himself. As a consequence he was open to ideas and to a young man who was full of ideas. In talking of his collaboration with Gorin, and Gorin's superior grasp of contemporary theory, Godard talks in terms of sound ('I was not aware of what had been recorded'), for it is sound which is at the centre of these experimental films. For Gorin, the focus on sound had many determinants – economic, political and technological.

The late sixties was a time when sound technology was in rapid development, in particular the ability to mix more than one channel into a track. Politically, there was the desire to reverse the general disdain for sound, a disdain reflected in the way that the sound recordist was always paid much less than a director of photography. There was also a genuine pleasure in didacticism. Economically, it was much easier to experiment with the sound than with the image. All this combined to place the emphasis on the editing and the sound rather than the shooting and the image, an emphasis that Godard was to retain when he returned to more conventional film-making. For Godard, the distrust of the image had a more personal component. He associates *Vent d'est* with the end of his relationship with Wiazemsky. The difference in age, and the same jealousy[43] that plagued his marriage with Karina, were significant factors, but the problem was also that both women had come to him as images – they were creations from the screen, not real women. In fact, Godard was not to move out of the flat in the rue Saint-Jacques (into which they had moved three days before the first of the May '68 riots) until the editing of *Jusqu'à la victoire* (Until Victory), but the making of *Vent d'est* seems to be an agreed watershed.

Raphaël Sorin holds up a book on Dziga Vertov on the set of *Vent d'est* in Rome, 1969.

So enthusiastic was Godard about the collaboration with Gorin that they decided to sign *Vent d'est* with the collective name of the Dziga Vertov group. Gorin had first mentioned the idea of a Dziga Vertov collective to Raphaël Sorin in early 1968, when Godard had asked him to write a script for the ill-fated twenty-four-hour project. Dziga Vertov was a Soviet film-maker of the revolutionary period whose work emphasised both editing and the importance of the current class struggle.[44] At one level, the choice of Vertov was a deliberate provocation. Didn't everyone know that Eisenstein was the great revolutionary film-maker? In 1969 the provocation was pronounced; Vertov was much less of a canonical figure then than he is now. But there were both political and aesthetic reasons for choosing Vertov. Politically, it enabled the condemnation of Eisenstein for his decision in 1924 to make a historical film about Potemkin rather than to concentrate on the class struggle. This fitted the Althusserian line that the Soviet revolution had only gone wrong in the mid-twenties. More importantly, the aesthetic distinction was between Eisenstein's notion of montage as primarily an editing process and the practice of Godard and Gorin, for whom the juxtaposition of disparate elements was necessary at every stage of the shooting, from the choosing of the material to be filmed to the filming, as well as in the so-called editing.

The idea of a collective was itself not unusual. The late sixties and early seventies saw attempts all over the West and at every level, from the domestic to the professional, to set up forms of organisation which were not based on the individual. The desire for such forms was broadly political, and the result of a disgust with the individualism of the West; their general catastrophic failure is a crucial element in the current inability to conceive of social relations except in their hyperindividualised form. To analyse either the desire or the failure in general is well beyond the scope of this book. But, for Gorin, the idea of a collective had been in the air for as long as he had been politically conscious, and both Chris Marker's collective Slon and Deleuze and Guattari's collaboration offered contemporary models.

There was also a specific resonance within film – an attack on the very idea of an author. At the same time as *Cahiers* had been promoting the idea of the author, Structuralism had been busy attacking it, and in 1967 both Barthes and Foucault published famous essays intended to displace the notion of the author as an autonomous individual consciousness. Barthes argued that the concept obscured the codes and the languages which a writer used and which he did not create. Foucault stressed that to talk of an unchanging author obscured the practices (legal, commercial, etc.) which defined the changing notion of an author.

However accurate these attacks were on the literary concept of the author inherited from the Romantics, much of the force was lost on *Cahiers*. *Cahiers* were the first to produce a theory of the author from the position of the audience, and as a result they stressed the specific codes of film (indeed it was through the codes that one found an author) and the legal and commercial practices that placed authors in relation to conditions of production and distribution. From another perspective, *Cahiers*'s emphasis on the author did glorify the individual in traditional Romantic terms, and if the Romantics had glorified the author at the expense of the reader, *Cahiers* added insult to injury by neglecting everybody else who worked on a film.

The question of how decisions are taken on a set was one that, according to Claude Nedjar, obsessed Godard from the mid-sixties on, and for Nedjar the excitement of the Dziga Vertov group was that, for once, the decisions were not vested in a single individual.[45] In an interview that he gave to Mike Dibb in 1968 while shooting the Eve Democracy sequence for *One Plus One*, Godard makes clear how much he dislikes the director making all the decisions in a 'fascist' manner. The Utopian ideal is that all fifty members of the crew must participate. For Godard, this Utopian ideal is not abandoned until the early eighties and the experiences of *Passion* and *Prénom Carmen*. What is never abandoned is the idea of collaboration. In retrospect, for Godard, collaboration was the key to the New Wave, and with Gorin he found someone whose desire to collaborate was as great as his own.

The great problem confronting the collaboration, a problem that Gorin characterises in terms of 'anguish', was that of the audience. The enormous weakness of the Dziga Vertov position was that it assumed that a revolutionary politics would provide another audience. One could criticise the audience of *Gone with the Wind* for accepting a false unity of sound and image, but this criticism depended on the possibility of another audience, a militant audience for whom the screen would be a blackboard and the soundtrack merely the beginning of a conversation. In fact, when Godard and Gorin made a film which genuinely tried to address student militants, not only did the commissioning broadcaster refuse to show it – on the by now predictable grounds that it was not political enough – it also failed to find any political audience whatsoever. The title *Lotte in Italia* may summon up images of students and workers clashing with police but, for the Dziga Vertov group, the struggle is always the struggle between sound and image. More than thirty years later, it still amuses Gorin that the film was shot almost entirely in Paris, because the whole thrust of its analysis is that it is impossible to 'see' a social situation. If the young Italian student who is the protagonist of the film is to become a revolutionary, it is through repetitively working through a very small number of images until by reflecting on them she understands how her subjectivity is constituted by the class struggle.[46]

The film is easily the most politically and theoretically coherent work of the Dziga Vertov group, at least in part because it is almost entirely based on Althusser's own reaction to May '68 in his essay 'Ideology and Ideological State Apparatuses'.[47] Althusser came with his wife to see the film in the editing room at the rue de Rennes and, according to Gorin, wept.

However moved Althusser was, he hardly constituted a large audience. The only place that such an audience could be found was on American campuses. When Godard had toured with *La Chinoise* in 1968, his trip had included a stop at the Pacific Film Archive, where the curator Tom Luddy had organised a full retrospective. Luddy had been a student at Berkeley, itself the epicentre of the anti-war movement, and was associated with the Maoist Progressive Labour Party. He accompanied Godard to Los Angeles, where King Vidor, Jean Renoir and Fritz Lang were present at a screening of *La Chinoise*, and they also went to a Free Huey Newton rally at Oakland jail.[48]

Luddy became Godard's American connection, and it was he who organised the first of a series of Dziga Vertov tours in the spring of 1970. There was a financial rationale to this. The television commissions were not lucrative, and the $1,000-a-venue speaking fee that Luddy arranged was a significant addition to Dziga Vertov funds. For Gorin, at least, it satisfied a desperate need for an audience. As one reads the accounts of Godard and Gorin's visits in the underground press of the day it can hardly be said that the audience was all that appreciative but an audience it was and one which certainly claimed a shared radicalism.

America provided a partial answer to the problem of the audience, but a much more satisfactory solution, as the revolutionary tide ebbed in both the United States and France, was to film a real revolution. The 1967 Arab/Israeli war had violently radicalised the Palestinians. After two decades of waiting for the Arab states to solve their problems, the Palestinians found themselves without the Left Bank of the Jordan, which had been occupied by the Israelis. A whole range of revolutionary factions sprang up in Jordan and began to create a state within a state.

Godard and Gorin agreed to a request from the Arab League to make a film about the Palestinian situation, and in early 1970 they spent considerable time in Jordan, with Godard often flying back to France to see Wiazemsky. For the Dziga Vertov group, there could be no question of just 'finding images', the mistake of *British Sounds* and *Pravda*; the crucial effort was to 'build' them, to practise montage before the shooting. But these efforts were hampered by the fact that neither Godard nor Gorin spoke Arabic. They found themselves time and time again listening to a long and complicated speech, only for

Godard and Jean-Pierre Gorin in Palestine for the shooting of *Jusqu'à la victoire*, 1970.

the interpreter to translate it in five words: 'We will struggle until victory.'

Eventually, *Jusqu'à la victoire* became the title of the film, but before they could complete the editing, the money from the Arab League ran out and they had to accept a commission from German television to make a film on the Chicago conspiracy trial, when, following the riots at the Democratic Convention of 1968, an array of radicals were put on trial on trumped-up charges. In interviews on American campuses at that time, Godard and Gorin make clear that they had little interest in *Vladimir et Rosa*, as they entitled it, except as a way of paying for the Palestinian film, and this attitude comes across in what is clearly the least interesting of the Dziga Vertov experiments.

But if *Vladimir et Rosa* was a hastily assembled mess, a much worse fate awaited *Jusqu'à la victoire*. As Godard and Gorin filmed and edited, the political situation grew more and more volatile, with many Palestinian voices calling for a revolutionary overthrow of King Hussein and the seizing of the Jordanian state as a prelude to a generalised war on Israel. Indeed, so volatile was the situation that Godard asked Claude Nedjar, who was now acting as producer for all the Dziga Vertov films, to provide an armoured door to the editing room.[49] By this time Godard had moved out of the flat in the rue Saint-Jacques and was sleeping in the editing room. This very immediate conjunction of life and work, like many other elements of the Dziga Vertov period, was to bear fruit later. In retrospect Godard saw it as a kind of imitation of his father's clinic.[50] Events in Jordan moved very quickly. In the autumn Hussein launched a pre-emptive strike against the Palestinian revolution, and many Palestinians died in a month which still bears the name Black September. The victory of the revolution had turned into the bitterest of defeats.

By now much of the initial enthusiasm of *Vent d'est* had worn off. There was a desire on both Godard and Gorin's part to add to the group, and efforts were made with Gérard Martin and Nathalie Biard, Gorin's former lover, to increase the active participation of the group, but these were unsuccessful.[51] Ultimately, in a state of some disillusionment, they decided to make a mainstream film.

One of the major emphases of the Dziga Vertov group was the

primacy of production, but their films had been unseen; now they would make a film which would be distributed. In the early part of 1971, together with the help of the charismatic producer Jean-Pierre Rassam, they put together a film, *Tout va bien*, financed by Gaumont, which would consider the class struggle in France four years on from 1968. Yves Montand, one of the great stars of French cinema, was cast together with Jane Fonda, then at the highest point of her career.[52] Both were known left-wing activists. Such was the power of Godard's name and so attractive the prospect of making a mainstream political film with him that they both agreed to work for no fee upfront and a share of the profits.

There was also an American end to the deal, and on 9 June 1971, Godard and Gorin were due to fly to New York to sign contracts with Frank Yablans of Paramount. They met at the rue de Rennes, where Gorin discovered that he'd left his passport at home. They agreed to meet at the airport, but first Godard wanted to go to a bookstore and buy *Meti* – a text of Brecht's. Christine Aya, the editor who was working with them at the time, offered to give Godard a ride on her motorbike. 'Don't do that,' joked Gorin, 'you'll have an accident.' At the bottom of the rue de Rennes a turning bus trapped both the bike and Godard under its front wheel. Godard's pelvis was broken, his skull fractured, and his body lacerated. On the first night in the hospital Gorin was told that he was certain to die. It took six days for him to recover consciousness, and Godard was to be in and out of hospital for more than two years. The editor was also badly injured. For Godard it was, 'the logical end of '68'.

But there was still unfinished business. Most important for Gorin was the question of Godard's medical insurance. Rassam had telephoned him to say that Jane Fonda was backing out: 'She has evolved and doesn't want to work with men.' If she pulled out the film would collapse, and Godard would not be covered. Gorin flew to see her and persuaded her to stay in the film. By December, although still under treatment and with further stays in hospital ahead of him, Godard was ready to start shooting. The plot of *Tout va bien* is simple: a couple – he is a film director, she a radio reporter – go to visit a factory as part of her assignment to file a report on the current state of France. While there, they become involved in a factory occupation and are imprisoned with the boss in his own office. Such 'sequestrations' were a favourite gauchiste tactic after 1968. The effect of the visit induces the couple to reflect on their own lives historically and the film ends by generalising their discovery for the whole of France.

The structure of the film is in some ways similar to *Vent d'est* and *Lotte in Italia*, but the content is fiction, however distanced. The presiding genius of the film is not Althusser, but Brecht. We are aware of the camera, always fixed or deliberately travelling, with no pans or zooms; we are aware of the staging – the factory looks like a set – and we are aware of the actors, of both Montand and Fonda as characters, but characters not very far from their public personae. The film constantly demonstrates the conditions of its own production, not least in the opening credit scene where the cost of each element is written out from a steadily diminishing cheque book. The Dziga Vertov determination to edit before shooting meant that the workers in the factory were young unemployed actors. Godard and Gorin felt that if they used workers, they would be so overawed by stars that the film would not portray any of the proletarian/bourgeois friction and resentment that was to animate the central scene. Put unknown actors with stars, though, and the camera would have something to record.

Thirty years on the film wears well. The Brechtian devices actually succeed – providing both distance and engagement – and the film provides a very accurate picture of the dissatisfactions of work, both in factory production and in the audiovisual media. The problem, however, remains the politics. Where Maoist class struggle and Althusserian ideology have failed, the film offers a final sequence in which gauchistes ransack a supermarket (another favourite contemporary tactic). In many ways, the film functions as an elegy for a historical moment, but it lacks the courage of its own insights which would involve a much more radical critique of gauchiste politics.

In between the editing of the film and its release, a young Maoist militant, Pierre Overney, was shot dead outside a Renault factory. His funeral became the last great demonstration of May. Godard told Gorin that this was the audience for their movie, if only they could find a way

Godard looks through the latest issue of
the Maoist journal *La Cause du peuple*
at the printer's before it goes on sale,
Paris, November 1970.

to reach them. But Althusser remarked, perhaps with more prescience, that the mourners were
there 'to bury gauchisme'.[53] *Tout
va bien* never managed to decide
whether it was there to bury or to
praise, and its ending glorifies the
violence which was one of the
most unappealing features of
gauchisme. Indeed, as late as
1980 Godard was to say, 'Even
now the terrorists are still for me
the inheritors.'[54]

The shoot of *Tout va bien*
was an unhappy one, and on
its release it was a critical and
commercial disaster. As if to
complete a woeful circle, Godard
and Gorin's next film, *Letter to
Jane*, was a vicious attack on
their recent star. The film is
composed of a single still – a photograph of Jane Fonda in North
Vietnam. The commentary, the 'Letter to Jane', analyses the photograph
in terms of the contemporary media's representation of the world. It also
analyses the photograph in terms of film history – the way in which
Fonda's expression, which resembles that of her own father Henry, is
the acting equivalent of the New Deal: benign liberal concern.

For Gorin, the film is still one of the few examples of a study of the
history of film-acting, and he defends the brilliance of the analysis. But
at the time it was perceived as a vicious attack by two men on a woman
who was given no chance to respond. Thirty years on, it seems to
confirm what Anne Wiazemsky remembers as the 'misogyny' of the
Dziga Vertov group. Godard talked directly about the group's relation
to women in an American interview:

The basis for *Struggles in Italy* was our attempt to organise our personal lives with our wives. We had problems as individuals, but these related to the general problem. So we deliberately chose a subject which was strongly related to our ideology, because even when you speak to a woman you are in love with, or the woman speaks to you, this is ideology. We tried, and it was a complete failure, because we finished the movie alone, and our wives thought of it, at that time, as only our work – you know, 'this is your job. I have my job too, and this is your job.' We tried to make the movie in order to raise the problem – not to solve it, but just to raise it – to say, 'This is our job from a technical point of view, yeah, but from a more general point of view it's our life.' Trying to work with our wives on movies, when they are not especially interested in movies, was correct at that moment.[55]

The stills photographer on *Tout va bien* was a young Swiss woman, Anne-Marie Miéville (credited under her married name of Anne-Marie Michel), whom Godard had first met in 1970. Their relationship had intensified during his period in and out of hospital after the motorcycle accident, and Godard was now keen to find ways in which to achieve the idea of a real studio, one which would include both Miéville and Gorin. The revolution was over, and the discussions were about what kind of company structure was needed to realise their film-making ambitions. Gorin confesses that these business discussions bored him, but they ended with the setting up of a company, Tout Va Assez Bien (Everything is just about OK), of which he was the legal representative.

The company had two initial projects, a film by him with the title *Ailleurs immédiat* (Elsewhere Immediately), and one by Godard entitled *Moi, Je* (I, Myself). The final injunction of *Tout va bien* was 'to think oneself historically', and both films were attempts to do this, but with questions of subjectivity and sexuality now woven deeply into questions of politics and history. Gorin's title came from Georges Bataille, the great theorist of the erotic who had died at the beginning of the sixties, but whose thought had been crucial for Foucault, for Derrida, for Barthes and for the magazine *Tel Quel*. *Ailleurs immédiat* was the first TVAB film to go into production.

Film sets are notorious for their sexual chaos. *Ailleurs immédiat*, with
eroticism as its topic and with Gorin playing the lead as well as directing,
was always likely to set chaotic records. The lead actress, who had been
having an affair with Gorin, switched her affections to another woman
in the cast, and when both women decided that the director was
behaving in a sexist manner, the shoot exploded.[56] Gorin fled to
California, where Tom Luddy was to look after him and find him a
job, and the Dziga Vertov group was history.

It's difficult to find a Maoist in the twenty-first century. Once the
Great Helmsman was dead, the dreadful realities of the Great Leap
Forward and the Cultural Revolution slowly began to emerge. When
China and Vietnam went to war at the end of the seventies, Marxist-
Leninism became a historical term. To complete the picture, Mao's
doctor published a memoir[57] that made clear the truth of Lord Acton's
dictum, 'power tends to corrupt, and absolute power corrupts absolutely'. But if one thinks of Mao's great slogan that one must count on
one's own forces, if one thinks of the Maoist emphasis on refusing the
divorce between intellectual and manual work, or on the need to find a
different balance between the country and the city, one might argue that

Jean-Paul Sartre and Godard at a press conference in Paris, February 1971.

Godard's life since 1968 shows that however few of Mao's texts he read, he read them with great attention. And there was perhaps an even more enduring legacy. French Maoism had defined itself as a 'New Resistance', arguing that the country was still occupied by capital. This is an identification which Godard has never relinquished. The idea that cinema has been occupied, an occupation which he must resist, is one of the enduring themes of Godard's interviews for the last three decades.

As for the Dziga Vertov films, they were made for an audience that didn't exist at the time, and it is hard to imagine them finding a real one now. Their politics seem grotesque, if not offensive, but it is difficult to think of a more comprehensive critique of the audiovisual world of information, a world whose dominance is far greater now than when they were made. Godard has developed rather than abandoned their theses. The break that Godard made in 1968 has never been renounced; it has been enlarged and intensified. Their films do not generate much pleasure, but anyone wishing to make a documentary is either consciously or unconsciously going to use techniques, strategies and procedures which are analysed with wit and brilliance in the Dziga Vertov work. The collaboration with Gorin is acknowledged by both as a real collaboration. For Godard, Gorin kept him going when he was stuck, 'it was a way of still being in the business'. Gorin says of Godard, 'I gave him hope when he didn't have any.'

As for May '68 itself, who knows what future generations may find in this extraordinary moment – into what millenarian lineages it may yet be woven, into what banal litany of tragic idiocy it may yet disappear? Godard has said that in reality the New Wave was the Last Wave, and '68 certainly seems to bear more relation to an insurrectionary past (there had been barricades in Paris almost every decade from 1789 on) than to the media future. For Raphaël Sorin, now head of the publishers Fayard, his generation has failed to deliver – in literature, in politics, or in philosophy. Certainly, if one thinks back to the moment at the Ecole Normale Supérieure in the mid-sixties, when Robert Linhart was producing the *Cahiers Marxistes-Léninistes* and Jacques-Alain Miller was producing *Cahiers pour l'analyse* (both of whom were classmates of

Gorin and Sorin at Louis le Grand), it would have been difficult to
believe that Linhart's place in the history books would be a footnote to
May,[58] and Miller's a footnote in the history of psychoanalysis.[59]
Possibly even more surprising, and more difficult to explain, would
be the way in which the thinkers of that moment (particularly Foucault
and Derrida) became a paralysing academic orthodoxy in the United
States.

Perhaps the real legacy of May '68 is a set of questions. At its most
important level the student movement was anti-authoritarian – a refusal
to be policed sexually or aesthetically. In many ways it was very
successful, but that was because it was going with the grain of capitalism
and not against it. And May dismally failed to produce alternative
structures. The disastrous failure of thousands of collectives all over the
Western world bears eloquent witness to the inability to find new forms
of authority. If all authority had been removed, how did one regulate
disagreements when revolutionary correctness made disagreement impossible?

Godard and Gorin's original business arrangement stipulated that the
money would be split 50/50 – after (no surprise here) deductions to pay
off Godard's back taxes. When Gorin fled, he left the company behind
him. Much later, Godard rang him in Los Angeles and told him that he
really needed to come back to Paris to deal with it. For Gorin, the
questions of rent and wages did not amount to much and should have
been dealt with by Godard; Godard says, 'there was a need to wash up,
to empty the ashtrays which Gorin – as all the militants I knew – didn't
want to do'.

In the end, Tout Va Assez Bien was wound up as 'fraudulently
bankrupt', to use the French legal term, and Gorin was banned from
commercial activity for three years. Sometime after this Gorin, now
teaching in California, was told that *Tout va bien* had played on French
television. He rang Godard to ask for his share of the money. The row
was so bitter that Gorin put down the phone.

The Arrière-Boutique:
Anne-Marie Miéville and Rolle

On 1 December 1973, Anne-Marie Miéville became the legal representative of a company with the name of Sonimage. The name was new but
the company, previously called Anouchka, had been in existence since
November 1963. The company's main activity had been producing
Godard's films, and from 1964 onwards its name often appears in the
producer credits. Although Anouchka produced other directors' films,
notably those of Bitsch and Eustache, its main function was to secure a
major stake in the commercial success of Godard's own films.

In its first phase of activity, it was managed by Phillippe Dussart, who
looked after the finances of almost all of Godard's films. At this point
the company functioned as an adjunct to Godard's existing activities. In
June 1968, the date of Godard's definitive break with commercial
cinema, Dussart was replaced by Anne Wiazemsky. But in the period
from 1968 to 1973, Anouchka films (although a co-producer of *Lotte in
Italia* and *Tout va bien*) did not assume the major producing function
for Godard's films; that role fell to Claude Nedjar and Jean-Pierre
Rassam. The company's change of name and Wiazemsky's replacement
by Miéville in December 1973 marked a new determination to control
every aspect of production. It is the most public sign of the beginning of
Godard's longest lasting and most productive relationship.

Anne-Marie Miéville was born on 11 November 1945 in Lausanne, and
when she assumed control of Sonimage she was living in Paris at 76,
Boulevard Saint-Michel. In an interview to accompany a 2002/2003
North American tour of her films, she talks of her family background
as 'petit-bourgeois' and describes a home in which feelings were not easily
expressed. Music was the great exception to this general rule and music

Anne-Marie Miéville and Godard in *Après la réconciliation*, 2000.

played an extremely important role in Miéville's formation. When she left Lausanne and moved to Paris as a young woman, she even enjoyed a brief career as a singer. Godard met her in 1970, when she had become a photographer and had a young daughter. Their close relationship was intensified in the aftermath of his crash when, according to Gorin and others, he felt alone and abandoned; Miéville was a constant support. She was the stills photographer on *Tout va bien* and by the end of that film, if not earlier, their desire to work together had become a determination.

The partnership has been remarkable both in its duration and in its productivity. It has not precluded Godard's close collaborations with others (Romain Goupil on *Sauve qui peut*, for example, or Peter Sellars on *King Lear*), nor other romantic attachments (most notably with Myriem Roussel), but for more than thirty years this most solitary of men has formed a union based on the most intimate of alliances. In the very early stages of this biography, Miéville told me that Godard had written to her every day since she had first met him. To speculate about their relationship without that correspondence would be futile, but what I can say with certainty is that my own brief contact with them both and everything that I have learnt in writing this book confirms that this relationship has been absolutely central to Godard's existence for the past thirty years.

In their endless discussions about the cinema and culture when they were working together, Godard told Gorin that he had always thought of himself as an essayist and that the figure he most identified with, the person he most wanted to emulate, was Montaigne. Michel de Montaigne is one of the great figures of the European Renaissance, a man who withdraws from his contemporary world of religious conflict (in which he played a significant role as Mayor of Bordeaux and mediator between the French Crown and Henri de Navarre) to produce a new form, the essay, in which general topics – friendship, the New World, intolerance – are treated from a personal perspective. In Montaigne's famous introduction to the essays, he says, 'I myself am the subject of my book', and his resolve to test everything against his own personal experience, to insist that any argument must come back to the ground of his own being, makes clear why Godard feels so close to him. 'To show and to show myself showing', one of Godard's most succinct formulations of his fundamental aesthetic, could almost be Montaigne's.

There is, however, a big difference. Montaigne, in order to carry out his own intellectual project, constructed at the centre of his castle a huge library – a physical refuge from the world, a place to which he could withdraw and think, a place which he named his 'arrière-boutique', his back room. But this arrière-boutique was explicitly masculine. It was a place from which his wife and daughter were excluded – 'ni femme ni fille.'[1] Over the past twenty-five years, Godard has constructed his own arrière boutique in the small Swiss village of Rolle, but he has constructed it with a woman, and it is unthinkable without her. It is Miéville who rescued him from the political and aesthetic dead-end in which he found himself in the early seventies. The strategic use of their company, and its investment in its own equipment, was crucial to that rescue. When in 1987 Godard took Don Boyd, the producer, to a celebratory lunch in Rolle after the completion of his

Anne-Marie Miéville in *Après la réconciliation*, 2000.

contribution to the multi-authored film *Aria* he told Boyd that he was the only film-maker in the world who could shoot on any day of the year, and he said that he owed this incredible creative freedom to Miéville.

Here and Elsewhere

One of the remarkable features of Godard's career is that he never ever stops making films. Ever since 1954, when he made his first short, he has made one if not more films in almost every year. The only break in this incredible productivity comes between 1972 and 1974. There are practical reasons for this. The long recuperation and frequent hospitalisations after his accident, the move from Paris to Grenoble and the setting up of new business structures all had a role to play. Perhaps more pertinent, however, was the voyage back to zero he embarked on with

Miéville, a voyage much more radical than any he had hitherto undertaken.

The original Bazinian premiss had been that cinema was the art of the real, that the technology of the camera provided a new set of aesthetic possibilities, and that the filmic image offered a new aesthetic dispensation for the West. Godard had always stressed the crucial role of subjectivity in this new objective art – the positioning of the camera was crucial. But as the image became more and more stereotyped, as it became the crucial cement of an ever more rapacious and unjust world, Godard abandoned hope in it, opting for an imaginary politics which would link him to suffering humanity, and for an elaborated soundtrack which would provide the correct way of reading the image. There undoubtedly was a moment, however brief, when this hope was linked to a widespread generational revolt in France, but this revolt, tied to failed models of revolution, evaporated.

The Maoism that Godard espoused had always stressed the global nature of revolution, and that went hand in hand with a number of analyses which saw the Third World, increasingly the site of the most unacceptable exploitation by capital, as the logical base of the revolution that would transform the world. For Godard the cinephile, this was a moment in which it looked as though Third World film-makers – Rocha in Brazil (*Terra em Transe*) and Solanas in Argentina (*The Hour of the Furnaces*) would be the most obvious names – were destined to create the new cinemas that the press book for *La Chinoise* had attempted to summon into being. *Jusqu'à la victoire* was not to be just another Dziga Vertov film – it would be the film which would justify the other experiments by providing an image of the Palestinian and Arab world never seen before. The importance of its collapse should not be underestimated. When Chris Marker dropped into the Dziga Vertov editing room in September 1970, Godard told him, 'The film is in pieces, just like Amman.' It was Miéville who was to put the pieces together again, and this process took her a very long time. At the end, Godard discovered a new and hesitant faith in the image, though this faith would involve a very much more profound recognition of death than had been available to the creator of Michel Poiccard.

Ici et ailleurs, the film Miéville and Godard made from the abandoned fragments of *Jusqu'à la victoire*, takes the form of a conversation – a man and woman discuss the images that unwind before us. It is this conversation which provides the new balance between sound and image. If the Dziga Vertov group had used conversations, they were didactic; one voice was given a necessary prominence and the sound was harsh and strident. In *Ici et ailleurs*, the voices are soft. Rather than dictating to us what the images mean, they attempt to discover what meaning they might have. The mistake of the earlier film was that the sound was too loud – every image was reduced to a set of political slogans. The film-makers may have gone to the Middle East, but the soundtrack that they brought with them meant that they were unable to see their own images. The structure of the Dziga Vertov film, with its Maoist emphasis on the people and the armed struggle, had failed to engage the reality of what had been shot. Many of those they photographed would die in the bloody battles of Black September. This simple fact of death – a death now evident in the images but rendered invisible by the original soundtrack – is what redeems the images even as it renders the original film null and void. As the voice-over of the final film emphasises, 'The actors in this film were filmed in danger of death.'

This dominance of sound, which ruined the initial project, is not an individual foible – it is the very foundation of Western politics. In one of the crucial sequences of the film, a young Palestinian girl declaims a poem and, as Miéville points out, the gestures and intonations she is using take us right back to the French Revolution and the politicians of the Convention. If we can declare the young girl innocent, the form of political theatre that she is imitating is less so. For it is a form which insists on one voice dominating another, and it is that dominance of sound – running from domestic rows to Hitler's speeches – which becomes the key to understanding why everywhere things 'are going badly'.

The analysis is radical, and the new video imagery which can mix pictures is used to mix Hitler into the conventional litany of the Russian Revolution and the Popular Front. Hitler led a popular revolution, and that revolution is not outside the history that we must figure out. The film is constantly trying to add together the great dates of canonical leftist history: 1789 – the French Revolution; 1917 – the Russian Revolution; 1936 – the Popular Front; 1968. But as an adding machine tries to compute these dates, the film makes increasingly clear that they avoid too much of our history. Indeed, the addition is even more complex, for the State of Israel comes out of this European history. But the film does not offer a new political analysis; the attempts to juxtapose political images are hesitant and tentative. What is certain is that Hitler and the concentration camps must be at the centre of any political understanding; they should not be understood as exceptions, but rather as providing the very model of the political processes which confront us.

In order to understand them, however, we must understand the domestic space – for example the French family gathered around the television – which the initial film ignored. To the fragments of the revolutionary film of 'elsewhere', Miéville and Godard add footage of 'here', of contemporary France – a man, woman and children in the most mundane of contemporary housing. The man is a militant 'poor revolutionary fool, a millionaire in images of revolution', and the task is to find a way out of the stereotyped flow of images which determine that all we see in the lens of the camera is the image that we bring to the viewfinder, exactly the problem of the original Dziga Vertov project. In this analysis the political militant is no different from any other consumer enslaved to a flow of images which he has neither created nor edited.

Ici et ailleurs is a classic feminist work; it argues that any politics must start from the domestic space of the family. The argument, however, is not based on a simple moralism but on an analysis which links our global political relationships to our familial conflicts. The key mediating term is the image. The reason we cannot understand the 'elsewhere' of Palestine is because we do not understand the 'here' of France. But to understand our 'here' in France, we must understand how others always constitute our 'elsewhere'. And to understand this we must understand what it is to put images together, we must find our place in the chain of images; only then may we find an answer to the question of how we might make our own image.

'Here' – a family watches television,   'Elsewhere' – a young Palestinian prepares
from *Ici et ailleurs*, 1976.   for death, from *Ici et ailleurs*, 1976.

Ici et ailleurs is also a programmatic piece; its project provides a framework for understanding both Godard and Miéville's work of the next three decades. If its dominant politics is feminist, the theory which informs it is psychoanalytic. Psychoanalysis came late and hesitantly to France (it was, after all, both a German as well as a Jewish science). In the post-war years, however, Jacques Lacan began to elaborate a radical form of psychoanalysis hostile to any kind of therapeutic normativity. It was inspired by the heretical surrealism of Georges Bataille (Lacan married Bataille's first wife) and, like Bataille, fundamentally influenced by Kojève's reading of Hegel, in which self and other are functions of the same intersubjective dialectic.[2]

Lacan is at his most brilliant as he maps this Hegelian dialectic on to the psychoanalytic world of partial objects. The breast and the other who responds to the cry of hunger surge out of the undifferentiated world of sensation, as the faeces separates itself from our body under the command of another. In both cases it is language which provides the key term within which both object and other are constituted. In making language central to our psychic constitution, Lacan was following Lévi-Strauss's anthropology and the notion that there was a 'symbolic' field which constituted the world of social meaning as opposed to the 'imaginary', which was the realm of personal subjectivity. But whereas for Lévi-Strauss access to this symbolic field is possible in any exchange, for Lacan, firm Freudian that he is, it is sexuality and, specifically, the incest taboo which constitute the symbolic field of the human. It is the

Oedipal drama which moves the infant from the imaginary dyadic world of I–Thou to the symbolic world in which it is figured by a 'he' or a 'she'.

Lacan is never cited by name in Godard's work, and in *Week-end* Godard demonstrates a hostility to psychoanalysis which seems to have reflected his views at the time.[3] But after the mid-seventies, his references to psychoanalysis become much more frequent and less hostile. This must in large part be due to Miéville's experience of psychoanalysis, but it is worth noting that a considerable number of Maoist militants used Lacanian analysis as their route back into a social order that they had uncompromisingly rejected. Indeed, *Moi, Je*, the title of the abandoned film of 1973, is a psychoanalytic title. For a Lacanian analyst, the aim of the psychoanalytic cure is to enable the patient to speak for him or herself (to say 'Moi, Je') instead of constantly speaking from someone else's viewpoint (I, as my father wants me; I, as my mother wants me, etc.).

The interest in psychoanalysis is particularly intense in the early eighties when there was a project to film the case history of Dora.[4] Godard's lack of direct interest in Lacan may derive from Lacan's conception of the image, which is as the false and delusive ground of the imaginary unity of the self. For Godard, the image is Bazinian, an image which is not rendered into a unity by a consciousness. It is this image that from *Ici et ailleurs* on Godard will use for his own analysis.[5]

Grenoble

If psychoanalysis is the theory which informs Miéville and Godard's work, it does not primarily inform it as theory. The dominance of sound had also been a dominance of theory, and the return to the image was above all a return to practice. Godard had already developed his technical grasp of editing with what he'd learnt from Christine Aya when she was working with him in the Dziga Vertov group. Now both he and Miéville took lessons from Willy Lubtchansky in their offices at Barbès Rochechouart, while working on *Ici et ailleurs*. Lubtchansky had been Kurant's assistant on *Masculin Féminin* and had shot *Un Film comme les autres* (A Film Like Any Other). He was to work on several Godard projects over the next two decades, including *Nouvelle Vague*. There was also a new technology, video, which was beginning to offer fresh possibilities for the image. As early as *La Chinoise* Godard had tried to use video for the self-criticism sequences, but by the early seventies video had made enormous technical strides which genuinely enabled new work on the image, and above all new forms of montage.

At this time, Miéville and Godard were still looking for a more collective project, and they decided to set up an atelier in Grenoble together with an ex-Maoist militant, Gérard Martin, and an expert in video technology, Gérard Teissèdre. The move to Grenoble was, in the first instance, a move away from Paris, a centre which was felt too dominating, too metropolitan, too central. It was necessary to move to the margins to try and find a new way of producing images, which would differ from the conventional industry which Godard had definitively abandoned and the militant cinema which had proved so blind.

Grenoble had several advantages; it had the workshops of Beauviala, the most innovative producer of cameras in the world (with whom Godard would collaborate on the Aaton, a 35 mm camera that would be as portable and light as an 8 mm); it also had a mayor who was interested in bringing cultural industries to the town; but perhaps above it all, it had the Alps. Certainly a return to the Alps was a very strong motive for Gérard Martin. He had grown up in the more remote reaches of the French Alps and had come to Paris in 1961 with the idea that he was going to be a painter. If Gorin represented the high intellectual end of Maoism, Martin was the practical militant. Martin's ambition to be a painter did not last long. He soon became involved, almost despite himself, in both the student and the film world. He cordially disliked the student environment, but his involvement in it was a necessity if he was to avoid military service. The French academic world is full of 'competitions', and Martin became a competition expert, claiming to have sat fifty-four different competitions and been successful in fourteen, in subjects as diverse as fine arts, law and philosophy. Rather than follow established courses, he prepared for these exams in a self-help group of fellow marginals. One of his successes was passing the entrance exam to the state film school, IDHEC (Institut des hautes études cinématographiques), in 1966, but constitutionally opposed both to authority and to theory, he did not stay there long. His real entry into film had come earlier by way of bit parts. With long hair and a Fu Manchu moustache, he was spotted by a producer playing pinball in Montparnasse and then found himself cast in a variety of minor criminal roles. But what interested him in the film-making process was the technical aspect, and he soon began to train himself in all aspects of film-making.

His interest in the practice of film-making went hand in hand with an ever growing political militancy. For a time, Martin hung out with the Situationists. The Situationists remain perhaps the most fertile source of ideas from the Parisian sixties. Their leader and principal theorist was Guy Debord. Debord's life shadows Godard's – when the young Godard was finding a classical cure for modernism in the cinema, the young Debord, through a group called the Lettrists, was pushing an ultra-modernist line which would refuse all art as bourgeois in favour of events that would scandalise and disrupt the bourgeois order. In the sixties Debord developed one of the most powerful restatements of Marxism, in which the image replaced the commodity as the central relationship of capitalism. But Situationism and Debord were above all devoted to sectarian disputes.

Martin, in the great tradition of Debord's movement,[6] was soon excluded for his dislike of their hyper-intellectualism. His commitment to practice and his belief that it was the working class who would transform the social order soon had him working with the Maoists. He was also one of the first people to work in video. A friend came back from Japan with one of the first black-and-white video cameras, and they used it to make militant anti-Vietnam-war videos. Although he had met Godard on a visit to the set of *Deux ou trois choses que je sais d'elle*, their friendship began at the end of May 1968. The film industry responded to the May events by calling an Estates General of Cinema, in which a new basis for a socially responsible industry would be hammered out. Both Godard and Martin would arrive up to an hour

early for the meetings, and it was in the café beforehand that Godard
and Martin recognised their joint interest in technology and practice,
and an aversion to the hot air of the Estates General. Martin would often
take Godard to shoots at occupied factories, where Godard functioned
as Jean-Luc the sound man.

Although Godard and Martin had various conversations about
possible collaborations during the Dziga Vertov period (indeed Martin
participated in some of the films), it was only with the end of the dream
of proletarian revolution that they settled on a joint venture. If there was
a disappointment in the failure of the working class to live up to
revolutionary aspirations, there remained an extraordinarily critical
vision of society, and a determination to struggle against the regime
of 'the generalised lie' which made up the media. Godard's slogan at this
time was 'instead of making films, we'll make cinema' – the idea was to
intervene in the circulation of the image without making recognisable
forms, for the recognisable forms were now all unusable.

The possibility of realising this programme came with the temporary
ascendancy of Jean-Pierre Rassam at Gaumont. Rassam was the most
charismatic of producers, a man of prodigious charm and appetite who
would end up dead from an overdose in 1985, but who for a brief
moment in the early seventies was producing Godard and Bresson as
well as hits like Marco Ferreri's *La Grande bouffe*. There is an
unforgettable picture of Rassam, under the name of Mazar, in Jean-
Jacques Schuhl's novel *Ingrid Caven*. The novel reflects on Mazar's fate
after he has been found dead:

> So Mazar had lost. He'd nearly won, he'd come within an inch, but he lost
> finally confronted by Seydoux, the pure hardline unbudgeable protestant
> capital. It was Mazar who had introduced him into the scam and who had
> very quickly been thrown out. Classic. But he lost because he was determined
> to have fun. And those to whom he'd given a leg up, those who he'd
> introduced before he was thrown out, Seydoux, Toscan du Plantier who
> he'd called Tocard du Planton, they couldn't bear to see this baroque
> exuberance, this 'madness', a certain art of living. It was necessary to clean
> up, to get rid of these images, which no one talked about any more, better

boredom. This guy who jumped on to the table with joy at the Carlton, seeing on the board the hit parade of films, the numbers for *La Grande Bouffe* rose vertiginously as a guy wrote out the numbers in chalk. And Mazar shouted 'I'm the king of French cinema' and he was just about to get there.[7]

There was a brief moment when this most charming of drug addicts looked set to gain control of the huge production house of Gaumont while still in his early thirties. Rassam's ascendancy proved short-lived, but it was crucial for the Grenoble venture. In 1973, French cinemas still had newsreels. They had long ago lost their raison d'être to television and were very nearly a hundred per cent subsidised by the state, but this seemed a perfect slot in which to make cinema rather than films. The idea was that Sonimage would provide material for the newsreel slot and Rassam agreed to equip the Grenoble studio at 2, rue de Belgrade. Even if Rassam had retained control at Gaumont, newsreels were just about to vanish for ever from cinema screens. Thus, at least in Martin's retrospective judgment, the Grenoble experiment was doomed from the beginning, with both its patron and its raison d'être gone. Martin's memory of the time is one of intense solitude, with Sonimage having no real connections with the town. Some days Godard would talk non-stop, others he would not talk at all. Beauviala was occupied with his own problems and the Sonimage team felt isolated in Grenoble.

The immediate financial crisis was solved by Godard's old friend, Georges de Beauregard. Together de Beauregard and Godard put a proposal for a remake of *Breathless* to the CNC, though the only element it would have in common with the original film was its budget, small in 1959 and miniscule in 1975. *Numéro deux* was a truly astonishing return to the cinema. Using non-professional actors and video technology, Godard made a home movie which was as far from the genres and stars of the cinema as it was possible to get. Images originally recorded on video were filmed in different combinations and sizes to produce an analysis of the modern family. The film is of an extraordinary density, juxtaposing feminist texts by Germaine Greer with the sex education of children and a grandfather's memoirs of lunatic exploits in the Third International.

- à mon avis, papa c'est une
  usine.
- à mon avis, maman c'est un
  paysage.

- c'est mon cul, c'est ma
  cuisine, c'est mes enfants,
  tu vois Pierrot, il y en
  a trop et en même temps
  c'est pas assez.

Pierre Oudry and Sandrine Battistella in promotional cards from *Numéro deux*, 1975.

If the originality of both image and sound gives the film a kind of optimism, its content is almost unbearably pessimistic. The couple trapped within the domestic space dominated by consumption are totally blocked; the woman Sandrine's constipation functions as the primary metaphor for the whole film. But in the analysis of the blockage, in the relentless reflexivity and video manipulation of the image, Godard does make a second version of *Breathless*. If the image can do no more than witness our suffering, it can at least do that.

The companion piece to *Numéro deux* is *Comment ça va?*, which examines, through a long discussion between a union militant and his gauchiste secretary (played by Anne-Marie Miéville), the use of the image in our society. If what is wrong at home is that there is no possibility of bringing work home except in the form of exhaustion and alienation, what is wrong with the image is that it is only ever used as an illustration of a text – there is nowhere for the image to be seen.

For Gérard Martin, in retrospect, Grenoble was a failed venture from the moment Rassam lost power at Gaumont. His own rather jaundiced view of the town seems to be echoed by Miéville and Godard in a snatch of dialogue in *Sauve qui peut*, where the residents of Grenoble are the recipients of some gratuitous abuse. Martin returned to Paris after a series of petty arguments, which covered everything from credits to whose turn it was to clean the toilets. When Sonimage finally closed its offices in Grenoble later in 1977, the technician Teissèdre felt that he had not been treated properly and took the company to court.

But before they left for Switzerland, Miéville and Godard were to undertake a first series of documentaries for television.

Television

In 1974, the Gaullists had been beaten in the presidential election by Valéry Giscard d'Estaing. A neo-liberal by ideology, Giscard d'Estaing was keen to distance himself from some of the more obviously author-itarian aspects of the Gaullist state, and one of his first actions was to break up the state monopoly of the ORTF into a number of semiautonomous units. One of these, the Institut National de l'Audiovisuel, was charged with a research and development function, and it was to be the key broker in the two long television series (eighteen hours in all) that Sonimage were to produce between 1976 and 1978.

Within film itself, particularly Hollywood film, television almost always functions as the realm of the false. Film is what takes us behind the television screen to see what is really happening, from *Nashville* to *Broadcast News*, from *Network* to the *Truman Show*. This fictional falsity is paralleled by a real competition in which television is figured as domestic and dull against the erotic and exciting world of film. While the idea of leaving television to work in film is a natural progression, the reverse trajectory seems almost perverse. But it is important to realise that Godard shares none of the elaborate snobbery about television which is so standard a part of cinema. It is a little remarked fact that for its first six issues *Cahiers du cinéma* announced itself as a journal of film and television, and Bazin clearly believed that the educational possibilities of television were a crucial element in the democratic possibilities offered by the image. More immediately for Godard, his hero Rossellini had abandoned the cinema for television in 1962, and throughout the sixties had devoted himself to a series of films which chronicled the major moments of Western civilisation, from Socrates through Augustine to the Medici and Pascal.

If *Le Gai savoir* and most of the Dziga Vertov films had been produced with television money, the television audience had been completely ignored in their production. But the burden of the argument of *Ici et ailleurs* had been the necessity to focus on the domestic audience for television, and it was this audience that Sonimage tried to address with *Six fois deux (Sur et sous la communication)* made in Grenoble and *France tour détour deux enfants* made in Paris and Rolle. If narrative is the major structuring device in film – the story constantly telling us the meaning of the image – television orders its much more heterogeneous material through direct address. The announcer who tells us what we have just seen and what we are about to see fixes the image for us.

Not surprisingly, Sonimage's first series of programmes eschew direct address altogether. The frame of the programme is simply provided by footage of a cassette being loaded into a video player. We then watch two fifty-minute segments – the first is a theoretical reflection on the image and the second is a long interview with a single figure. The density of the analysis of the first part and the refusal to use any of the normal techniques of the interview (no interviewer to identify with, the camera in a fixed position with no reverse shots) means that these programmes require an intensity of attention which is the complete reverse of 'normal' television. But then normal television is part of that regime of the image which erases our specific being to place us as part of a normal audience. This is the theme of the second and densest of all the theoretical reflections, the *Leçons de choses* (Lessons of Things). It ends by reflecting on a rainbow ('the image of an image'). The rainbow depends on the specific position of the observer in relation to the light source. This makes it the emblem of all images – for all of them you must ask 'when and where you were there' and 'when and where there was light'. It is these straightforward questions which are erased by a regime of the image which summons the spectator to a pre-existent place and which pretends that there is no source for a light which bathes everything in clarity and allows of no shadows. In *Six fois deux*, the divisions of the programmes are taken from the divisions of French primary education in which there are two types of lesson – lessons about things, in which the child engages with the world, and lessons about words, in which the child learns about language. In the second programme the lessons about words is an interview with Godard himself.

As with all the other interviews, this is shot from a fixed position, but it is a fixed position where Godard's face is often obscured by shadow, by the interviewers and by the writing (often quotations from Brecht) which scrolls across the screen for much of the interview. The ability to write directly on the image is one of the great boons of video. Godard had started the practice when filming the simple *Film-tracts* at Dumage's photographic studio in the rue Littré in May 1968. The rules of this agitprop cinema were simple. Anybody could shoot 100 ft of film on the fixed 16 mm camera – assembling different material on the billboard that faced the camera. There was no second thought and no editing, but it was here that Godard started writing directly on the image (indeed his own

Film-tracts can be identified by this use of writing). Video allowed a real development of this writing within the image, in a way which draws attention to the image's construction – to when and where you were there.

Godard's interview, and its written commentary, stresses his solitude and the difficulty of making images which are anything more than stereotypes. If all we are addressing is undifferentiated spectators, then the organisation of sound and image will be unbelievably limited. The interview is conducted by journalists from *Libération*, a newspaper which grew directly from the failures of Maoism, and is one of the few visible traces of 1968 in French public life. Godard had really with-drawn from the world of the spectacle in the period 1968–1976. This series and this interview mark his return, but he returns as Jean-Luc rather than as Godard. There had always been a strong element in Godard which refused generalisation, and this is now accentuated. As he talks to the journalists from *Libération*, he refuses to engage with questions of a general kind, questions which stress that, as Godard, he can work in television in a way that no one else can and therefore he cannot function as a model for others. Godard refuses the terms of such questions, always returning with the response that he, Jean-Luc, does what he can do, it is for others to do what they can do. There is no generalisation from the specific.

The interview with *Libération* is, in retrospect, the first sketching of a public persona which will appear again and again on French television screens over the next quarter of a century. If the visibly angry Godard of the late seventies and early eighties has been replaced by a much mellower character in recent years, both refuse all generalities in favour of specifics. The role that Godard has allotted himself, perfected in films like *Prénom Carmen*, *Soigne ta droite* and *King Lear*, is that of the Fool, the licensed destroyer of convention and ceremony, the figure who, even in the banal world of celebrity television, asks the viewer when and where he or she is watching this, when and where the light is there.[8]

If *Libération* is to become one of the privileged interlocutors from the seventies to the present another is *Cahiers du cinéma*. *Cahiers*'s initial post-1968 politicisation took place in relation to the Communist Party and accentuated a development which had become clear under Rivette's editorship. This led to a break with the Maoist Godard, who took his name off the masthead and gave the transcript of *British Sounds* to a breakaway Maoist rival, *Cinéthique*. But *Cahiers* was to follow Godard, not least because of the Dziga Vertov films, which become a talisman for a possible future for a political cinema. By late 1971, and in the wake of Phillippe Sollers's *Tel Quel*, *Cahiers* had declared its Maoist allegiances. By this time Maoism, never a major political movement, was all but finished. For two years, *Cahiers* wallowed in a political trough – fewer and fewer issues appeared, and all analysis of film was subordinated to the political struggle. This moment culminated at Avignon in the summer of 1973, when a mere fifty people turned up for the political mass meetings which had become the major purpose of the review. An alliance was formed between the militant Serge Toubiana and the critic Serge Daney to take the magazine back to a readership defined by the cinema rather than politics. Godard's films remained a crucial reference for *Cahiers* – and arguably Godard's films had been a crucial factor in the magazine's history in the early seventies (C2:185–263) – but there had been no contact between Godard and *Cahiers* since he had dissociated himself from the magazine in the summer of 1968, as part of his generalised break with the world of Parisian mandarins.

At the beginning of 1976, and as part of a whole cycle of meetings with the film-makers who had made *Cahiers*'s reputation, Daney and Toubiana went to visit Godard in Grenoble, which was Toubiana's home town. Toubiana and Daney were received in a unilluminated dusk, and listened to Godard talk about his projects in both film and television. This visit (which Toubiana describes as having made a 'profound impression') was a prelude to a renewed period of collaboration which culminated in Miéville and Godard guest-editing the 300th issue of *Cahiers* in 1979.

It was *Cahiers du cinéma* which immediately reacted with the greatest interest to the screening of *Six fois deux*. The French programmers had taken fright at these unusual programmes and had buried them in the August schedules. The reviewers took their cue from this and most talked of them as technically inept or very cheap. Godard seems to have been genuinely surprised by the hostile reception they received. Four years later he told *Le Monde*, in an interview dated 30 March 1980, how surprised he had been by *Six fois deux*'s reception: '*Le Gai savoir* was a little infantile and provocative but I was astonished that *Six fois deux* was not received as a serious piece of work, the critics looked for provocation where there was none' (G 1:404).

Cahiers asked the philosopher Gilles Deleuze to comment on the television programmes. Deleuze was one of the philosophical figures most involved with French *gauchisme*. He had taken a chair of philosophy at Vincennes in 1969, and in 1972 had published with the radical psychoanalyst Félix Guattari a volume entitled *Anti-Oedipus*, a stinging attack on the orthodoxies of Lacanian analysis which became a short-lived bible of the ultra-left.[9] Deleuze obviously took the programmes seriously:

> Like many people I was moved – and that's a lasting emotion. I can say how I picture Godard. He's a man who works a lot, so he is, necessarily, completely alone. But his is not just any solitude, it's an extraordinarily populous solitude, populated not by dreams, fantasies or projects, but by action, things and even people. A multiple creative solitude. It's by drawing on the depths of this solitude that Godard can be a force by himself alone, but also work in tandem with several other people. He can deal on equal terms with anyone, from officials or organisations to a cleaning lady, a worker or madmen and -women. In his TV programs, Godard's questions are always direct. They disturb us, the audience, but not the people to whom he asks them. When he talks to lunatics he doesn't talk like a psychiatrist, like another lunatic, or like someone acting crazy. When he talks to workers he's not a boss, or another worker, or an intellectual, or a producer with actors. This isn't at all because he is trying to impersonate artfully every tone, but because his solitude gives him a great capability, a great populatedness. In a certain sense, it's always about being a stammerer. Not a stammerer in his speech but a stammerer in language itself. Generally, you can only be a foreigner in another language, but here, it's rather a matter of being a foreigner in your own language. Proust said that the great books are necessarily written in a sort of foreign language. It's the same with Godard's program; he's even perfected his Swiss accent for the purpose. It's this creative stammering, this solitude that gives Godard his force.[10]

If *Six fois deux* did find some viewers like Deleuze, the general reaction was dismissive. In some ways Godard's surprise at this reaction may seen disingenuous – Sonimage's refusal to use the most basic conventions of television make *Six fois deux* extremely arduous viewing. But the message of the series is clear: we live in a world that we cannot see or understand, in which the image is contaminated at every moment by the money with which it is bought and sold. Our individual being in the world – the moment that we find ourselves here – remains unilluminated; we cannot find the light. Sonimage's second attempt at television, *France tour détour deux enfants*, was obviously designed to avoid some of the criticisms levelled at *Six fois deux*; it also seems to bear much more clearly the marks of Miéville's collaboration. Designed as twelve half-hour programmes to be shown daily over two weeks, *France tour détour deux enfants* employs many of the most familiar of television's devices – above all repetition and direct address – in its investigation of the world.

The focus of the programmes are two small children, and it is their passage through a normal day which is used as a way of investigating the reality of France. But if the structure resembles a conventional programme, the content is anything but conventional, whether it be

Albert Dray as the presenter, with screen stills from *France tour detour deux enfants*, 1979.

Godard's questioning of the children, the documentary footage of the children's day (always shot from a fixed camera and always fixed on the child) or the brief and complex essays that punctuate the programmes.

In the programmes, the adults are always referred to as 'monsters', and the series uses the children to try to understand the monstrous world in which we live. These twelve programmes offer a new confidence in the image – we do in fact see the daily world of the child in a fresh light – but that image is above all an image of solitude, a solitude rooted in biology and reinforced by society. The forms of communication which should enable us to speak to one another are so fixed in routine and so stereotyped that they are all but impossible to use. As if to prove Godard's point, the programmers sat on *France tour détour deux enfants*, eventually broadcasting them in four slots (three programmes a slot) dedicated to great film directors.

Sonimage's attempt to make television differently was rewarded by their being treated as though they had made films. This was a hugely important watershed for Godard. Throughout the sixties and seventies, Godard frequently spoke about television as a desirable alternative to film; after the Sonimage experiments, television is usually referred to by Godard as the most evident example of a completely degraded use of the image. For a decade from 1968 to 1978, almost all of Godard's money had come from television, and in the period between 1976 and 1978, Sonimage had really attempted to produce television. Indeed, at this time, Sonimage accepted a commission from the new Mozambique government to help plan a new kind of television station.[11] But after 1980 television dropped entirely from Godard's agenda. If television money continued to be used, it was now to make films.

Sauve Qui Peut

In 1978 it was Miéville who advised Godard to return to the cinema, and an opportunity presented itself in Hollywood. Fresh from the triumph of *Apocalypse Now*, Coppola's American Zoëtrope had purchased a studio in Los Angeles and was busy turning it into a studio of all the talents, a dream as old as United Artists. Coppola's first attempt, based in San Francisco, at running a studio fuelled by creativity rather than money had crashed in the late sixties, but he had directed his way back to a position where he could start again. He had recruited Tom Luddy as part of his team after their successful ventures in the screening of silent movies.[12] Luddy had kept in touch with Godard throughout the seventies and was delighted to offer him the possibility of making his way back into films. Godard had become obsessed with the story of Bugsy Siegel, the mobster who built Las Vegas, and was particularly intrigued by the impossibility of shooting a film about Siegel's life: who would play the Hollywood stars who were Siegel's friends? Godard produced several scripts for the film which he called simply 'The Story'. They are beautiful works of art in themselves, using the photocopier as a way of cutting together still images of his chosen stars, Diane Keaton and Robert de Niro. The film is set in the present, and Bugsy Siegel, like other elements of Hollywood history, functions only as background to a much more basic story: 'There is a story between us. As with everybody, the story comes from him and enters her. And there, inside, one loses the trace. And then it comes out again, a child is born, and one finds it outside. And then one sees anew the story' (G:1:418).

Godard's tale of a couple meeting by chance on a shoot in Las Vegas six years after they separated is a compelling one – the figure of the blind daughter is particularly haunting. (An abbreviated version of the script was published in the 1985 edition of *Godard on Godard*.) The project was finally to founder due to Keaton's lack of interest, but Godard had already prepared a French film instead, *Sauve qui peut (la vie)*.

In the huge number of interviews that Godard gave around the launch of *Sauve qui peut (la vie)*, he rarely failed to speak of it as a 'second first film'. There can be few examples in art or culture (Wittgenstein's return to philosophy after the *Tractatus* might be one) where a great artist or thinker comes back for a new beginning, but *Sauve qui peut* is exactly that.

In the films before '68, Godard had been pre-eminently a film-maker of the city. If both sea and sky had illuminated *Contempt* and *Pierrot le fou*, the countryside, if it appeared at all in films like *Les Carabiniers* and

Nathalie Baye in *Sauve qui peut (la vie)*, 1980.

Week-end, appeared as alien territory. *Sauve qui peut* is a hymn to the beautiful Swiss countryside to which he had just returned, the country-side of his childhood. Indeed, the opposition between town and country provides one of the most important of the film's themes. When the male protagonist meets his estranged ex-wife to pay her monthly cheque, their daughter is struggling over an essay on the blackbird, describing how in one country after another it has changed its habitat and behaviour in order to become a city rather than a country bird. The father suggests a final paragraph which claims that the history of the last two hundred years should be understood in terms of this change, which is much more important than any political transformation.

For his return to cinema, Godard equipped himself with a story elaborated with the help of Buñuel's screenwriter, Jean-Claude Car-rière,[13] and three of the biggest stars of French cinema: Jacques Dutronc, Nathalie Baye and Isabelle Huppert. The film is an extraordinary mix of exhilaration and despair – the exhilaration coming from the beauty and

Jacques Dutronc in *Sauve qui peut (la vie)*, 1980.

force of the images, the despair from a society in which no one is free, except the banks, and from a vision of male sexuality as inevitably damaged and damaging.

The film covers the last days in the life of Paul Godard, a film-maker separated from his wife and daughter, and breaking up with his girlfriend Denise (Nathalie Baye). Denise is intent on moving to the country, and the opening section of the film (entitled 'Imagination') follows her. The second section of the film ('Fear') focuses on Dutronc. One night he picks up a prostitute (Isabelle Huppert), and we then enter the third phase of the film ('Commerce'), in which Huppert plies her trade and looks for a flat in which to live. The film ends with Huppert talking to Baye as she rents her flat, while Dutronc is run over by a car as his wife and daughter walk away from him.

If Godard returns to prostitution as a major theme, the interest of the film is no longer in the mystery of feminine sexuality but in the violence and brutality of male sexuality, always desperate to fix women in a

Isabelle Huppert in *Sauve qui peut (la vie)*, 1980.

fetishised place. One of the central scenes of the film is that in which Huppert joins with another prostitute to perform a complicated scenario which requires an exact alignment of bodies and voices, according to the fantasy of the boss who has ordered it. The film makes explicit that this alignment of sound and image, this freezing of desire so that it can be consumed, is exactly the operation of commercial cinema. When Huppert bumps into an old schoolfriend in one of the anonymous hotel corridors where she conducts her business, the schoolfriend gives her an address where she can find work. The address is 15, rue du Nord, the building in Rolle to which Miéville and Godard had moved in 1976, with their studio on the ground floor and their apartments above. When Huppert finds the address, she discovers a man at an editing table who offers her huge sums of money to travel around the world doing nothing.

Godard's dissatisfaction with the cinema had been made very clear to me in the period when he was making this film. He had invited me to attend two days of the shooting as part of the preparation for a short book that I was writing about him. When I went to meet him for the first time in the spring of 1979, the ostensible reason for my visit was to acquire the non-theatrical rights to Sonimage's television work for the British Film Institute; in fact the primary reason for my visit was to obtain an interview for a BFI collection of essays on his post-1968 work. Although Godard had been interviewed a great deal in the period before 1968, and although he was to be interviewed even more in the years to come, there were very few interviews with him in the period following 1968. Indeed there appeared to be a fog of rumour which suggested that anyone who asked him for an interview was taking their life into their hands. But there was no living film-maker and few living artists who I was more keen to hear first hand.

My first year at university coincided with May 1968, and my intellectual life had been profoundly affected by French politics and culture. Indeed, I had spent a year at the Ecole Normale Supérieure between 1972 and 1973 studying with Althusser. When I returned, I was asked to join the board of *Screen*, the magazine for the Society for Education in Film and Television. The British Film Institute was perhaps the only British institution fundamentally affected by the events of May, and a series of bruising institutional battles had resulted, in 1971, in new funding for *Screen*, a magazine charged with the explicit task of developing a theory of film. Early work had included translations from *Cahiers* and *Cinéthique*, and by 1973 the magazine was keen to develop its own positions. I was delighted to join this intellectual endeavour and thrilled to find that Godard was the central point of reference.

My first encounter with Godard had taken place in January 1967 when, as a seventeen-year-old who had just left school, I found myself in Paris for a night en route to Geneva, and had to pick a film to go and see. As my French was non-existent, I chose *Made in USA*, assuming that I would find an English-language film. My mistake was irrelevant as I discovered in Godard's use of colour and light possibilities in the image that I had never dreamt of. But if I was saturated in Godard's films when I joined *Screen*, I was no cinephile. As a teenager in London in the sixties, both pop music and television had meant much more to me than the cinema. *Screen*, and particularly its editors Sam Rhodie and Ben

Marianne Faithfull in *Made in USA*, 1966.

Brewster, gave me the most wonderful education as we tried to elaborate a theory of politics and cinema. *Screen*'s aesthetic was a version of *Tel Quel* and *Cahiers* – a dismissal of representation and identification in favour of a use of the image which introduced contradiction and change. In attempting to hold together modernism and Marxism, our crucial reference was Brecht, rejecting both socialist realism on the one hand and bourgeois aesthetics on the other. As with *Cahiers* at that period *Screen*'s directors were Godard, Oshima and Straub – but above all, Godard.

After an initial burst of amazing productivity, *Screen*'s project ran into the problem that in the cinema audiences continued to demand representation and identification, whatever the pleasures of contradiction and conflict. More specifically for me, the political project of Eurocommunism ran aground as events in Portugal, France and Italy made clear the impossibility of linking a Leninist party to democratic institutions. If modernism had promised a fresh start which would relinquish the exclusions of bourgeois culture, this promise was broken in the reality of a newly dominant popular culture devoted to a regime of representation and identification, which was much more wearisome than the bourgeois culture it had replaced.

I had therefore abandoned my investigation of modernism, and particularly the attempt at a political reading of James Joyce, to go back to the sixteenth and seventeenth centuries and the moment of formation of both national languages and national literatures, in the hope that this would provide a clearer perspective on the incomprehensibility of the present. But a chance to get my hands on Sonimage's mysterious television work (which had never been seen in Britain) and to interview Godard was too good to miss. However one wished to configure the contemporary, Godard would be a key reference. Simon Hartog, who had worked very closely with Frelimo, the national liberation movement in Mozambique, and who knew Godard because of their shared contacts in that country, advised me to put money in my purse if I was going to Rolle. Luckily the BFI wanted to acquire the television programmes, and so I travelled with their cheque and contract in my pocket. Godard asked me to meet him in the waiting room of the train station in Nyon.

Godard is small of stature and speaks in a very soft and low voice, but the force of his presence is remarkable. I was not surprised in the course of research for this book to discover that both Bernardo Bertolucci and Serge Daney had vomited on their first encounter with him. It is, of course, difficult to discount the aura of fame, but Godard has none of the attitude or assumptions of the famous. He does, however, have absolutely no time at all for the phatic communication of normal social intercourse. Either there is something specific to talk about or there is no point in talking. I now realised why Simon Hartog had advised me to come with business to discuss. But the business, and this was also characteristic, was dealt with very efficiently and unbelievably quickly. I then found myself stammering out a request for an interview to accompany the BFI's book. 'Will this be a proper book?' he asked. 'Yes' was the only possible answer. 'If it is a proper book then you can come to my office and have access to whatever papers you wish, you can visit the set of my next film and I will do whatever interviews you require.'

In retrospect, it is obvious that the former press agent for Fox was preparing for the huge publicity circus that was going to accompany his return to the cinema. Some eighteen months later, Tom Luddy was to write an internal Zoëtrope memo about the early success of *Sauve qui peut* in the United States: '. . . part of the credit for the success must go to

Godard the promoter . . . He really exhausted himself, spending about
12–14 full days, on 2–3 trips to New York in September and October,
on interviews, TV tapings, photo sessions etc.' An academic book was
simply a minor tie-in in what was to be a major campaign. For me at the
time, the transformation of Godard the political hermit shunning
publicity, to Godard the commercial film-maker encouraging a book,
was much more baffling. Baffling or not, I made a series of phone calls to
England and by the time I was on my way the next day to the little town
of Rolle, the collection of essays had been abandoned in favour of a
'real' book on the unseen Godard of the previous decade.

Rolle is a small town of about 4,000 inhabitants situated between
Nyon and Lausanne on Lake Geneva. Although it is tiny, it is just off a
motorway which is only half an hour from Geneva airport. It is also on
the main Lausanne–Geneva railway, and it was to the train station that I
made my way the next day. The rue du Nord runs parallel to the main
street in Rolle, one block up the hill. Number 15 is a completely
unremarkable modern apartment building in which one is surprised
to find any sort of office. The large front room was full of audiovisual
equipment of various kinds, and behind it was a working office,
impeccably neat and tidy, with shelf after shelf of books. The only
decoration was a photo on his desk of Miéville and her daughter turning
into the narrow alleyway which runs from the main street to the rue du
Nord. Once the meeting had begun, Godard spent a considerable
amount of time looking for material on his previous films – there
was absolutely no material from before 1968 – Godard obviously
regarded these films as belonging to another time. There was also
surprisingly little from the Dziga Vertov films, but there was an
abundance of material on the current projects, particularly the beautiful
scripts of 'The Story'.

Just before the end of our meeting, Miéville returned from a bicycle
ride. A strikingly beautiful woman in her mid-thirties with a polite Swiss
manner, her effect on Godard was palpable. Although he had been
extremely courteous on both days, his manner was withdrawn, and I got
the sense I was distracting him from a compelling internal world. This
initial impression was to be confirmed in all my later meetings with him,

but the appearance of Miéville transformed him. He shone with pleasure as he introduced her, and I felt the rare sensation that I was witnessing love. Even discounting my rather nervous and star-struck state, the effect of Miéville's presence on him was remarkable. The only other occasions on which I saw him so visibly engage with the world was in the presence of small children (who he evidently loves and who respond in kind), and in a more minor key, sport on the television, particularly tennis.

Six months later I returned to Switzerland for the first week on the shoot of *Sauve qui peut*. The first day I attended the filming of one of the opening scenes in the hotel. Shooting finished early and Godard assembled the crew for a discussion, which consisted of an extraordinary monologue by Godard on the relations between time and money. Using examples as diverse as the history of Hollywood and the complimentary chocolates provided by the hotel management, Godard came back again and again to the fact that the forms of financing for films meant that one never had any time to reflect properly on what one was doing.

The talk was notable in a number of ways. It remains to this day the best single analysis that I have ever heard of what one might term the labour process of the film industry. But it was far from being a bullet-point presentation. Ellipses were followed by digressions to the point that one became embarrassingly convinced at times that these were psychotic ramblings. Time and time again, however, the argument would reassert itself – it was crucial at each moment to reflect on all technical and professional decisions, to engage fully even in the most minor of tasks in order to produce a film that would be worthy of the labour devoted to it.

What was even more embarrassing was that the crew were expected to engage with this discourse; something that they were visibly unable to do. When, after the shoot was finished, Godard told me that he had argued with all the technicians, I was surprised, for it was clear that they all admired him only this side of idolatry. With the benefit of hindsight, however, it is clear that the demands that he was placing on the crew were beyond reason, and if there should be no doubting his desire to work collectively, which he expressed again and again in the seventies

Renato Berta, Anne-Marie Miéville and Godard on the shoot of *Sauve qui peut (la vie)*, 1979.

and eighties, there can also be no doubt that the terms Godard set for collective work were entirely personal.

On the second day, the shoot was of a traditional Swiss game called Hornuss played in a remote village in the Swiss hinterland. Hornuss involves hitting a small ball hundreds of yards down a field, where men waving huge bats of wood attempt to block it. A railway ran alongside the field and Godard's ideal shot would have opened on a train and then panned round to the game; city and country, modernity and tradition caught in one vision. The assistant director, Romain Goupil, had a timetable and thus knew when the infrequent trains would arrive. But Godard refused to direct the Hornuss players; if he wanted to catch the train and the game in a single shot, he would have to catch it by chance. There could be no question, as his increasingly heated exchanges with Goupil made clear, of organising the players for the shot. In fact, train and players evaded the camera, and the establishing shot in the final film is simply of the Hornuss field itself.

The sequence comes at the beginning of the film as Nathalie Baye seeks to move to the country. She comes to the Hornuss field to find an old friend of hers, an ex-gauchiste who has taken over the family-owned local newspaper, to see if he can offer her work. Their dialogue turns on the abandonment of revolutionary dreams, and is part of the major theme of the demise of politics which runs through the opening of the film. Godard became increasingly agitated as the scene was shot again and again, finally exploding in total rage at the actor playing the journalist. He hated the oversentimental and cloying tones with which the actor was investing the discussion of the past – the journalist should be thinking about seducing Baye. The violence of Godard's outburst was truly shocking – the poor actor wandered around visibly distressed and muttering, 'I didn't know I was trying to seduce her.' From the outside it was obvious that Godard's rage stemmed from the fact that he did not want to tell the actor what to do, and indeed the specific suggestion of seduction was not the real point – he wanted the actor to produce something which would ring true. What he certainly did not want was another version of benign liberal concern.

Another observer of the Hornuss game that day was Paule Muret, the girlfriend of the cameraman Renato Berta. Godard had asked Muret to take on the role of Dutronc's ex-wife, and she was observing the proceedings to help her make up her mind. She had spent the previous weeks and months hearing stories of Godard's rages and had been unable to understand why nobody in the crew reprimanded him. But now she saw that the rages were not the capricious self-indulgence of a 'great director' with a menial, but were like the rage of a six-year-old child unable to tie his shoelaces. Such genuine frustration at the facts of existence was outside the sphere of any reprimand. Despite the violence of the day, she agreed to take the part.

The final stage in the process was when Godard came to London for the premiere of the film which opened a complete retrospective of his films at the National Film Theatre, and for the publication of my book. In the two days that he was in London, two things were evident. The first was the energy and commitment he invested in the publicising of the film – from the most minor radio interview to the on-stage presentation at the National Film Theatre, this was work that had to be done. The second was his complete indifference to normal social conventions. This ranged from the visibly startling – when asked by a feminist journalist why he had taken prostitution for his theme, he replied straightforwardly that prostitution had always been a problem in his life;[14] through the disconcerting – in all social gatherings where he was not required to answer specific questions he simply withdrew into an asocial silence which could freeze a room instantly; to the hilarious – when a waiter informed us that we could not drink in the Savoy bar without ties, Godard told him, without a beat, 'Don't worry I've just bought the hotel.'[15]

Godard's visit to England was simply part of a process which had started in May 1980 with the presentation of *Sauve qui peut* at the Cannes Film Festival, and which was to conclude in October with the launch of the film in the United States. It announced his return to the world of cinema and a return which was successful both critically and commercially. *Sauve qui peut* took over a million dollars in its twelve-week Paris run, and this result was repeated internationally. The film did not win a prize at Cannes, for which Godard blamed Kirk Douglas who was on the jury, but it received an enormous amount of publicity, not least for the explicit sex scenes which took advantage of the liberal-isation of the censorship laws allowing the production of legal porno-graphy from the early seventies onwards.

But if Godard had returned to the cinema, he had not returned to his former life. In interviews given at the time of Cannes, Godard was extremely bitter about Belmondo, who had refused to help him with *Sauve qui peut*.[16] Even more bitter were his final exchanges with Truffaut. In 1973, and with almost no contact since the break of 1968,[17] Godard had written to Truffaut to ask for financial help as he and Gorin prepared their films after *Tout va bien*. The letter was not of the traditional begging kind as it began with a ferocious attack on Truffaut's most recent film *La Nuit américaine* – a film starring Jacque-line Bisset which took film-making for its subject. Godard claimed it was a deeply dishonest film and he called Truffaut a liar: 'Liar, because the shot of you and Jacqueline Bisset the other night [at the restaurant] is not in your film and one asks why the director is the only one who doesn't screw in *La Nuit américaine*?' This lack of personal honesty, the refusal

to put himself in the film, is linked directly in Godard's letter to a failure
to understand Europe and the concentration camps. The letter ends:

> Because of the films of Malle and Rassam who produce expensive movies
> (like you), the money that was reserved for me has been swallowed up by
> the Ferreri . . . and I'm stuck. The film costs about 20 million and is
> produced by Anouchka and TVAB films (the company owned by Gorin
> and me). Could you enter into co-production with us for 10 million? For 5
> million? Considering *La Nuit américaine*, you ought to help me, so that
> the public doesn't get the idea that we all make films like you. You aren't a
> liar, like Pompidou, like me, you speak your own truth. In exchange, if
> you like, I can sign over my rights to *La Chinoise*, *Le Gai savoir* and
> *Masculin Féminin*. If you want to talk it over, fine.[18]

The original manuscript of Truffaut's reply is clearly a document of great
emotion, the pencil digging deeply into nearly twenty continuously written
pages. Truffaut's complaints against Godard range from his treatment of
Jean-Pierre Léaud, Janine Bazin, and Mireille Darc, to his failure to turn up
to sell the Maoist newspaper *La Cause du peuple* when it had been banned.
But the specific attacks, often difficult to understand – the letter is one of
genuine emotion – are merely fuel for an attack on Godard's position
of moral and political superiority which, for Truffaut, is nothing other
than a mask for an egotism which wishes always to be centre stage:

> Here you are, in 1973, as fond as ever of making grand gestures and
> spectacular announcements, as arrogant and dogmatic as ever, secure on
> your pedestal, indifferent to others, incapable of simply and unselfishly
> giving up a few hours of your time to help someone. Between your interest
> in the masses and your own narcissism there's no room for anything or
> anyone else . . . You need to play a role and the role needs to be a
> prestigious one; I've always had the impression that real militants are like
> cleaning women, doing a thankless, daily but necessary job. But you,
> you're the Ursula Andress of militancy, you make a brief appearance, just
> enough time for the cameras to flash and then you disappear again,
> trailing clouds of self-serving mystery.[19]

The violence of the exchange is hardly surprising. The autobiographical force of Truffaut's first film, the determination to record a life, had fast given way to films much more within the tradition attacked by Truffaut the young critic. The distance between Truffaut and Godard was not a matter of personal whim, but the resulf of fundamental aesthetic and economic choices.

With *Sauve qui peut* Godard wrote again to Truffaut. The Parisian release of *Sauve qui peut* coincided with new films by Rivette, Chabrol and Truffaut, and Godard now suggested a public discussion:

> Couldn't one really make a 'conversation'? Whatever our differences, it would interest me to hear in our own voices what our cinema has become. We could certainly find a 'moderator' that we'd all agree to. We could make it a book, at Gallimard or elsewhere. I'd be happy to invite you for one or two days to Geneva. I would like, if it were possible, to show a little bit of my 'localisation'. Perhaps a meeting like that, one on one, would be felt as too violent, with four it would be possible to diminish the potential difference and a bit of current could pass. In friendship all the same.

Truffaut's reply was cutting:

> Your invitation to Switzerland is extraordinarily flattering when one knows how precious your time is . . . Your letter is amazing and your pastiche of the 'political' style convinces. The finale of your letter will remain one of my happiest findings: 'Friendship all the same'. Thus you show that you don't bear a grudge for having called us thugs and crooks to be avoided like the plague. As for me I agree to come to your localisation – what a pretty expression . . . when I think of all the hypocrites who would say simply: my house – but it is a privilege that I want to share with others, let's say four or five persons who could note what you say and broadcast it everywhere. I ask you thus to invite at the same time as me Jean-Paul Belmondo. You've said that he's frightened of you and it's time to reassure him. I'd also very much like to see Vera Chytilova, denounced by you as 'revisionist' in her own country under

Soviet occupation. Her presence at your conference seems necessary to me, because I am sure that you'll help her to get her exit visa. And why neglect Loleh Bellon who you called a real bitch in Télérama. Finally, don't forget Boumboum, our old friend Braunberger who wrote to me the day after your phone call: ' "Dirty Jew" is the only insult that I cannot bear'. I await your response without excessive impatience because if you've become one of Coppola's groupies, you'll be pressed for time and you don't want to ruin the preparation of your next autobiographical film whose title I think I know: 'A Shit is a shit'. (T:712–713)

The old relationships were not rekindled, but the base in Rolle and the partnership with Miéville were to endure. Before the move to Grenoble, Godard had changed house and office with incredible frequency. What is striking from 1976 onwards is continuity – Godard moved his working studio one block in the early nineties, and both Miéville and Godard moved from their apartments in the rue du Nord to houses in the town, but Rolle itself has remained the base of their operations for a generation.

There have also been enduring production relationships. Alain Sarde developed the relationship begun on *Sauve qui peut* and has been Godard's French producer through the subsequent decades. Ruth Waldburger, the unit production manager on *Passion*, set up a Swiss production company in the late eighties which has been as regular a partner as Sarde. Perhaps the most frequent name on Godard's credits is that of François Musy for sound. Musy's relationship goes well beyond individual films as it is he who provides Godard with the technical back-up for the increasingly complex equipment which allows Godard so much autonomy.[20]

The shoot for *Sauve qui peut* had been based in Rolle and run with a small crew. Its success led to

Alain Sarde and Godard at Roland-Garros, 28 May 2001.

a much bigger production, the technically ambitious *Passion*, and to Godard's return to a studio for the first time since *Contempt*. The dream of an American film had faded slowly. Godard liked his trips to Zoëtrope and even rented an apartment in Santa Monica for a time. He had a real attachment to his assistant Brooks Riley and a genuine enjoyment of Tom Luddy's company. But Zoëtrope itself was in trouble as Coppola recreated Las Vegas on a Hollywood set for *One from the Heart*.[21] Coppola's legendary photographer, Vittorio Storaro, and production designer, Dean Tavoularis, were set to work on Godard's next movie, which would be shot in France and Switzerland. And it was on the set of *One from the Heart*, the day before it finished shooting, that time was found for Godard to orchestrate a strikingly beautiful shot of a crane moving through a complicated arabesque. There is a shot which resembles it in the final movie, but Godard's fragment from Hollywood can itself be seen as part of the videoscript for the film *Scénario du film 'Passion'*. But Storaro and Tavoularis were not to work on the finished film; in a pattern inherited from *Sauve qui peut* and intensified on *Passion*, Godard pushed all his relationships with technicians to breaking point, and Storaro and Tavoularis were discarded early in the process. Thus Raoul Coutard found himself contacted by the *Passion* production office to see if he was available to work on a Godard film after a break of more than a decade. Having made clear that he would always be available for a Godard film, Coutard was determined to get to the studio in Billancourt well in advance on his first day of shooting. But when he arrived he found that Godard – unshaven and with dark glasses (both bad signs for Coutard) – was already there. This reunion after so many years was not of the most emotional – Godard remarked that they'd tried all the leading cameramen in the world, but none were available. Coutard said nothing.

Their reunion was to lead to the film *Passion* which is, for me, the greatest and also the most beautiful of Godard's work. The phrase Godard had used for the title of his previous film, 'Sauve qui peut', is the signal that a ship and its crew and passengers no longer constitute a collectivity with duties and obligations – the precise English translation is 'every man for himself'. And *Sauve qui peut* had very clearly placed

Ingres's *The Bather*, recreated in *Passion*, 1982.

itself in a time after politics. In *Passion*, Godard returned to analyse the failure of politics. The film juxtaposes a factory and a film set, and the two worlds meet in a hotel owned by Hanna Schygulla. Her husband, Michel Piccoli, owns the factory, while she is having an affair with the film director, Jerzy. Jerzy is also involved with a worker in the factory, Isabelle Huppert, a young Catholic militant who is trying to organise the workers into a strike.

The film has both too many stories and too few. There is the story of the strike, the story of the marriage, the story of Piccoli's business. But each of these is told in abbreviated, almost farcical scenes. Meanwhile, on a huge film set, many of the most classic paintings of European art (from Rembrandt's *The Night Watch* and Ingres's *The Bather* to Delacroix's *The Fall of Constantinople* and El Greco's *The Virgin and the Immaculate Conception*) are being recreated. The film is in financial crisis; Laszlo Szabo – perhaps Godard's most constant actor – is the beleaguered producer trying desperately to extract a story from his director that will enable him to raise the money to keep the production going.

Jerzy Radziwilowicz setting up a crane shot for *The Fall of Constantinople* by Eugène Delacroix on the set of *Passion*, 1982.

Passion is one of the great works of European modernism. Modernism is most familiarly known as the turning of the focus on to the form and medium of art itself. Perhaps the most canonical examples are Picasso's Cubism or Joyce's experiments with language. The classic critical formulation is the Russian Formalist Victor Shlovsky's: 'the laying bare of the device'. Without wishing to rearrange the canon or to doubt Shlovsky's critical genius, it would be a mistake to understand modernism as some arid formalism, because the turn to the form is caused by a crisis of the audience. In practical terms, the audience for art explodes at the end of the nineteenth century as universal literacy and the new forms of printing join together with the invention of the Lumière brothers to create audiences on a scale which beggar all historical comparison. But these new audiences clarify the constraints imposed by the demands of genre and spectacle, demands no longer sanctioned by classical precept or aristocratic authority, but imposed by the working of a very visible market. It is this market, with its ready-made meanings, which is rejected by modernism, determined to engage the audience in the construction of meaning itself. And in this rejection of meanings, modernism rejects not simply the commodity-dominated culture of the present but also the terms of Western European art since the Renaissance, now seen as impossibly exclusive. The paradox of modernism is thus that it offers a totally democratic view of art – the determination to turn every aspect of both world and self into matter for art – in forms which require a level of attention and commitment which limits the audience to a mere handful.

Passion's staging of the paintings makes clear how Western art has focused on meanings: on the burgher politics of Rembrandt's *Night Watch*; on the historical subjects of Delacroix; on the religious paintings of El Greco. But *Passion* is not interested in the meanings of these paintings. It is interested in their organisation of space and in the light which can render the everyday reality of the sun over Lake Geneva, or the movements of Isabelle Huppert as she works in the factory, just as luminous.

The original Bazinian position had solved the problems of modernism by finding the genuine presence of art in the great popular form of film. But that art is largely dependent on the dominance of a small elite of producers and critics, an elite which is threatened and displaced by the new forms of television which force Hollywood to integrate more with finance capital. This process, which stretches from the early fifties to the release of *Jaws* in 1975, accelerates just at the moment that Bazin's young disciples begin to make films in the early sixties. From 1963 on, the key thinker for Godard is no longer Bazin but Brecht. For it is Brecht who tries to square the circle of modernism and popularity by linking the growing recognition of form, and the failure of the current audience, to a future political transformation. In retrospect it is evident that Godard's '68 solution, which was to abandon the traditional circuits of distribution, their aesthetic constraints no longer embraced as a new classicism but rejected as debased stereotypes, was the exact opposite of Truffaut's determination to make his small company financially viable. The bitterness of their exchanges is not simply the result of the closeness of their friendship but also of their profound disagreement over their joint heritage.

Godard's abandonment of politics – Jerzy says at the beginning of the film 'one must give up the idea that one can save oneself by saving the world' – was not a return to the Bazinian cinema defined by Rohmer as linking direct access to the real with the accepted genres of cinema. Instead, as Jerzy takes on the sacrificial position of the artist, what emerges is a modernist Bazin: after he has rejected politics, Jerzy admits that 'one must register everything'. What is left is the camera, but the camera must be stripped of all its rules, all its stories, if it is to fulfil its historic mission to let us see the world.

In Godard, radical change and the reusing of material are not contradictions but rather the definition of the method. In *Passion*, we find the workers' discussion from *British Sounds*, the eating of the soup from *Lotte in Italia*, and the old man with his mad memories of the Third International from *Numéro deux*. But the proletarian struggle is now seen to be as bankrupt as every other tradition, a point made even more savagely in an early treatment where the workers strike against Huppert's attempts to organise them.

The politics which was to save art is simply a narcotic with which to dull the senses. In my first proper conversation with Godard, I asked him what he thought of politics. In an excessive theatrical gesture of a kind he rarely uses, he mimed injecting a huge syringe into his arm. 'Some people take drugs, some people take politics.' If the revolutionary claim that 'the poor are usually right' remains, and if Miéville and Godard continue to lend their name to the struggle to recognise the rights of asylum seekers, politics as a system of belief, or as a code to organise life and art, is simply evasion.

And what comes back in the place of politics are Coutard's twin themes of death and the impossibility of love. But now the impossibility of love is not entirely projected on to the too desirable body of the woman, and death involves a study of the ancestors. The adolescent fixation on the treachery of women and the heroism of the doomed individual gives way to a more adult concern with questions of masculinity and society. It is the dead-ends of masculine sexuality and the Western tradition of art and religion which now provide the colours for Godard's palette.

Frame still of Hanna Schygulla in *Passion*, 1982.

Sauve qui peut had investigated the dead-end of a masculine sexuality offered by the father: 'I borrowed my father's name for 90 minutes to be less frightened of women.' And the most chilling aspect of this film is that sex can only be experienced by women as suffering.[22]

If *Passion* attempts to produce an acceptable relationship, it is outside any terms that are conventionally understood. Huppert, the prostitute of *Sauve qui peut*, becomes the virgin of *Passion*, and it is around this figure of the desired and sexualised virgin that the film plays out its climax, after Jerzy has rejected the claims of Hanna Schygulla and conventional sexual experience. Godard's treatment of Schygulla on the set was extremely harsh; Coutard recalls one morning when Schygulla turned up visibly exhausted by a night of passion. Coutard attempted to add some light to mask some of the more evident wrinkles, but Godard stopped him with a comment delivered to anyone who wished to hear, 'She's been screwing all night – let everybody see the wrinkles on her face.' Despite Godard's harshness, Schygulla has never been photographed more beautifully, wrinkles and all, and the scene in which Jerzy plays and replays the video he has taken of her face is not only deeply moving but makes as clear as possible why Godard wanted to capture a moment outside the narrative of film or the frame of a picture, a moment in which we can see a face.

The end of the film holds out the vision of some impossible sexual union less explicitly anal than the desire to find 'another passage' which will leave no trace, in some impossible blend of the carnal and the spiritual. Godard continued to investigate this sublimation in *Prénom Carmen*, the film that he shot the following year. *Passion* was a tremendous financial failure. Despite a huge release, as befitted its budget, it earned barely $300,000 in the five weeks following its Parisian release as against more than $1,000,000 that *Sauve qui peut* had taken in twelve.

Godard told me at the time that the whole experience of filming had been intensely disagreeable, and it is a constant theme of the interviews he gave around its release. Coutard found Godard much changed from the film-maker he had worked with in the sixties. Then he had often been short-tempered and irritable but also frequently apologetic, always ready with flowers or a drink to excuse his own behaviour. Now there were no apologies and Coutard noted that he seemed to take real pleasure in his bad temper.

Godard's immediate response was to make *Prénom Carmen* a 'small film'. The studio and the huge crews gave way to a crew even more slimmed down than that for *Sauve qui peut*. When Isabelle Adjani, who had been cast in the role of Carmen, arrived at the hospital where the opening scenes were to be shot, her entourage of hairdressers, make-up artists and assistants filled two cars; Godard's entire crew for camera and sound filled one. Having unloaded their equipment and set it up, Coutard began to measure the light around Adjani's face. Adjani, who had never seen a lighting cameraman handle equipment before, was convinced that Coutard was an unqualified grip, burst into tears and left both the set and the film. She was afraid that Godard's methods would not render her beautiful enough and, at the very last moment, the unknown Maruschka Detmers had to replace the superstar Adjani. This

Maruschka Detmers and Jacques Bonaffé in *Prénom Carmen*, 1983.

was a severe financial blow, which was compounded when the delay in filming meant that the string quartet in which Myriem Roussel plays had to shift their dates. Godard had rowed very badly with the quartet and Coutard says they were delighted to take their revenge.

The film sets Bizet's *Carmen* to Beethoven's Late Quartets, and juxtaposes the fatal sexual passion of Joseph for Carmen with his 'different' relationship with his girlfriend Myriem. If the explicit modernism of *Passion* has given way to the most skeletal of generic thrillers, it is Godard himself, as 'Uncle Jean' the film-maker desperate to remain in the hospital, who introduces at the narrative level the reflection on the form of cinema. 'Can I', he asks his nurse at the beginning of the film, 'stick my finger up your ass until I've counted to thirty-three?' At the end he turns to the nurse, now his assistant on the film set which has also doubled as a heist scene, and says, 'I've counted to thirty-three.'

Art as the sublimation of sexuality – as that impossible depiction of a penetration that will leave no trace – is the alternative to a sexuality which is absolutely fatal. Carmen, taking her English line from

Godard in *Prénom Carmen*, 1983.

Preminger's black production of the story, *Carmen Jones*, that both Miéville (who wrote the script) and Godard loved so much, tells Joseph 'If I love you, that's the end of you.' And the end of physical passion has perhaps never been better or more terribly represented in the cinema than in the scene where Joseph, violently rejected sexually by Carmen, slumps over the television as Tom Waits's 'Ruby's Arms' swells on the soundtrack. For Coutard it is this film, rather than *Passion*, which is Godard's greatest – its balancing of light in the shots of Detmers taken at the very edge of dusk in the apartment in Brittany is nowhere excelled in his work, its statement of the great themes of death and the impossibility of love never more poignant. The scene where Joseph collapses helpless to the flow of Carmen's desire as Tom Waits sings on the soundtrack of the impossibility of staying in his much beloved Ruby's arms must rate amongst the greatest and most unbearable of love scenes in the cinema.

Carmen ends with the caption, 'In memoriam small movies'; this film is in fact another farewell to the cinema that Godard found more and more intolerable. His fights with the diminished crew were more violent. 'He was even very disagreeable with me', says Coutard, and his relationship with Detmers – unwillingly made to strip to the skin for the camera – was as bad as if not worse than those with other women who had figured female desire for him. When Mo Teitelbaum had talked with Godard about the sequence of the naked woman in *British Sounds*, Godard had emphasised how important pubic hair was to the nudity, how crucial it was for a genuine acceptance of the body. In *Prénom Carmen*, whatever the terrible human relationship endured by actress and director, Godard portrays a woman's body in the beauty of youth, with its full weight of sexuality and eroticism, without falling into the

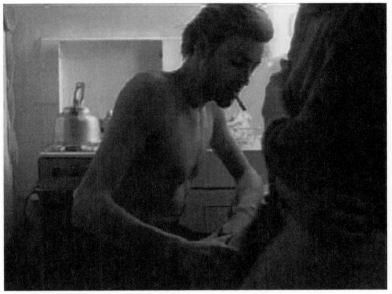

Jacques Bonaffé in *Prénom Carmen*, 1983.

pornographic. Perhaps the young Stephen Daedalus's aesthetic theory in *A Portrait of the Artist as a Young Man* comes closest to giving us the right terms: 'The feelings excited by improper art are kinetic, desire or loathing. Desire urges us to possess, to go to something; loathing urges us to abandon, to go from something. These are kinetic emotions. The arts which excite them, pornographical or didactic, are therefore improper arts. The aesthetic emotion (I use the general term) is therefore static. The mind is arrested and raised above desire and loathing.'[23]

However successful *Carmen* was for the audience – and it won multiple prizes at Venice in the autumn of 1983 – it was also another ending, as Godard made clear at the time in an interview he gave to the magazine *American Film*:

The film started from an economic need when I feared *Passion* was going to be a commercial failure. So I tried to organise another picture and then there was the possibility to sign a contract with Adjani if we would do a Carmen, and Anne-Marie Miéville was very interested in Otto

Preminger's *Carmen Jones* at that time. I, too, liked *Carmen Jones* immensely. I realised that you couldn't do Carmen without music but I couldn't do it with Bizet's music which would be just like a photocopy. And I realised that the real subject of Carmen is the music and the body, and the script comes from that realisation – the lovemaking between music and the body.

Q: You said that you got ill during *Passion* and it nearly killed you.

A: *Carmen* killed me even more.

Q: Why?

A: Oh, the crew and the way they thought you made movies. They were against the movie, so we made the movie against the crew. Like the captain of a ship, like Captain Ahab.

Q: In *Sauve qui peut (la vie)* there were no real problems.

A: Yes, there were, but I was equal to the crew in strength and imagination, and now I am not as strong. I am weaker than the crew.[24]

In the discussion that I had heard on the set of *Sauve qui peut*, Godard repeated again and again that the major trouble with film-making came from the fact that once the money was committed, it had to be spent and spent fast. There was no possibility of stopping, reflecting, starting again, although from *Prénom Carmen* onwards, Godard would almost always work exactly like this. There was an immediate exception in 1984 when, in order to finance '*Je vous salue, Marie*', he had to make the star vehicle *Détective* with Johnny Hallyday and Nathalie Baye, but from the mid-eighties on, Godard makes his movies at his own rhythm and in his own time. The vast majority of his work is shot within a few kilometres of Rolle, and on a completely flexible timescale.[25] This rhythm of production is only possible because Godard refuses to treat his budgets as any normal producer would. Very few film-makers are now able to make a film without calculating the expenditure in advance in incredible detail. Of course there are contingencies, and much of the technical skill of film production is in giving the director the greatest degree of choice within an apparently very detailed budget. But to be able to spend money as the film itself develops is almost impossible.

Nathalie Baye in *Détective*, 1985.

Jean-Pierre Léaud in *Détective*, 1985.

Godard refuses to submit such budgets. Like a small artisan, he will quote a price and then deliver his product without accounting for it, which means that he is widely suspected of pocketing most of his budgets. But these suspicious minds neglect the fact that any surplus money is immediately used for other projects or more equipment, for owning equipment rather than hiring it is another way of escaping the tyranny of the budget. Over the years, Godard has been supported by Gaumont, but there is no doubt that much of his own money has been spent this way: 'A film which costs four million can be made for three. At that point one can invest a million in equipment – an enormous sum. I think we are the company which, in percentage terms, invests more than any other in equipment. And that's another idea that comes from Rossellini.'

Godard has certainly not always made money on his films and, like any great artisan, he has been known to spend his own money to perfect a project. His first shoot of his contribution in 1987 to the multi-part film *Aria* so displeased him that he shot it again at his own expense. The British director, Don Boyd, who produced the film, was astonished that Godard wanted to re-shoot what he saw as perfect footage, and even more astonished when Godard said he would pay for it himself. Godard finally edited the re-shot film in one perfectly prepared session in Rolle, where the film was assembled at the editing table before Boyd's eyes. Boyd was amazed by the complexity of the equipment, above all by the sound, and by the originality with which video and film were linked together. Godard was visibly nervous as he assembled the film shot by shot with an assistant, and even more nervous as he then ran the eleven-minute film in its entirety. Boyd was ecstatic at what he saw. He had on several occasions given up on the Godard contribution, and did not hide his incredible pleasure at what Godard had produced; Godard hugged him in thanks.

At the celebratory lunch in one of Rolle's small restaurants, described earlier, Godard explained his method of production and the centrality of his partnership with Miéville.[26] The level of Godard's mastery of the production process is without obvious parallel in the history of the cinema. This is not just a question of the ownership and access to the technology, but also of the control of the money in the form of expenditure. Although no external budgets are produced, there are internal budgets and Hervé Duhamel, Godard's assistant in the late eighties, remembers Godard sitting down and, without hesitation, writing out an entire budget including separate line items for each tax. Godard also often produces the daily schedule complete with directions to the location.

When Boyd saw the results of the second shoot for *Aria*, he understood why Godard had been so dissatisfied with his first effort, and why he had described it as 'badly directed'. Godard had chosen Armide's recitative aria from act two scene five of Lully's 1686 opera *Armide*. The story is taken from Tasso's *Gerusalemme Liberata*, and Armide is singing of her desire for the French knight, Renaud, and her wish to kill him because he has refused her advances. Godard sets his film in a bodybuilding gym where two beautiful young women try unsuccessfully to seduce or to kill two bodybuilders insulated in their male narcissism.[27] The force of the film comes from the beauty of the women who try hopelessly to engage the attention of the bodybuilders but, as Boyd realised when he saw the final version, that beauty must be unselfconscious. In the first shoot, Godard had allowed or encouraged the young women to flaunt their physical attraction, to turn themselves into masculine fetishes.

Aria can be seen as a coda to '*Je vous salue, Marie*', a film which solves the impasses of masculine sexuality by recording the physical beauty of the woman's body in a situation where the masculine desire to control and penetrate has been forbidden. In an age where sexual desire has become the single most important element in the stimulation of economic demand, it seems incredible to choose the story of Joseph and Mary for a film focused on the body. But in a highly influential book of 1977, *L'Evangile au risque de la psychanalyse*, Françoise Dolto, a leading Lacanian psychoanalyst and child therapist, had made a new version of the traditional Christian argument for the Holy Family as the ideal couple. The lack of sexual union is not a barrier to this idealisation because it makes explicit the most essential element of the Lacanian theory, that fatherhood is a metaphorical state.

Freud's account of the Oedipus story had stressed the rivalry between father and son, but it is Lacan who emphasised that in so far as the son remains in this state of rivalry, fantasising a position of pure phallic power, he is constantly at risk of psychosis, of being unable to distinguish between symbol and reality. It is the moment at which the child recognises that the father is himself caught up in the circuits of desire, and that his possession of the phallus is dependent on the desire of the mother, that we find the deepest of hatreds that sunders father and son. But this is also the moment when the father himself is symbolised, and the name of the father marks the place where a dead father allows desire to live. Fatherhood is this symbolic function, which no individual can assume, and for which Joseph is a perfect example.

Godard's reliance on Dolto is very considerable, and her words punctuate Godard's own explanation of the film: 'This extraordinary couple help us to discover the depth of feelings in a meeting between an ordinary man and an ordinary woman.'[28]

Mary was played by Myriem Roussel. Godard had met Roussel on the set of *Passion*, in which she is the naked girl in the pool who allows Jerzy to contemplate 'the universal wound'. Godard cast her as Joseph's 'different' girlfriend in *Carmen*, but with '*Je vous salue, Marie*' she becomes the undisputed star of the film. Godard's relationship to Roussel was extremely close. In 1985, Alain Bergala brought out a collection of Godard's writings and interviews which updated a much inferior edition published early in 1968. The volume was prefaced with a biography in pictures to which Godard contributed the final two pages. One grouped Roussel with Karina and Wiazemsky as 'those who had counted in the image'; the other was a portrait of Miéville 'who had counted in life'. Roussel described their relationship thus:

> I met Godard on *Passion*. I was an extra for the paintings. One girl was ill and I was asked to replace her. Afterwards we began to talk. He had a very old project which was the story of a father and daughter. We worked on this project in video. Then in the meantime we made *Prénom Carmen* together. Then it became clear that the project could not be realised, because it demanded far too much personally that I was certainly incapable of and perhaps he was too. It was a project which was a little

like an analysis: to use daily life to make a film. We thus abandoned it to make '*Je vous salue, Marie*'. You have to live things before you film them. I think that posed too many problems, that we should both have had to live things that we didn't really need. You have to be incredibly strong to live all that and know how to use it for work. That's where I in the end preferred to separate . . . To use myself from what I could be, to what I am for work, but not to utilise my daily life for that, to fashion a daily life for that.[29]

Godard's commitment to '*Je vous salue, Marie*' and his efforts to raise money reached as far as England. He asked me whether I could try to get money from the newly established Channel 4, and I was lucky enough to discover that the channel was keen to fund some new Godard work. When Channel 4 had been set up in 1982, it had bought the Other Cinema's entire back catalogue, which included nearly all of Godard's films since 1968, and they had been waiting for an opportunity for a Godard season. The new film would provide one. Godard had asked for $100,000 to which Channel 4 was agreeable, but they wanted something more – an original documentary for which they would provide an additional $60,000. I had been so impressed by the television work of the late seventies that I persuaded Channel 4 to give the commission for the documentary to both Miéville and Godard, rather than to Godard alone.

Godard wanted an idea for the documentary, and I suggested that he and Miéville could make a film on Britain – a 'British

Anne-Marie Miéville and Godard in *Soft and Hard*, 1985.

Images' to complement his *British Sounds* of sixteen years earlier. I even produced a treatment for such a work. But when Godard had received the money and finished '*Je vous salue, Marie*', there followed a long period of procrastination which resulted in Godard and Miéville making a documentary which reflected on their own lives in Rolle – *A Soft Conversation between Two Friends on a Hard Subject* or, for short, *Soft and Hard*.

It would be easy to take a cynical view and suggest that considerations of cost and time meant that the British topic was always a mere fiction, but one could just as well argue that the British topic did not in the end mean much to Miéville and Godard. The passage from reflecting on Britain to reflecting on their own lives was not a devious or hypocritical one – ideas were genuinely pursued until the moment at which they caught fire. The cynical and the friendly interpretations are probably not genuine alternatives; they are better grasped as two sides of an indivisible coin.

The length of time taken in the production meant that I was not involved in the final stages when Tony Kirkhope of the Other Cinema, which provided the production company, and Rod Stoneman, the commissioning editor at Channel 4, hurried the documentary down to the wire.[30] In fact it was Rod Stoneman who became Godard's primary English interlocutor, not least because he had the most at stake in getting the documentary finished on time for the already scheduled season. Stoneman recalls:

> What struck me most about Jean-Luc – from our first meeting in the Pâtisserie Valérie in Old Compton Street – was the absolute continuity between Godard's imaginative and discursive work and his life. With other film-makers there was often a pause and a change of gear as they moved from the creative work to the financial business. Not with Jean-Luc who moved with a immediate gentle irony between one and the other without a break. Also he was, if not egoless, relatively unconcerned with his status. Other famous film-makers might make an effort to be almost ordinary but you inevitably noticed the effort – Jean-Luc had no concern with how he was being regarded. By and large directors are linear in speech and behaviour, Jean-Luc was always non-linear.

Over the next few years I went and saw him several times in Rolle and ended up buying the first episodes of the *Histoire(s) du cinéma* as well as *Grandeur et décadence d'un petit commerce du cinéma* and Miéville's *Mon cher sujet*. I'll never forget one occasion on which I had to take a taxi to Geneva airport and didn't have enough money – Jean-Luc threw a handful of notes on the table with an extraordinary gesture that indicated that the money might pass through him but it wasn't a preoccupation of his – and all this without the slightest shift of gear.

He was always very solicitous about my first son, who was born at that time. In fact as Jean-Luc knew Adam had been born a couple of days after a visit to Rolle there was a certain poignancy in his kind concerns. There's a line in *Soft and Hard*: 'So I'm making pictures instead of making children. Does that stop me being a human being?' The evolution of *Soft and Hard* was very easy – it seemed sensible for me to have the meditation closer to home. The finished programme offered an extraordinary glimpse into a way of looking at the world, playing between the passing events of History and everyday life. Their ways of understanding – the 'despair of art', politics, relationships and creativity – were, of course, remarkable. I felt that the consideration of pornography and technology might have been more developed and imagistically richer if we'd had more time, but we had the deadline of the Godard season and I was happy with the result – although I felt that Godard himself felt there was something unfinished about it. There was some argument about how we would present the finished programme. Jean-Luc wanted it dubbed, as he was concerned that subtitles distract from the image. But I managed to persuade him that, in terms of British television and the traditions of synch speech in our cultures, subtitling would be 'less worse' for the piece. In fact he checked Orla Kustow's draft subtitles with rare precision.

One thing I remember very clearly was that when one night he put me up in his flat in Rolle there were no books at all in his bedroom. It struck me as a very ascetic and pure space for someone who lived amongst written texts – as all his films indicate.

'Je vous salue, Marie' brings to an end the cycle of films begun with *Sauve qui peut (la vie)*. If it was necessary to shoot *Détective* to finance

his everyday story of the divine, he would never again make a film within the constraints of the dominant film industry. Over a period of more than a decade, Godard made a series of films beginning with *King Lear* and ending with *For Ever Mozart*; all were shot with minimal crews and most of them in the environs of Rolle.

They contain much that is brilliant and wonderful, from Caroline Champetier's beautiful photography of dawn over Lake Geneva, to Godard's own extraordinary performance as the idiot in *Soigne ta droite*, but in all these films there is, and it is there in '*Je vous salue, Marie*' itself, something irreducibly private in the conjunction of the images, an attempt to bring together too much, a density of reference which leaves the films as fragments. Alain Bergala, whose magnificent editorial efforts have given us two volumes of *Jean-Luc Godard par Jean-Luc Godard*, considers, in an article of real subtlety and learning, that these films work as a whole – an entire work in which the whole is more than the sum of its parts. Bergala's thesis may well be true, but there can be no doubting his other assertion, that from the late eighties onwards Godard's major creative commitment was to his video history of the cinema *Histoire(s) du cinéma*.[31]

These *Histoire(s)* have a long incubation dating from Godard's first days as a critic, and it is certain that their spiritual begetter is Henri Langlois. At the time of Langlois's death in 1978, he had been expected at the University of Montreal to give lectures on the history of the cinema. Godard took his place and delivered a series of lectures published in book form as *Introduction à une véritable histoire du cinéma*. Godard's teaching method was to show extracts of one of his own films with other relevant films: *Contempt* with *Man with a Movie Camera*, *The Bad and The Beautiful* and *Day for Night*; *Week-end* with Tod Browning's *Dracula*, *Germany, Year Zero* and *The Birds* etc. The lectures are extraordinarily interesting in themselves, and they constitute a summary of his views on cinema at exactly the moment that he moves to Rolle. However, there is a constant complaint running through them about the inadequacy of the method he is using: there should be a way to undertake a history of the image with the image, to narrate visually the history of cinema.

In 1988, Godard surprised me by asking me if I wished to see some work in progress. I was surprised, because after '*Je vous salue, Marie*' he never volunteered any information about the films that he was working on, even to complain about them. From my very marginal perspective, I had the impression that they were now becoming unwelcome if financially necessary chores. But what I saw was not a film; indeed, it defied any simple characterisation. It was an extraordinary montage of both image and sound which could be classified as a history of cinema, but equally it seemed to be a history of the twentieth century. Documentary footage, particularly of the Second World War and the concentration camps, was juxtaposed with clips of a wide array of films. The imagery was further complicated by quotation from the legacy of Western art and inflected by a soundtrack which drew on a huge range of both popular and classical music. At the centre of this flow of sounds and images is the figure of Godard himself in his studio at Rolle, reading, writing, editing. It seemed to me on this very first viewing, and the initial impression has not left me, that Godard was now working on a new level.[32]

Montage had always been his key to the cinema, a placing together of two images, of two sounds, to make a new meaning. This operation is not in fact dependent on the technology of the cinema, but it is cinema which discovered this operation – for Godard it is *the* discovery of the cinema.[33] Now, thanks to the technology of video and to the generosity of Freddy Buache in the Swiss archive in Lausanne, Godard was able to develop Langlois's Cinémathèque of the 1940s and its endlessly inventive programming in a new direction. He could now undertake a montage of the twentieth century which juxtaposed the personal, the fictional, and the documentary in a way which simply ignored the usual assumptions of priority or importance of one element over another. History is always history for a particular person, and the history of the real and its fictions are not dissociable in the way that most written history assumes. Godard himself says of the programmes:

> I had a plan that I never changed, it was the name of the eight programmes. I knew that the first episode, *All the Histories*, would show

that cinema immediately took possession of everything. Next I showed that its way of working was very solitary, it is the episode that I have called *A Solitary History* . . . Then *The Cinema Alone*, which shows that in fact the cinema has been the only form to both film history and little stories, little musical comedies, little gags, screwball stuff which everybody has thought worthless since the twenties.

After that I show that the cinema is men filming women. There is something fatal there. It is the history of beauty which, in painting as in literature, has always been linked to women, and not to men. Thus it's *Fatal Beauty*. Then it is *The Currency of the Absolute*, which comes from Malraux. There is therefore a kind of absolute to which you have to account: you have to pay. Then, still under the influence of Malraux, there is *The Answer of Darkness*, since the cinema comes from the dark. Then it is *The Control of the Universe*, the aspect linked to economic power (although it is treated in a different manner). The end is *The Signs Amongst Us*: the cinema is a sign and the signs are among us. It is the only one which has given us a sign. The others have given us orders. The cinema is a sign to interpret, to play with, you've got to live with it. (G2:16–1)[34]

Godard's emphasis on interpretation and play is crucial to understanding the *Histoire(s)*. It might seem possible to complain that Godard has missed many of the most important moments at which the history of the twentieth century is the history of the cinema; for example, the role of early newsreels in the astonishing outburst of nationalism that ensured that the outbreak of war in August 1914 was to signal the end of Europe; the extraordinary moment when Laurence Olivier brings stage to screen and Henry V fights both the last great imperial war and Nazism; the importance of the Hollywood blacklist in limiting the potential of the American cinema in the post-Second World War years; the paradox by which the blaxploitation movies of the early seventies were never given a chance to develop because of the devastating politically correct attack launched on them.[35] Such topics (except perhaps the Hollywood blacklist) do not interest Godard. What interests him is his cinema, the cinema of Langlois and the cinema of the New

Two pages from a working document for the *Histoire(s) du cinéma*.

FOR LIFE

OH !
TEMPS

TO GIVE BACK TO CINEMA

WHAT IT STOLE FROM IT

(LOUIS DELLUC)

Wave. The *Histoire(s) du cinéma* allow 'the eye to negotiate for itself'. They allow both us and Godard to refind within these images a real heritage. Godard's *Histoire(s)* are genuinely a new way of presenting history. The advent of video technology means that there can be a new kind of reflection on the image in which the most private of identifications and the most public of images can be conjugated together.

The originality of the *Histoire(s)* makes them extremely difficult to describe, and any description runs the risk of making them sound like some kind of academic puzzle of 'hunt the reference', in which the half-glimpsed shots and transposed images have to be identified. It is certainly true that these histories invite commentary. Within a year of their being completed, the great French scholar Jacques Aumont had produced a magnificent book devoted to them, and they had been featured in a special number of *Art Press*. There is every likelihood that this is only a start.[36] But fascinating as such studies are, they risk obscuring the extraordinary force of the *Histoire(s) du cinéma*. The important point is that each sound and image is only incidentally a quotation or reference; their real function is as the direct material of the story Godard is telling, a story which is deeply personal, but which is also the story of us all.

It is perhaps worth looking at the most discussed sequence from the very first part, when Godard juxtaposes an Elizabeth Taylor smile from George Stevens's *A Place in the Sun* with footage of the concentration camps. On the soundtrack, Godard relates how Stevens was one of the first to film the camps, and he analyses the force of Taylor's smile in terms of Stevens's desire to celebrate life after this experience of death. On the one hand this scene fits into the major theme of the histories – that the cinema is guilty for allowing the camps to happen, for not recording history accurately enough either to stop the killing from happening or to understand what happened. At the same time, the sequence is simply one of the most startling of memento mori. The skull is always there beneath the skin, even if the skin is as young and beautiful as Elizabeth Taylor's.

The enormous achievement of the *Histoire(s)* is to have married these levels, the historical – the general theses of the centrality of film to the history of the twentieth century – and the formal – the looting of the archive of cinema to provide an abstract pattern of existence. While the *Histoire(s)* are an immense historical excavation, they are also patterns of sound and image which engage and illuminate on their own terms.

While the *Histoire(s)* appeared through the early nineties, I was working for most of the year at the British Film Institute. My days on the *Sauve qui peut* shoot in the autumn of 1979 had been an important part of my own shift of emphasis from academic work to practical production. If those autumn days in Switzerland are clear to me in retrospect, what was clear at the time was that, however much I might have written about the cinema, I understood very little about film-making. But from 1985 to 1989 I was Head of Production at the British Film Institute and made good some of the deficiencies in my education. I was then asked to take over the whole of the BFI's publishing and educational activities with the aim of building the kind of education that Bazin had sketched out a generation earlier.

One immediate task was to develop a television arm. We published books and magazines on films – why should we not make television programmes? What was intended as a tiny initiative suddenly found itself overtaken by planning for the centenary of cinema, due in 1995. Channel 4 wanted us to provide a memorable anniversary, and we ended up producing sixteen films around the world. Each film was a great director's personal view of their own national cinema, with Martin Scorsese's history of American cinema as our flagship.

Channel 4 of the nineties was not the Channel 4 of the eighties, and the only clear instruction I received was that we were not to commission an incomprehensible Godard. British television, which in its own way had been as creative and enjoyable a place as classic Hollywood, had also been totally dominated by the producers rather than the consumers of programmes. There had been bitter rivalry and competition between BBC and ITV, but it took place in a context within which producers sought to please themselves and their peers as much as their audience. Channel 4 had not challenged this system, but instead had expanded its horizons. But with Margaret Thatcher's Broadcasting Act of 1990, and the advent of cable and satellite, this system was coming to an end.

So I didn't even argue for Godard. I approached another obvious choice, Bertrand Tavernier, a great critic and director of more conventional taste. A year of amusing and instructive conversations made clear that, much as he was tempted, even Tavernier was daunted by the prospect of presenting a history of French cinema in fifty minutes. At this point I told Channel 4 that I would have to ask Miéville and Godard. I thought they were the only directors who might possibly accomplish the commission in the short time now available, but also they were the only directors I knew well enough to ask while admitting that Tavernier had been our first choice.

BFI TV was meant to make up only a small part of my duties, which most importantly involved making film central to every level of education from primary to graduate school. When the 'Century of Cinema' project ballooned into life, I had to find a partner to run it with me, and I was lucky enough to persuade Bob Last to collaborate. His time as a manager of punk rock groups had left him with a keen grasp of the problems of copyright. Copyright was key because from an economic point of view the sixteen programmes involved little more than the exchange of the copyright on the clips used in the programmes, with the initial and crucial value being provided by Scorsese's choice of extracts from classic Hollywood.

Godard presciently understands copyright as a crucial artistic and political issue. Most legal discussions turn around differences between the French and the Anglo-Saxon systems, with the French being held to favour the author, while the Anglo-Saxon favours the owner of the copyright. What differences there are pale into insignificance beside the fact that neither system allows the audience any rights whatsoever. But in a world where we are entertained from cradle to grave whether we like it or not, the ability to rework image and dialogue, light and sound, may be the key to both psychic and political health. What is certain is that the work that Godard accomplished with *Histoire(s) du cinéma* would be more or less impossible for any other individual on the planet. When Rod Stoneman bought the first two episodes for Channel 4, the head lawyer decided that although one might argue that there were 'gross breaches of multiple copyrights', they would be broadcast without clearing these rights under the protection of the 'fair dealing' provision of the British copyright act, which allows a limited amount of quotation for the purposes of criticism.

Even if such individual bravery is to be commended, its effects will always be local. It is impossible to imagine broadcasters across the world daring to take on the massive entertainment corporations which understand their copyrights to be their most significant economic asset.

When John Milton wrote *Areopagitica*, his classic defence of free speech, the only part of the censorship bill he excused from censure was that which preserved 'justly every man's Copy to himself.'[37] It may seem simply an amusing paradox that the first bill in England to introduce copyright is famous for Milton's attack on its other provisions which prevented the free circulation of ideas. But three and a half centuries on it is neither amusing nor a paradox, for copyright is now one of the major obstacles to the free development and exchange of ideas.

In so far as people think of copyright, they imagine (as did the drafters of Milton's bill) an individual handing on to their children and grandchildren a right which then expires. In fact two thirds of global copyrights are now owned by six corporations. Even when the copyright rests with an individual, that individual may in the twenty-first century have amassed royalties beyond the dreams of those early Protestant capitalists trying to define a new property right. Should the Rolling Stones still own 'Satisfaction' when they have already earned many millions from it and when, if I wished to make any record of my own life, it would be impossible not to use it and yet impossible to afford the cost of permission? There is little doubt that these questions will become more pressing throughout this century. Godard's obsession with copyright is not merely an individual idiosyncrasy but rather a real understanding of the contemporary realities of sound and image.

These realities were the everyday work of 'The Century of Cinema', and Bob Last's experience was crucial to that work. We divided responsibilities for each of the sixteen productions, and for Miéville and Godard we decided that Bob should take full control. Bob Last recalls the experience:

The first time I talked to Godard on the phone I felt this wave of Dickensian misanthropy and felt, then, as I did during other phone calls, like an importunate car dealer. He said 'of course, if you ask me then I must do it – but it is completely impossible'. At our initial lunch in Rolle I had the strong feeling that he was enjoying our unease. We needed to get some kind of treatment from him to convince the money and yet we knew there was no point in asking him for so unGodardian an entity. I was astonished by the sophistication of his mixing studio in Rolle and indeed sound seemed a dominant theme in all my dealings with him. I learnt two things from that first lunch: I learnt that he saw himself as above all else a French film-maker where I had thought of him as engaging with a more international space. And what went along with that was a kind of French government line that one needed to put up the euro-bureaucratic barriers against an American monoculture. I found it very surprising that someone as smart and interesting had so fixed a view of the situation. The second thing was that we were going to be working from an unusual starting point – a world wherein any productive action was to be considered fundamentally impossible yet he, Godard, was condemned to try. Our series was suddenly a chain gang peopled by movie-makers and we were the prison guards. Somewhat to my surprise he did come up with a treatment which was about the fact that no one now really remembered French cinema. In the treatment this was going to involve going to famous locations of French cinema – like Pigalle from *Bob le flambeur* – and seeing what people knew of the great films of French cinema. In the end he dropped that idea in favour of getting Michel Piccoli to come down to Rolle and gently roasting him about his presidency of the committee charged by the government to celebrate the centenary. I always knew that with Godard you got lucky or you didn't and I thought we got lucky. When he asked if he could delay delivery to fit in with Piccoli's schedule, I was more than happy.

We'd been much more worried about whether the clips he was using would be properly cleared for worldwide delivery and a lot of time had gone into preparing a watertight contract which specified that forty per cent of the budget would be spent on clips. We were completely stumped when he said that he'd be using no clips that he didn't own and asked for

BFI TV
Head: Colin MacCabe
BY FAX TO : 44 21 825 4824

BRITISH FILM INSTITUTE

CELEBRATING THE MOVING IMAGE

December 9th 1993

Sonimage Suisse
15 rue du Nord
Rolle
Switzerland

British Film Institute
21 Stephen Street
London W1P 1PL.

Telephone 071 255 1444
Telex 27624 BFILDNG
Fax 071 436 7950

Registered Charity

Dear Anne-Marie and Jean-Luc,

100 YEARS OF CINEMA

I have faxed separately covering all our detailed
discussions. I now have to ask you your thoughts on a
broader issue.

We have still not concluded our negotiations with
Canal Plus and in the meantime we feel obliged to
think about all possible ways of funding your
programme, which as you know we are extremely keen to
have as part of our series.

One possibility is ARTE and this would inevitably
involve the issue of French rights to "Anne-Marie
Miéville and Jean-Luc Godard's 100 Years of Cinema",
as well as the rights to the the rest of our series.
Our discussions with Sonimage to date have been on the
basis that you would hold the French rights to your
programme. If it became appropriate for BFI TV to
include some or all French rights in our discussions
with third parties, what would Sonimage's view be and
what price would Sonimage put on them ?

Very best regards,

Yours,

BOB LAST

*one mexican
dollar if the
deal is signed
before 23 de-
cembre
Sincerely yours
jeanluc godard*

The British Film Institute exists
to encourage the development
of film, television and video in
the United Kingdom, and to
promote knowledge, under-
standing and enjoyment of the
system of the moving image.
Its activities include: the
National Film and Television
Archive; the National Film
Theatre; the Museum of the
Moving Image; the London
Film Festival; the production
and distribution of film and
video; funding and support for
regional activities; Library and
Information Services; Stills,
Posters and Designs; research;
Publishing and Education; and
the monthly Stills and Sound
magazine.

Patron
HRH The Prince of Wales
KG KT OCB

Chairman
Jeremy Thomas

Director
Wilf Stevenson

Assistant Director
Michael Prescott

Correspondence between Godard and the British Film Institute during the production
of *2 x 50 ans du cinéma français*.

BFI TV
Head: Colin MacCabe

BRITISH FILM INSTITUTE

bfi

CELEBRATING THE MOVING IMAGE

FAX TO: 21 825 48 24
  DATE:9 February 1994
  PAGE: 1 of 1
  FAO: Jean Luc Godard

Dear Jean Luc

Re: Anne Marie Mieville and Jean Luc Godard's 100
Years of French Cinema

I am pleased to confirm that we have now received the
confirmation we required from ARTE/La Sept.

I will prepare a letter agreement between BFI TV and
Peripheria (Suisse) reflecting our discussions to
date. I shall fax this to you on Friday and courier
hardcopies at the same time.

I have instructed preparation of a bankers draft for
$60,000, 20% of the $300,000 budget. This cheque will
be ready on Monday and couriered to you on receipt of
a signed agreement. The draft will be drawn on Lloyds
Bank and will be calculated in US$. If you would like
it drawn in a different currency please let Esther
Johnson in my office know.

Very best regards.

Bob Last

" but from thine eyes my
Knowledge I derive,
and, constant stars, in
them I read such art, "

British Film Institute
21 Stephen Street
London W1P 1PL

Telephone 071 255 1444
Telex 27624 BFILDNG
Fax 071 436 7950

Registered Charity

the forty per cent to be advanced straight away. It was a brilliant move
and to this day if you asked me whether it was a scam to avoid cost and
effort or an aesthetic strategy linked to his theme of the forgetting of the
movies I couldn't answer. It was both at the same time – cash theory
instead of critical theory – something I could respond to given my punk
days in the seventies. Corresponding with him was a lot of fun. Every
letter was written and from the opening 'Dear still just friends' the tone
would be set. As with all small businessmen delays in payment drove him
nuts but he was always reasonable if you explained the situation. He was
a deal-maker. Right at the end he felt that he wasn't being technically
consulted about the projection at Cannes – again he was particularly
worried about the sound – and he wrote to Gilles Jacob saying that he
wasn't being allowed final cut. But he copied the letter to us. His concern
did seem very enigmatic in technical terms, but here was a man whose
films had more to say about the detailed impact of technology on his work
than most, so I tried hard to address his concerns. As with other elements
of the production, a problem would arise, we'd work to solve it, the
production would move forward again but always on the unspoken

understanding that Jean-Luc
was reserving the right to come
back after some other twist or
turn and tell us that it hadn't
been a solution at all. It was
hilarious sitting with all the
dignitaries of French cinema
as Godard demonstrated that
the emperor of the centenary
had no clothes.

It was at the time of 2 × 50 ans
du cinéma français that Godard
showed me two treatments, one
for For Ever Mozart and one for
Nous sommes tous encore ici by
Miéville. Of his own treatment, I

Tanks breasting the hill at
Anthy in For Ever Mozart, 1996.

could make nothing at all. That Sollers was still a point of reference, that European politics – and above all the appalling and frightening events in former Yugoslavia – continued to be a major focus, all this was clear, but the film to be shot was a mystery buried deep in an enigma.[38]

Miéville's treatment was by contrast a model of clarity. In three parts, the first was a dramatisation of part of Plato's *Gorgias*, one of the first treatments in Western philosophy of the question as to why the strong should not dominate the weak, in which the roles of Socrates and Calliclès would be played by women; the second used an extract from Hannah Arendt's *The Nature of Totalitarianism*, which deals with solitude and loneliness, and which would be spoken by a man; and the third was a portrait of a contemporary couple.

I told Godard that I found Miéville's film much better thought through than his own effort. Reading the treatment of *For Ever Mozart*, you could see a companion piece to *Nouvelle Vague* (1990) and *Hélas pour moi* (1993), where the complexity and range of the material gathered together was, amongst other things, an indication of a lack of interest in the feature film as a form. Indeed, one could make a paradoxical argument that '*Je vous salue, Marie*' marked the passing within the company of the feature-film baton from Godard to Miéville.

Godard in *Nous sommes tous encore ici*, 1997.

Miéville had made shorts from the late seventies, but they had remained largely invisible. Godard decided to change this by making Miéville's short, *Le Livre de Marie* (The Book of Mary), a physically integral part of his own film '*Je vous salue Marie*'. If you wanted to see '*Je vous salue, Marie*', you had to see

Bernadette Lafont (left) as Socrates and and Aurore Clément (right) as Calliclès in *Nous sommes tous encore ici*, 1997.

Miéville's short which preceded it. Miéville's film, a small masterpiece, follows a young girl as she moves between her separated parents. It eschews all the familiar intensifiers of cinema, the close-up and the dramatic scene, in favour of accuracy of representation and a delicacy of editing. As a picture of a child attempting to hold together two parents that have broken – that most modern of conditions – it is difficult to imagine anything better. This short had been followed by *Mon cher sujet* (1989), a portrait of three generations of women, and *Lou n'as pas dit non* (1994), an account of the dissolution of a relationship inspired by the correspondence between Lou Andreas-Salomé and Rainer Maria Rilke, as well as further shorts.

At first glance and in brief description these films can sound soft and lyrical, but they are also hard and tragic; the isolation of human beings can rarely have been portrayed with as sympathetic or as cold an eye. In *Nous sommes tous encore ici*[39] two of the roles are taken by Godard, who proves amongst his other talents to be a very good actor.[40] In conventional terms, Godard already had acting credits – he had starred in an early Rohmer short and had appeared briefly in his own and other films, and with Karina he had acted in the silent film sequence in Varda's *Cléo de 5 à 7*. Perhaps more importantly, since *Deux ou troix choses que je sais d'elle* in 1967, his very recognisable voice has been an important element in many of his films, and in the eighties he had turned in major performances in *Prénom Carmen, King Lear* and *Soigne ta droite*.

Miéville's film opens with a sequence from the end of Plato's *Gorgias*. Gorgias is a historical figure, one of the most famous rhetoricians of his day. The dialogue rehearses Socrates's concern to assert the claims of truth and philosophy over argument and rhetoric, and it culminates when the fictional figure of Calliclès takes the argument to its logical conclusion – rhetoric's indifference to truth and justice merely reflects a world in which the strong should dominate the weak, in which the satisfaction of the passions is the only good. Calliclès simply states at greater length, and with more sophistication, the question which Thrasymachus poses at the beginning of the *Republic*, which is one of the central questions of Western philosophy: why it is not in the interest of the strong to dominate the weak.[41] By transposing the gender and the time of the dialogue, Miéville shifts the political question from the state to the couple. Socrates's argument that the only good life is one in which the passions are dominated by a notion of reasonable conduct, in which wisdom and knowledge are the supreme virtues, is transposed from the public space of Athenian politics to the domestic space of the contemporary West.

Arendt's *Origins of Totalitarianism* remains the single most important work of political philosophy in the twentieth century. Miéville focuses not on its broad sweep of European history, but on passages which contrast the richness of solitude and the poverty of isolation for the individual. Now a male voice animates a female text, and furthermore, it is Godard's voice, a voice which has spoken to us for so long about his solitude. This sequence is remarkable for it requires Godard to forgo his very marked discontinuous forms of speech in order to deliver a continuous philosophical discourse. His ability to deliver the text, and he delivers it well, while retaining something of his own hesitancy in language, is a performance of the very highest order – the actor holding text and self in a genuine montage. It is surely not impertinent to think that no director other than Miéville could have elicited such a reading.

In taking two of the most famous texts of political philosophy and focusing them both on the individual rather than the state, Miéville remains true to the themes of *Ici et ailleurs* and the slogan which ends the number of *Cahiers* which they jointly edited: 'On whom does repression depend – on us; on whom does liberation depend – on us.'[42] Politics starts in the home and the question of the dominance of the strong and the weak, the question of creative solitude or disabling isolation are questions that start with the couple. The couple that we now meet in the third section of the film (the woman is played by Aurore Clément from the first section and the man by Godard) are obviously long used both to each other's company and to each other's weaknesses. Their conversation combines the quotidian – shall we go for a walk? shall we go for a trip? – with the most fundamental questions of work and love – what is the relation between life and art? what constitutes love? While the tone, both verbal and visual, could hardly be more controlled, the content is frequently painful. Godard's, 'It's incredible how much you hate me', or Clément's resort to a casual pick-up, make clear that the extraordinary level of connection between the couple is very far from conventional ideas of married bliss. At the same

Aurore Clément and Godard in *Nous sommes tous encore ici*, 1997.

time, there is a moving conclusion when Godard pledges his love. *Nous sommes tous encore ici* is a major work in a minor key.

It was during this period that I first broached the possibility of Miéville and Godard taking on a commission from the British Film Institute and the Museum of Modern Art. In 1992 I had worked on a retrospective of Godard's work since 1975 at the Museum of Modern Art in New York. The crucial force behind the retrospective and its accompanying book was Mary Lea Bandy, Curator of Film and Media at MoMA. My new work at the British Film Institute had led our paths to cross, and we had discovered a shared passion to redefine the way in which the history of cinema was exhibited and curated. It was obvious that the first wave of cinémathèques, museums and institutes had to find new ways to show film in the age of video and DVD, and such new ways involved a complete rethinking of the place of cinema in relation both to history and the other arts. Bandy remembers the adventure:

> I'd always loved Godard's films but what really surprised me was the first time I saw his videos and saw that he had mastered the medium of video as well. And that probably was the main impetus that made me want to put on the retrospective: to see the films and the videos together. And

Anne-Marie Miéville and Godard at the Sarlat Festival, 2000.

what riches we saw, above all the *Histoire(s) du cinéma* which I consider
one of the great gifts of an artist to his particular public, a rich legacy.
What was fascinating as we put the book together was Godard's generous
loan of photographs, sketches, and notebooks for the catalog which
spurred my thinking about his approach to image-making as a collagist.
And then I listened to Godard at a press conference in Cannes for further
episodes in the *Histoire(s) du cinéma*, where he said that at the end of the
twentieth century, we were finally beginning to grasp the nineteenth. And
that linked with the sense of loss and anger as he observed the end of a
political era in *Allemagne 90 neuf zéro*. And that gave rise to the idea
which came up in conversation with Colin: why not ask Miéville and
Godard to reflect on the arts at the end of the twentieth century and the
place of cinema in relation to the other arts?

I'll never forget when he came to New York to discuss the project and
we went to dinner with Celeste Bartos. I said to Godard 'This is the first
film I've ever produced and I've persuaded Celeste to fund it.' And his face
assumed a tremendously mournful expression and he sighed, 'Pauvre
Celeste'. But he was charming at the dinner as he was throughout the
production. He is not a man for small talk but he is a remarkly acute
observer so one always feels a little bit on guard. He can be extremely

funny but it is a mordant wit that keeps one constantly on guard. Anyone who has seen his short film on Woody Allen (*Meeting Woody Allen*) can see how subversive and witty he can be – definitely a little bit alarming.

I talked with Godard about the use of audio and visual clips and images, and I understood that his notion of fair use was a political and aesthetic act of appropriation: he uses them not as subjects in themselves, not as representations or copies to be studied as in catalogs; nor are they to be taken literally any more than are the extracts of texts and music. Rather, they serve to be transformed into his own audiovisual poetry and philosophy and commentary – they are but man-made elements that exist, I supposed, like words – found objects to be arranged as he desired, in a new form of literature, in chapters or exercises. Of course they are citations, quotes – they are I think the pipes and newspapers, the ropes and violins and absinthe glasses that compose early twentieth century Cubist collages.

I always felt that he had the very highest comprehension of beauty and that he had made a lot of sacrifices to preserve the purity of his vision. And there was also a sense, which went with this, of a monastic anger. But above all there was a tremendous integrity: a total commitment to his art.

At the beginning of *The Old Place*, the title that Miéville and Godard gave to their MoMA commission, in a classic self-reflexive moment, Godard reads from the contract for the film: 'The producers shall examine any object or subject, ordinary or extraordinary in order to reveal, by chance and with painstaking care any trace that may remain of what we call art. That is to determine if art is myth (légende) or reality.' It is perhaps not necessary to say that the exact clause is a fabrication but, as so often with Godard, the fabrication reveals the truth. Mary Lea Bandy's and my interest in commissioning the film from Miéville and Godard had arisen from our need to find a way to play our part in the transformation of our institutions. The time of Langlois was dead. If video had enabled Godard to see cinema anew, it had assassinated cinémathèques. And if a generation of marginals and deviants had found in cinema an authority and a tradition, the cinema that they had found was now also dead, a victim of the technological and economic advance that had brought it to light.

To orient ourselves in this new situation why not ask Godard, the greatest figure of the last generation of cinema? And given the clarity of the extraordinary work that they had accomplished together, why not ask Miéville? Celeste Bartos, one of the great patrons of the Museum of Modern Art and a long-time friend of the British Film Institute, whose generosity had saved 'The Century of Cinema' at a very early stage, was delighted at the idea. My own delight when it became clear that the project would go ahead was slightly tempered by my two previous experiences of *Soft and Hard* and *2 × 50 ans du cinéma français*. I expected a very rocky ride as we progressed from initial idea to final work of art.

I was completely wrong. Miéville's and Godard's re-definition of the project was a more intelligent version of what we had asked for. And indeed when Godard thanked me, on his and Miéville's behalf, for the commission, he also thanked me for the idea, which he said had turned out to be very useful in solving problems that they had both been thinking about.

It is difficult for me to claim much critical objectivity, but I consider *The Old Place* to be the finest of all the Miéville/Godard essays. As their two voices, so familar now over the years, answer back and forth across the images, as the soundtrack swells and falls, the question very simply posed is: What is Art in the twentieth century? And the question is posed in the shadow of death, of biological death and of the death of the century. If we understand Godard's Maoism as a desperate attempt to sustain the possibility (albeit virtual) of a contact between art and audience, *The Old Place* brings to a new level of achievement the choice of *Ici et ailleurs*, that is, to break the impasse of artist and audience, of the one and the many, through conversation – the necessity of dialogue. It is this dialogue which sustains *The Old Place* – a conversation so secure in its rhythms that it is able to confront any subject. And if we do not see the couple speaking, we do in a remarkably composed shot see Miéville and Godard sitting together in the studio in Rolle looking at the screen, their eyes, the only feature illuminated, negotiating for themselves.

One of the opening clips of *The Old Place* comes from the close of *The Magnificent Ambersons*, as Major Amberson contemplates his approaching end. It is a perfect example of Godard's use of quotation, because it is not at all necessary to know Welles's film to get the full force of the quotation. Like Major Amberson, like Godard, like the century, we confront a death which poses the most urgent of questions without any of the conventional props of our existence. The opening sections rehearse a number of deaths of art, from the concentration camps to the society of the spectacle. But these deaths are not elaborated from a pessimistic point of view: they are the realities from which we must begin to ask our questions. Like the *Histoire(s) du cinéma*, the tone is not tragic but elegiac. But these elegies, these celebrations of the dead, do not look back but forward.

The way forward is above all by new forms of juxtaposition, by developing the possibilities of montage which is the foundation stone of Godard's faith in the cinema. To use the words of Pierre Reverdy, which Godard has quoted again and again in the last two decades: 'The image is a pure creation of the mind, it cannot be born from a comparison, but comes from the bringing together of two distant realities . . . An image is not powerful because it is brutal and fantastic, but because the association of ideas is distant and true.'[43]

As these two voices rise and fall over their montages of the twentieth century and its arts, there is a wholesale rejection of much of contemporary culture and art. The modernist breaking of convention merely leads to a simple commercialisation of art in which the image is reduced to its contextual discourses. But the faith in art which has endured from the joyous discovery of the cinema is still there. Significantly, it is Miéville who makes the final statement: 'Nevertheless I feel that there is something that resists, something original, that the origin will always be there, and that it resists.'

Miéville then relates the Borges story taken from Burton's notes to the *Thousand and One Nights*, of the A Bou A Qou. The A Bou A Qou lives at the bottom of the Tower of Victory, from which one can regard the most marvellous landscape in the world. At the approach of each pilgrim, he comes to life and accompanies them up the stairs which begin to glow with an interior light. The light only reaches its full illumination if the pilgrim reaches the top of the stairs. When the pilgrim descends, the A Bou A Qou tumbles down to the bottom where its inert being awaits the next pilgrim. In an unusual emphasis Godard adds a final word: 'If we thought it good to finish the film with this text, it is because the text illustrates the film' ('c'est qu'il en est l'illustration').

Before *The Old Place* was delivered and as *Nous sommes tous encore ici* was being shot, edited and released, Godard was bringing the *Histoire(s) du cinéma* to a close in a multimedia release. On 9 October 1998, Gallimard bought out a four-volume boxed set of books;[44] a month later, on 6 November, Gaumont released the final version of all eight chapters on video,[45] and in December ECM produced a five-CD audio version of the work.

It is not possible to find a comparison to Godard's *Histoire(s)* in cinema or television, but there is good reason to compare it to James Joyce's *Finnegans Wake*. *Finnegans Wake* takes the whole of history and language for its subject and uses montage as its basic creative principle, but a montage which operates within the individual word. It attempts to tell the story of all human history and also records one individual life. Towards the end of his life and partly in reaction to a Parisian fashion started largely by Derrida and Sollers, Jacques Lacan turned to Joyce, who had been a figure of his own Parisian youth. Lacan devoted his 1975 seminar to Joyce, under the title of 'Le sinthomme'. 'Sinthomme' is the sixteenth-century spelling of the French word for 'symptom', and Lacan uses it because it gives him a pun between symptom and holy man ('saint homme'). Lacan needs this concept of the sinthomme to account for what he sees as a crucial third category to complement the opposition of neurosis and psychosis.

From the perspective of Lacanian psychoanalysis, the psychiatric distinction between the neurotic and the psychotic is understood in relation to the Oedipus complex. The neurotic is someone who has accepted the possibility that he or she could be different, that he or she could be she or he. The little boy or little girl posing the question of their own origin, of the desire that has produced them, confronts the fatal question of whether they could be a different gender ('what did my parents really want?'). That confrontation, which both Freud and Lacan name castration, determines the child's access to the world of the symbolic – the human world where words symbolise things and where the sexes define each other. This is the world of exchange.

Of course, this entry to the symbolic is always resisted, because it involves a narcissistic wound (if only in fantasy) to the original unified image of our self and body. It is this necessary wounding which makes us all neurotics, producing around this wound a symptom (hysterical or obsessional according to choice) which denies this possibility of difference. Lacan makes this crystal clear when he says that 'the Oedipus is the symptom.'[46] The alternative is psychosis, that is, the rejection of the very possibility of castration, of the symbolic itself. Here, to use the famous formulation, 'what has been rejected in the symbolic returns in the real', in the hallucinations and deformations of reality which are the consequence of the psychotic's inability to understand the separation between word and thing.

Lacan's seminar on the 'sinthomme' produces a third category, the neurotic whose symptom is to interrogate the symbolic itself. At risk of drowning in psychosis, Joyce finds in an excavation of the cultural tradition itself a substitution for an earthly father who is too weak and a heavenly father who is too strong. The whole question of my parents' desire and its role in my being, repressed by the neurotic and disavowed by the psychotic, is recast by the 'sinthomme' in terms of the relation to the social and cultural itself. It is here that Lacan's pun pays off, for the artist who uses his symptom to interrogate the symbolic, who takes for his aim the liberation of his self and his community at the same time is a holy man, a saint.

There are obvious parallels between Lacan's analysis of Joyce and Godard's *Histoire(s) du cinéma*. In the years from *Sauve qui peut* to *King Lear*, Godard had been obsessed with the symbolic – on the one hand referring to incest and on the other to religion. The incest taboo is one of the defining features of the human condition.[47] The fact that there are endless attempts to explain it in functional terms, as a genetic or economic imperative, merely emphasises the extent to which it is the very constitution of the human. And if incest took up one pole of Godard's interest, religion took up the other.

From Huppert's cry at the opening of *Passion*, 'O Lord, O Lord why hast thou forsaken me?' it might be easy to imagine that Godard, in tune as ever with the Zeitgeist, was hitching his cart to the monotheistic fundamentalism which as Bob Dylan presciently remarked was 'A Slow Train Coming', and which in Christian, Judaic and Islamic forms has dominated global politics ever since. From a French perspective, it should be stressed that Godard remained generally indifferent to media posturing around the rediscovery of religion by what was called 'la nouvelle philosophie' – a movement aptly summarised by *Time* magazine's headline, 'God is dead, Marx is dead and I'm not feeling too well myself'. Nor did he share Soller's assessment of the election of Pope John Paul II in 1978 as the greatest geo-political development since Mao's launching of the Cultural Revolution. But there is little doubt that when Godard did pick up on Christianity through Solidarity in 1980 and through Dolto's 1977 book, it was Catholicism as much as Protestantism which took his interest.

There are two points to be made about this concern with Catholicism. First, it is European culture and the European past which now obsess Godard, and that culture and that past are Catholic as well as Protestant. Second, however, Godard's interest in religion is profoundly Protestant. He has little interest in the content of religious beliefs – questions about that are brushed aside with some irritation. What is in question is belief itself, the faith that Luther defined and Calvin emphasised as the only essential element in one's relation to God. But while it is clear that '*Je vous salue, Marie*' finds a formal solution in a story which both forbids and licenses desire, there can be little doubt that the succeeding films – and particularly *King Lear*, where Godard reads the relationship between Lear and his daughters in terms of incest – reveal how formal and temporary that solution was. In a perceptive article, Richard Brody sees Godard's personal appearances in his films of the mid-eighties as an indication of his difficulty in knowing where to put himself in the picture.[48] It is interesting to note that it is in this period that Godard also showed some minor interest in biographical projects, both my own plan for a book and Alain Bergala's proposed biographical programme for television, which got as far as the first day of shooting before being abandoned.

There can be little doubt that the *Histoire(s) du cinéma* provided the form in which Godard could pursue the question of the symbolic, of his own place in society or, to put it another way, of his faith in the cinema in relation to the European faith of his fathers – the faiths of art and science and religion. It is not surprising that from now on there is no need for him to appear in his own films or to be interested in biographical projects. Now he has a way of finding his own place in the image, of finding in the story of cinema a paternal function which will acknowledge the death of the fantasy of absolute power while offering a model of how that death does not entail the renunciation of all desire.[49]

These most schematic of formulations do scant justice to works of such complexity and beauty which, until the copyright laws are changed or routinely violated, will remain without rival or comparison. But to understand these works as profoundly autobiographical is to do no more than state the obvious. At the end of the third section, in a magisterial reflection on his cinematic youth, Godard recites the names of Une Vague Nouvelle: 'Becker, Rossellini, Melville, Franju, Jacques Demy, Truffaut . . . yes, they were my friends.' The posthumous reconciliation with Truffaut was hard. When Caroline Champetier, then working for Sonimage, told Godard in 1984 that Truffaut was ill with an inoperable brain tumour, Godard's immediate reaction was, 'That's what happens if you read so many bad books.' However, when I asked him in 1988 if he missed Truffaut, he admitted that, although his death had not affected him at first, he was now beginning to miss him. The *Histoire(s)* treat Truffaut at some length, particularly in the long conversation with Serge Daney which occupies much of 2A, and the analysis developed there is restated in more concise form in *2 × 50 ans du cinéma français*. Truffaut is related to the cinema primarily through criticism and not through his films, but it is criticism which Godard holds to be the specific French contribution to the cinema. This criticism stretches back to Diderot and makes France the country which has reflected most deeply on the image and Truffaut the greatest representative of this tradition in Godard's generation.

The final section of the fourth chapter, *The Signs Amongst Us*, is

THE ARRIÈRE-BOUTIQUE: ANNE-MARIE MIÉVILLE AND ROLLE   319

dedicated to Anne-Marie Miéville and to Godard himself ('moi-même'). The opening section is one of the greatest evocations of love in European literature or cinema, a montage which includes footage of Karina and Wiazemsky over a text which sketches the impossibility of recalling the moment of love without it passing from the memory to the imagination. The final section and the whole *Histoire(s)* end with an acknowledgement of how privileged Godard has been to be able to film and live in France. But it is also an acknowledgement that the France in which he lives is a 'totally and permanently' corrupt society. Cinema is both hope and illusion, a promise of what was to come and a testament of what has been. As often in the *Histoire(s) du cinéma*, it is not simply the complexity of sound and image which astonishes, but the complexity of a thought which, from within the most realistic and pessimistic account of the twentieth century and its art, asserts an enduring flame. The last lines of the *Histoire(s)*, which rhyme back across twenty-five years to the project for the film *Moi, Je*, are pure lyric:

> If a man
> If
> a man
> travelled across
> paradise
> in a dream
> and received a flower
> as proof
> of his passage
> and on awakening
> he found
> that flower
> in his hands
> what is to be said
> I was
> that man[50]

Envoi

On 15 May 2001, I sat in the Grand Palais in Cannes for the screening of Godard's *Eloge de l'amour*. This was his first feature film in four years and the first since he had completed the *Histoire(s) du cinéma*. In recent years Cannes, like many other such events, runs a video display inside the theatre of the celebrities gathering outside. I had not seen Godard in more than two years. *The Old Place* had been intended to contribute to a renewed debate about the possibilities of the British Film Institute, but

Godard embraces Johnny Hallyday as he accepts an honorary César, Paris, February 1998.

by the time it was finished, the British Film Institute had been abolished in all but name. After its election in May 1997, New Labour appointed Alan Parker as Chairman of the British Film Institute. Parker's loathing of the BFI had been on record for over twenty years, and he duly stripped it of its production and graduate education functions and made it a subordinate client of a newly created industry body.[1] Godard had been both sympathetic and helpful when I left the Institute, but soon after he made it clear that he doubted there would be any more joint ventures. Truth to tell, I now had no reason to do business with him and, fond as I was of the old brute, I'd never thought that he found my company irresistible. And so instead of a snatched conversation to discuss the latest project in the hubbub of Cannes, I was able to regard him at my leisure on the video screen.

He had celebrated his seventieth birthday the previous December after a decade which had seen many honours, the most prominent of which were the Adorno prize of 1995 and in 1998 a César for the Nouvelle Vague which he had accepted with every sign of emotion. He had also continued to create controversy – collaborations with both La Fémis, the National Film School, and the TNP, the French National Theatre, had ended in familiar tears. The collaboration with Fémis had given his and Miéville's company a new name. Sonimage had had to be abandoned in the eighties when another company claimed prior rights to the name. The company was briefly called JLG Films, but this hardly reflected Miéville's role, and it was Jack Lang, the socialist Minister of Culture who, while brokering the deal with Fémis, suggested that as they were on the periphery, they should call themselves Périphéria.[2]

At Cannes, Godard had always seemed angry or resigned, actively annoyed or passively suffering the circus of the festival. But the figure who stood at the bottom of the steps of the Grand Palais looked quite different. Happy might perhaps be too strong a term, but serene would not. His ease with his actors as he gathered them to make the ascent, the distant but real familiarity with which he greeted his old contemporary, Gilles Jacob, at the top of the stairs, and his pleasure in the day were all palpable. Despite even these signs,

Godard gives his César acceptance speech, Paris, February 1998.

Bruno Putzulu, Cécile Camp and Godard at a photocall for *Eloge de l'amour*,
Cannes 2001.

nobody could have expected a 'normal' film. As Godard himself says: 'I
wish I could do a normal picture, normally, but with me, I don't know
why, it's not possible.'

The hatred of the simplifications of narrative, the belief that stories had
to be lived before they were told, the conviction taken as much from
Bresson as from Bazin that the performance before the camera must be
real, all this means that Godard is forever excluded from the greatest
achievements of narrative cinema. But if he is not a novelist, he is the
greatest essayist and one of the greatest poets that the cinema has known.

When I asked Philippe Sollers whether he agreed that Godard was the
great French poet of the twentieth century, he looked at me as if I were
an uncultured rustic. When I corrected myself and said, 'after Valéry', he
obviously regarded me as dangerously demented. But one has only to
read Godard's stammering words on the death of de Beauregard or to
open the volumes of *Histoire(s) du cinéma* or the transcripts that he has
published at POL,[3] to see that Godard is not only a poet, but a great

poet. In the POL publications and the *Histoire(s) du cinéma*, the text is transcribed from the film. But the text is not set on the page in relation to characters or stage directions. Quotations are not distinguished from original material. The text is merely broken up into phrases. The word 'phrase' indicates both a grammatical category below the level of the sentence and a unit of music linked to the individual improvisation of jazz. The words sit on the page, outside any final syntactic configuration, awaiting the breath of the reader to blow them into life.

When Joyce finished *Finnegans Wake* in 1939 he planned a very simple work. Death came first. After the huge European complexities of the *Histoire(s) du cinéma*, *Eloge de l'amour* is a simple French story. A young man Edgar, played by Bruno Putzulu, is pursuing (that most Sartrean of terms) 'a project'. Edgar is clearly a sympathetic version of Godard's younger self; he spends a great deal of time reading from a blank Mallarméan book of himself and manages not only to talk the Godardian talk but also to make a fair stab at a Godardian walk. Godard himself appears briefly on a bench in Paris overhearing two young lovers. And the structure of the film seems to pose an older Godard trying to synthesise the wisdom of age for the young of today. As with the young Godard of the late forties, the project has not yet found its medium – is it a play, a novel, an opera, a film? But the film's theme is simple: love and death. The love is that of Perceval for Eglantine, that courtly love in which the man renounces the possibility of enjoying the body of the woman. It was in courtly love that Lacan found the most accurate figuring of desire, because it makes clear the impossibility of actually possessing the sexual object. But if Perceval is content with this love, Eglantine is not. She dies.

This story is set in a breathtakingly beautiful black-and-white Paris, the Paris of the new millennium shot as though it were the late forties. The film remembers, after so many years, Godard's great love of Paris, and it comes as no surprise that Balzac, Godard's great model as a recorder of Paris, is a prominent reference. The Paris through which Edgar moves in his desire to tell the story of love is a world where not only art is bought and sold, but bodies too. If courtly love figures one side of the sexual equation, on the other are the beloved brothels of

Georges Bataille, churches in which the sacramental exchanges of flesh and money are daily performed. The beautiful woman in the rue de Rivoli with nothing but underwear beneath her smart coat could have stepped out of the pages of *Madame Edwarda*, Bataille's pornographic novel set in the brothels and streets of Paris. It was a world with which Godard was familiar both through Balzac – whose *Splendeurs et misères des courtisanes* describes that world in Paris of the 1830s – and through Jean-Pierre Melville, who introduced him to the world of scortatory lust in the 1950s.

The press book describes the first part of *Eloge de l'amour* thus:

> Someone we hear but don't see talks of a project entitled 'Eloge de l'amour', which deals with the four key moments of love: the meeting, the physical passion, the quarrels and separation, the reconciliation. These moments are seen through three couples: young, adult and elderly. Is the project to be a play, a film or even an opera? A sort of servant or assistant always accompanies the author of the project.
>
> Adults pose a real problem. Unlike old people or young people, an adult is hard to define without telling a story. The author of the project finally meets an extraordinary young woman. In fact they had already met three years earlier when Edgar had by chance been present during a discussion between some Americans and the young woman's grandparents. When he comes to tell the young woman that his project is on, Edgar learns that she has died.

The second part of the film opens on an orange sea breaking out of a yellow sky. We are in the world of colour, but of over-exposed video, of colour that is more than colour. It is an insistent theme of Godard's history that he has always been at the cutting edge of technology – from the lightweight cameras and portable recorders of the early sixties to the video technology of the seventies and eighties. But the digital developments of the last twenty years have been all but ignored. *Histoire(s) du cinéma* is punctuated by the sounds of the typewriter and the editing table, both technologies rendered redundant by the computer. When we were making *2 × 50 ans du cinéma français*, one of Godard's running jokes was that he was not on Bill Clinton's digital superhighway. At Cannes in 1997, he was even more direct in his judgment, 'Digital is like hotdogs or cigarettes – it's a technique' (G:2:412). The contempt for digital technology is never referred to the Bazinian premiss which is at the base of Godard's aesthetic, but rather related to an ever greater distinction between culture (the world of commerce) and art (the world of the individual).

In fact, Godard's use of video in this film (and *Eloge de l'amour* is the first film where video and film are really used together since *Numéro deux*)[4] is, as always, technologically innovative, but it is the innovation of the artisan rather than the production engineer. The method used has been developed with Julien Hirsch, who had worked as Caroline Champetier's assistant on *Hélas pour moi* and other projects. There is in fact a genealogy of assistants that goes back to Willy Kurant, the one cinematographer other than Coutard whom Godard used in the period between *Breathless* and *Week-end*. Lubtchansky was Kurant's assistant, Champetier was Lubtchansky's assistant, Hirsch was Champetier's assistant. In this succession one can discern Godard's desire to take on someone who, as he said when recruiting Champetier, 'knows something but not too much'. One of Godard's *bêtes noires*, from the earliest days, is the technician who has turned his knowledge into a set of rules – the assistant is less likely to have committed this cardinal sin.

Godard's method of working and his care for the equipment means that he develops relations with the camera assistants in a way that is unusual among directors. Thus Julien Hirsch was not too surprised to be telephoned out of the blue by Godard. What did surprise him, however, was that Godard had seen a small movie he had worked on called *Drancy avenir*, and had noticed a particular effect where they had used material originated on video. Hirsch explained to Godard that budgetary constraints had not allowed the use of the very expensive process of digitising video on to film. Instead, Hirsch had simply experimented with filming the video off the monitor. Godard asked him to come to Rolle and experiment further, and together they produced the remarkable colour world of the second half of the film. What is striking about the method is that what the camera records is not what the eye sees on the video. To discover the right settings on the video was a long and arduous process.

The second half of the film is set two years earlier, thus following

Godard's dictum that a film needs a beginning, a middle, and an end – but not necessarily in that order. The black-and-white Paris of Godard's youth is juxtaposed with the oversaturated colour of Brittany, to which he fled as a child as the Germans occupied Paris in that terrible summer of 1940[5].

From Eglantine and Perceval to Tristan and Iseult, the film never leaves its theme of love and death. But love and death have always to be remembered, and the effort to remember the love of country and the deaths associated with it is the effort to understand what it was to resist. But these efforts of memory are set against others. The press book summarises the second half:

> Two years earlier. Sent by Hollywood producers, a bureaucrat from the American Embassy in Paris meets with an old couple who had fought in the Resistance. He offers to buy the rights to their love story and their combat against the Nazi occupiers. The grandfather has asked his grand-daughter, a lawyer in training, to look over the contract – she is the same young woman that we met in the first part. Edgar happens to be present. He is there to interview a historian friend of the grandfather's about de Gaulle and the Free French in London. This all takes place in one night with various heated discussions. The real question in fact is to know if an American superproduction today has the right to dramatise all the great hopes that came out of the end of World War Two.

All narrative summaries of Godard's films are misleading because the films proceed by montage rather than story. Here the montage is between the American present and the French past. For Godard, this past is always both personal and public. The Edgar who stares in the window is the serious young man studying the reality of the Free French and the place of Catholics in the resistance. But he is also the child trying to calculate his place in the circuit of his parents' desire. The obscurity of the relationship of the couple who run the Resistance network is historical – what did they tell their controllers about each other? – but it is also structural: the opacity of any parents' relationship to any child. It is here that Godard develops a theme which has been building throughout the nineties, that of the relationship between grandparents and grandchildren. For of course the opacity of our parents' desire is nothing less than the complexity of understanding their place within the chain of their own parents' desire.[6] Some recent psychoanalysis has focused on how repressed historical trauma in the generation of the grandparents reappears in the grandchildren.[7] Godard now privileges this jumping of generations, and relates it to Miéville's grandchildren. In an interview in the *Eloge de l'amour* press book, when questioned about the serenity of the film he says, 'That comes from age and also the contacts I have with Anne-Marie's grandchildren.'

It is this transmission from grandparent to grandchild, this passing of the secret of resistance, which is now challenged by the American cinema eager to buy and sell memories. Godard's anti-Americanism has been pretty constant since the anti-Vietnam campaigns of the mid-sixties. It is also one of the most serious weaknesses of his later work. When the New York Film Critics' Circle wanted to honour him in 1995, he refused the honour, giving a list of nine aspects of American cinema which he had been unable to influence. Top of the list was the failure 'to prevent Mr Spielberg from reconstructing Auschwitz'. The filming of the camps has been at the centre of Godard's concerns from the very first. The failure to prevent or record the camps is one of the major, if not *the* major, theme of the *Histoire(s)*. From very early on, Godard held that the only way to film the camps would be from the perspective of the home life of one of the guards. Spielberg's *Schindler's List* is, for Godard's aesthetic, a genuine obscenity. It is impossible to film the camps now, because it is impossible to starve actors to the point of death. It is impossible to film the camps because the narratives we impose on them, which 'explain' them, are necessarily misleading and actually prevent understanding.

For Godard, the issue is clear-cut. I myself am less sure. To a child growing up in an Irish home in London in the fifties, the camps were considered the major topic that had to be addressed in any attempt to define an ethical or political life. This has always been my own position. I was astonished when, four decades later, I took my daughter to see *Schindler's List,* and she informed me that I had never discussed the matter with her; my certainty that I had instructed my children was false. Of course, Godard would argue that nothing can be learned from the Spielberg film, which can respect neither the light in front of the camera nor the spectator in front of the screen. It is true that Spielberg's films are generally execrable; it is true that *Saving Private Ryan*'s reduction of the Normandy landings to the attempt to save a single life shows an unbearable contempt for history; it is true that the final scene of *Schindler's List*, in which Liam Neeson melodramatically bemoans his inability to have saved more Jews, demonstrates beyond doubt that Spielberg has no interest in Schindler's heroism. However, it is not clear that Spielberg's film does not function as a genuine reminder. And there are films like *Duel* or the first half of *Minority Report* which also clearly show that Spielberg has prostituted genuine talent.[8]

But if the threat of Hollywood cinema is as great as Godard claims, he has now become incapable of seeing anything other than this threat. The man who loved Tashlin does not appear to have seen *The Simpsons*. For all its weaknesses, *Fight Club* was a genuine attempt to penetrate American madness, and *Three Kings* an effort to ask real questions about Desert Storm. Even a film as poor as *The Quiet American* asks why Americans will soon be afraid to walk any streets in the Third World.[9] The problem here is that Godard's blindness runs very deep. *Eloge de l'amour* indulges in the crudest kind of chauvinism, which opposes the honest French to the perfidious Anglo-Saxons. The mistake goes back a long way and can be seen at its clearest in *King Lear*.

The story of the making of *King Lear* was by and large an unhappy one. In May 1985, Menahem Golan, desperately seeking cultural credibility for a huge expansion of his Cannon empire, signed up Godard over a lunch in Cannes to make a film on Lear for a million dollars. To get the film off to a good start, the dollar immediately lost about a third of its value, and Godard, who had not read Shakespeare's text, never seemed to be able to get past the first page. An enormous number of candidates were touted for the part of Lear, from Clint Eastwood to Norman Mailer. There is a hilarious book to be written on Godard's various visits to Los Angeles luminaries. My favourite is an appointment with Tony Curtis. Tom Luddy, who as producer had the unenviable task of mediating between Golan and Godard, recalls Curtis, perma-tan in place, receiving Godard in his studio amongst a dozen of his paintings, finished and unfinished. After some desultory chat, Godard stepped forward to say softly that obviously Mr Curtis had no interest in the uncertain part he was being offered in an uncertain film. Curtis too stepped forward and oblivious to Godard's self-deprecation, announced with a Hollywood shake of the hand, 'Monsieur Godard – I'll do the picture.'

Luddy had considerable experience of Godard's Rossellinian approach to deal-making from the days at Zoëtrope, when Godard had endlessly swapped one picture for another. His favourite story concerns *Sauve qui peut (la vie)*. Godard had used some of Charles Bukowski's stories for scenes in *Sauve qui peut (la vie)*, and thought it would be best to clear the rights. Bukowski was contacted and agreed, provided that the several thousand dollars were delivered to him at the Los Angeles racetrack. Godard set out with the money in a holdall, and then in conversation with Bukowski he added a twist. He didn't want Bukowski to be unable to sell the rights to his book in the future, so they agreed that Bukowski would say that he had originally heard the stories from Godard who thus owned those underlying rights, allowing him to make the film but leaving Bukowski unencumbered to sell the rights in the future. The story illustrates Chabrol's view that 'for Jean-Luc to be happy there must be something crooked [escroquerie] in the deal'.

The 'escroquerie' at Cannes was that, while the contract on the napkin said that Godard was going to film *King Lear*, nothing specified that it would be Shakespeare's. The writer specified was Norman Mailer. Godard had been reading Mailer for a long time, and *Prénom Carmen* has several quotations from his work. Luddy found Mailer unwilling to commit – he was both worried about the difficulties of collaborating with Godard and about his own projects. In particular, Mailer had a movie he wanted to direct called *Tough Guys Don't Dance*. Luddy suggested to Golan that the clever thing to do would be to link the two films. Golan rang Luddy as he was lunching with Mailer. In those dear dark days before mobile phones, Luddy had to take the call at the bar. 'Go back to your table', said Golan, 'and tell Mr Mailer he has a two-picture deal with Cannon.' The addition of Mailer did not really provide the impetus the project needed, and his exit from the picture after one day of shooting is recorded at the beginning of the film.[10]

The real force of the picture came from Peter Sellars. A genuine wunderkind, Sellars had been wowing theatrical audiences since he was an undergraduate at Harvard in the late seventies, and he turned up at the Zoëtrope studio linked to a long-term Coppola project to turn Kerouac's *On the Road* into a movie. Sellars had directed *King Lear* at Harvard and indeed had stepped in at the very last moment to take the part of Lear himself, so he knew the play backwards. It was Sellars who suggested Molly Ringwald to Godard; it was Sellars who was to record Ruth Maleczech and David Warrilow in Philip Glass's New York recording studio; it was Sellars's enthusiasm which kept the project going.

The shoot was, to use Tom Luddy's phrase, a 'train wreck', but it says something of Godard's mastery of the medium that, according to Sellars, Godard used every foot he shot. In fact, much of *King Lear* is mesmerising. Godard may not have got past the first scene, and he may have focused on Cordelia's repetitive utterance of 'Nothing', but the first half hour of the film brings that scene to magnificent life. And his soundtrack, in which Maleczech and Warrilow's readings of *King Lear* are used to the greatest effect, is a masterpiece. Even Godard's idiosyncratic reading of Lear's relationship with Cordelia as incestuous might have proved fruitful if explored more fully. The core of disturbed sexuality which animates the great tragedies and which is only calmed in the late plays by those dutiful and sexless daughters, as 'chaste as unsunned snow', is certainly susceptible to being read in terms of incest. But it must also be said that Godard cannot weave into a film his heartrending opening or the brilliant soundtrack or the intriguing incestuous reading. He tries to hold the film together with one of his greatest roles, Professor Pluggy. Pluggy, his hair a Rastafarian mass of electronic coils, is desperately seeking the solution which will reclaim the culture that has been lost in the disaster of the modern world. In death, he brings together the figures of Jesus and the Romantic artist to redeem time. The religious themes that have been building since *Passion*, which form a continuous motif in Godard's later work, are condensed in a quotation attributed to St Paul, 'The image will be redeemed at the time of the resurrection.'[11] Pluggy's death seems to merge the vision of sacrifice which lurks in every Christian male with a traditional Romantic Agony and the most basic human fantasy of quickening the dead.

All this is a long way from Shakespeare. Having Léos Carax and Julie Delpy mince through some Vaudois woods, pursued by models borrowed from a commercial he was then shooting, captures little of the force of that opposition between court and heath which is so fundamental to Shakespeare's imagination. And Godard's complete inability to engage with Shakespeare's text is obvious from his treatment of the macro-politics of the play. Shakespeare is, of course, the great poet of the hatred between the English and the French. The chaos of Lear's universe is captured at the political level by the fact that Cordelia comes back to England at the head of a French army.[12] But such complications are too much for Godard. Abandoning Shakespeare and summoning a theatrical white horse, he takes refuge at the end of the film in that most patriotic of French figures – the Maid of Orleans, Joan of Arc. The easy equation of the English occupation of France and the American occupation of the cinema brings the film to a rather lame conclusion.

Eloge de l'amour is an incomparably greater work than *Lear* and certainly signals a renewed engagement with the form of the feature film. But the second half of the film turns on an identification of England and America which may owe something to General de Gaulle, but very little to any serious examination of the differences which from the 1650s on sunder the American colonies from England. If anti-Semitism has been well described as the socialism of fools, then anti-Americanism is the radicalism of idiots. While there can be no doubting the mortal danger of much of American foreign and economic policy, there can also be no doubting that changes in these policies are going to be crucially dependent on this fact being recognised by Americans. Much of what Godard says about the United States is extraordinarily acute, particularly on the key role of cinema in America's global economic dominance. But the cartoon nature of his American characters soon palls and the stereotypes become borderline offensive.

And besides, Godard's interest is no longer there; the wound has turned into a scar, and his imagination is now dominated not by the American films of his youth, but by an obsession with and romanticisation of the French Resistance. One can sympathise deeply with his desire to find the memories to convey a history more telling than current versions, which leave Europe unreconciled with its past. But the details perplex. The emphasis on Catholicism and Péguy (a figure who links Christian mysticism to French republicanism), the centrality of a conversion from Judaism to Catholicism in the Ravensbrück concentration camp, and the absolute opposition, carried over from the *Histoire(s)*, of the state and love are all difficult themes to weave into an alternative history of Europe – they remain exclusively French.

Godard has been as hard at work as ever since his seventieth birthday and the completion of *Eloge de l'amour*. As this book goes to press I have deliberately not seen his short film on Switzerland, *Liberté et patrie*, nor learnt anything about the feature he is about to shoot. But one can be certain that they will have sound and image of incredible beauty. The soundtrack of *Eloge de l'amour* takes to new heights the composition of music dialogues and effects, and the fresh images still do fresh images beget. When I asked Caroline Champetier to explain the beauty of Godard's images, she talked very eloquently about the way in which the light source originates in the image and thus exceeds it. Coutard more prosaically emphasised that Godard's images were never postcards. In both descriptions, the emphasis is on a relation between frame and image which always asks the spectator to see more, to recognise the position from which he or she must negotiate, to see afresh.

It might be usual to end such a book with a prediction of Godard's position in the canon of the future, a final estimate of his place in film history. But it is not simply Godard's continuing productivity which prevents such an assessment. We are still chidren of the European Renaissance, that moment when figures as diverse as Erasmus and Montaigne reached back to the tutor cultures of Greece and Rome to figure the immortality of the artist. Five hundred years later the problem is not the past and the immortality of the artist, but the future and the mortality of the world. That same moment in European history was also the beginning of a process of political and technological development which is now set fair to destroy the planet. If I were to pronounce on the security of Godard's reputation into the future, I would have to be more certain of that future than I am.

One could argue that Godard's commitment to, and respect for, the image are critical to the planet's future because any optimistic perspective must include genuine attempts to transform our audiovisual media into real souces of information, attempts for which Godard's lessons are crucial. But such an argument must also reckon the difficulty of Godard's art and the necessarily small size of the audience. Godard himself said in a press conference for the *Histoire(s)* in Cannes that he and Miéville's audience can most accurately be described as 100,000 friends around the world.

Efforts in the twentieth century to link avant-garde art to a progressive politics have all been dismal failures. Godard's description of his relationship to his audience in terms of friendship alters the terms of those political discourses. From the Romantics on, when Shelley promised to legislate for humanity, art has been promising to deliver the world. If we reject the humanist claim on eternity and the political promise of aesthetic salvation, then perhaps all that is left is individual witness. I do know that in writing this book I committed myself to looking again and again at Godard's work. The life often became tiresome; we are all, like the dog returning to its vomit, condemned to repeat within a sadly limited repertory. But the work never failed to intrigue, to illuminate and to inform. Much of it is extremely difficult to obtain. Much of it requires repeated viewings before it begins to yield its treasure. Some of it is very uneven. But the worst is never less than intelligent, and the best is the best there is.

Godard sitting on a bench overhearing two lovers in *Eloge de l'amour*, 2001.

Filmography

Researched and compiled by Sally Shafto

In a filmography it is customary to list films by their release dates and this filmography generally conforms to this rule. (As a point of reference, the release dates, unless otherwise noted, refer specifically to their release in Paris.) Occasionally, however, some of Godard's films were released several years later than their year of production. This is true of some of the short films and the sketch films. It is also true of the films made during his militant period 1968–1971 (which, although they were distributed in France by Claude Nedjar's company Nef Diffusion and on American college campuses by Grove Press, did not benefit from an immediate regular commercial release) and true too of some of the Grenoble work. Other notable examples include: *Le Petit soldat*, finished in 1960, but not released until January 1963, and *King Lear* (1987) which, despite an original brief run in New York, did not open in France until March 2002. In such instances, the films have usually been listed by their date of production. If the exact date of release and/or date of production was not known, this has been left blank, and the film is listed under the date generally attributed to it (e.g. Miéville's *Faire la fête*). With regard to the dating of the *Histoire(s) du cinéma*, early versions of the first chapters were in circulation from 1989, but in this filmography the *Histoire(s) du cinéma* have all been dated to 1998, the year when Godard, with Gaumont, released their final version on video-cassette and published the accompanying volumes with Gallimard.

A review of the credits in Godard's films reveals absences and inconsistencies. Although his short films from the 1950s have credits, from his first feature film, Godard showed himself chary of traditional film credits. His second film likewise is *sans générique*, but this may be due to the censorship and banning of *Le Petit soldat* for two and a half years. His third film *Une Femme est une femme* carries exuberant, if highly selective, credits that begin as a fairy tale: 'Il était une fois – Beauregard-Eastmancolor-Ponti . . .' In contrast, the credits of *Vivre sa vie* and *Bande à part* are extensive. *Masculin Féminin* has strictly minimal credits, split between the beginning of the film (production credit) and the end (actors, director of photography and sound engineer). *Deux ou trois choses que je sais d'elle*, and *La Chinoise* are without credits, thus both recalling his first two films and presaging his militant period. In *Week-end* four title cards ('Interdit aux moins de 18 ans/Les Films Copernic présentent/Un film égaré dans le cosmos/Un film trouvé à la ferraille') precede the title; no other credit information is given. The films that followed *Week-end* and up until *Tout va bien* are, except for an authorial credit, without technical credits. *Pravda*, for example, one of the films that Grove Press circulated in the US, carries a single credit: Made by 'Jean-Luc Godard and the comrades of the Dziga Vertov Group'.[1] *Tout va bien*, the film which ends this phase of Godard's career, opens with comprehensive credits emphasising film as a collaborative enterprise. In the Grenoble period that followed, the credits are once again spare. *Comment ça va?*, for instance, opens on the following text: 'Un film entre l'actif et le passif', and refuses all credit information, including a title card.

Since 1980 the credits of Godard's films have moved away from naming individual positions, often preferring instead a more generic title covering the field: for instance, the use of the word 'image' to indicate the director of photography and assistants, or 'son' to designate the sound engineer and assistants. Thus, under the heading 'Images' in the credits of *Nouvelle Vague* nine names are listed, which seems like a lot until it is understood that Godard has here included also the continuity person, the key grip and assistants and the gaffer and assistants. Miéville's credits have likewise followed this tendency. For instance, in *Lou n'a pas dit non*, nine names follow the heading of 'Photography'. While the ordering of names in *Nouvelle Vague* seems obvious (the director of photography and two assistants followed by the continuity person etc.), the order of the names in *Lou n'a pas dit non* seems random, or perhaps more democratic (that is, they are listed neither in terms of importance nor alphabetically). In this instance, consultation of the technical credits for this film submitted to the Centre National de la Cinématographie (CNC) assisted me in partially determining the contribution of several of the technicians.

In the filmography to *Jean-Luc Godard par Jean-Luc Godard*, vol. 2, the title 'assistant à la mise-en-scène' is used instead of 'assistant réalisateur' from *Détective* onwards. I have followed this usage which both distances the position from the director, and resonates with the *Cahiers du cinéma* critics' emphasis on mise-en-scène in the 1950s. Already in two early shorts, *Charlotte et Véronique* and *Une Histoire d'eau*, Godard uses the phrase 'mise-en-scène par' to indicate his role. The credit that Godard gives himself in *Vivre sa vie* signals its importance for him: 'Pensé, dialogué, tourné, monté, bref: mise-en-scène par J.L. Godard.'

Since the credits in the films themselves are often incomplete, I have consulted other existing filmographies, as well as, when available, the crew lists circulated by the production company. The technical credits submitted to the CNC, which are not necessarily one hundred per cent accurate, have also been consulted when available.[2] Occasionally, mention is made in the accompanying footnotes of the technical credits submitted to the CNC, particularly, for example, in the case of the Dziga Vertov period, when the credits submitted to the CNC differ from the understood authorship of these films.

In addition to interviewing numerous persons who have worked with Godard, I consulted the credits in the films/videos themselves, the technical credits on file at the CNC, *Le Film français*, and the technical credits and posters available at the Bibliothèque du Film (BiFi, Paris). Publications consulted for this filmography are marked 'F' in the general bibliography.

Sally Shafto

Standard Positions on a Film Crew

The following is a brief listing of positions on a standard film crew. When relevant, Godard's own practices have been noted. An asterisk following the title in French indicates that it is a position requiring the professional working card of the Centre National de la Cinématographie.

Director or Film-maker: In French 'cinéaste', 'réalisateur', or 'metteur en scène'.*
The person who has the overall responsibility for creating a film.

Assistant Director: In French 'assistant réalisateur'.*
The right hand of the director throughout the making of a film. (In the credits for *Vivre sa vie*, Godard credits Bernard Toublanc-Michel as just that: 'le bras droit'.) Although the responsibilities of this position are administrative rather than creative, it is nevertheless a position highly valued by Godard. In a 1967 interview Godard cites, albeit obliquely, the importance of his assistant director, Charles Bitsch, at the time: 'I don't have a screenwriter, but I have perhaps someone better, someone that a Preminger does not have and whom I need. An assistant with whom I can speak, who is both my friend and my assistant, who doesn't just help with the film but who helps me because he lives the film while I am creating it. A Preminger does not have that, he has people whom he pays, who work for him.'[3]

Director of Photography: In French 'directeur de la photographie', or 'chef opérateur'.*
The person responsible for lighting (thus making an important contribution to the general look of a film) and shooting of a film. Works in close collaboration with the director. Usually supervises the further processing of filmed material up to the completion of the work print ('étalonnage de la copie zéro'). Often advises the director on the most appropriate film stock to use.

Camera Operator or Cameraman: In French 'cadreur' or 'caméraman'.*
The person who assists the director of photography in using and maintaining the camera. Moves the camera according to the latter's directions and carries out his or her instructions. As the title indicates in French, the *cadreur* 'frames' the shot. Raoul Coutard always combined the job of director of photography and camera operator.

Focus-puller: In French 'pointeur' or '1er assistant'.*
The person responsible for focusing the shot.

Second Assistant:
The person who loads the cameras with film.

Continuity: In French, 'la scripte'.*
The person responsible, during the shoot, for taking detailed production notes which serve to prevent lapses in the continuity of dialogue, action, set dressing, props, or wardrobe.

Sound Engineer: In French 'ingénieur du son'.*
Technician and creative collaborator responsible for the recording of the direct sound. René Levert and William R. Sivel specialised in the recording of direct sound, whereas Antoine Bonfanti and later François Musy did both direct sound and mixing. Jacques Maumont specialised in post-synchronisation mixing.

Godard's first two features, shot with the portable but noisy Cameflex Eclair, were post-synchronised. *Une Femme est une femme*, shot in studio and with a Mitchell, allowed for synch sound.

Boom Operator: In French 'perchman'.*
Technician who, working under the sound engineer, operates a mechanical arm from which a microphone is suspended.

Mix: In French 'mixage'.
The process of combining separate sound tracks into a single track.

Gaffer or Electrician: In French 'chef électricien'.
Working under the supervision of the director of photography, the person responsible for providing electrical equipment and ensuring the supply of electricity.

Key Grip: In French 'chef machiniste'.
The person responsible for overseeing the set-up of the camera support equipment.

Editor: In French 'chef monteur/se'.*
The person who, following the script and in creative co-operation with the director, selects, arranges, and assembles the scenes; controls the synchronisation of picture and sound, and supervises the further technical processes.

Assistant Editor: In French 'assistant monteur/se'.*
Assists the editor in editing a film.

Art Director: In French, 'chef décorateur'.*
The person who designs, in creative collaboration with the director, all settings and properties, and oversees the realisation of designs, structures, make-up, and costumes. A position rarely filled on Godard's film crews.

In the credits of *Sauve qui peut (la vie)* Romain Goupil is listed (in English) as 'art director'. Godard's use of this title, however, does not strictly conform with the traditional job description, and for William Lubtchansky, a director of photography on that film, Goupil served as the assistant director. In fact, Goupil worked in close collaboration with Godard for a year on the film, assisting in a variety of roles (collaborating on the screenplay, scouting out locations, and serving as an intermediary between Godard and the rest of the film crew), and as such his responsibilities surpassed that of an assistant director. In crediting Goupil as art director on *Sauve qui peut (la vie)* and Anne-Marie Miéville as art director on *Nouvelle Vague*, Godard emphasises their contribution as not just administrative but also creative. Given the importance Godard attaches to the creation of his images, the naming of Goupil and Miéville in this position seems honorific, indicating their overall creative contribution.[4]

Costume Designer: In French 'costumière'.
The person who chooses, in creative collaboration with the director, the costumes to be worn by all the characters in a given film.

Wardrobe Person: In French 'habilleur/se'.
The person responsible for the physical maintenance of the clothes worn during a shoot. Traditionally, a professional film team includes both a costumer designer and wardrobe person. Godard has occasionally collaborated with costume designers (Jacqueline Moreau, and particularly Gitt Magrini), but has also frequently worked only with a 'habilleur/se', thus emphasising, once again, his artistic authority over a given film.

Make-up Person: In French 'maquilleur/se'.*
The person responsible for the alteration of the appearance of actors by use of cosmetics or transformation, in order to achieve the effect desired by the director.

Producer: In French 'producteur'.
The person bearing the ultimate administrative and financial responsibility for a film.

'Producteur Délégué' (difficult to translate properly into English):
When there is more than one producer involved in both business and creative matters, one takes lead responsibility for the production of the film. On *Contempt*, there were three producers, and Georges de Beauregard was the producteur délégué. Similarly, there were three production companies involved in the producing of *Tout va bien*, and Jean-Pierre Rassam was the producteur délégué.

Executive Producer: In French 'producteur exécutif'.
This person is usually the top executive in the production company making the film. The executive producer follows the development of a film from pre-production till the film is finished, and is usually not involved in the day-to-day running of the production, but may take an active role in supervising the producer. In several of Godard's films produced by his production company Anouchka Films (*Bande à part, Une Femme mariée,* and *La Chinoise*) Godard was the producer, with Philippe Dussart acting as the executive producer.

Production Manager: In French 'directeur de production'.*
The person responsible for the daily running of a film production, according to the
directions and requirements of the director, and working in close collaboration with the
producer and assistant director.

In *Bande à part, Une Femme mariée* and *La Chinoise*, films produced by Godard's
production company Anouchka Films with small budgets and straightforward shooting
schedules, Philippe Dussart was both the executive producer and the production manager.

Production Coordinator: In French 'régisseur' or 'régisseur général'.*
Works under the supervision of the production manager in a concrete way during the
shoot.

A Jean-Luc Godard and Anne-Marie Miéville Filmography

1955 Opération 'béton'. 35 mm, 20 minutes.
Release: May 1955. Filmed: The Grand Dixence Dam, Switzerland, 1954.
Director: Jean-Luc Godard. Screenplay: Jean-Luc Godard. Photography: Adrien Porchet.
Music: Bach, Handel. Editing: Jean-Luc Godard.
Camera: Cameflex Eclair. Film Stock: Kodak.
Cast: Workers on the Grand Dixence Dam, Switzerland, 1954.
Production Company: Actua Film.
Note: The voice-over is often attributed to Godard.

1956 Une Femme coquette. 16 mm, 10 minutes.
Release: 25 April 1956. Filmed: On location in Geneva, 1955.
Director: Jean-Luc Godard. Screenplay: Hans Lucas (Jean-Luc Godard), after a short story
'*Le Signe*' by Guy de Maupassant. Photography: Hans Lucas (Jean-Luc Godard). Music:
Bach, Handel. Orchestra directed by Pierre Colombo. Editing: Hans Lucas (Jean-Luc
Godard).
Camera: Paillard. Film Stock: Kodak 3-X. Lab: Cinégram, Geneva.
Cast: Maria Lysandre, Roland Tolmatchoff, Jean-Luc Godard.
Production Company: Jean-Luc Godard.

1957 Charlotte et Véronique, ou Tous les garçons s'appellent Patrick. 35 mm, 21
minutes.
Release: 6 May 1959. Filmed: On location in Paris, August or September 1957.
Director: Jean-Luc Godard. Screenplay: Eric Rohmer. Photography: Michel Latouche.
Music: Beethoven, Pierre Monsigny. Sound Mix: Jacques Maumont. Editing: Jean-Luc
Godard and Cécile Décugis.

Cast: Jean-Claude Brialy, Anne Colette, Nicole Berger.
Production company: Les Films de la Pléiade. Producer: Pierre Braunberger.
Note: The title of this film is often reversed (*Tous les garçons s'appellent Patrick –
Charlotte et Véronique*), or simply called *Tous les garçons s'appellent Patrick*. The title
card of the film is *Charlotte et Véronique, ou Tous les garçons s'appellent Patrick*. The
credits are handwritten by Godard.

1958 Une Histoire d'eau. 35 mm, 20 minutes.
Release: 3 March 1961. Filmed: In a flooded region of Paris by Truffaut, during the
winter of 1957–1958. Truffaut subsequently abandoned the footage.
Mise-en-scène: Jean-Luc Godard. Screenplay: François Truffaut. Photography: Michel
Latouche. Sound Mix: Jacques Maumont. Editing: Jean-Luc Godard.[5]
Dedication: Mack Sennett.
Cast: Jean-Claude Brialy (the man), Caroline Dim (the woman), Jean-Luc Godard
(narrator).
Production Company: Les Films de la Pléiade. Producer: Pierre Braunberger.
Production Manager: Roger Fleytoux.

1958 Charlotte et son Jules. 35 mm, 20 minutes.[6]
Release: 3 March 1961. Filmed: Godard's hotel room, rue de Rennes, 1958.
Director: Jean-Luc Godard. Screenplay: Jean-Luc Godard. Photography: Michel La-
touche. Music: Pierre Monsigny. Sound Mix: Jacques Maumont. Editing: Jean-Luc
Godard.[7]
Lab: Eclair.
Dedication: Jean Cocteau.
Cast: Anne Colette (Charlotte), Jean-Paul Belmondo (Jean, Charlotte's old lover), Gérard
Blain (Charlotte's new friend). Belmondo's voice dubbed by Godard.
Production Company: Les Films de la Pléiade. Producer: Pierre Braunberger. Production
Manager: Roger Fleytoux.

1960 A Bout de souffle [Breathless]. 35 mm, 90 minutes.
Release: 16 March 1960. Filmed: Marseilles, and interiors and exteriors in Paris 17
August–30 October 1959.
Director: Jean-Luc Godard. Screenplay: based on an original treatment by François
Truffaut. Artistic and Technical Advisor: Claude Chabrol. Assistant Director: Pierre
Rissient. Photography: Raoul Coutard,[8] Claude Beausoleil. Set Photographer: Raymond
Cauchetier. Make-up: Phuong Mattret. Music: Martial Solal, Mozart. Sound Mix:
Jacques Maumont. Editing: Cécile Décugis, Lila Herman.
Camera: Cameflex Eclair.[9] Film Stock: Gevaert and Ilford.
Dedication: Monogram Pictures.
Cast: Jean Seberg (Patricia Franchini), Jean-Paul Belmondo (Michel Poiccard, alias
Laszlo Kovacs), Daniel Boulanger (Police Inspector Vital), Henri-Jacques Huet (Antonio

Berrutti), Roger Hanin (Carl Zombach), Van Doude (journalist Van Doude), Parvulesco
(Jean-Pierre Melville), Richard Balducci (Tolmatchoff), Liliane David (Liliane), Claude
Mansard (used-car dealer), Gérard Brach (studio photographer), Michel Fabre (second
police officer), André S. Labarthe (interviewer), Jean Herman (soldier who asks for a
light), Jean Douchet (passer-by), Jean Domarchi (man attacked in the restroom).
Production Companies: Société Nouvelle de Cinématographie, Productions Georges de
Beauregard. Producer: Georges de Beauregard.
Prize: Jean Vigo Prize, 1960,[10] Best direction Berlin Film Festival, and the German
Critics' Prize awarded to Raoul Coutard for the Photography 1960.
Note: The CNC required that the scene of President Eisenhower and President de Gaulle,
in a car on the Champs-Elysées, be removed. Upon release, the film was forbidden to
anyone under 18.

1960 Le Petit soldat. 35 mm, black and white, 88 minutes.
Release: 25 January 1963. Filmed: In and around Geneva, 4 April–early May 1960.
Director: Jean-Luc Godard. Screenplay: Jean-Luc Godard. Technical Advisor:
Claude Chabrol. Assistant Director: Francis Cognani. Script Continuity: Suzanne
Schiffman. Photography: Raoul Coutard, Michel Latouche. Music: Maurice Leroux.
Sound Mix: Jacques Maumont. Editing: Agnès Guillemot, Nadine Marquand, Lila
Herman.[11]
Cast: Michel Subor (Bruno Forestier), Anna Karina (Véronica Dreyer), Henri-
Jacques Huet (Jacques), Paul Beauvais (Paul), Laszlo Szabo (Laszlo, member of FLN),
Georges de Beauregard (OAS leader), Jean-Luc Godard (bystander at railroad
station), Gilbert Edard.
Production Companies: Société Nouvelle du Cinéma, Rome-Paris Films. Producers:
Georges de Beauregard, Carlo Ponti.
Note: Le Petit soldat was banned until January 1963 by the French Board of Censors
and the Minister of Information.

1961 Une Femme est une femme. 35 mm, Franscope, 84 minutes.
Release: Presented at the Berlin Film Festival 1 July 1961, and released 6 September 1961.
Filmed: Studio Saint Maurice, and exteriors Paris, November 1960–January 1961.
Director: Jean-Luc Godard. Screenplay: Jean-Luc Godard, after an idea of Geneviève
Cluny. Assistant Director: Francis Cognani. Script Continuity: Suzanne Schiffman.
Photography: Raoul Coutard, Claude Beausoleil. Still Photography: Raymond Cauche-
tier. Art Direction: Bernard Evein. Costumes: Jacqueline Moreau. Make-up: Jackie
Reynal. Gaffer: Fernand Coquet. Key Grip: Roger Scipion. Grip: Bernard Largemains.
Sound: Guy Villette. Music: Michel Legrand ('Angela's Song' by Legrand and Godard).
Sound Mix: Jacques Maumont. Editing: Agnès Guillemot, Lila Herman.
Film Stock: Kodak Eastmancolor. Cameras: Mitchell (in studio); Cameflex (exteriors).
Lab: GTC.
Cast: Anna Karina (Angéla), Jean-Claude Brialy (Emile Récamier), Jean-Paul Belmondo

(Alfred Lubitsch), Marie Dubois (Suzanne), Marion Sarrault (second prostitute), Nicole Paquin (first prostitute), Jeanne Moreau (Herself), Ernest Menzer (cabaret manager), Catherine Demongeot.

Production Company: Rome-Paris Films. Producers: Georges de Beauregard, Carlo Ponti. Production Manager: Philippe Dussart. Assistant Production Manager: Marcel Georges.

Prize: Special Jury Prize, and Best Actress Prize to Anna Karina for her role, Berlin Film Festival 1961.

1962 La Paresse. Sketch in **Les Sept péchés capitaux.** 35 mm, Dyaliscope, 15 minutes.

Release: 7 March 1962. Filmed: Paris, September 1961.

Director: Jean-Luc Godard. Screenplay: Jean-Luc Godard. Assistant Director: Marin Karmitz. Photography: Henri Decae, Jean-Paul Schwartz. Still Photography: Marilu Parolini. Music: Michel Legrand. Sound: Jean-Claude Marchetti, Jean Labussière. Editing: Jacques Gaillard.

Camera: Debrie. Film Stock: Kodak. Lab: GTC.

Cast: Eddie Constantine (Himself), Nicole Mirel (Herself, the starlet).

Production Companies: Les Films Gibé, Franco-London Films, Titanus. Producer: Joseph Bergholz. Production Manager: Jean Lavie.

Note: Other sketches in *Les Sept péchés capitaux* by Sylvain Dhomme, Philippe de Broca, Jacques Demy, Edouard Molinaro, Roger Vadim, and Claude Chabrol.

1962 Vivre sa vie: film en douze tableaux. 35 mm, black and white, 90 minutes.

Release: Presented at the Venice Film Festival 28 August 1962, and released 20 September 1962. Filmed: On location Paris, February–March 1962.

Director: Jean-Luc Godard. Screenplay: Jean-Luc Godard, based on the book *Où en est la prostitution* by Judge Marcel Sacotte, and Edgar Allan Poe's 'The Oval Portrait'. Assistant Directors: Bernard Toublanc-Michel, Jean-Paul Savignac. Script Continuity: Suzanne Schiffman. Photography: Raoul Coutard, Claude Beausoleil, Charles Bitsch. Still Photography: Marilu Parolini. Costumes: Christiane Fageol. Hairdresser: Simone Knapp, designs by DeAlexandre. Make-up: Jackie Reynal. Gaffers: Ferdinand and Pierre Coquet. Key Grip: Jean Philippe. Travelling: Bernard Largemains. Sound: Guy Villette. Music: Michel Legrand, with song ('Ma Môme, elle joue pas les starlettes') by Jean Ferrat. Sound Mix: Jacques Maumont. Editing: Agnès Guillemot, Lila Lakshmanan. Film Stock: Kodak XX. Camera: Mitchell. Lab: Eclair.

Dedication: 'Aux films de série B'.

Cast: Anna Karina (Nana Kleinfrankenheim), Sady Rebbot (Raoul), André S. Labarthe (Paul), Guylaine Schlumberger (Yvette), Gérard Hoffman (man to whom Nana is sold), Monique Messine (Elisabeth), Paul Pavel (photographer), Peter Kassowitz (Nana's boyfriend, voice dubbed by Godard), Eric Schlumberger (Luigi), Brice Parain (Himself), Henri Attal (Arthur), Gilles Quéant (client), Odile Geoffroy (barmaid), Laszlo Szabo (wounded man), Gisèle Hauchecorne (concierge), Marcel Charton (policeman), Dimitri

Dineff (Dimitri), Jean Ferrat (Himself), Jean-Paul Savignac (soldier in bar), Jacques Florency (man in cinema).
Production Company: Films de la Pléiade. Producer: Pierre Braunberger. Production Manager: Roger Fleytoux.
Prize: Special Jury Prize and Italian Critics' Prize, Venice Film Festival 1962, and German Critics' Prize for the best foreign film.

1963 Le nouveau monde. Sketch in **RoGoPaG.** 35 mm, black and white, 20 minutes.
Release (in Italy): 6 March 1963. Filmed: In Paris, November 1962.
Director: Jean-Luc Godard. Screenplay: Jean-Luc Godard. Assistant Director: Charles Bitsch, Jean-Paul Savignac. Script Continuity: Suzanne Schiffman. Photography: Jean Rabier, Roger Delpuech, P. Willemin. Still Photography: Marilu Parolini. Sound: A. Hervé. Boom Operator: G. Manneveau. Music: Beethoven. Editing: Agnès Guillemot, Lila Lakshmanan.
Cast: Alexandra Stewart (Alexandra), Jean-Marc Bory (the narrator), Jean-André Fieschi, Michel Delahaye, Radio Voice-over by André S. Labarthe.
Production Companies: Arco Film, Cineriz, Société Lyre Cinématographique. Producer: Alfredo Bini. Production Manager: Yves Laplache.
Note: *RoGoPaG* was banned in Italy ten days after its release. Subsequently re-released with cuts and new title: *Laviamoci il cervello (Let's Wash Our Brains)*. Other sketches by Roberto Rossellini, Pier Paolo Pasolini, and Ugo Gregoretti.

1963 Les Carabiniers. 35 mm, black and white, 80 minutes.
Release: 31 May 1963. Filmed: Paris outskirts, December 1962–January 1963.
Director: Jean-Luc Godard. Screenplay: Jean-Luc Godard, Jean Gruault, and Roberto Rossellini. Based on Benjamin Joppolo's play *I Carabinieri*, adapted to the French stage by Jacques Audiberti. Assistant Directors: Charles Bitsch, Jean-Paul Savignac. Script Continuity: Suzanne Faye. Photography: Raoul Coutard, Claude Beausoleil, Georges Liron. Still Photography: Marilu Parolini. Make-up: Jackie Reynal. Wardrobe Person: Mme. Caudrellier. Decors: Jacques Fabre. Military Props: Roger Bollengier. Gaffer: Fernand Coquet. Key Grip: Roger Robert. Sound: Bernard Orthion. Music: Philippe Arthuys. Sound Mix: Jacques Maumont. Editing: Agnès Guillemot, Lila Lakshmanan. Camera: Cameflex and Arriflex.[12] Film Stock: Kodak XX. Lab: GTC.
Dedication: Jean Vigo.
Cast: Marino Masé (Ulysse), Albert Juross (Michel-Ange), Geneviève Galéa (Vénus), Catherine Ribeiro (Cléopâtre), Gérard Poirot (first carabinier), Jean Brassat (second carabinier), Alvaro Gheri (third carabinier), Barbet Schroeder (car salesman), Jean Gruault (Bébé's father), Jean-Louis Comolli (soldier with fish), Odile Geoffroy (revolutionary citing poem), Catherine Durant (woman in film-within-film), Jean Monsigny (soldier), Gilbert Servien (soldier), Wladimir Faters (revolutionary), Roger Coggio and Pascale Audret (couple in car).
Production Companies: Marceau Films, Cocinor Films, Rome-Paris Films, Laetitia.

Producers: Georges de Beauregard, Carlo Ponti. Production Manager: Roger Scipion. Note: Handwritten credits by Godard.

1964 Le Grand escroc. Sketch in **Les Plus belles escroqueries du monde.** 35 mm, Franscope, Color, 25 minutes.
Release: 14 August 1964. Filmed: Marrakesh, January 1963.
Director: Jean-Luc Godard. Screenplay: Jean-Luc Godard. Assistant Director: Charles Bitsch. Photography: Raoul Coutard, Claude Beausoleil, Georges Liron. Make-up: Jackie Reynal. Sound: André Hervé. Music: Michel Legrand. Sound Mix: Antoine Bonfanti. Editing: Agnès Guillemot, Lila Lakshmanan.
Lab: GTC.
Cast: Jean Seberg (Patricia Leacock), Charles Denner (the swindler), Laszlo Szabo (police inspector), Jean-Luc Godard (narrator in voice-over; also seen wearing a fez).
Production Companies: Ulysse Productions, Lux-C.C.F., Primex Films, Vidès Cinematografica, Toho/Toawa, Cesar Film Productie. Producer: Pierre Roustang. Production Manager: Philippe Dussart. Assistant Production Manager: Bernard Taisant.
Note: Godard's sketch cut from Paris premiere in August 1964. Other sketches in *Les Plus belles escroqueries du monde* by: Roman Polanski, Ugo Gregoretti, Claude Chabrol, Hiromichi Horakawa.

1963 Le Mépris [Contempt]. 35 mm, Franscope, 110 minutes.
Release: 27 December 1963. Filmed: On location in Rome and Capri (Villa Malaparte) April–June 1963; additional shots Paris, autumn 1963.
Director: Jean-Luc Godard. Screenplay: Jean-Luc Godard, after Alberto Moravia's novel *II disprezzo*. Assistant Director: Charles Bitsch.[13] Photography: Raoul Coutard, Alain Levent.[14] Still Photography: Ghislain Dussart. Script Continuity: Suzanne Schiffman. Costumes: Tanine Autré. Sound: William R. Sivel. Music: Georges Delerue. Sound Mix: Jacques Maumont. Editing: Agnès Guillemot, Lila Lakshmanan.
Film Stock: Kodak Eastmancolor. Lab: GTC.
Cast: Brigitte Bardot[15] (Camille Javal), Michel Piccoli (Paul Javal), Jack Palance (Jeremy Prokosch), Fritz Lang (Himself), Giorgia Moll (Francesca Vanini), Jean-Luc Godard (Assistant Director to Lang), Linda Veras (a siren).
Production Companies: Rome-Paris Films, Films Concordia, Compagnia Cinematografica Champion. Producers: Carlo Ponti, Joseph E. Levine. Associate Producer: Georges de Beauregard. Production Managers: Philippe Dussart, Carlo Lastricati.
Note: Partial credits for the film are announced in a voice-over in the opening scene. Upon release, the film was forbidden to anyone under 18.

1964 Bande à part. 35 mm, 95 minutes.
Release: Presented at the Berlin Film Festival 5 July 1964, and released 5 August 1964.
Filmed: On location in Paris, 17 February–17 March 1964.
Director: Jean-Luc Godard. Screenplay: Jean-Luc Godard, after Dolores and Bert

Hitchens's novel *Fool's Gold*. Assistant Directors: Jean-Paul Savignac, Pierre Delanjeac. Photography: Raoul Coutard, Georges Liron, Théodore Robichet. Still Photography: Marilu Parolini. Script Continuity: Suzanne Schiffman. Make-up: Jackie Reynal. Costumes: Christiane Fageol. Hair Stylist: Janou Pottier. Gaffer: Fernand Coquet. Key Grip: Bernard Largemains. Grip: Roger Schleich. Sound: René Levert. Boom Operator: Robert Cambourakis. Music: Michel Legrand. Sound Mix: Antoine Bonfanti. Editing: Agnès Guillemot, Françoise Collin.

Cameras: Arriflex[16] and Mitchell. Film Stock: Kodak XX. Lab: GTC.

Cast: Anna Karina (Odile), Claude Brasseur (Arthur), Sami Frey (Franz), Louisa Colpeyn (Mme. Victoria), Chantal Darget (Arthur's aunt), Ernest Menzer (Arthur's uncle), Danièle Girard (English teacher), Michèle Seghers and Claude Makowski (students in English class), Georges Staquet (soldier), Michel Delahaye (doorman at language school), Peter Kassowitz, Guards of the Louvre Museum, Godard in voice-over.

Production Companies: Anouchka Films, Orsay Films. Producer: Jean-Luc Godard. Executive Producer: Philippe Dussart. Production Manager: Philippe Dussart. Assistant Production Manager: Maurice Urbain.

Note: Working title was 'Sammy, Arthur, and Anouchka'. In the credits, Godard signs the film: 'Jean-Luc Cinéma Godard'.

1964 Une Femme mariée: Fragments d'un film tourné en 1964. 35 mm, 98 minutes. Release: Presented at the Venice Film Festival 8 September 1964, and released 4 December 1964. Filmed: In Paris, interiors mostly at Elysées 2, and Orly Airport, June–July 1964.

Director: Jean-Luc Godard. Screenplay: Jean-Luc Godard. Includes: adapted scene from Racine's *Bérénice* and monologue from Louis-Ferdinand Céline's novel *Mort à crédit*. Assistant Directors: Claude Othnin-Girard, Hélène Kalouguine, Jean-Pierre Léaud. Script Continuity: Suzanne Schiffman, Catherine Savignac. Photography: Raoul Coutard, Georges Liron,[17] Jean Garcenot. Still Photography: Marilu Parolini. Decors: Henri Nogaret.[18] Props: Joseph Gerhard. Wardrobe Person: Laurence Clairval. Gaffers: Fernand Coquet, Henri Schickel. Key Grip: Bernard Largemains. Grip: Roger Schleich. Sound: René Levert, Antoine Bonfanti.[19] Boom Operator: Robert Cambourakis. Music: Beethoven, Claude Nougaro, and song by Sylvie Vartan. Sound Mix: Antoine Bonfanti, Jacques Maumont. Editing: Françoise Collin, Agnès Guillemot,[20] Andrée Choty. Lab: GTC.

Cast: Macha Méril (Charlotte Giraud), Bernard Noël (Robert, the lover), Philippe Leroy (Pierre, the husband), Roger Leenhardt (Himself), Rita Maiden (Mme. Céline, the maid), Margaret Le Van and Véronique Duval (Two women at the pool), Christophe Bourseiller (Nicolas, the little boy), Georges Liron (the doctor).

Production Companies: Anouchka Films, Orsay Films. Producer: Jean-Luc Godard. Executive Producer: Philippe Dussart. Production Manager: Philippe Dussart. Assistant Production Manager: Maurice Urbain.

Note: The film was presented at the 1964 Venice Film Festival as *La Femme mariée*. Due to censorship, the film was released that December under the title: *Une Femme mariée*. The film was originally forbidden to anyone under 18.

1965 Montparnasse-Levallois: un action film. Sketch in *Paris vu par* . . . 16 mm, 18 minutes.
Release: Presented at the Cannes Film Festival 19 May 1965, and released on 13 October 1965. Filmed: Montparnasse (in the studio of sculptor Philippe Hiquilly) and Levallois, December 1963–January 1964.
Director: Jean-Luc Godard. Screenplay: Jean-Luc Godard, based on a story by Jean Giraudoux in *Contes du lundi*, and told by Jean-Paul Belmondo in *Une Femme est une femme*. Photography: Albert Maysles. Still Photography: Marilu Parolini. Sound: René Levert. Music: Philippe Arthuys. Editing: Jacqueline Raynal.
Film Stock: Ektachrome. Lab: LTC.
Cast: Johanna Shimkus (Monika), Philippe Hiquilly (Ivan, the sculptor), Serge Davri (Roger, the garage mechanic).
Production Company: Films du Losange. Producer: Barbet Schroeder. Associate Producer: Patrick Bauchau.
Note: According to the credits, this sketch is a 'film organisé par Jean-Luc Godard'. Other sketches in *Paris vu par* . . . by Claude Chabrol, Jean Douchet, Eric Rohmer, Jean Rouch, Jean-Daniel Pollet.

1965 Alphaville: une étrange aventure de Lemmy Caution. 35 mm, 98 minutes.
Release: 5 May 1965. Filmed: January–February 1965, on location in Paris in the most futuristic buildings: Maison de la Radio, Palais des Expos, etc.
Director: Jean-Luc Godard. Screenplay: Jean-Luc Godard. Assistant Directors: Charles Bitsch, Jean-Paul Savignac, Hélène Kalouguine, Jean-Pierre Léaud. Photography: Raoul Coutard, Georges Liron. Still Photography: Georges Pierre (colour), Marilu Parolini (black and white). Make-up: Jackie Reynal. Key Grip: Bernard Largemains. Grip: Roger Schleich. Sound: René Levert. Music: Paul Misraki. Editing: Agnès Guillemot.
Film Stock: Ilford HPS. Camera: Mitchell and Cameflex. Lab: GTC.
Cast: Anna Karina (Natacha von Braun), Eddie Constantine (Lemmy Caution), Akim Tamiroff (Henri Dickson), Howard Vernon (Professor Léonard Nosferatu, alias von Braun), Laszlo Szabo (chief engineer), Michel Delahaye (von Braun's assistant), Jean-André Fieschi (Professor Heckel), Jean-Louis Comolli (Professor Jeckell), Christa Lang, Jean-Pierre Léaud, and Alpha 60.
Production Companies: Chaumiane, Filmstudio. Producer: André Michelin. Production Manager: Philippe Dussart.
Prize: Best Film, Berlin Film Festival, 1965.
Note: Working title of the film was 'Alphaville: une nouvelle aventure de Lemmy Caution'.

1965 Pierrot le fou. 35 mm, Techniscope, 112 minutes.
Release: Presented at the Venice Film Festival 29 August 1965, and released 5 November 1965. Filmed: On location in Paris, and in the south of France (Hyères) June–July 1965. Director: Jean-Luc Godard. Screenplay: Jean-Luc Godard, based on the novel *Obsession* by Lionel White. Assistant Directors: Philippe Fourastié, Bernard Toublanc-Michel, Alexis Poliakoff, Jean-Pierre Léaud. Script Continuity: Suzanne Schiffman. Photography: Raoul Coutard, Georges Liron, Jean Garcenot. Still Photography: Georges Pierre (colour), Marilu Parolini (black and white). Costumes: Gitt Magrini. Wardrobe Person: Laurence Clairval. Make-up: Jackie Reynal. Hair Stylist: Triestine Sarnelli. Decors: Eric Simon.[21] Gaffer: Fernand Coquet. Grip: Roger Robert. Sound: René Levert. Boom Operator: Robert Cambourakis. Music: Antoine Duhamel. Songs: 'Ma ligne de chance' and 'Jamais je ne t'ai dit que je t'aimerai toujours' by Duhamel and Bassiak. Sound Mix: Antoine Bonfanti. Editing: Françoise Collin, Andrée Choty.
Cameras: Cameflex and Arriflex. Film Stock: Eastmancolor. Lab: LTC.
Cast: Jean-Paul Belmondo (Ferdinand Griffon), (Belmondo's double: Maurice Auzel), Anna Karina (Marianne Renoir), Georges Staquet (Franck), Dirk Sanders (Marianne's brother or lover), Raymond Devos (man on pier), Graziella Galvani (Mrs Griffon), Roger Dutoit (gangster), Hans Meyer (ganster), Jimmy Karoubi (dwarf, gangster), Christa Nell (Mme. Staquet), Pascal Aubier (second brother), Pierre Hanin (third brother), Princess Aïcha Abadie (Herself), Samuel Fuller (Himself), Alexis Poliakoff (sailor), Laszlo Szabo (political exile from Santo Domingo), Jean-Pierre Léaud (young man in cinema).
Production Companies: Rome-Paris Films, Société Nouvelle de Cinématographie, Dino de Laurentiis Cinematografica. Producers: Georges de Beauregard and Dino de Laurentiis. Production Manager: René Demoulin. Assistant Production Managers: Roger Scipion, Roger Ferret.
Note: Original title was 'Le Démon de 11 heures'. Upon release, the film was forbidden to anyone under 18.

1966 Masculin Féminin: 15 faits précis. 35 mm, 110 minutes.
Release: 22 April 1966. Filmed: In Paris and Stockholm,[22] 22 November–13 December 1965.
Director: Jean-Luc Godard. Screenplay: Jean-Luc Godard, loosely based on two short stories by Guy de Maupassant ('La Femme de Paul' and 'Le Signe'), LeRoi Jones's *Dutchman*, and Vauthier's *Prodigues*. Assistant Directors: Bernard Toublanc-Michel, Jacques Barratier.[23] Script Continuity: Elisabeth Rappeneau. Photography: Willy Kurant,[24] William Lubtchansky,[25] Jean Orjollet. Still Photography: Marilu Parolini. Gaffer: Pierre Cornier. Grip: Bernard Largemains. Sound: René Levert. Music: Francis Lai, J.J. Debout, Mozart. Sound Mix: Antoine Bonfanti. Editing: Agnès Guillemot, Geneviève Bastid.
Cameras: Arriflex and Mitchell. Film Stock: Kodak 4X. Lab: GTC.
Cast: Jean-Pierre Léaud (Paul), Chantal Goya (Madeleine), Marlène Jobert (Elisabeth), Michel Debord (Robert), Catherine-Isabelle Duport (Catherine-Isabelle), Eva Britt

Strandberg ('She' in the film-within-film), Birger Malmsten ('He' in the film-within-film), Elsa Leroy (Miss Nineteen-Year-Old, Elsa), Françoise Hardy (companion to the US officer in car), Brigitte Bardot and Antoine Bourseiller (couple rehearsing in café), Chantal Darget (in extract from 'Le Métro Fantôme').

Production Companies: Anouchka Films, Argos Films, Svensk Filmindustrie, Sandrews. Producer: Anatole Dauman. Executive Producer: Philippe Dussart. Production Manager: Michel Choquet.

Note: Upon release, the film was forbidden to anyone under 18.

1966 Made in USA 35 mm, Techniscope, 90 minutes.

Release: Shown at London Film Festival 3 December 1966, and released 21 January 1967. Filmed: On location in Paris, and Paris outskirts July–August 1966.

Director: Jean-Luc Godard. Screenplay: Jean-Luc Godard, based on Richard Stark's novel *The Juggler*. Assistant Directors: Charles Bitsch, Claude Baaka, Jean-Pierre Léaud, Philippe Pouzenc. Script Continuity: Suzanne Schiffman. Photography: Raoul Coutard, Georges Liron, Jean Garcenot. Set Photographer: Marilu Parolini. Make-up: Jackie Reynal. Sound: René Levert. Music: Schumann, Beethoven. Song: 'As Tears Go By' by Mick Jagger and Keith Richards, sung by Marianne Faithfull. Sound Mix: Jacques Maumont. Editing: Agnès Guillemot, Geneviève Letellier.

Film Stock: Eastmancolor. Lab: LTC.

Dedication: 'A Nick (Ray) et Sam (Fuller) qui m'ont élevé dans le respect de l'image et du son'.

Cast: Anna Karina (Paula Nelson), Laszlo Szabo (Richard Widmark), Yves Afonso (David Goodis), Jean-Pierre Léaud (Donald Siegal), Jean-Claude Bouillon (Inspector Aldrich), Kyoko Kosaka (Doris Mizoguchi), Ernest Menzer (Edgar Typhus), Elaine Giovagnoli (dentist's assistant), Rita Maiden (woman who gives information to Paula), Marianne Faithfull (Herself), Rémo Forlani (worker in bar), Sylvain Godet (Robert MacNamara), Jean-Pierre Biesse (Richard Nixon), Claude Baaka (man with Marianne Faithfull), Philippe Labro (Himself), Marc Dudicourt (barman), Alexis Poliakoff (man with notebook), Roger Scipion (Dr Korvo), Danièle Palmero (chambermaid in hotel), Isabelle Pons (journalist), Philippe Pouzenc (policeman), Fernand Coquet (bill poster), Miguel (dentist), Annie Guégan (young woman in bandages), Marika Perioli (young woman with dog), Jean-Philippe Nierman (policeman), Charles Bitsch (taxi-driver), Daniel Bart (policeman), Jean-Luc Godard (voice of Richard Politzer).

Production Companies: Rome-Paris Films, Anouchka Films, S.E.P.I.C. Producer: Georges de Beauregard. Production Manager: René Demoulin. Assistant Production Manager: Roger Scipion.

1967 Deux ou trois choses que je sais d'elle. 35 mm, Techniscope, 90 minutes.

Release: 17 March 1967. Filmed: In Paris region, 8 August–8 September, 1966.

Director: Jean-Luc Godard. Screenplay: Jean-Luc Godard, based on 'La Prostitution dans les grands ensembles', articles by Catherine Vimenet in *Le Nouvel Observateur*, 29 March and 10 May 1966. Assistant Directors: Charles Bitsch, Isabelle Pons. Script

Continuity: Suzanne Schiffman. Photography: Raoul Coutard, Georges Liron, Jean Garcenot. Still Photography: Marilu Parolini. Costumes: Gitt Magrini. Wardrobe Person: Dora Balabanow. Hair Stylist: Renée Guidet. Make-up: Jackie Reynal. Gaffer: Fernand Coquet. Key Grip: Edmond Frees. Sound: René Levert. Boom Operator: Robert Cambourakis. Music: Beethoven. Sound Mix: Antoine Bonfanti. Editing: Françoise Collin, Chantal Delattre.

Film Stock: Kodak Eastmancolor.

Cast: Marina Vlady (Juliette Jeanson), Roger Montsoret (Robert Jeanson), Anny Duperey (Marianne), Jean Narboni (Roger), Raoul Lévy (John Bogus), Christophe and Marie Bourseiller (Christophe and Solange Jeanson), Joseph Gehrard (Mr Gérard), Helena Bielinic (woman in bathtub), Robert Chevassu (electricity meter reader), Yves Beneyton (one of Juliette's clients), Jean-Pierre Laverne (author), Blandine Jeanson (student), Claude Miller (Bouvard), Jean-Patrick Lebel (Pécuchet), Juliet Berto (woman talking to Robert in café), Anna Manga (woman in basement), Benjamin Rosette (man in basement), Helen Scott (woman playing pinball), Jean-Luc Godard (narrator in voiceover).

Production Companies: Anouchka Films, Argos, Les Films du Carrosse, Parc Film. Producers: Anatole Dauman, François Truffaut. Executive Producer: Philippe Dussart. Production Manager: Philippe Senné. Assistant Production Managers: Claude Miller, Jean-Patrick Lebel.

Prize: Femina prize 1976.

1967 Anticipation (*ou* L'Amour en l'an deux miller 2000). Sketch in Le Plus vieux métier du monde (*ou* L'Amour à travers les âges). 35 mm, 20 minutes.

Release: 21 April 1967. Filmed: On location in Paris, and at Orly Airport, November 1966.

Director: Jean-Luc Godard. Screenplay: Jean-Luc Godard. Assistant Directors: Charles Bitsch, Claude Miller. Script Continuity: Lydie Doucet. Photography: Pierre Lhomme and Service de Recherches du Laboratoire, LTC,[26] Gilbert Duhlade, Testa-Rossa. Still Photography: Raoul Foulon. Make-up: Jackie Reynal. Hair Stylist: Renée Guidet. Costumes: Gitt Magrini. Wardrobe Person: Andrée Demarez. Props: Jean Gosse. Gaffer: Jacques Touillaud. Key Grip: Edmond Frees. Sound: René Levert. Boom Operator: Robert Cambourakis. Music: Michel Legrand. Editing: Agnès Guillemot, Geneviève Letellier.

Film Stock: Kodak Eastmancolor. Lab: LTC.

Cast: Jacques Charrier (male space traveller, John Demetrios), Anna Karina (Miss Conversation, Eléonor Roméovitch, called Natacha), Marilu Tolo (Miss Physical Love, Marlène), Jean-Pierre Léaud (bellboy), Daniel Bart, Jean-Patrick Lebel.

Production Companies: Les Films Gibé, Francoriz, Rialto Films, Rizzoli Films. Producer: Joseph Bergholz. Production Manager: André Cultet. Assistant Production Managers: Tonio Suné, Maurice Magalon.

Note: Other sketches in Le Plus vieux métier du monde by Franco Indovina, Mauro Bolognini, Philippe de Broca, Michaël Pfleghaar, Claude Autant-Lara.

1967 La Chinoise. 35 mm, 90 minutes.

Release: Presented at the Avignon Festival 3 August 1967, and released 30 August 1967.
Filmed: On location in Paris (apartment of Antoine Bourseiller) and Nanterre, 6 March–
11 April 1967.
Director: Jean-Luc Godard. Screenplay: Jean-Luc Godard. Assistant Directors: Charles
Bitsch, Isabelle Pons. Script Continuity: Suzanne Schiffman. Photography: Raoul Cou-
tard, Georges Liron, Jean Garcenot. Still Photography: Marilu Parolini. Costumes: Gitt
Magrini. Wardrobe Person: Laurence Clairval. Make-up: Jackie Reynal. Gaffer: Fernand
Coquet. Key Grip: Edmond Frees. Sound: René Levert. Boom Operator: Robert Cam-
bourakis. Music: Stockhausen, Schubert, Vivaldi. Sound Mix: Antoine Bonfanti. Editing:
Agnès Guillemot, Delphine Desfons, Christine Marsollier (intern).[27]
Camera: Mitchell and Cameflex. Film Stock: Eastmancolor. Lab: Eclair.
Cast: Anne Wiazemsky (Véronique), Jean-Pierre Léaud (Guillaume), Michel Semeniako
(Henri), Lex de Bruijn (Kirilov), Juliet Berto (Yvonne), Omar Diop (Omar), Francis
Jeanson (Himself), Blandine Jeanson (Blandine), Elaine Giovagnoli.
Production Companies: Productions de la Guéville, Parc Films, Simar Films, Anouchka
Films, Athos Films. Executive Producer: Philippe Dussart. Production Manager: Philippe
Dussart. Assistant Production Managers: Claude Miller, Jean-Patrick Lebel.
Prize: Special Jury Prize, Venice Film Festival 1967.
Note: Final title card 'Fin d'un début'.

1967 *Caméra-Œil* [Camera Eye]. Sketch in **Loin du Viêt-Nam**, 16 mm, 15 minutes.

Release: Presented at the Montreal Film Festival 28 August 1967; New York Film
Festival, October 1967, and released 13 December 1967. Filmed: In Paris, June 1967, in
Michèle Rosier's apartment, about the same time as the sketch *L'Amour*.[28]
Director: Jean-Luc Godard. Screenplay: Jean-Luc Godard. Assistant Director: Charles
Bitsch. Photography: Alain Levent, Armand Marco. Sound: Antoine Bonfanti. Music:
Fano. Sound Mix: Antoine Bonfanti. Editing: Ragnar, Jacqueline Meppiel, Chris Mar-
ker.[29]
Film Stock: Kodak Eastmancolor.
Cast: Jean-Luc Godard.
Production Companies: Groupe S.L.O.N., Sofracima. Production Manager: Andrea
Haran. Producers: Jean-Luc Godard and Chris Marker.
Note: *Loin du Viêt-Nam* was refused by the Venice Film Festival. Other sketches shot for
Loin du Viêt-Nam by Alain Resnais, William Klein, Joris Ivens, Chris Marker, Agnès
Varda, Claude Lelouch. Varda's sketch was not included in the final version.

1967 L'Amour. Sketch in **La Contestation**. 35 mm, Techniscope, 26 minutes.

Release: Presented at the London Film Festival 24 November 1967; Berlin Film Festival
5 July 1969, and released in June 1970. Filmed: In 1967 on Michèle Rosier's roof garden
in Paris.
Director: Jean-Luc Godard. Screenplay: Jean-Luc Godard. Assistant Directors: Charles

Bitsch, Isabelle Pons, Jean-Pierre Rassam. Script Continuity: Elisabeth Rappeneau. Photography: Alain Levent, Armand Marco, I. Guergov. Gaffer: Georges Boisrond. Key Grip: Jean L'Herrou. Sound: Guy Villette. Boom Operator: Jean Bareille. Music: Giovanni Fusco. Sound Mix: Antoine Bonfanti. Editing: Agnès Guillemot, Delphine Desfons.
Film Stock: Kodak Eastmancolor.
Cast: Christine Guého (She), Catherine Jourdon (female witness), Nino Castelnuovo (He), Paolo Pozzesi (male witness).
Production Companies: Castoro Films, Anouchka Films. Producer: Carlo Lizzani. Production Manager: Philippe Senné. Assistant Production Manager: Jean-Patrick Lebel.
Note: Italian release version of Godard's sketch known as *L'Aller et retour des enfants prodigues, Andate e ritorno dei figli prodighi*. The film was meant to be a dialogue between Marxists and Christians, and the original Italian title of all the sketches was *Vangelo 70 (Evangile 70)*. The title was subsequently first changed to: *Amore e rabbia*, and following the events of May 1968, to *La Contestation*. The film was not released in France until 1970. See Marcel Martin's review, *Les Lettres françaises*, 10 June 1970. Other sketches by: Bernardo Bertolucci, Pier Paolo Pasolini, Carlo Lizzani, Marco Bellocchio, Elda Tattoli.

1967 Week-end. 35 mm, 95 minutes.
Release: 29 December 1967. Filmed: In the Paris area September–October 1967.
Director: Jean-Luc Godard. Screenplay: Jean-Luc Godard. Assistant Directors: Claude Miller, Isabelle Pons. Script Continuity: Suzanne Schiffman. Photography: Raoul Coutard, Georges Liron, Jean Garcenot. Still Photography: Marilu Parolini. Props: Angelo Rizz. Costumes: Gitt Magrini. Hair Stylist: Mimi Chaperon. Gaffer: Fernand Coquet. Key Grip: Edmond Frees. Sound: René Levert. Boom Operator: Urbain Loiseau. Music: Antoine Duhamel, Mozart. Song by Guy Béart 'Allô, allô, tu m'entends'; Jean-Pierre Kalfon playing the drums, and song sung by Valérie Lagrange. Sound Mix: Antoine Bonfanti. Editing: Agnès Guillemot, Odile Faillot, Christine Aya (intern).
Film Stock: Eastmancolor. Lab: Eclair.
Cast: Mireille Darc (Corinne), Jean Yanne (Roland), Jean-Pierre Kalfon (FLSO leader), Valérie Lagrange (his companion), Jean-Pierre Léaud (Saint-Just, and man in phone booth), Georges Staquet (tractor driver), Yves Beneyton (FLSO member), Paul Gégauff (pianist), Daniel Pommereulle (Joseph Balsamo), Virginie Vignon (Marie-Madeleine), Yves Afonso (Tom Thumb), Blandine Jeanson (Emily Brontë, and young woman in farmyard), Ernest Menzer (cook), Juliet Berto (woman in car crash, and FLSO member), Jean Eustache (hitchhiker), Laszlo Szabo (Arab), Helen Scott (woman in car), J. C. Guilbert (Monsieur Jojot), Isabelle Pons, Michel Cournot, Anne Wiazemsky.
Production Companies: Films Copernic, Comacico, Lira Films, Ascot Cineraïd. Production Manager: Ralph Baum. Assistant Production Manager: Philippe Senné.
Note: Originally entitled 'Le Week-End', the film was unofficially retitled *Week-end* upon its release. The title was officially changed in 1988 at the request of Gaumont. Final title

cards: 'Fin de conte/Fin de cinéma'. Upon release, the film was forbidden to anyone under 18.

1968 Film-tracts nos. 7, 8, 9, 10, 12, 13, 14, 15, 16, 23, 40.[30] 16 mm, 3 minutes each. Release: Shown non-commercially in student assemblies, factories on strike, and other venues in 1968. Filmed: May–June 1968, photo studio Dumage rue Littré, Paris; Godard's apartment, rue Saint-Jacques.[31]
Director: Jean-Luc Godard. Photography: Armand Marco, William Lubtchansky.
Film Stock: Kodak XX 7222. Camera: Beaulieu.
Producer: Jean-Luc Godard.
Note: Originally intended to be collective works (and thus not of individual authorship) Godard's film-tracts are recognisable by his distinctive handwriting, over the still images. These short films are often called ciné-tracts (many are so titled). This filmography prefers to call Godard's contributions 'film-tracts', in accordance with his own titling. Each film begins with a shot identifying the film stock ('Kodak double-X type 7222 pour appareils 16 mm seulement,') over which Godard has written 'film tract' and its individual number. They are available for viewing at the Forum des Images, Paris.

1968 Film-tracts. 16 mm, 3 minutes each.
Release: shown non-commercially in student assemblies, factories on strike, and other venues in 1968. Filmed: May–June 1968, photo studio rue Littré, Paris.
Director: Alain Jouffroy. Photography: Jean-Luc Godard.
Note: Jouffroy shot two or three film tracts with Godard's help.

1968 Rouge, film tract No 1968. 16 mm, 3 minutes.
Release: shown non-commercially in student assemblies, factories on strike, and other venues in 1968. Filmed: May or June 1968.
Director: Gérard Fromanger. Photography: Jean-Luc Godard.
Note: See Gérard Fromanger, 'Il faut créer un Vietnam dans chaque musée du monde', *Jeune, dure et pure! Une histoire du cinéma d'avant-garde et expérimental en France*, eds. Nicole Brenez and Christian Lebrat (Paris and Milan: Cinémathèque Française and Mazzotta, 2001), pp. 336–338. Fromanger subsequently did another version with Marin Karmitz.

1968 Un Film comme les autres. 16 mm and 35 mm, 100 minutes.
Release: 1971 by Nef Diffusion. Filmed: Paris, May 1968, the University of Vincennes, and Flins, July or August 1968.
Director: Jean-Luc Godard,[32] with the group ARC and Jacques Kébadian. Screenplay: Jean-Luc Godard. Photography: William Lubtchansky.[33] Editing: Christine Aya.
Film Stock: Ektachrome, and black and white.
Cast: Three students from Nanterre, and two workers from the Renault Factory at Flins. Godard's voice is heard on the soundtrack.

Production Company: Anouchka Films.
Note: The film is often (incorrectly) listed as a Dziga Vertov film.

1968 One A.M. (One American Movie). 16 mm, unfinished.
Filmed: In New York City, Newark, New Jersey, and Berkeley, California, November 1968.
Directors: Jean-Luc Godard during the shoot; D.A. Pennebaker and Richard Leacock for release version. Photography: Richard Leacock. Music: Jefferson Airplane.
Film Stock: Ektachrome.
Cast: Rip Torn, Tom Hayden, LeRoi Jones, Jefferson Airplane, Eldridge Cleaver, Black Panthers, Jean-Luc Godard, Anne Wiazemsky, Richard Leacock, Tom Luddy, Paula Madder, Mary Lampson.
Note: In March 1970, Godard and Gorin went to New York to edit the footage. They ultimately abandoned the project because they felt in conflict with Leacock and Pennebaker's style (Lesage). Pennebaker and Leacock subsequently edited the footage, with the title *One P.M.*

1968 One Plus One. 35 mm, Eastmancolor, 99 minutes.
Release: Presented at the London Film Festival 29 November 1968, and released 7 May 1969. Filmed: In Olympic Recording Studios, London, and exteriors London and Sussex, June–August 1968.
Director: Jean-Luc Godard. Screenplay: Jean-Luc Godard. Assistant Directors: Isabelle Pons, Tim Van Rellim, John Stoneman. Script Continuity: Valerie Booth. Photography: Anthony Richard. Camera Operator: Colin Corby. Make-up: Linda De Vetta. Sound: Arthur Bradburn, Derek Ball. Music: Mick Jagger and Keith Richards. Song: 'Sympathy for the Devil'. Sound Mix: Antoine Bonfanti. Editing: Ken Rowles, Agnès Guillemot, Christine Aya.
Cast: Rolling Stones (Mick Jagger, Keith Richards, Brian Jones, Charlie Watts, Bill Wyman), Anne Wiazemsky (Eve Democracy), Iain Quarrier (Fascist porno bookseller), Frankie Dymon, Jr. (Himself), Bernard Boston (Himself), Sean Lynch (narrator), Danny Daniels, Clifton Jones (black power militant), Ilario Pedro, Roy Stewart, Limbert Spencer, Tommy Ansar, Michael McKay, Rudi Patterson, Mark Andrew, Karl Lewis, Niké Arrighi, Françoise Pascal, Joanna David, Monica Walters, Glenna Forster-Jones, Elizabeth Long, Jeanette Wild, Harry Douglas, Colin Cunningham, Graham Peet, Matthew Know, Barbara Coleridge.
Production Company: Cupid Productions. Producers: Michael Pearson, Iain Quarrier. Executive Producer: Eleni Collard. Production Managers: Clive Freedman, Paul de Burgh.
Note: The producer brought out a slightly different version of *One Plus One* with the title *Sympathy for the Devil*, and with a complete rendition of the song at the end of the film. Godard disowned this version.

1969 Le Gai savoir. 35 mm, 91 minutes.
Release: Presented at the Berlin Film Festival 28 June 1969. Filmed: Joinville Studios, December 1967–January 1968 (edited after June 1968).
Director: Jean-Luc Godard. Screenplay: Jean-Luc Godard, based (loosely) on Rousseau's *Émile*. Title is translation of Nietzsche's *Die Fröhliche Wissenschaft*. Photography: J. L. Picavet. Georges Leclerc. Music: Revolutionary Songs, especially Cuban. Editing: Germaine Cohen.[34]
Camera: Cameflex. Film Stock: Eastmancolor. Lab: LTC.
Cast: Juliet Berto (Patricia Lumumba), Jean-Pierre Léaud (Émile Rousseau).
Production Companies: Originally ORTF (French Radio-Television), later Anouchka Films, Bavaria Atelier. Production Manager: Philippe Dussart.
Note: ORTF sold their rights back to Godard. French censors forbad its showing on French television or in commercial cinemas. Certain cuts were demanded by the Commission de Contrôle des Films Cinématographiques (6 February 1969).

1969 British Sounds.[35] 16 mm, 52 minutes.
Release: Distributed by Grove Press in the US and Nef Diffusion in France. Filmed: England, March 1969.
Director: Dziga Vertov Group. Screenplay: Jean-Luc Godard and Jean-Henri Roger. Photography: Charles Stewart. Sound: Fred Sharp. Sound Mix: Antoine Bonfanti. Editing: Christine Aya.[36]
Film Stock: Eastmancolor.
Cast: Production line of MG sports car, British Motor Co., students from Oxford, students from Essex, feminist from *Black Dwarf* paper, a group of militant workers from the Dagenham area. Godard's voice on soundtrack.
Production Company: Kestrel Productions for London Weekend Television.[37]
Note: First of the films made retrospectively under the collective title of the Dziga Vertov Group.

1969 Pravda. 16 mm, 58 minutes.
Filmed clandestinely in Czechoslovakia, June 1969.[38] Edited several months later. Some images taken off Czech television.
Director: Dziga Vertov Group. Photography: Paul Bourron. Editing: Christine Aya.[39]
Film Stock: Agfa Gevaert. Lab: C.T.M.
Cast: Jean-Pierre Gorin (Vladimir Lenin) in voice-over, and a woman's voice (Rosa Luxembourg).[40] Voice-over in English.
Production Company: Grove Press, and Centre Européen Cinéma Radio Télévison (CERT) for German TV. A documentary section of the Czech Cinematographic Institute paid for the shoot. Producer: Claude Nedjar.
Note: 'Pravda' means truth in Russian.

1970 Vent d'est. 16 mm, 100 minutes.

Release: Presented at the Cannes Film Festival 6 May 1970, and subsequently distributed by Nef Diffusion. Filmed: On location in Italy, and in studios, 16 June–16 July 1969. Director: Dziga Vertov Group.[41] Screenplay: Jean-Luc Godard, Daniel Cohn-Bendit, Sergio Bazzini. Photography: Mario Vulpiani, Mario Bagnato, Paul Bourron. Decors: Lucianna Levi. Costumes: Lina Nerli Tavani. Assistants: Isabelle Pons, Gianni Amico, Raphaël Sorin. Sound: Antonio Ventura, Carlo Diotalevi. Sound Mix: Antoine Bonfanti. Editing: Christine Aya.

Film Stock: Eastmancolor 7254.

Cast: Gian Maria Volonté (cavalryman), Anne Wiazemsky (woman in petticoat), Marie Dedieu, Glauber Rocha (Himself), José Varela (guide), George Götz, Fabio Garriba, Jean-Luc Godard, and film crew (Themselves), Allen Midgette (Indian), Marco Ferreri, Paolo Pozzesi (union representative), Vanessa Redgrave (woman with movie camera), Daniel Cohn-Bendit (Himself), Franco Bucceri, Marco Vergine.

Production Companies: Compagnia Cinematografica Champion, Polifilm, Anouchka Films, Film Kunst. Producers: Georges de Beauregard, Gianni Barcelloni, Ettore Rosboch. Director of Production: Roberto Giussani. Production Assistant: Raniero di Giovanbattista.

1970 Lotte in Italia.[42] 16 mm, 76 minutes. In Italian.

Release: Bergamo September 1970. Filmed: Paris (Godard and Wiazemsky's apartment, rue Saint-Jacques), and Italy, December 1969.

Directors: Dziga Vertov Group. Screenplay: Dziga Vertov Group. Photography: Armand Marco. Sound Mix: Antoine Bonfanti. Editor: Christine Aya.[43]

Film Stock: Eastmancolor. Camera: Debrie.[44] Lab: Eclair.

Cast: Commentary spoken by Christina Tullio Altan (Paola), Anne Wiazemsky (store clerk), Jérôme Hinstin (young man), Paolo Pozzesi (narrator).

Production Companies: Cosmoseion for Italian Radio and Television,[45] Anouchka Films. Producer: Gianni Barcelloni.

1970 Jusqu'à la victoire (Méthode de pensée et travail de la révolution palestinienne). 16 mm, unfinished. Later incorporated into *Ici et ailleurs* (1976).[46]

Filmed: Palestine, 1969–1970.[47]

Director: Dziga Vertov Group. Photography: Armand Marco.

Film Stock: Eastmancolor.

1971 Vladimir et Rosa. 16 mm, colour. 103 minutes.

Release: Hyères Film Festival 1971; New York 16 April 1971. Filmed: Paris, autumn 1970.

Director: Dziga Vertov Group. Photography: Armand Marco and Gérard Martin. Sound Mix: Antoine Bonfanti. Editor: Christine Aya,[48] Chantal Colomer.[49]

Cast: Jean-Luc Godard (Vladimir), Jean-Pierre Gorin (Rosa), Anne Wiazemsky, Juliet

Berto, Ernest Menzer, Yves Afonso, Larry Martin, Claude Nedjar. Voice-over in French by Jean-Pierre Gorin and Jean-Luc Godard.
Lab: C.T.M.
Production Companies: Munich Tele-Pool for German Television,[50] Grove Press. Producer: Claude Nedjar.

1972 Tout va bien. 35 mm, 95 minutes.
Release: 28 April 1972. Filmed: In Epinay Studio (1 February–23 February 1972), and Paris outskirts (17–31 January 1972; 24 February–6 March 1972).
Directors: Jean-Luc Godard and Jean-Pierre Gorin. Screenplay: Jean-Luc Godard, Jean-Pierre Gorin. Photography: Armand Marco, Yves Agostini, Edouard Burgess. Still Photography: Alain Miéville, Anne-Marie Michel.[51] Assistant Directors: Isabelle Pons, Jean-Hughes Nelkene. Script Continuity: Marie-Noël Bon. Sets and Art Direction: Jacques Dugied, Olivier Girard, Jean-Luc Dugied. Gaffers: Louis Parola, Robert Beulens, José Bois. Grips: Ferdinand Rocquet, André Saudemont, Eugène Delsuc, Marcel Mercier. Special Effects: Jean-Claude Dolbert, Paul Trielli, Roger Jumeau, Marcel Vantieghem. Sound: Bernard Orthion, Gilles Orthion. Music: Eric Charden, Thomas Rivat, Paul Beuscher. Song: 'Il y a du soleil sur la France'. Sound Mix: Antoine Bonfanti. Editing: Kenout Peltier, Claudine Merlin.
Camera: Mitchell (studio) and Cameflex (exteriors). Film Stock: Kodak Eastmancolor. Lab: Eclair (Epinay).
Cast: Yves Montand (Him), Jane Fonda (Suzanne), Vittorio Caprioli (boss of factory), Jean Pignol (1st representative of the CGT), Pierre Oudry (Frédéric), Elisabeth Chauvin (Geneviève), Anne Wiazemsky (Leftist woman), Marcel Gassouk (2nd representative of the CGT), Didier Gaudron (Germain), Michel Marot (Communist Party representative), Huguette Miéville (Georgette), Luce Marnaux (Armande), Natalie Simon (Jeanne), Ibrahim Seck.
Production Companies: Anouchka Films, Vicco Film, Empire Film. Associate Producer: Jean-Pierre Rassam. Director of Production: Alain Coiffier. Assistant Production Managers: Armand Barbault, Volker Lemke, Jacques Perrier, Philippe Venault.
Note: Title card at the end of the film in red-white-blue: 'C'était un conte pour ceux qui n'en tiennent aucun'.

1972 Letter to Jane: An Investigation about a Still. 16 mm, colour, 52 minutes.
Release: Never released in France.[52] Screened in Frankfurt, 6 November 1974. Filmed: Auditel editing, Avenue du Maine, Paris. Camera: Debrie.
Directors: Jean-Luc Godard, Jean-Pierre Gorin. Screenplay: Jean-Luc Godard, Jean-Pierre Gorin.
Cast: Voice-over commentary spoken in English by Jean-Luc Godard and Jean-Pierre Gorin; with still photographs, principally one of Jane Fonda from the magazine *L'Express* (31 July–6 August 1972).
Production: Jean-Luc Godard, Jean-Pierre Gorin.

1976 Ici et ailleurs. 16 mm and video, 60 minutes.
Release: September 1976. Filmed: Palestine 1970, and Paris early seventies.
Directors: Jean-Luc Godard and Anne-Marie Miéville. Photography: Armand Marco, William Lubtchansky.[56] Video: Gérard Teissèdre. Editing: Anne-Marie Miéville.
Cast: Commentary spoken by Jean-Luc Godard, Anne-Marie Miéville.
Production Companies: Sonimage, Institut National de l'Audiovisuel, Gaumont. Producers: Jean-Pierre Rassam, Anne-Marie Miéville, Jean-Luc Godard. Production Manager: Stéphane Tchalgadjieff.
Cameras: Shibaden FP 1200, Eclair ACI, and Debrie CX. Film Stock: Kodak Eastmancolor.
Note: Incorporates recycled footage shot by Godard and Gorin for the unfinished *Jusqu'à la victoire*.

1975 Numéro deux. 35 mm and video, 88 minutes.
Release: 24 September 1975. Filmed: Sonimage studio, Grenoble, 17 February–15 May 1975.
Director: Jean-Luc Godard. Screenplay: Jean-Luc Godard and Anne-Marie Miéville.[53] Photography: Gérard Martin.[54] Kinescopage: William Lubtchansky.[55] Technical collaborators: Gérard Martin, Milka Assaf, Gérard Teissèdre. Sound: Jean-Pierre Ruh. Song: Léo Ferré. Editing: Jean-Luc Godard, Anne-Marie Miéville.
Filmstock: Eastmancolor. Cameras: Arriflex and video. Lab: Eclair.
Cast: Sandrine Battistella (Sandrine), Pierre Oudry (her husband), Alexandre Rignault (Grandfather), Rachel Stefanopoli (Grandmother), Marine Martin (Vanessa).
Production Companies: Sonimage, Bela, Société Nouvelle du Cinématographie. Producers: Georges de Beauregard, Jean-Pierre Rassam. Associate Producers: Jean-Luc Godard and Anne-Marie Miéville. Production Manager: Marcel Mossotti.
Note: The film's original title was 'Numéro 2 – A Bout de souffle'. Upon release, the film was forbidden to anyone under 18.
Giuffrida and the Fiche technique at the BiFi list Miéville as co-director; *Jean-Luc Godard par Jean-Luc Godard*, vols 1 & 2, and Lesage do not. Miéville is cited as co-screenwriter in *Jean-Luc Godard par Jean-Luc Godard*, vols 1 & 2; the technical credits submitted to the CNC (28 February 1975) list only Godard as screenwriter.

1976 Six fois deux (Sur et sous la communication). Video. Six programmes of 100 minutes, each divided into two segments.
Release: France 3 originally programmed *Six fois deux* on Sunday evenings between 25 July and 29 August 1976. Filmed: Sonimage studio, Grenoble.
Directors: Jean-Luc Godard and Anne-Marie Miéville. Screenplay: Jean-Luc Godard and Anne-Marie Miéville. Photography: William Lubtchansky, Dominique Chapuis. Technical Collaborators: Gérard Teissèdre, Joël Mellier. Still Photography: Anne-Marie Miéville. Assistant Director: Philippe Rony. Editing: Jean-Luc Godard and Anne-Marie Miéville.

Titles of individual episodes: 1. Y'a personne/Louison, 2. Leçon de choses/Jean-Luc, 3. Photo et compagnie/Marcel, 4. Pas d'histoires/Nanas, 5. Nous trois/René, 6. Avant et après/Jacqueline et Ludovic.

Production Companies: Institut National de l'Audiovisuel, Sonimage. Producers: Michel Raux, Jean-Luc Godard. Production Manager: Louisette Neil.

Note: Farassino, Guiffrida, and Lesage list Miéville as co-director, *Jean-Luc Godard par Jean-Luc Godard*, vols. 1 & 2, do not.

1978 Comment ça va? 16 mm and video, colour, 78 minutes.

Release: Presented at the Venice Film Festival August 1976, and released 26 April 1978.

Filmed: Grenoble May 1975–January 1976.

Directors: Jean-Luc Godard and Anne-Marie Miéville. Screenplay: Jean-Luc Godard and Anne-Marie Miéville. Photography: William Lubtchansky. Music: Jean Schwartz.

Cast: Michel Marot, Anne-Marie Miéville.

Camera: Eclair ACL. Video: Sony. Film Stock: Kodak Eastmancolor 7247.

Production Companies: Sonimage, Bela, Société Nouvelle du Cinématographie, Institut National de l'Audiovisuel. Producer: Jean-Pierre Rassam. Production Manager: Marcel Mossotti.

Note: Lesage, Farassino, Guiffrida, and Fiche technique at the BiFi list Miéville as co-director; *Jean-Luc Godard par Jean-Luc Godard*, vols. 1 & 2, do not.

1978 Papa comme maman. 35 mm, short film.

Director: Anne-Marie Miéville.

1979 Scénario de 'Sauve qui peut (la vie)': Quelques remarques sur la réalisation et la production du film. Video, 20 minutes.

Filmed: Switzerland in 1979.

Production Companies: Sonimage, Télévision Suisse Romande.

1979 France tour détour deux enfants. 35 mm and video, 12 programmes, each 26 minutes.

Release: Presented at the Venice Film Festival August 1979. Presented on Antenne 2 in April 1980 by Jean-Claude Philippe in his Ciné-Club. Filmed: In the house of William Lubtchansky in Paris in 1978.

Directors: Jean-Luc Godard and Anne-Marie Miéville.[58] Screenplay: Jean-Luc Godard, Anne-Marie Miéville, freely adapted from G. Bruno's textbook for French school children: *Le Tour da la France par deux enfants.* Assistant Director: Philippe Rony. Photography: William Lubtchansky, Dominique Chapuis, Philippe Rony. Technical Engineer: Pierre Binggeli. Song: Julien Clerc.

Titles of individual episodes: 1. Obscur/Chimie, 2. Lumière/Physique 3. Connu/Géométrie/Géographie, 4. Inconnu/Technique, 5. Impression/Dictée, 6. Expression/Français, 7. Violence/Grammaire, 8. Désordre/Calcul, 9. Pouvoir/Musique, 10. Roman/Economic, 11. Réalité/Logique, 12. Rêve/Morale.

Cast: Camille Virolleaud, Arnaud Martin (the children), Betty Berr and Albert Dray (the television announcers), Godard (as off-screen interviewer), Evane Hanska (as barmaid in one segment).
Production Companies: Institut National de l'Audiovisuel for Antenne 2, Sonimage. Producers: Jean-Luc Godard and Anne-Marie Miéville.[59]
Note: Turin lists as co-directed by Miéville; Farassino, *Jean-Luc Godard par Jean-Luc Godard*, vols. 1 & 2, do not.

1980 Sauve qui peut (la vie). 35 mm and video, 87 minutes.
Release: Presented at the Cannes Film Festival May 1980, and released October 1980.
Filmed: Switzerland, autumn 1979.
Director: Jean-Luc Godard. Screenplay: Anne-Marie Miéville, Jean-Claude Carrière.
Assistant Director: Romain Goupil. Photography: William Lubtchansky, Renato Berta,[57] Jean-Bernard Menoud. Colour Consultant: Daniel Bernard. Still Photography: Anne-Marie Miéville. Sound: Luc Yersin, Oscar Stellavox. Music: Gabriel Yared. Sound Mix: Jacques Maumont. Editing: Anne-Marie Miéville, Jean-Luc Godard.
Cast: Isabelle Huppert (Isabelle Rivière), Nathalie Baye (Denise Rimbaud), Jacques Dutronc (Paul Godard), Roland Amstutz (a client of Isabelle's), Anna Baldaccini (Isabelle's sister), Fred Personne (another of Isabelle's clients), Nicole Jacquet, Dore de Rosa, Cécile Tanner (Paul's daughter), Michel Cassagne (Piaget), Paule Muret (Paul's ex-wife), Catherine Freiburghaus, Bernard Cazassuss, Eric Desfoissés, Nicole Wicht, Claude Champion, Gérard Battaz, Angelo Napoli, Serge Maillard, Marie-Luc Felber, Guy Lavoro, Michèle Gleiser, Maurice Buffat, Monique Barscha, Irène Foresheim, Serge Desarnault, Giorgiana Eaton.
Production Companies: Sara Films, MK2, Saga Productions, Sonimage, Centre National de la Cinématographie, ZDF, SSR, ORF. Executive Producers: Alain Sarde, Jean-Luc Godard. Associate Producer: Marin Karmitz.
Prize: Nathalie Boye, César for female supporting role. Décibel d'or to Jacques Maumont for the Sound Mix.
Note: Godard signs the film 'Un film composé par Jean-Luc Godard'.

1981 Troisième état du scénario du film 'Passion' (Le travail et l'amour: Introduction à un scénario). Video, 20 minutes.
Filmed: 1981.
Director: Jean-Luc Godard.

1982 Lettre à Freddy Buache (à propos d'un court-métrage sur la ville de Lausanne). Video (subsequently transferred to 35 mm), 11 minutes.
Release: May 1982. Filmed: Lausanne 1981.
Director: Jean-Luc Godard. Screenplay: Jean-Luc Godard. Photography: Jean-Bernard Menoud. Collaborators: Pierre Binggeli, Gérard Ruey. Sound: François Musy. Music: Ravel. Editing: Jean-Luc Godard.

Dedication: Robert Flaherty and Ernst Lubitsch.

Cast: Commentary spoken by Godard over images of Lausanne.

Production Company: Film et Vidéo Production.

Note: Commissioned by the city of Lausanne.

1982 Passion. 35 mm, 87 minutes.

Release: 26 May 1982. Filmed: Studios Boulogne-Billancourt, and Rolle, Winter 1981–1982.

Director: Jean-Luc Godard. Screenplay and Dialogues: Jean-Luc Godard. Assistant Directors: Alain Tasma, Gérard Ruey, Bertrand Theubet, Lee Colver. Photography: Raoul Coutard, André Clément, Jean Garcenot. Video: Jean-Bernard Menoud. Set Photographer: Anne-Marie Miéville. Advisor: Anne-Marie Miéville. Art Direction: Serge Marzolff, Jean Bauer. Script Continuity: Lydie Mahias. Costumes: Christian Gasc, Rosalie Varda. Wardrobe Persons: Bernard Minne, Rosemary Melka. Hair Stylist: Patrick Archambaud. Technical Advisor: Bernard Gruninger. Gaffers: Michel Vaucoret, Jean-Claude Basselet, Alain Cousseau, Jacques Guyot. Key Grips: Jean Hennau, René-Albert Pequignot, Gaston Verdonck, Frédérique Erni.

Painting: Yvon Aubinel. Sound: François Musy. Music: Mozart, Dvorak, Beethoven, Fauré, Ravel. Song: Léo Ferré. Sound Mix: Bernard Le Roux. Editing: Jean-Luc Godard.

Cast: Isabelle Huppert (Isabelle), Hanna Schygulla (Hanna), Michel Piccoli (Michel), Jerzy Radziwilowicz (the film director), Laszlo Szabo (the producer), Patrick Bonnel, Sophie Lucatchevsky, Jean-François Stévenin, Enzio Ambrosetti, Magali Champos, Myriem Roussel (deaf-mute niece of Michel), Barbara Tissier.

Film Stock: Kodak Eastmancolor. Lab: LTC.

Production Companies: Sara Films, Sonimage, Films Antenne 2, Film et Vidéo Production, Switzerland. Executive Producer: Alain Sarde. Production Managers: Martine Marignac, Catherine Lapoujade, Armand Barbault. Location Production Manager: Ruth Waldburger. Assistant Production Manager: Daniel Chevalier.

1982 Scénario du film 'Passion'. Video, 54 minutes.

Filmed: 1982.

Director: Jean-Luc Godard. Collaborators: Jean-Bernard Menoud, Anne-Marie Miéville, Pierre Binggeli, Studio Transvidéo.

Production Companies: JLG Films, Télévision Suisse Romande.

1982 Changer d'image (Changement ou Lettre à ma bien aimée). Video, 10 minutes.

Director: Jean-Luc Godard. Photography: Jean-Bernard Menoud.

Cast: Jacques Probst, Jean-Luc Godard.

Production Companies: Sonimage, Institut National de l'Audiovisuel.

1983 Prénom Carmen. 35 mm, 85 minutes.
Release: 7 December 1983. Filmed: Paris, and Paris outskirts; Trouville, January–February 1983.
Director: Jean-Luc Godard. Screenplay and adaptation: Anne-Marie Miéville. Assistant Director: Gérard Delayat. Photography: Raoul Coutard, Jean Garcenot, Jean-Bernard Menoud. Costumes: Renée Renard. Make-up: Laurence Azouy. Music: Beethoven quartets, recorded by the Prat Quartet. Song: 'Ruby's Arms' by Tom Waits. Sound: François Musy, Oscar Stellavox. Editing: Jean-Luc Godard, Suzanne Lang-Willar, Adeline Yoyotte-Husson.
Cameras: Aaton 35/8 and Arriflex. Film Stock: Kodak Eastmancolor.
Dedication: 'In memoriam small movies'.
Cast: Maruschka Detmers (Carmen), Jacques Bonaffé (Joseph), Myriem Roussel (Claire), Jean-Luc Godard (Uncle Jean), Christophe Odent, Hyppolite Giradot (Fred), Pierre-Alain Chapuis (inspector), Bertrand Liebert (guardian angel), Alain Bastien-Thiry, Jacques Villaret, Jean-Pierre Mocky.
Production Companies: Sara Films, JLG Films, Antenne 2 Films. Associate Producer: Alain Sarde. Production Manager: Bernard Bouix.
Prizes: Golden Lion, and Special Prizes to Raoul Coutard (Photography) and to François Musy (Sound), Venice Film Festival 1983.

1983 Petites notes à propos du film 'Je vous salue, Marie'. Video, 25 minutes.
Director: Jean-Luc Godard.
Cast: Jean-Luc Godard, Myriem Roussel, Thierry Rode, Anne-Marie Miéville.

1984 How Can I Love (A Man When I Know He Don't Want Me). 35 mm, 13 minutes.
Release: January 1984. Filmed: 1983.
Director: Anne-Marie Miéville. Assistant Director: Jacques Firmann. Screenplay: Anne-Marie Miéville. Photography: Francis Reusser. Music: Louis Crelier. Sound: François Musy. Editor; Anne-Marie Miéville.
Film Stock: Eastman Kodak. Labs: LTC and Cinégram (Geneva).
Cast: Harriet Kraatz, Jo Excoffier, Carlo Brandt, Dominique Stehle, François Germond, Antoine Basler.
Production Companies: JLG Films, Sonimage Suisse.

1985 'Je vous salue, Marie'. 35 mm, Eastmancolor, 72 minutes.
Release: January 1985. Filmed: beginning of January–mid February 1984.
Director: Jean-Luc Godard. Screenplay: Jean-Luc Godard. Photography: Jean-Bernard Menoud, Jacques Firmann. Music: Bach, Dvorak, Coltrane. Assistant Directors: Philippe Malignon, François Pélissier. Sound: François Musy. Editing: Jean-Luc Godard.
Cast: Myriem Roussel (Marie), Thierry Rode (Joseph), Philippe Lacoste (Angel), Juliette Binoche (Juliette), Johann Meyssen (the professor), Anne Gauthier (Eva), Malachi Jara Kohan (Jesus), Manon Andersen (child), Dick (Arthur), Georges Staquet (Marie's doctor).

Production Companies: Pégase Films, Radio Télévision Suisse Romande, JLG Films, Sara Films, Gaumont, Channel 4.
Note: This film is accompanied by Anne-Marie Miéville's short film *Le Livre de Marie*.

1985 Le Livre de Marie. 35 mm, 27 minutes.
Release: January 1985.
Director: Anne-Marie Miéville. Screenplay: Anne-Marie Miéville. Photography: Jean-Bernard Menoud, Caroline Champetier, Jacques Firmann. Art Direction: Ivan Niclass. Music: Chopin, Mahler. Sound: François Musy. Editing: Anne-Marie Miéville.
Cast: Bruno Cremer (the father), Aurore Clément (the mother), Rebecca Hampton (Marie), Copi, Valentine Mercier, Cléa Rédalier.
Production Companies: Pégase Films, JLG Films.
Note: This film is accompanied by Jean-Luc Godard's '*Je vous salue, Marie*'.

1985 Détective. 35 mm, Dolby stereo, 95 minutes.
Release: Presented at the Cannes Film Festival May 1985. Filmed: mid-August–20 September 1984.
Director: Jean-Luc Godard. Screenplay: Alain Sarde, Philippe Setbon, Anne-Marie Miéville. Dialogue: Alain Sarde, Philippe Setbon, Anne-Marie Miéville. Assistant à la mise en scène: Reynald Calcagni. Script Continuity: Hélène Sébillotte. Photography: Bruno Nuytten. Music: Schubert, Wagner, Chopin, Liszt, Honegger, Chabrier, Ornette Coleman, Jean Schwarz. Sound: François Musy. Editing: Marilyn Dubreuil.
Dedication: John Cassavettes, Edgar G. Ulmer, and Clint Eastwood.
Cast: Nathalie Baye (Françoise Chenal), Claude Brasseur (Emile Chenal), Johnny Hallyday (Jim Fox Warner), Stéphane Ferrara (Tiger Jones, the boxer), Eugène Berthier (the old manager), Emmanuelle Seigner (Grace Kelly, the fiancée), Cyril Autin, Julie Delpy, Laurent Terzieff (hotel detective), Jean-Pierre Léaud, Anne-Gisèle Glass, Aurèle Doazan, Alain Cuny (Mafia don), Pierre Bertin, Alexandra Garijo (little girl), Xavier Saint-Macary (book-keeper).
Production Companies: Sara Films, JLG Films. Producers: Alain Sarde, Jean-Luc Godard. Production Manager: Christine Gozlan. Casting: Dominique Besnehard.

1985 Soft and Hard (A Soft Conversation between Two Friends on a Hard Subject). Video, 52 minutes.
Directors: Jean-Luc Godard and Anne-Marie Miéville. Photography: Pierre Binggeli. Cast: Jean-Luc Godard, Anne-Marie Miéville.
Production Companies: Deptford Beach Production in association with Channel 4, JLG Films. Producer: Tony Kirkhope. Friend: Colin MacCabe.

1986 Grandeur et décadence d'un petit commerce du cinéma. Video and 35 mm, 52 minutes.
Filmed: 1986.

Director: Jean-Luc Godard. Screenplay: Jean-Luc Godard. Assistants à la mise en scène: Reynald Calcagni, Richard Debuisne. Photography: Caroline Champetier. Video: Serge Lefrançois (SFP), Pierre Binggeli (Transvidéo). Music: Leonard Cohen, Joni Mitchell, Bob Dylan, Janis Joplin, Arvo Pärt, Bela Bartok. Sound: François Musy, Pierre-Alain Besse. Editing: Jean-Luc Godard.

Dedication: Jack Lang.

Cast: Jean-Pierre Mocky (Jean Almereyda, called Jean Vigo), Marie Valéra (Eurydice), Jean-Pierre Léaud (Gaspard Bazin), Jean-Luc Godard, Anne Carrel, Françoise Desporte, Jean-Pierre Delamour, Jacques Pena, Jean Grécault, Jean Brisa, and the unemployed of ANPE.

Production Companies: TF1, Hamster Productions, Radio Télévision Lausanne, Télévision Suisse Romande, JLG Films, RTL. Production Secretary: Marie-Christine Barrière.

Note: Original title: *Chantons en chœur*.

1986 Meeting Woody Allen/JLG Meets Woody Allen. Video, 26 minutes.
Director: Jean-Luc Godard. Screenplay: Jean-Luc Godard. Sound: François Musy. Editing: Jean-Luc Godard.
Cast: Jean-Luc Godard, Woody Allen.
Production Companies: JLG Films, Cannes Film Festival.

1986 Faire la fête. 35 mm, 13 minutes.
Director: Anne-Marie Miéville. Photography: Jean-Bernard Menoud. Sound: Claudine Nougaret. Editing: Anne-Marie Miéville.
Cast: Anne Alvaro, Didier Flammand, Hélène Lapiower, Eric Wild.

1987 Armide. Sketch in **Aria**. 35 mm, 12 minutes.
Release: Presented at the Cannes Film Festival May 1987. Filmed: In a Paris gym.
Director: Jean-Luc Godard. Screenplay: Jean-Luc Godard. Assistant à la mise en scène: Reynald Calcagni. Photography: Caroline Champetier. Music: Opera by Lully (Aria: 'Enfin, il est en ma puissance'). Singers: Rachel Yakar, Zeger Wandersteene, Daniel Borst. Sound: François Musy. Editing: Jean-Luc Godard.
Cast: Marion Peterson (young woman), Valérie Alain (young woman); Jacques Neuville, Luke Corre, Christian Cauchon, Philippe Pellant, Patrice Linguet, Lionel Sorin, Jean Coffinet, Alexandre des Granges, Gérard Vives, Frédéric Brosse, Pascal Bermont, Bernard Gaudray, Dominique Mano, Patrice Tridian: bodybuilders.
Production Companies: RVP Production, Virgin Vision, Lightyear Entertainment. Producer: Don Boyd.
Note: Other sketches in *Aria* by Nicolas Roeg, Charles Sturridge, Julien Temple, Bruce Beresford, Robert Altman, Frank Roddam, Ken Russell, Derek Jarman, Bill Bryden.

1987 Soigne ta droite, ou Une place sur la terre. 35 mm, Dolby stereo 82 minutes.
Release: December 1987. Filmed: 1986.

Director: Jean-Luc Godard. Screenplay: Jean-Luc Godard. Assistants à la mise en scène: Richard Debuisne, Hervé Duhamel, Reynald Calcagni. Photography: Caroline Champetier, Jacques Loiseleux. Sound: François Musy, Joël Beldent. Music: The Rita Mitsouko. Sound Mix: Bernard Le Roux. Editing: Jean-Luc Godard, C. Benoit.

Cast: The Rita Mitsouko (Fred Chichin and Catherine Ringer), Jean-Luc Godard (the idiot and the prince), Jacques Villeret (the individual), Jane Birkin (the grasshopper), François Périer (the man), Michel Galabru (the admiral), Jacques Rufus (the policeman), Pauline Lafont (the golfer), Eva Darlan (the passenger), Philippe Khorsand (the passenger), Isabelle Sadoyan (the grandmother), Philippe Rouleau (the golfer), Raphaël Delpart (the businessman), Carina Baronne (the American), Jean-Pierre Delamour (steward), Catherine Houssay (stewardess), Jean Grécault, Eloïse Beaune (the mother), Laurence Masliah (classic lover), Bruno Wolkowith (classic lover), Agnès Sourdillon, Christian Labrousse, Jacques Pena, Mélissa Chartier, Valérie Morat, Guy Moeson, Kada Kader, Eddie Atangana. Film Stock: Eastman Kodak 5247. Labs: LTC and Schwarz (Berne).

Production Companies: Gaumont Production, JLG Films, Xanadu Films, Radio Télévision Suisse Romande. Producer: Ruth Waldburger. Production Manager: Hervé Duhamel. Casting: Françoise Ménidrey. Production Secretary: Marie-Christine Barrière. Prize: Louis Delluc Prize, 1987.

1987 King Lear. 35 mm, Dolby stereo, 90 minutes.

Release: March 2002. Filmed: Begun August 1986.

Director: Jean-Luc Godard. Screenplay: Jean-Luc Godard, after Shakespeare's play of the same title. Dialogue: Jean-Luc Godard and Peter Sellars. Assistant à la mise en scène: Hervé Duhamel. Photography: Sophie Maintigneux, Isabelle Czajka. Sound: François Musy. Editing: Jean-Luc Godard.

Cast: Norman Mailer (Himself), Kate Mailer (Herself), Burgess Meredith (Don Learo), Peter Sellars (William Shakespeare, the Fifth), Molly Ringwald (Cordelia), Jean-Luc Godard (Professor Pluggy), Freddy Buache (Professor Quentin), Léos Carax, Julie Delpy. Production Company: Cannon Group. Producers: Menaham Golan, Yoram Globus. Associate Producer: Tom Luddy. Executive Producer: Jean-Luc Godard.

1988 Ads for Girbaud or **Closed.**[60] Video, 10 ads between 15 and 20 seconds in length. Director: Jean-Luc Godard. Screenplay: Jean-Luc Godard. Photography: Caroline Champetier. Sound: François Musy. Editing: Jean-Luc Godard. Production Company: Marithé and François Girbaud.

1988 On s'est tous défilé. Video, 13 minutes. Director: Jean-Luc Godard. Screenplay: Jean-Luc Godard. Assistant à la mise en scène: Hervé Duhamel. Photography: Caroline Champetier. Sound: François Musy. Music: Honegger, Leonard Cohen, Mozart, Barbra Streisand, Sonny Rollins. Editing: Jean-Luc Godard. Production Company: Marithé and François Girbaud.

1988 Puissance de la parole. Video, 25 minutes.
Director: Jean-Luc Godard. Screenplay: Jean-Luc Godard. Assistants à la mise en scéne: Hervé Duhamel, Philippe Malignon. Photography: Caroline Champetier, Pierre Binggeli. Costumes: Laurence Guimdollet. Music: Bach, Bob Dylan, Beethoven, John Cage, Richard Strauss, César Franck, Maurice Ravel, Leonard Cohen. Sound: François Musy, Pïerre-Alain Besse, Marc-Antoine Beldent. Editing: Jean-Luc Godard.
Cast: Jean Bouise (Mr Agathos), Laurence Côte (Mlle. Oïnos), Lydia Andréi (Velma), Jean-Michel Iribarren (Franck).
Production Companies: France Télécom, JLG Films, Gaumont. Production Secretary: Marie-Christine Barrière.

1988 Mars et Vénus. 35 mm, short film. Director: Anne-Marie Miéville.
Production Company: The Louvre.

1988 Le Dernier mot/Les Français entendus par. Sketch in **Les Français vus par.** Video, 13 minutes.
Director: Jean-Luc Godard. Screenplay: Jean-Luc Godard, with text by Valentin Feldman. Assistant Director: Hervé Duhamel. Photography: Pierre Binggeli. Costumes: Catherine Leroy. Sound: Pierre Camus, Raoul Fruhauf. Music: Bach. Sound Mix: François Musy. Editing: Jean-Luc Godard.
Cast: André Marcon (Valentin Feldman), Hanns Zischler (son of a German officer), Catherine Aymerie, Pierre Amoyal (violinist, son of Feldman), Michel Radio, Luc Briffoch, Laurent Rohrbach, Gilles Laeser, Laurence Nanzer, Damien Nanzer.
Production Company: Erato Films. Executive Producer: Daniel Toscan du Plantier. Producer: Anne-Marie Miéville. Production Secretary: Marie-Christine Barrière.
Note: Commissioned for the tenth anniversary of the *Figaro* magazine. Other sketches in *Les Français vus par* by: Werner Herzog, Luigi Comencini, David Lynch, Andrzej Wajda.

1989 Le Rapport Darty. Video, 50 minutes.
Directors: Jean-Luc Godard and Anne-Marie Miéville. Screenplay: Jean-Luc Godard and Anne-Marie Miéville. Assistant Director: Hervé Duhamel. Photography: Hervé Duhamel. Sound and Sound Mix: François Musy. Editing: Jean-Luc Godard.
Cast: Voices of Anne-Marie Miéville and Jean-Luc Godard.
Production Companies: Gaumont, JLG Films.

1989 Mon cher sujet. 35 mm, 96 minutes.
Release: Presented at the Belfort Film Festival November 1989.
Director: Anne-Marie Miéville. Screenplay: Anne-Marie Miéville. Assistants à la mise en scène: Reynald Calcagni, Bernard Cassus. Photography: Jean-Paul Rosa da Costa, Jean-Bernard Menoud, Daniel Barrou, Martin Gressmann. Decors: Ivan Niclass, Fanny Gagliardini. Sound: Pierre Camus, Raoul Fruhauf. Music: Mahler, Mozart, Gluck, Fauré, Debussy. Song by Anne-Marie Michel.[61] Sound Mix: François Musy. Editing: Anne-Marie Miéville.

Cast: Gaële Le Roi (Angèle), Anny Romand (Agnès), Hélène Roussel (Odile), Yves Neff (Carlo), Hanns Zischler (Hans), Bernard Woringer (François), Marc Darnault (Auguste), Michel Ferrer (music teacher), David Cuinier (Louis as a baby), Michaël Gumener (Louis as a young boy), Catherine Cornuot (pianist), Pierre-André Sand (store owner), Christian Musitelli (doctor), Laurence Rochaix (Agnès's friend), Violaine Barret (woman in the country), Roland Amstutz.
Production Companies: Centre National de la Cinématographie, La Cinq, Les Films du Jeudi, JLG Films, Xanadu, Radio Télévision Suisse Romande. Production Assistants: François Roch, Catherine Thomas, Marie-Christine Barrière.
Prize: Grand Prize, Belfort Film Festival 1989, and 2nd Grand Prix de la création Glace Gervais pour le cinéma.

1990 Nouvelle Vague. 35 mm, 89 minutes.
Release: Presented at the Cannes Film Festival in May 1990, and released on 23 May 1990.
Filmed: Geneva, and Swiss countryside, 1 September–1 November 1989 (8-week shoot).[62]
Director: Jean-Luc Godard. Screenplay: Jean-Luc Godard. Assistant à la mise en scène: Emmanuel Finkiel. Script Continuity: Hélène Sébillotte. Art Director: Anne-Marie Miéville. Photography: William Lubtchansky, Christophe Pollock, Franck Messmer. Wardrobe Persons: Ingebord Dietsche, Marie-Françoise Perrochon, Mélusine Schamber. Hair Stylist: Patrick Villain. Make-up: Josée de Luca. Gaffer: James W. Howe. Sound: Henri Morelle, Pierre-Alain Besse, Miguel Rejas. Music: Hindemith, Meredith Monk, Patti Smith, David Darling. Sound Mix: François Musy. Editing: Jean-Luc Godard.
Cast: Alain Delon (Roger Lennox/Richard Lennox), Domiziana Giordano (Elena Torlato-Favrini), Roland Amstutz (the gardener), Laurence Côte (housekeeper), Jacques Dacqmine (managing director), Christophe Odent (Raoul), Laurence Guerre (Della), Joseph Lisbona (doctor), Laure Killing (doctor's wife), Véronique Müller (1st friend of Raoul), Maria Pitarresi (2nd friend of Raoul), Jacques Viallette (Schpountz, the factory boss), Raphael Delpard (the minister), Tatem Belkacem (maître d'hotel), Joe Sheridan (Bob Aldrich), Pascal Sablier (the Iranian), Violane Barret (gardener's wife), Brigitte Marvine (journalist), Steve Suissa (waiter).
Film Stock: Kodak.
Production Companies: Sara Films, Canal Plus, Périphéria, Films Antenne 2, Centre National de la Cinématographie, Sofica, Vega Film, Télévision Suisse Romande. Producer: Alain Sarde. Associate Producer: Ruth Waldburger. Production Managers: Christine Gozlan, François Roch. Assistant Production Manager: Claudia Sontheim, Hervé Duhamel.

1990 L'Enfance de l'art. Sketch in **Comment vont les enfants?** 35 mm, 8 minutes.
Directors: Jean-Luc Godard and Anne-Marie Miéville. Screenplay: Jean-Luc Godard, and Anne-Marie Miéville. Assistant à la mise en scène: Hervé Duhamel. Photography: Sophie Maintigneux. Music: Hindemith, Meredith Monk. Sound: Pierre-Alain Besse. Editing: Jean-Luc Godard.
Cast: Antoine Reves, Nathalie Kadem, Michel Benpoil, Denis Vallas, Nikolas Sukic.

Production Companies: C9 Communication, Vega Film for UNICEF. Executive Producer: Jean-Luc Godard.
Note: Other episodes of *Comment vont les enfants?* by: Lino Brocka, Rolan Bykov, Euzhan Palzcy, Ciron Duran, Jerry Lewis.

1991 Lettre à Thomas Wainggari (Indonésie). Sketch in the television programme **Contre l'oubli.** Video, 3 minutes.
Release: Premiered on Canal Plus 10 December 1991, and released in cinemas 11 December 1991.
Director: Jean-Luc Godard and Anne-Marie Miéville. Texts and voice-over by André Rousselet.[63] Photography: Jean-Marc Fabre. Music: Arvo Pärt. Editing: Jean-Luc Godard. Production Company: Amnesty International.
Note: Other sketches in *Contre l'oubli* by: Ch. Akerman, R. Allio, D. Amar, J. Beckar, J. Birkin, J.-M. Carré, P. Chéreau, A. Courneau, Costa Gavras, D. Dante, C. Denis, R. Depardon, J. Deray, M. Deville, J. Doillon. M. Franck, G. Frot-Coustaz, B. Giraudeau, F. Girod, R. Goupil, J.-L. Hubert, R. Kramer, P. Leconte, S. Moon, M. Piccoli, A. Resnais, C. Serreau, B. Tavernier, N. Trintignant.

1991 Allemagne 90 neuf zéro: Solitudes, un état et des variations. 35 mm and video, 62 minutes.
Release: Presented at the Venice Film Festival September 1991, and shown on Antenne 2 on 4 November 1991. Filmed: Berlin, Weimar, and France.
Director: Jean-Luc Godard. Screenplay: Jean-Luc Godard, adapted from *Nos Solitudes: Enquêtes sur un sentiment* by Michel Hannoun. Photography: Christophe Pollock, Andreas Erben, Stepan Benda. Wardrobe Persons: Alexandra Pitz, Julia Griep. Sound: Pierre-Alain Besse. Music: Bryars, Scelsi, Liszt, Mozart, Bach, Stravinsky, Hindemith, Beethoven, Shostakovich. Sound Mix: François Musy. Editing: Jean-Luc Godard.
Camera: Arriflex 35. Video for the archival shots (later transferred to 35 mm). Optic Dolby stereo. Film Stock: Kodak. Lab: Schwarz (Berne).
Cast: Eddie Constantine (Lemmy Caution), Hanns Zischler (Count Zelten), Claudia Michelsen (Charlotte/Dora), André S. Labarthe (Narrator), Nathalie Kadem (Delphine de Staël), Robert Wittmers (Don Quixote), Kim Kashkashian (Violinist), Anton Mossine (Russian), and Heinz Przbylski, Kerstin Boos, H.J. Jurgen, Uwe Orzechowici, Jochen Glichinski, Iva Svarcova, Elfi Gabel.
Production Companies: Antenne 2, Brainstorm Productions. Executive Producer: Nicole Ruelle. Production Managers: Romain Goupil, Hanns Zischler.[64] Assistant Production Managers: Frédéric Jardin, M. Schlichter. Production Secretary: Régine Provvedi-Wedekind.
Note: The title is often written as 'L'Allemagne, année 90 neuf zéro', and it is thus that Godard submitted it to the CNC. The film itself is titled *Allemagne 90 neuf zéro*.

1993 Parisienne People.
Director: Anne-Marie Miéville.
Note: Cited as screening at the Taormina Film Festival.

1993 Les Enfants jouent à la Russie. Video (Beta sp stereo), 60 minutes.
Director: Jean-Luc Godard. Screenplay: Jean-Luc Godard. Assistants à la mise en scène: Caroline Champetier, Thierry Bordes, Julien Hirsch. Photography: Caroline Champetier. Sound: Stéphane Thiébaud. Editing: Jean-Luc Godard.
Dedication: Giuseppe Cecconi. In Memory of Ira Barmak.
Cast: Laszlo Szabo (Jack Valenti, the Producer), Jean-Luc Godard (the idiot, Prince Mychkine), Aude Amiot (Anna Karina), Bernard Eisenschitz (Harry Blount), André S. Labarthe (Alcide Jolivet), Bénédicte Loyen, Marie Borowski.
Production Companies: Cecco Films in collaboration with the Russian State Television and Radio Company, Vega Films, JLG Films. Producers: Alessandro Cecconi, Ruth Waldburger.
Executive Producers: Giuseppe Cecconi, Alessandro Cecconi. Production Manager: Caroline Champetier.

1993 Hélas pour moi. 35 mm, Dolby stereo, 84 minutes.
Release: Premiered in a theatre in Auch (Gers), August 1993. Filmed: Switzerland, Summer 1992 (8-week shoot).[65]
Director: Jean-Luc Godard. Screenplay: Jean-Luc Godard, after Jean Giraudoux's play *Amphytrion 39*. Assistants à la mise en scène: Frédéric Jardin, Natalie Engelstein. Script Continuity: Agathe Grau. Photography: Caroline Champetier, Julien Hirsch, Laurent Hincelin. Music: David Darling, Bach, Holliger, Shostakovich, Beethoven, Tchaikovsky, Honegger, Kancheli. Sound: François Musy, Pierre-Alain Besse. Sound Mix: Bernard Le Roux. Editing: Jean-Luc Godard.
Cast: Gérard Depardieu (Simon Donnadieu), Laurence Masliah (Rachel Donnadieu), Bernard Verley (Abrahim Klimt), Jean-Louis Loca (Max Mercure), François Germond (pastor), Jean-Pierre Miquel (another pastor), Anny Romand (pastor's wife), Roland Blanche (drawing teacher, or bookseller), Marc Betton (doctor), Michel Barras (owner of the hotel for men), Pascale Vachoux (owner of the hotel for women), Christina Hernandez (waitress), Thierry Wegmuller (adolescent), Gilbert Isnard (roadmender), Monique Couturier (old servant), Vincent Siegrist (student of Latin), Stephan Elbaum (tennis player), Laurence Dubas (weeping woman), Jérôme Pradon (Miguel), Jean-Louis Caillat (Spaniard), Anne-Elise Bottiau (employee in video store), Harry Cleven (God), Manon Andersen (Ondine), Aude Amiot (Aude), Sophie Lukasik, Séverine Koller, Louis-Do de Lencquesaing, Raphaël Potier, Benjamin Kraatz (Benjamin), Véronique Varlet (student), Delphine Quentine (student), Veronika Beiweis (student), Laura Cabrera (student), Lorelei Rautermann (maid), Fabienne Chaudat, Vaness Boch, Yves Gaillard (client in video store), Monsieur Rolland (voice of God).
Production Companies: Les Films Alain Sarde, Vega Films, Périphéria, Télévision Suisse

Romande. With aid from the Départment Fédéral de l'Intérieur, Cofimage 4 and Investimage 4. Producer: Alain Sarde. Associate Producer: Ruth Waldburger. Production Managers: Catherine Mazières, Anne-Marie Faux. Production Manager: Claudia Sontheim. Casting: Jean-Luc Godard, with Julie Philippe.

1994 Je vous salue Sarajevo. Video.
Director: Jean-Luc Godard.

1994 Lou n'a pas dit non. 35 mm, 70 minutes.
Release: Montreal Film Festival. Filmed: France (Annecy), Paris (The Louvre), and Paris outskirts); Switzerland (Rolle, Lutry, Vevey).
Director: Anne-Marie Miéville. Screenplay: Anne-Marie Miéville. Assitants à la mise en scène: Reynald Calcagni, Gilles Bannier, Laetitia Masson. Photography: Jean-Paul Rosa Da Costa, Sophie Maintigneux, Katell Dijan, Isabelle Czajka. Decors: Ivan Niclass. Set Decorator: David Stadelman. Costumes: Marina Zuliani, Corinne Baerswyil. Choreographer: Jean-Claude Gallotta. Sound: Pierre-Alain Besse, Raoul Fruhauf. Music: Chopin, Shostakovich, Serge Houppin, Keith Jarrett, Mahler, Arvo Pärt, Rossini. Sound Mix: François Musy. Editing: Anne-Marie Miéville.
Lab: Eclair and Schwarz (Berne).
Dedication: Alain Miéville.
Cast: Marie Bunuel (Lou), Manuel Blanc (Pierre), Caroline Micla (Florence), Geneviève Pasquier (Suzanne), Métilde Weyergans (Isabelle), Harry Cleven (Théo), Wilfred Benaïche, Muriel Boulay, Delphine Rich, Anne-Marie Miéville in voice-over.
Production Companies: DF1, Sara Films, Périphéria, Vega Films, Canal Plus, Radio Télévision Suisse Romande. Executive Producer: Jean-Luc Godard. Production Manager: Joseph Strub. Assistant Production Manager: Eric Grandjean, Philippe Saal.
Prize: Shared grand prize at the Belfort Film Festival.

1995 JLG/JLG: Autoportrait de décembre. 35 mm, 62 minutes.
Release: 8 March 1995
Director: Jean-Luc Godard. Screenplay: Jean-Luc Godard. Assistant à la mise en scène: Thierry Bordes. Photography: Yves Pouliguen, Christian Jaquenod. Costumes: Marina Zuliani, Corrine Baersiwyl. Music: Arvo Pärt. Sound: Pierre-Alain Besse, Benoît Hilbrant. Editing: Jean-Luc Godard, Catherine Cormon.
Cast: Jean-Luc Godard, Geneviève Pasquier, Denis Jadot, Brigitte Bastien, Elizabeth Kaza, André S. Labarthe, Louis Séguin, Bernard Eisenschitz, Nathalie Aguillar.
Production Companies: Périphéria, Gaumont, JLG Films. Production Manager: Joseph Strub.

1995 Deux fois cinquante ans de cinéma français. Video, 50 minutes.
Directors: Anne-Marie Miéville and Jean-Luc Godard. Screenplay: Jean-Luc Godard and Anne-Marie Miéville. Assistant à la mise en scène: Gilbert Guichardière. Photography: Isabelle Czajka. Sound: Stéphane Thiebaud. Editing: Jean-Luc Godard.

Cast: Jean-Luc Godard, Michel Piccoli, Cécile Reigher, Estelle Grynspan, Dominique Jacquet, Patrick Gillieron, Xavier Jougleurx, Fabrice Dierx-Benard. Production Companies: British Film Institute, Périphéria. Executive Producers: Colin MacCabe and Bob Last. Production Manager: Philippe Saal.

1996 Plus Oh. Music video for France Gall.
Release: shown once on M6, 20 April, 1996.[66] Director: Jean-Luc Godard.

1996 For Ever Mozart. 35 mm, 84 minutes.
Release: 1996. Filmed: France and Switzerland, scheduled to begin August 1995.[67] Director: Jean-Luc Godard. Screenplay: Jean-Luc Godard. Assistants à la mise en scène: Gilbert Guichardière, Laurent Maillefer. Photography: Christophe Pollock, Katell Dijan. Decors: Ivan Niclass. Costumes: Marina Zuliani. Wardrobe Person: Nadine Butin. Music: David Darling, Ketil Bjornstad, Jon Christensen, Ben Harper, Gyorgi Kurtag, Beethoven, Mozart. Orchestra: Les Jeunes de Fribourg, Eric Cerantola. Sound/Mix: François Musy, Oliver Burgaud. Sound Mix: Bernard Le Roux. Special Effects: Georges Demetrau. Armourer: Maratier. Editing: Jean-Luc Godard. Cast: Madeleine Assas (Camille), Ghalya Lacroix (Rosette), Bérangère Allaux (actress in the film-within-film), Vicky Messica (film director), Frédéric Pierrot (Jérôme), Harry Cleven (great writer), Michel Francini (baron), Sabine Bail (baron's friend), Max André (advisor), Sylvie Herbert (mother), Cécile Reigher (cameraman), Dominique Pozzeto (intern), Valérie Delangre (baron's daughter), Xavier Boulanger (assistant director), Yasna Zivanovic (partisan), Nathalie Dorval (journalist), Daniel Krellenstein, Jean Grécault (tourist, owner of cinema), Béatrice Avoine (tourist, ticket-seller at the cinema), Marc Faure (minister), François Savioz (Red Cross representative), Valerio Popesco (officer), Euryale Wynter (Mozart), Gérard Baume (mercenary), Norbert Krief (mercenary), Eric Pichon (soldier), Boris Andersen (soldier), Cécile Caillaud, Alain Wilmet (soldier), Nedeljko Grujic (soldier), Dan Thorens (officer), Sarah Bensoussan (wife of the great writer), Karine Belly (friend of the assistant director), Alain Moussay (production manager), Stéphanie Lagarde, Zbiniew Horoks, André Lacombe (old assistant director), Stanislas Gaczol (director of photography). Production Companies: Avventura Films, Périphéria, Centre Européen Cinématographique Rhône-Alpes, France 2 Cinéma, Canal Plus, Centre National de la Cinématographie, Vega Films, Télévision Suisse Romande, Eurimages, DF1, ECM Records. Producer: Alain Sarde. Associate Producer: Ruth Waldburger. Production Manager: Hervé Duhamel, Philippe Saal.

1997 Nous sommes tous encore ici. 35 mm, 80 minutes.
(Release: February 1997. Filmed: France) Paris, Colombes, and Switzerland (Rolle, Lausanne). Director: Anne-Marie Miéville. Screenplay: Anne-Marie Miéville. Texts by Plato and Hannah Arendt. Photography: Christophe Beaucarne, Jean-Paul Rosa da Costa, Christophe Pollock. Decors: Ivan Niclass. Costumes: Marina Zuliani. Hair Stylist: Michel

Demonteix, Marie-France Thibault. Sound: Olivier Burgaud. Music: Christophe Gio-
vannoni, Shostakovich, Lester Bowie, Liszt, Schumann, David Darling. Sound Mix:
François Musy. Editing: Anne-Marie Miéville.
Lab: Eclair and Schwarz (Berne).
Cast: Aurore Clément (Socrates), Bernadette Lafont (Calliclès), Jean-Luc Godard (the
actor), David Amigoni, Vincent Babel, Daniel Geiser, Roland Vouillox, Colin Ledoux,
Robert Degennes, Yvette Gamet.
Production Companies: Périphéria, Les Films du Losange, Vega Films, Les Films Alain
Sarde, with Canal Plus, Télévision Suisse Romande, and the Vaudoise Foundation.
Production Manager: Joseph Strub. Assistant Production Managers: Pierre Amiard,
Véronique Farget, Gilbert Guichardière.

1998 Histoire(s) du cinéma 1A: Toutes les histoires. Video, 52 minutes.
Director: Jean-Luc Godard.
Dedication: Mary Meerson and Monica Tegelaar.

1998 Histoire(s) du cinéma 1B: Une Histoire seule. Video, 42 minutes.
Director Jean-Luc Godard.
Dedication: John Cassavettes and Glauber Rocha.
Production Companies: La Sept, France 3, Gaumont, JLG Films.

1998 Histoire(s) du cinéma 2A: Seul le cinéma. Video, beta stereo, 26 minutes.
Director: Jean-Luc Godard.
Dedication: Armand J. Cauliez and Santiago Alvarez.
Cast: Jean-Luc Godard, Serge Daney, Julie Delpy.
Production Companies: La Sept, France 3, JLG Films, Centre National de la Cinémato-
graphie, Radio Télévision Suisse Romande, Vega Films.

1998 Histoire(s) du cinéma 2B: Fatale beauté, Video beta stereo, 28 minutes.
Director: Jean-Luc Godard.
Dedication: Michèle Firk and Nicole Ladmiral.
Cast: Sabine Azéma.
Production Companies: Gaumont, Périphéria, Centre National de la Cinématographie,
Femis.

1998 Histoire(s) du cinéma 3A: La Monnaie de l'absolu. Video, 26 minutes.
Director: Jean-Luc Godard.
Dedication: Gianni Amico and James Agee.
Cast: Alain Cuny.
Production Companies: Périphéria, Centre National de la Cinématographie, Femis.

1998 Histoire(s) du cinéma 3B: Une vague nouvelle. Video, 27 minutes.
Director: Jean-Luc Godard.
Dedication: Frédéric C. Froeschel and Nahum Kleiman.
Production Companies: Périphéria, Centre National de la Cinématographie, Femis.

1998 Histoire(s) du cinéma 4A: Le Contrôle de l'univers. Video, 27 minutes.
Director: Jean-Luc Godard.
Dedication: Michel Delahaye and Jean Domarchi.
Cast: Alain Cuny.
Production Companies: Gaumont, Centre National de la Cinématographie, Femis, Périphéria.

1998 Histoire(s) du cinéma 4B: Les Signes parmi nous. Video, 34 minutes.
Director: Jean-Luc Godard.
Dedication: Anne-Marie Miéville and Jean-Luc Godard.
Production Companies: Gaumont, Centre National de la Cinématographie, Femis, Périphéria.

1999 The Old Place: Small Notes Regarding the Arts at Fall of 20th Century. Video, 49 minutes.
Release: Presented at the Cinémathèque Française, January 1999.
Directors: Anne-Marie Miéville and Jean-Luc Godard. Music: Ketil Bjornstad, David Darling, Tomasz Stanko, Léo Ferré, Keith Jarrett, Saluzzi. Editing: Anne-Marie Miéville and Jean-Luc Godard.
Cast: Voice-over commentary spoken by Jean-Luc Godard and Anne-Marie Miéville.
Production Companies: The Museum of Modern Art, New York, Périphéria. Executive Producers: Mary Lea Bandy and Colin MacCabe.

2000 Après la réconciliation 35 mm, 74 minutes.
Release: 27 December 2000. Filmed: Paris.
Director: Anne-Marie Miéville. Screenplay: Anne-Marie Miéville. Photography: Christophe Beaucarne. Decors: Dominique Roubaud. Costumes: Florence Sadaune, Maïka Guézel. Make-up: Marie-France Thibault. Sound: François Musy. Music: Tomasz Stanko, Arvo Pärt, Lester Bowie, Shostakovich, Keith Jarrett, Saint-Saëns. Sound Mix: François Musy. Editing: Anne-Marie Miéville.
Lab: LTC.
Cast: Claude Perron (Cathos), Anne-Marie Miéville (the woman), Jacques Spiesser (Arthur), Jean-Luc Godard (Robert), Xavier Marchand (youth on rollerblades), Patrick Gruss (circus trainer).
Production Companies: Avventura Films, Périphéria, Vega Films, Radio Télévision Suisse Romande. Producer: Ruth Waldburger. Production Manager: Jean-Paul Battaggia. Assistant Production Manager: Bruno Amestoy.

2000 L'Origine du XXième siècle: à la recherche de siècle perdu. Video, 17 minutes. Director: Jean-Luc Godard. Photography: Julien Hirsch. Music: Hans Otte. Sound: François Musy, Gabriel Hafner. Editing: Jean-Luc Godard. Production Companies: Vega Films, Canal Plus.

2001 Eloge de l'amour. 35 mm and video, 90 minutes.
Release: Presented at the Cannes Film Festival in May 2001, and released 16 May 2001. Filmed: January 2000 in Brittany, Paris.[68]
Director: Jean-Luc Godard. Screenplay: Jean-Luc Godard. Assistants à la mise en scène: Christophe Rabinovici, Fleur Albert. Photography: Christophe Pollock, Julien Hirsch. Costumes: Marie-France Thibault. Sound: Christian Monheim. Music: David Darling, Ketil Bjornstad, Arvo Pärt. Sound Mix: François Musy, Gabriel Hafner. Editing: Raphaëlle Urtin.
Cast: Bruno Putzulu (Edgar), Cécile Camp (Elle), Jean Davy (grandfather), Françoise Verny (grandmother), Philippe Loyrette (servant), Audrey Klebaner (Eglantine), Jérémy Lippmann (Perceval), Claude Baignières (Mr Rosenthal), Rémo Forlani (Maître Forlani), Mark Hunter (journalist), Bruno Mesrine (magician), Djelloul Beghoura (Algerian), Serge Spira (the homeless person), Violeta Ferrer (woman), Valérie Ortlieb (woman), Stéphanie Jaubert (young girl), Jean-Henri Roger (mayor's assistant), Jean Lacouture (historian).
Film Stock: Kodak. Lab: LTC.
Production Companies: Périphéria, Télévision Suisse Romande, Arte France Cinéma, Avventura Films, Vega Films, Canal Plus. Producer: Alain Sarde. Associate Producer: Ruth Waldburger. Production Manager: Jean-Paul Battagia.

2002 Dans le noir du temps. Sketch in **Ten Minutes Older: The Cello.**
Release: Presented at the Toronto Film Festival 28 August 2002.
Director: Jean-Luc Godard. Screenplay: Anne-Marie Miéville. Director of Photography: Julien Hirsch. Music: Arvo Pärt. Sound: François Musy.
Producers: Ulrich Felsberg, Nicolas McClintock, Nigel Thomas.
Note: Other sketches in *Ten Minutes Older: The Cello* by Bernardo Bertolucci, Claire Denis, Mike Figgis, Jiri Menzel, Michael Radford, Volker Schlöndorff, Istvan Szabo.

2002 Liberté et patrie. Short film.
Directors: Jean-Luc Godard, Anne-Marie Miéville. Screenplay: based on text by Charles-Ferdinand Ramuz.

Select Bibliography

No director has been more written about than Godard, and he has been very well served by his critics. The first book written on him in 1963 by Jean Collet remains a useful introduction, as does Richard Roud's first English language text. In the eighties and nineties there was an extraordinary flowering of French criticism both directly on Godard and on the Nouvelle Vague in general. I am heavily indebted to the work of Antoine de Baecque, Michel Marie, Jacques Aumont, Alain Bergala, Serge Toubiana, Marc Cerisuelo.

Julia Lesage's *Jean-Luc Godard: A Guide to References and Resources* provides a comprehensive bibliography to 1979. An update of that work would fill several volumes. This bibliography contains only texts cited in the book or of direct use in its composition. Sources used by Sally Shafto for the filmography are marked 'F'.

Where there is no page reference and the work cited is available in many editions both in French and English (e.g. Balzac's *La Cousine Bette* or Freud's *The Interpretation of Dreams*) then it is not included in the list of 'Other Works'.

Interviews

The most important source of information in the book is interviews. In each case I have given the month or months in which the interview was conducted. In some cases the interview gave rise to a continuous conversation and those are marked with an asterisk. 'T' indicates a telephone conversation.

Mary Lea Bandy (November 2002), Charles Bitsch (February 2002*), Alain Bergala (September 2002), Antoine Bourseiller (May 2002), Caroline Champetier (September 2002), Michel Clerc (March 2002), Raoul Coutard (February 2002*), Marcel Dreyfus (February 2002), Claude Godard (August 1991*), Rachel Godard (December 1988), Véronique Godard (1989*), Jean-Pierre Gorin (April 2002), Agnès Guillemot (March 1993), Julien Hirsch (September 2002), Gilles Jacob (January 2002 T) Anna Karina (February–April 2002), Bob Last (November 2002), Michel Latouche (February 2002), Richard Leacock (May 2002) Willy Lubtchansky (August 2002 T), Tom Luddy (April 2002*), Chris Marker (April 2002*), Georgia Moll (June 2002), Paule Muret (September 2002), Claude Nedjar (July 2002), Bulle Ogier (June 2002), D.A. Pennebaker (April 2002), Isabelle Pons (March 2002), Adrien Porchet (April 2002 T), Jackie Reynal (April 2002 T), Pierre Rissient (January 2002), Jean-Henri Roger (September 2002*), Jean Rosset (September 2001/February 2002), Suzanne Schiffman (March 1993), Barbet Schroeder (June 2002), Peter Sellars (May 2002), Philippe Sollers (May 2002), Raphaël Sorin (August 2002), Rod Stoneman (November 2002), Irving Teitelbaum (July 2002), Mo Teitelbaum (July 2002), Roland Tolmatchoff (February 2002*), Serge Toubiana (March 2002), Ruth Waldburger (September 2002 T), Anne Wiazemsky (May–August 2002).

Texts by Godard

Godard, Jean Luc. *Godard on Godard*. Ed and trans. Tom Milne. (London: Secker and Warburg, 1972).
Introduction à une véritable histoire du cinéma (Paris: Éditions Albatros, 1980).
Jean-Luc Godard: Articles, essais, entretiens. Introduction and notes by Jean Narboni (Paris: P. Belfond, 1968).
Jean-Luc Godard par Jean-Luc Godard. Vol. 1 1950–1984. Ed. Alain Bergala (Paris: Cahiers du cinéma, 1985).
Jean-Luc Godard par Jean-Luc Godard. Vol. 2 1984–1998. Ed. Alain Bergala. (Paris: Cahiers du cinéma, 1998).

Articles and Books about Godard

Adair, Gilbert. 'Gilbert Adair from London'. *Film Comment* 17.3 (May–June 1981): pp. 4, 6.
Aumont, Jacques. *Amnésies: fictions du cinéma d'après Jean-Luc Godard* (Paris: POL, 1999).
    ed. *Pour un cinéma comparé: influences et répétitions*. Conférences du Collège de l'art cinématographique (Paris: Cinémathèque française, 1996).
    'Godard: The View and the Voice'. *Discourse* 7 (1985): pp.42–65.
    'Beauté, fatal souci: Note sur un épisode des *Histoire(s) du cinéma*'. *Cinémathèque* no. 12 (1998): pp.17–25.

'Godard peintre'. In *L'oeil interminable: Cinéma et peinture* (Paris: Librairie Séguier, 1989), pp.223–247.

de Baecque, Antoine. 'A la recherche d'une forme cinématographique de l'histoire'. *Critique* 632–633 (2000): pp.154–165.

Bassan, Raphaël. 'Jean-Luc Godard'. *Revue du cinéma* no. 90 (January 1984): pp.25–30.

Bellour, Raymond, with Mary Lea Bandy (eds.). *Jean-Luc Godard Son+Image, 1974–1991* (New York: The Museum of Modern Art, 1992) F.

Bergala, Alain. 'Enfants: Ralentir'. *Cahiers du cinéma* 301 (June 1979): pp. 28–33.

'Hélas pour moi, ou du présent comme passé légèrement corrigé'. *Cinémathèque* 5 (1994): pp.19–27.

Nul mieux que Godard (Paris: Editions Cahiers du cinéma, 1999).

Bergala, Alain and Léos Carax. 'Jean-Luc Godard: *Sauve qui peut (la vie)*: une Journée de tournage'. *Cahiers du cinéma* 306 (December 1979): pp.32–37.

Bergala, Alain, Serge Daney and Serge Toubiana. 'En attendant Passion: Le Chemin vers la parole'. *Cahiers du cinéma* 336 (May 1982): pp.5–14, 57–60, 63–64.

Bertolina, Gian Carlo. 'Filmografia', in *Visuel: dossier Jean-Luc Godard* (Turin: Franco-Italian Cultural Centre, 1982), pp.21–33, F.

Biette, Jean-Claude. 'L'Encrier de la modernité'. *Cahiers du cinéma* 375 (September 1985): pp.x–xi.

'Les Enfants de Godard et de Pasiphaé'. *Trafic* 15 (1995): pp.118–130.

'Godard et son histoire du cinéma'. *Cahiers du cinéma* 327 (September 1981): pp.v–vi.

Bonitzer, Pascal. 'Dieu, Godard, le zapping'. *Trafic* 8 (1993): pp.5–12.

Bordwell, David. 'Godard and Narration'. *Narration in the Fiction Film* (London: Methuen, 1985), pp.311–336.

Braunberger, Pierre. *Pierre Braunberger: Producteur. Cinéma-mémoire*. Préface de Jean-Luc Godard. Propos recueillis par Jacques Gerber (Paris: Centre National de la Cinématographie, and Centre Georges Pompidou, 1987), F.

Brody, Richard. 'An Exile in Paradise'. *New Yorker*. 20 November 2000. pp.62–76.

Brown, Royal S., ed. *Focus on Godard*. (NJ: Prentice-Hall, 1972).

Buache, Freddy. 'De Godard à Jean-Luc'. *Revue belge du cinéma* 14 (1985): pp.50–62.

Cerisuelo, Marc. *Jean-Luc Godard* (Paris: L'herminier/Quatre-Vents, 1989), F.

Collet, Jean. *Jean-Luc Godard* (Paris: Seghers, Collection Cinéma d'Aujourd'hui, 1963). Rev. ed. By Jean Collet and Jean-Paul Fargier. (Paris: Editions Seghers, 1974).

Dixon, Wheeler Winston. *The Films of Jean-Luc Godard* (Albany: SUNY Press, 1997).

Douin, Jean-Luc. *Godard* (Paris: Rivages, 1989).

Duras, Marguerite and Jean-Luc Godard. 'Duras–Godard: Un Dialogue tendre et passionné.' *Cinéma* (Paris) 422 (December 1987): pp.6–7.

Durgnat, R. 'Jean-Luc Godard: His Crucifixion and Resurrection'. *Monthly Film Bulletin* 52.620 (September 1985): pp.268–271.

Eco, Umberto. 'Do-It-Yourself Godard'. *Harper's* (May 1993): pp.24–26.

Eisenschitz, Bernard ' "Une Machine à Montrer l'Invisible": Conversations à propos des *Histoire(s) du cinéma*.' *Cahiers du cinéma* 529 (1998): pp.52–56.

Farassino, Alberto. *Jean-Luc Godard/2* (Milan: Il Castoro, 1996), pp.111–135, F.

Forbes, J. 'Jean-Luc Godard: 2 into 3'. *Sight and Sound* 50.1 (1980–1981): pp.40–45.

Frodon, Jean-Michel. 'Jean-Pierre Rassam: un provocateur dans le cinéma français', calendar program of the Cinémathèque Française, May–June 2002, pp.6–10, F.

Gerber, Jacques. *Anatole Dauman. Argos Films Souvenir Ecran* (Paris: Centre Georges Pompidou, 1980), F.

Gianvito, John, and Maryel Lockey. *Jean Luc Godard's 'Hail Mary': Women and the Sacred in Film* (Carbondale and Edwardsville: University of Illinois, 1993), F.

Goodwin, Michael, Tom Luddy and Naomi Wise. 'The Dziga Vertov Film Group in America: An Interview with Jean-Luc Godard and Jean-Pierre Gorin'. *Take One* vol.2., no.10 (March–April 1971).

Guzzetti, Alfred. *Two or Three Things I Know about Her* (Cambridge: Harvard UP, 1981).

Harcourt, Peter. 'Calculated Approximations of Possibilities: Rhetorical Strategies in the Late Films of Jean-Luc Godard'. *Cineaction* 48 (1998): pp.8–17.

Hoberman, Jim. 'He-e-ere's Jean-ee: TV à la Godard'. *Village Voice*. 28 April 1986, pp. 45–46.

'Jean-Luc Godard: Picasso, Marx, and Coca-Cola'. *Artnews* 92.2 (February 1993): pp.57–58.

Ishaghpour, Youssef. 'Archéologie du cinéma et mémoire du siècle'. Dialogue I. *Trafic* 29 (1999): pp.16–35.

'Archéologie du cinéma et memoire du siècle'. Dialogue II. *Trafic* 30 (1999): pp.34–53.

Jacob, Gilles. 'Alphaville' *Cinema* 65.97 (June 1965) pp.115–118.

'Pierrot le fou: selection du Godard's Digest' *Cinema* 65.101 (October 1965) pp.100–104.

'Du cinema atonal des marmottes' *Cinema* 67.113 (February 1967) pp.68–86.

Jameson, Fredric. 'High-tech Collectives in Late Godard'. In *The Geopolitical Aesthetic: Cinema and Space in the World System* (Bloomington: Indiana UP, 1992), pp.158–185.

Jousse, Thierry. 'Lettre à Jean-Luc Godard'. *Cahiers du cinéma* 471 (1993): pp.30–32.

'Melancholia: JLG/JLG'. *Cahiers du cinéma* 489 (1994): p.36.

Kernan, Margot. 'Jean-Luc Godard Shows a New Film and a New Interest in Hollywood', *Washington Post* (14 September 1980).

Klawans, Stuart. 'Jean-Luc Godard: Son + Image'. *The Nation*. 23 November 1992, pp.642–644.

Kwietniowski, Richard. 'Between Love and Labour? Godard's *Scenario of the Film "Passion"*. *Screen* 24.6 (1983): pp.52–69.

Lesage, Julia. *Jean-Luc Godard: A Guide to References and Resources* (Boston: G.K. Hall, 1979).

Leutrat, Jean-Louis. *Des traces qui nous ressemblent: Passion de Jean-Luc Godard* (Seyssel: Éditions Comp'Act, 1990).

Loshitzky, Yosefa, *The Radical Faces of Godard and Bertolucci* (Detroit: Wayne State University Press, 1995).

MacBean, James Roy. 'Every Man for Himself: An Open Letter to Godard'. *Jump Cut* 31 (March 1986): pp.8–12.

MacCabe, Colin. *Godard: Images, Sounds, Politics* With Laura Mulvey and Mick Eaton. (London: British Film Institute/MacMillan, 1980).

'Every Man For Himself'. *American Film* 9.8 (June 1984): pp.30–35.

Marie, Michel. *Le Mépris* (Paris: Nathan, 1990).

A Bout de souffle (Paris: Nathan, 1999).

Monaco, James. *The New Wave: Truffaut, Godard, Chabrol, Rohmer, Rivette* (New York: Oxford University Press, 1976).

Moullet, Luc. 'Jean-Luc Godard'. *Cahiers du cinéma* 106 (April 1960).

Narboni, Jean. 'Jean-Luc Godard à Avignon: "Laissez rêver la ligne"' *Cahiers du cinéma* 316 (October 1980): pp.8–9.

Païni, Dominique. 'Cinéma prénom musique'. *Cahiers du cinéma* 356 (February 1984): pp.vi–vii.

Prieur, Jérôme and Alain Bergala. '*France/tour/détour/deux/enfants*'. *Cahiers du cinéma* 301 (June 1979): pp.24–33.

Rancière, Jacques. 'La sainte et l'héritière: A propos des *Histoire(s) du cinéma*'. *Cahiers du cinéma* 536 (1999): pp.58–61.

Rosenbaum, Jonathan. 'Godard in the 90s: an interview, argument, and scrapbook'. *Film Comment* 34.5 (September–October 1998): pp.52–61.

'Jean-Luc, Chantal, Danièle, Jean-Marie and the Others'. *American Film* 4.4 (February 1979): pp.52–56.

'Le vrai coupable: Two Kinds of Criticism in Godard's work'. *Screen* 40.3 (1999): pp. 316–322

Roud, Richard. *Godard*. 2nd ed (London: Thames and Hudson, 1970).

Shafto, Sally. 'Saut dans le vide: Godard et le peinture'. *Cinémathèque* 16 (1999): pp. 92–107.

Ut Pictura Cinema: The Strange Adventure of Jean-Luc Godard. (PhD, University of Iowa, 2000).

Silverman, Kafa and Harun Farocki. *Speaking about Godard* (New York: New York University Press, 1998).

Sollers, Phillipe. 'Godard/Sollers: L'Entretien'. *Art Press* 88 (January 1985): pp.4–9.

'JLG/JLG: Un cinéma de l'être-là'. *Cahiers du cinéma* 489 (1994): pp.37–39.

Sontag, Susan. 'Godard' in *Styles of Radical Will* (London: Martin Secker and Warburg, 1969), pp. 147–189.

Sterritt, David. *The Films of Jean-Luc Godard: Seeing the Invisible* (New York: Cambridge University Press, 1999).

ed. *Jean-Luc Godard: Interviews* (Jackson: University of Mississippi Press, 1998).

Suchet, Simone. 'Produire Godard: être un partenaire et un manager (Interview with Alain Sarde)', *CinémAction* 52 (July 1989), pp.90–91.

Taubin, Amy. 'Death and the Maiden, Jean-Luc Godard at MOMA: the Video Years'. *Village Voice* 24 November 1992, pp.45–46.

Temple, Michael and James S. Williams, eds. *The Cinema Alone: Essays on the Work of Jean-Luc Godard 1985–2000* (Amsterdam: Amsterdam University Press, 2000).

Toubiana, Serge. 'Les hasards arbitraires'. *Cahiers du cinéma* 262–263 (January 1976).

Vianey, Michel. *En attendant Godard* (Paris: Bernard Grasset, 1966).

White, Armond. 'Double Helix: Jean-Luc Godard'. *Film Comment* 32.2 (1996): pp.26–30.

Witt, Michael. *On Communication: The Work of Anne-Marie Miéville and Jean-Luc Godard as Sonimage from 1973–1979*. Unpublished thesis.

In 2002–2003, there is a retrospective of Anne-Marie Miéville's cinema touring in the USA and Canada. See: www.pro-helvetia.ch/film/projekt.html

Special Issues on Godard

'Dossier: Jean-Luc Godard'. Special issue of *Cinématographe* 95 (December 1983).

'Jean-Luc Godard, le cinéma'. Special issue of *Revue belge du cinéma* 22/23 (1988).

'Jean-Luc Godard, les films'. Special issue of *Revue belge du cinéma* 16 (1986).

'Le Cinéma selon Godard'. Special issue of *CinémAction* 52 (July 1989).

Collet, Jean. *Jean-Luc Godard* (Paris: Seghers, Collection. Cinéma d'Aujourd'hui, 1963).

'Passion'. Special issue of *Avant-Scène* 380 (April 1989).

'Spécial Godard – Trente Ans depuis'. Special issue of *Cahiers du cinéma* 437 (November 1990).

'Nouvelle Vague'. Special issue of *Avant-Scène* 396–397 (November–December 1990).

'Spécial Godard: *Les Carabiniers, Pierrot le fou*, et les films invisibles'. Special issue of *Avant-scène* 171–72 (July–August 1976), F.

'Special Godard'. Special issue of *Art Press* 4 (December 1984–February 1985).

'Spécial Godard'. Special issue of *Avant-Scène* 323–324 (March 1984).

'The Godard Dossier'. Special issue of *Screen* 40.3 (Autumn 1999).

Special issue of *Wide Angle* 1/3 (1976).

Other Works

Andrew, Dudley. *André Bazin* (New York: Oxford University Press, 1978).

Althusser, Louis. *L'Avenir dure longtemps* (Paris: Stock/IMEC, 1992).

'Ideology and Ideological State Apparatuses (Notes Towards an Investigation).' *Lenin and Philosophy and Other Essays*. Trans. Ben Brewster (London: New Left Books, 1971).

Aubert, Jacques, ed. *Joyce avec Lacan* (Paris: Navarin Editeur, 1987).

Baecque, Antoine de. *Cahiers du cinéma: Histoire d'une revue.* 2 vols. (Paris: Cahiers du cinéma, 2001).

Baecque, Antoine de, and Charles Tesson. *La Nouvelle Vague.* (Paris: Cahiers du cinéma, 1999).

Baecque, Antoine de, and Serge Toubiana. *François Truffaut.* 2nd ed. (Paris: Gallimard, 2001).

Bardèche, Maurice and Robert Brasillach. *Histoire du cinéma* (Paris: Denoël et Steele, 1935).

Bardot, Brigitte. *Initiales BB* (Paris: Bernard Grasset, 1996).

Bataille, Georges. *Eroticism* (London: Penguin 2001).

Bazin, André. *Le Cinéma de l'Occupation et de la Résistance* (Paris: Union Générale d'Éditions, 1975).

'Comment peut-on être Hitchcocko-Hawksien' *Cahiers du cinema* 44 (February 1955): pp.17–18.

'De la politique des auteurs' *Cahiers du cinéma* 70 (April 1957): pp.2–11.

'En marge de L'érotisme au cinéma'. *Cahiers du cinéma* 70 (April 1957): pp.27–31.

'Six personnages en quete d'auteurs' *Cahiers du cinéma* 71 (May 1957).

Bazin, André and Jacques Doniol-Valcroze. 'Entretien avec Jacques Flaud'. *Cahiers du cinéma* (May 1957).

Beauregard, Chantal de. *Georges de Beauregard: Premier sourire de Belmondo . . . dernier de Bardot* (Paris: Lacour/Colporteur, 1991).

Bercot, Martine and André Guyaux, eds. *Dictionnaire des Lettres Françaises* (Paris: Librairie Générale Française, 1998).

Berthet, Frédérique. *Anatole Dauman, un producteur dans le cinéma français (1950–1998). Contribution à une histoire economique du culturel.* Unpublished thesis (Université de Paris 3, 2001).

Bertin-Maghit, Jean-Pierre. *Le Cinéma Français sous l'occupation* (Paris: Presses Universitaires de France, 1994).

Bessy, Maurice, Raymond Chirat, André Bernard. *Histoire du cinéma français: Encyclopédie des films 1961–1965* (Paris: Pygmalion, 1991), F.

Histoire du cinéma français: Encyclopédie des films 1966–1969 (Paris: Pygmalion, 1992), F.

Bonjour, E., H.S. Offler, and G. R. Potter. *A Short History of Switzerland* (Oxford: Clarendon, 1952).

Bourseiller, Christophe. *Vie et mort de Guy Debord 1931–1994* (Paris: Plon 1999).

Brialy, Jean-Claude. *Le Ruisseau des singes* (Paris: Robert Laffont, 2000).

Chabrol, Claude. *Et pourtant je tourne.* Ed. René Marchand (Paris: Robert Laffont, 1976).

'Compte-rendu de la matinée du 22 janvier 1921 au cinéma du Colisée'. *Journal du ciné-club* 4. 28 January 1921.

Cowie, Peter. *Coppola* (London: Faber and Faber 1998).

Deleuze, Gilles and Félix Guattari. *Anti-Oedipus: Capitalism and Schizophrenia*. Preface by Michel Foucault. Trans. Robert Hurley, Mark Seem, and Helen R. Lane (New York: Viking, 1977).

Dreyfus, Marcel. *Souvenirs de Nyon* (Geneva: Slatkine, 1999).

Durant, Philippe. *Belmondo* (Paris: Robert Laffont, 1993).

Ecksteins, Modris. *Rites of Spring: The Great War and the Birth of the Modern Age* (London: Macmillan, 2000).

Ellmann, Richard. *James Joyce* (Oxford: Oxford University Press, 1983).

Feuille d'Avis de Lausanne. 26 April 1954.

Frappat, Hélène. *Jacques Rivette, secret compris* (Paris: Cahiers du cinéma, 2001).

Gallagher, Tag. *The Adventures of Roberto Rossellini: His Life and Films* (New York: Di Capo Press, 1998).

Gance, A. 'Qu'est-ce que le cinématographe? Un sixième art'. *Ciné-journal* 185. 9 March 1912.

Garrisson, Janine. *Les Protestants au XVIe siècle* (Paris: Fayard, 1988).

Gauthier, Christophe. *La Passion du cinéma: Cinéphiles, ciné-clubs et salles specialisées à Paris de 1920 à 1929* (Paris: AFRHC, 1999).

Gerber, Jacques, ed. *Pierre Braunberger, producteur: Cinémamémoire* (Paris: Centre National de la Cinématographie/Centre Georges-Pompidou, 1987), F.

Gudet, Pierre. Private communication of June 2002 on Nyon and the Collège de Nyon in the war years.

Guiffrida, Daniela. 'Filomografie', *Jean-Luc Godard: Un Hommage* (Turin: Centre Culturel Français, Museo Nationale del Cinema, 1990) F.

Hamon, Hervé and Patrick Rotman. *Generation* (Vol. 1,): *Les Années de rêve* (Paris: Le Semil, 1987). *Generation* (Vol. 2): *Les Années de poudre* (Paris: Le Semil, 1987).

Holzmann, Gunter. *On dit que j'ai survécu quelque part au delà des mers* (Paris: Editions La Découverte, 1997).

Houssiau, Bernard J. *Marc Allégret, découvreur de stars, sous les yeux d'Andre Gide*. (Yens./Morgues: Editions Cabédita, 1994).

Jeancolas, Jean-Pierre. 'Cinéma, Censure, Contrôle, Classement'. In *La Censure en France à l'ère démocratique*. Ed. Pascal Ory (Paris: Editions Complexe, 1997). *Histoire du cinéma français* (Paris: Nathan, 1995).

Johnson, Samuel. 'Preface to Shakespeare'. *Johnson as Critic*. Ed. John Wain (London: Routledge, 1973).

Joyce, James. A *Portrait of the Artist as a Young Man* (London: Penguin, 1992). *Finnegans Wake* (London: Faber & Faber, 1975).

Julien, Isaac and Colin MacCabe. *Diary of a Young Soul Rebel* (London: British Film Institute, 1991).

Kael, Pauline. *Kiss Kiss Bang Bang* (New York: Atlantic Little Brown, 1966).

Karina, Anna. 'Anna Karina et Jean-Luc Godard: Les Enfants Terribles'. Interview. *Studio* 67 (November 1992): pp.122–126.

Kaufman, Vincent. *Guy Debord: la revolution au service de la poesie* (Paris: Fayard 2001).

Klifa, Thierry. 'Isabella Hubert: ma vie d'actrice', *Studio Magazine* 181 (September, 2002).

Kojève, Alexandre. *Introduction à la lecture de Hegel* (Paris: Gallimard 1979).

Langlois, Georges P. and Glenn Myrent. *Henri Langlois: premier citoyen du cinéma* (Paris: Denoël, 1986).

Langlois, Henri. *Etudes cinématographiques* 38–39 (Spring 1965).

Leenhardt, Roger. *Les Yeux ouverts: entretiens avec Jean Lacouture* (Paris: Le Seuil 1979).

L'Herbier, Marcel. *Intelligence du cinématographe* (Paris: Editions Correa, 1946).

Locarno Film Festival Catalogue, Locarno, 1994, pp.54–65, 154–55, F.

MacCabe, Colin. 'Cultural Vandalism', *Screen International* 2001.

James Joyce and the Revolution of the Word, 2nd edition (London: Palgrave, 2002).

Magny, Joël. *Eric Rohmer.* 2nd ed. (Paris: Editions Payot et Rivages, 1995).

Malraux, André. *Esquisse d'une psychologie du cinéma* (Paris: Gallimard, 1996).

Marie, Michel. *La Nouvelle Vague* (Paris: Nathan, 1997).

Marx, Karl. *Capital: A Critique of Political Economy.* 3 Vols. (London: Penguin, 1984).

Mayer, Arno. *Why Did the Heavens Not Darken?: The 'final solution' in History* (New York: Pantheon, 1988).

McGilligan, Patrick Fritz Lang. *The Nature of the Beast, A Biography* (New York: St Martin's Press, 1997).

Michelson, Annette, ed. *Kino-Eye: The writings of Dziga Vertov* (Berkeley and Los Angeles: University of California Press, 1984).

Milton, John. *Complete Prose Works* (New Haven: Yale University Press, 1959).

Montaigne, Michel. *Oeuvres Complètes.* Textes Établis par Albert Thibaudet et Maurice Rat. Introduction et notes par Maurice Rat (Paris: Gallimard, 1962).

Mulvey, Laura. *Citizen Kane.* (London: British Film Institute, 1992).

Nimier, Roger. *Le Hussard bleu* (Paris: Gallimard, 1950).

Olmeta, Patrick. *La Cinémathèque de 1936 à nos jours* (Paris: CNRS, 2000).

Paisson, Edouard. *Le Voyage d'Edgar* (Paris: Grasset, 1938).

Petric, Vlada. *Constructivism in Film: The Man with a Movie Camera* (Cambridge: Cambridge University Press, 1987).

Pivasset, Jean. *Essai sur la signification politique du cinema: L'exemple français, de la Libération aux événements du mai 1968* (Paris: Editions Cujas, 1971).

Reverdy, Pierre. *Le Gant de crin.* 1927 (Paris: Flammarion, 1968).

Richards, David. *Played Out: The Jean Seberg Story* (New York: Random House, 1981).

Rivette, Jacques. 'Lettre à Rossellini'. *Cahiers du cinéma* 1955.

Rohmer, Eric. 'La "Somme" d'André Bazin'. *Cahiers du cinéma* 91. January 1959.

Rouch, Jean. *Dziga Vertov* (Paris: Editions Champs Libres, 1971).

Roud, Richard. *A Passion for Films: Henri Langlois and the Cinémathèeque Française* (New York: Viking Press 1983).

Rowbotham, Sheila. *Promise of a Dream: Remembering the Sixties* (London: Penguin, 2000).

Rushdie, Salman. *The Satanic Verses* (London: Viking, 1988).

Sadoul, Georges. *Dziga Vertov*, preface by Jean Rouch (Paris: Editions Champs Libres, 1971).

Sartre, Jean-Paul. 'Quand Hollywood veut faire penser . . .' *L'Écranfrançais*, August 1945.

Savage, Jon. *Teenage* (London: Chatto and Windus, Forthcoming).

Schama, Simon. *Citizens* (London: Penguin, 1989).

Schuhl, Jean-Jacques. *Ingrid Caven* (Paris: Gallimard, 2000).

Seaford, Richard. 'Thunder, Lightening and Earthquake in The Bacchae and The Acts of the Apostles' in *What is a God?*, ed. A. B. Lloyd (London: Duckworth, 1997) pp.139–151.

Shakespeare, William. *King Lear*. Ed. R. A. Foakes. (London: Arden Shakespeare, 1977).

Steinberg, Jonathan. *Why Switzerland?* 2nd ed. (Cambridge: Cambridge University Press, 1996).

Torok, Maria and Nicholas Abraham. *The Shell and the Kernel: Renewals of Psychoanalysis*. Ed. and trans. Nichola T. Rand (Chicago: University of Chicago Press, 1994).

Thomson, David. *The New Biographical Dictionary of Film* (New York: Knopf 2003).

Truffaut, François. *Correspondence*. Ed. Claude de Givray and Gilles Jacob. (Rennes: 5 Continents/Hatier, 1988). English trans. Gilbert Adair (London: Faber and Faber, 1988).

'Positif; Copie zero' *Cahiers du cinéma* 79 (January 1958).

Valéry, Paul. *Œuvres*. 2 vols. Ed. Jean Hytier (Paris: Gallimard, 1960).

Vidal, Gore. *Screening History* (Cambridge: Harvard University Press, 1992).

Vlastos, Gregory. *Socrates, Ironist and Moral Philosopher* (Cornell: Cornell University Press, 1991).

Wake, Sandra and Nicola Hayden, eds. *Bonnie and Clyde* (London: Lorrimer, 1972).

Winock, Michel. *Le Siècle des intellectuels* (Paris: Points, 1999).

Zizek, Slavoj, ed. *Selected Writings of Lenin from 1917* (London: Verso, 2002).

Documentaries

Paparazzi. Dir. Jacques Rozier. Filmes du Colisee, 1964

Cinéma de notre temps: Jean-Luc Godard ou le cinema au defi. Prod. Janine Bazin and Andre S. Labarthe. ORTF, 1965

Doniol-Valcroze, Jacques. 'Interview with Jean-Luc Godard', in: 'Pour le plaisir', dir. Roger Stéphane, ORTF, 1965

Chambre 12, Hôtel du Suède. Dir. Claude Ventura and Xavier Villetard. La Sept/Télé Europe, 1993.

The Typewriter, The Rifle and The Movie Camera. Dir. Adam Simon. BFI TV, 1996

Howard Hawks: American Artist. Dir. Kevin MacDonald. BFI TV, 1997

Baadasssss Cinema. Dir. Isaac Julien. Minerva Pictures, 2002

Notes

Preface

1. When referring to Godard's and others' films, I have used English titles when they have real currency, as with *Breathless* and *Contempt*. Otherwise I use the French titles.

1 Gods and Demi-Gods: The Monods and the Godards

1. Samuel Johnson, 'Preface to Shakespeare', *Johnson as Critic*, ed. J. Wain (London and Boston: Routledge & Kegan Paul, 1973), p.153.
2. Paul Valéry *Oeuvres* 1 edition établie par Jean Hytier (Gallimard: Paris, 1957), p.49–50.
3. ibid.
4. Georges Godard used his revolver for protection when he went to Antwerp to buy diamonds.
5. Janine Garrisson, *Les Protestants au XVIe siècle* (Paris: Fayard, 1988), p.37.
6. If anti-Semitism was unusual amongst Protestants, who had historically often been lumped with Jews as undesirable outsiders, it was not at all unusual in France. Indeed France both before and after the Dreyfus affair was a country in which violent anti-Semitism was a part of the political and intellectual landscape. Of course, anti-Semitism is not a doctrine or a creed but a mess of prejudices and inadequacies which has no genuine intellectual or political core. Julien-Pierre Monod's anti-Semitism should not make him, as many French anti-Semites were, an accomplice of the Judeocide, to use the term from Arno Mayer's book *Why Did the Heavens not Darken?: The 'final solution' in History* (New York: Pantheon, 1988). If Godard's grandfather was enough of a figure of the right to be seized in the savage days of revenge after Le Clerc's army had liberated Paris in 1944, he was released almost as quickly. I have been told nothing to suggest that his anti-Semitism ever passed from word to act.
7. Marcel Dreyfus, *Souvenirs de Nyon* (Geneva: Slatkine, 1999), p.70.
8. Godard, in an interview in December 1988, remembered two separate periods in France after June 1940. Family and school records suggest very strongly that there was only one such period stretching from June 1940 to October 1940 which was divided into a initial stay in Brittany and then a further period at Vichy, from which it would have been easier to get back to Switzerland.

9. E. Bonj, H. S. Offler and G. R. Potter, *A Short History of Switzerland* (Oxford: The Clarendon Press, 1952), pp.367–378.

10. Marcel Dreyfus, op.cit, p.55

11. The school had many supply teachers during the war years because of the number of masters on military service. According to Pierre Gudet, a classmate of Jean-Luc's, this led to a certain relaxation of discipline. Written communication of June 2002 on Nyon and the Collège de Nyon in the war years.

12. Pierre Gudet mentions *Goodbye Mr Chips* and *Robin Hood* as the two films that 'all the adolescents of that time' would have seen.

13. It should be noted, however, that in his acceptance speech for the Adorno prize on 17 September 1995, Godard links his interest in the concentration camps to the 'love of Germany' transmitted to him by his father (G2:404).

14. There were two troops of Scouts at Nyon, one Catholic and one Protestant. The majority of Scouts came from well-off families because of the cost of the uniforms and the outings. Gudet, op.cit.

15. Jean-Luc Godard, *Introduction à une véritable histoire du cinéma* (Paris: Éditions Albatros, 1980), p.74.

16. He also claims to have registered at the Institut de Filmologie (G2:41).

17. Luc Moullet, *Cahiers du cinéma* 106 (April 1960), p.26.

18. Gunter Holzmann, *On dit que j'ai survécu quelque part au delà des mers* (Paris: Éditions La Découverte, 1997), p.155, quoted in Sally Gately Shafto *Ut Pictura Cinema: The Strange Adventure of Jean-Luc Godard*, PhD, University of Iowa, 2000, p.81.

19. Godard wrote to Truffaut at the time of *Breathless* proposing a film set in Panama 'which I know well' [quoted in Michel Marie *A Bout de souffle* (Paris: Nathan, 1999) p.34] – it is perhaps surprising in a film-maker who has taken so much raw material from his own life that the South American journey has not left more obvious traces in his films.

20. There is an almost unbelievable end to this tale. Late one night in the summer of 1970, as Godard and Gorin were editing their unfinished film *Jusqua'à la victoire*, there was a ring at the door and a doctor appeared whom Gorin had met at a congress in Cuba. He announced that he was touring psychiatric hospitals in Europe seeking out the files of famous people and then returning them to the former patients. He presented Godard with his file.

21. *Feuille d'Avis de Lausanne*, Monday 26 April 1954, p.16

2 'The Cinema Is not a Bad School': André Bazin and the *Cahiers du cinéma*

1. Even Lenin's famous quotation was not quite so positive in its original context. Post-Soviet researches in Lunacharsky's archives record Lenin making the remark in exasperation as Lunacharsky made yet another request for some film-maker: 'Of

course, of course, Anatoly Vassilievich, cinema is the most important of the arts, isn't it?'

2. A. Gance, 'Qu'est-ce que le cinématographe? Un sixième art', *Ciné-journal* 185. 9 March 1912, reproduced in M. L'Herbier *Intelligence du cinématographe* (Paris, 1946), pp.91–92.

3. Christophe Gauthier, *La Passion du cinéma: Cinéphiles, ciné-clubs et salles specialisées à Paris de 1920 à 1929* (Paris: AFRHC, 1999) pp.23–24.

4. 'Compte-rendu de la matinée du 22 janvier 1921 au cinéma du Colisée' in *Le Journal du ciné-club* no.4, 28 January 1921, p.4.

5. E.J.H. Greene, *T.S. Eliot et la France* (Paris: Boivin, 1951), p.10.

6. Richard Roud, *A Passion for Films: Henri Langlois and the Cinémathèque Française* (New York: Viking Press, 1983), p.16.

7. Henri Langlois, *Etudes cinématographiques* 38–39 (Spring 1965), p.42. Later in the same interview, Langlois makes clear what is at stake: 'I am persuaded that a return to Surrealism, to its sources and its endings is the only hope of a cinematographic renewal. And that's why one must . . . go back to the Surrealist manifesto, because it remains explosive provided you read it with eyes which are in excellent condition.'

8. Richard Roud, op.cit., p.17.

9. Richard Roud, op.cit., p.34.

10. The scale of de Gaulle's achievement was brought home to me as a student at the Ecole Normale Supérieure when on 18 June 1973 I attended a seminar by Louis Althusser on Marx's *Critique of Political Economy*. Leaving Marx somewhat in his wake, Althusser gave us an extended meditation on, to use Althusser's own telling phrase, 'the only man to have saved a bourgeoisie twice'. His references were to both 1940 and 1958.

11. Unfortunately the archives of the Lycée Buffon were destroyed in the student riots of 1968 to make exact dating even more difficult.

12. Jacques Vilaines, *Sud Ouest Bordeaux Dimanche*, 30 August 1967.

13. Jean-Claude Brialy, *Le Ruisseau des singes* (Paris: Robert Laffont, 2000), p.120.

14. Jacques Gerber, editor. *Pierre Braunberger, producteur: Cinémamémoire,* (Paris: Centre Georges-Pompidou/Centre National de la Cinématographie, 1987), p.166.

15. Bernard J. Houssiau, *Marc Allégret, découvreur de stars: sous les yeux d'André Gide* (Yens s./ Morgues: Editions Cabédita, 1994), p.187.

16. Sally Shafto, op.cit., pp.10 and 83.

17. Joël Magny, *Eric Rohmer* (Paris: Editions Payot et Rivages, 1995), p.9. Rohmer himself told me: 'I did not want to mix things up.'

18. Gégauff was a crucial figure in the *Cahiers* family as Rohmer was to stress movingly in the special December 1984 issue of *Cahiers*, published after Truffaut's death. 'La vie, c'était l'écran', *Cahiers du cinéma*, p.18.

19. Joël Magny, op.cit., p.10.

20. The story goes that de Gaulle was informed before a demonstration that the police intended to arrest Sartre. His response 'You don't arrest Voltaire', even if apocryphal, attests to Sartre's position.

21. See Annie Cohen-Solal, *Sartre 1905–1980* (Paris: Gallimard, 1985) pp.121–124.

22. Dudley Andrew, *André Bazin* (New York: Oxford University Press, 1978), p.45.

23. For more on Leenhardt see the compelling set of interviews, *Les Yeux ouverts: entretiens avec Jean Lacouture* (Paris: Le Seuil, 1979).

24. See Dudley Andrew, op.cit., pp.38–60.

25. ibid, p.57.

26. While Head of Research at the British Film Institute I initiated a project to publish Bazin's Collected Works. Most unusually, I asked Godard's advice because I was worried that hero worship was blinding me to the fact that very few Complete Works deserve publication. Equally unusually Godard hesitated before replying 'Yes, you should do it.' When New Labour, after its election in 1997, determined to finish with the British Film Institute as the kind of critical and intellectual centre which Bazin had argued was necessary for any genuine development of film as an art, it was fitting that the projected Collected Works was the first of many projects to be axed. It was not axed because of a lack of money; instead the aim was the explicit subordination of all inquiry and education to the needs of the industry.

27. Eric Rohmer, 'La "Somme" d'André Bazin', *Cahiers du cinéma* 91 (January 1959), p.31.

28. The advent of digital technology marks a real technological break with the cinema that André Bazin theorised. Whether we will come to recognise cinema from 1895 until 1982 as Bazinian cinema – a different medium, defined by its chemistry, from the post-digital screen, defined electronically – is still a moot point. What is certain is that there seems to be a real audience resistance to digital effects which may yet prolong Bazin's axiom. Whatever the future will bring, Godard's films are part of Bazinian cinema.

29. Sartre's political analysis is as faulty as his formal one. Laura Mulvey shows brilliantly in her *Citizen Kane* how Welles's film articulates a pro-interventionist position in an America hesitating about joining the war against fascism. *Citizen Kane* (London: British Film Institute, 1992).

30. Dudley Andrew, op.cit., pp.84–85.

31. André Bazin, 'Pour une critique cinématographique' in *Le Cinéma de l'Occupation et de la Résistance* (Paris: Union Générale d'Éditions, 1975), p.69.

32. 'There is no longer any need to apologise for snobbism. In the modern world of anonymous business, snobbery is the philanthropy of imbeciles. As the mass of those unconscious philanthropists cannot find in themselves the real workings of their opinions, the problem comes back to an effective politics of snobbery in the more general perspective of a politics of cinema', op.cit., p.78.

33. Dudley Andrew, op.cit., p.155.

34. The term the 'Schérer gang' was sometimes used to describe all the young critics of the early fifties. I have used it here to emphasise the links which bound Rohmer, Rivette and Godard together before the encounter with Truffaut.

35. Interview with Charles Bitsch, February 2002.

36. For fuller details on Truffaut, see Antoine de Baecque and Serge Toubiana, *François Truffaut* 2nd edition (Paris: Gallimard, 2001) and Antoine de Baecque, *Cahiers du cinéma: Histoire d'une revue*, 2 vols (Paris: Cahiers du cinéma, 2001) especially vol.1. pp.89–126.

37. François Truffaut, *Correspondance*, lettres recueillies par Gilles Jacob et Claude de Givray. Notes de Gilles Jacob. Avant propos de Jean-Luc Godard (Rennes: 5 Continents/Hatier, 1988) p.8.

38. Indeed, Truffaut's biographers claim that Truffaut and Godard were enamoured of the same girl, Liliane Litvin (T:105–107). But Godard says that it was only Truffaut who was in love. Truffaut would use his own experiences of Liliane Litvin for his second Antoine Doinel film, *Antoine et Colette* (T:361).

39. Godard can have been no more than eighteen and probably younger when he submitted these articles.

40. Dudley Andrew op.cit, p.91.

41. 'Certainly it was a sign that I wished to hide, to be prudent. But not at all because of my family, it was rather because of literary ambition, because at the time my ambition was to publish a novel with Gallimard. I admired Astruc because he'd done that' (G:1:9).

42. There is, however, a perceptive reading of Godard's criticism in Marc Cerisuelo, *Jean-Luc Godard* (Paris: L'herminier/Quatre-Vents, 1989).

43. Perhaps the most eloquent testimony to this can be found in Gore Vidal's *Screening History* (Cambridge: Harvard University Press, 1992)

44. See Howard Hawks: *American Artist*, dir. Kevin MacDonald, 1997.

45. 'I even stole from *Cahiers*, that's why I disappeared for a while.'

46. Interview, Roland Tolmatchoff, March 2002.

47. Telephone interview with Adrien Porchet, April 2002.

48. Gégauff tells a similar story of events in 1950: 'I saw Jean-Luc steal at one of the shoots. There were these old ladies who were accompanying their granddaughters and the old ladies had handbags. Jean-Luc didn't have a penny at the time. He'd bust up with his father or something, he was in a totally black poverty. And he smoked like a chimney. So one day an old lady digs around in her handbag and finds a thousand francs missing . . . A terrible scandal breaks out and everybody's looking at Jean-Luc. Everybody tells him "Listen you idiot – give the 1,000 francs back." And he got furious and said that he'd leave and all that. And then people realised (I wasn't there but Momo (Rohmer) told me) that Jean-Luc who had no money or cigarettes pulls out a pack of Gauloises from his pocket. Momo said to him 'You have a pack of cigarettes – how did you pay for them?" Godard said – "Oh I found them in an old pocket." Then everybody went for him. A pack of Gauloises cost at the time 65 francs, something like that, and the next day the old lady opened her bag and finds a thousand francs less 65 francs, that's to say 935 francs.' 1967/68 interview with Paul Gégauff by André S. Labarthe, Jean Eustache and Bernadette Lafont published in *LimeLight*, June 1997, pp.56–65.

49. Interview, Jean-Luc Godard, December 1988.
50. *Cahiers du cinéma* no.33 March 1954, p.42.
51. Bazin himself contributed two excellent articles indicating the excesses of the *politique des auteurs* 'Comment peut-on être Hitchcocko – Hawksien', *Cahiers du cinéma* 44, February 1955, pp.17–18, 'De la politique des auteurs', *Cahiers du cinéma* 70, April 1957, pp.2–11.
52. Claude Chabrol, *Et pourtant je tourne* (Paris: Robert Laffont, 1976), pp.69–87.
53. Claude Chabrol, op.cit., p. 102.
54. Joël Magny, op.cit., p.11.
55. Chantal de Beauregard, *Georges de Beauregard: Premier sourire de Belmondo . . . dernier de Bardot* (Paris: Lacour/Colporteur, 1991), p.70.
56. There is no doubt that in taking montage for his subject, Godard was attempting to break a lance with the 'inoubliable' Bazin.
57. Jean-Claude Brialy, *Le Ruisseau des singes* (Paris: Robert Laffont, 2000) pp.102–108. Brialy claims that Godard was in the car with Bitsch and Chabrol, Godard says he was not.
58. Michel Marie, *A Bout de souffle* (Paris: Nathan, 1999), p.11.

3 A Certain Tendency of French Film Production: The New Wave of Karina and Coutard

1. Godard insists that this slogan is, in fact, Griffiths', but I have been unable to locate the original.
2. It should be noted that two of these interviews, those with Rossellini and Renoir, were in fact fabrications: 'It was at *Arts*. We needed interviews and then people wouldn't do them and it was difficult to arrange. As the magazine liked the idea of the interviews, I made them up – saying to myself: the ideas won't be false' (G1:13). While Godard is committed to the most rigorous honesty in his films, in life he lies all the time with the peculiarity, as one of his long-term assistants perspicaciously remarked, that there is absolutely no effort to pretend that he is not lying.
3. 'Six personnages en quête d'auteurs', *Cahiers du cinéma* 71, May 1957, p.18.
4. The original English translation confuses the second baccalauréat (the equivalent of English A Levels) with the *agrégation* for which there is no English equivalent. Each year, the Ministry of Education announces the numbers of posts vacant in the different subjects (philosophy, French, English, maths etc.) and organises a competitive exam. Success, which requires concentrated study in a form for which there is no Anglo-Saxon equivalent, rewards you with a well-paid job for life. Both Sartre and Derrida famously failed their aggrégation at their first attempt and we have already seen that Bazin's failure led, in the particular circumstance of the war, to him abandoning teaching. Kast was another of those who failed to join the state education system because of the war.
5. It says something about the paralysing nature of the division between literature and

cinema in the academy that one can find no such history. Michel Winock's impressive *Le Siècle des intellectuels* (Paris: Points, 1999) contains one reference to Truffaut – as a signatory to a petition on the Algerian war – and none to Godard. The otherwise extremely accurate entry for 'Hussard' in *Dictionnaire des Lettres Françaises*, ed Martine Bercot and André Guyaux (Paris: Librairie Générale Française, 1998) does not mention the crucial role of Truffaut and the other *Cahiers* critics in the last years of the hussard magazine *Arts*. Stupefyingly there is not even an entry for Bazin, whose only rival as a critic in the post-war years in France is Roland Barthes.

6. The term 'hussard' came from Nimier's second novel *Le Hussard bleu*, published in 1950. The process by which an insult is turned into a badge of honour is well summarised by Salman Rushdie in *The Satanic Verses* 'to turn insults into strengths, whigs, tories, Blacks all chose to wear with pride the names they were given in scorn'. (London: Viking, 1988) p.93.

7. Charles Maurras (1886–1952) was the most significant right-wing thinker in Europe in the first half of the twentieth century.

8. Antoine de Baecque and Serge Toubiana, op.cit., pp.168–173. In the concluding sentence de Baecque and Toubiana are perhaps too ready, from a left-wing perspective, to identify Maurras and the Action Française with the Hussards. In this they are following Kast who did talk of Maurrasisme in relation to Truffaut (ibid p.173) in 1954. But Kast was a crucial ten years older than Truffaut and in any case there was a deep antipathy between the two. There is a hilarious account of Kast and Truffaut arguing furiously, seated back to back in the *Cahiers* offices with their supporting troops ranged in front of them.

9. The first edition of this work, written with his brother-in-law Maurice Bardèche, was published in 1935 by Denoël and Steele. (2nd edition revised and updated in 1943.)

10. François Truffaut, 'Positif; Copie zéro' *Cahiers du cinéma* 79 (January 1958), p.62.

11. Jean-Pierre Bertin-Maghit, *Le Cinéma Français sous l'occupation: Le Monde du cinéma français de 1940 à 1946* (Paris: Orban, 1989) pp.22–23.

12. There is a parallel story unfolding in England from the thirties onwards, but it is one of unremitting failure.

13. André Bazin and Jacques Doniol-Valcroze, 'Entretien avec Jacques Flaud', *Cahiers du cinéma*, May 1957, p.4.

14. André, Malraux, *Esquisse d'une psychologie du cinéma* (Paris: Gallimard, 1996), p.19. For a fascinating and thorough account of the economics of the Nouvelle Vague see Frédérique Berthet, *Anatole Dauman, un producteur dans le cinéma français (1950–1998) Contribution à une histoire économique du culturel* (unpublished thesis Université de Paris 3, 2001). On Malraux, in particular see ibid pp.129–140.

15. For an account of the making of these films see Claude Chabrol, op.cit., pp.135–145, and Jean-Claude Brialy, op.cit., pp.118–119 and 135–136.

16. For Chabrol's retrospective assessment see the entertaining and informative documentary about *Breathless, Chambre 12, Hôtel de Suède* (dir. Claude Ventura and Xavier Villetard, 1993).

17. See Jon Savage, *Teenage* (London: Chatto and Windus, forthcoming) for the definitive history of the 'generation gap'.

18. Morgenstern was Truffaut's father-in-law and Madeleine Morgenstern leaves no doubt that in financing *Les Quatre cents coups*, Morgenstern thought that he was fulfilling a family obligation rather than making an investment (T:253).

19. Beauregard's reputation as a 'coureur de femmes' is a theme of his daughter's book on him. During the shoot of *Breathless* Beauregard turned up with a producer friend delighted at the prospect of seeing Virginie Uhlman take off her bra. Godard, who had gone to great lengths to find an actress willing to appear nude, decided not to ask the actress to undress. Interview Pierre Rissient, January 2002.

20. There is not space in this book to deal with all the aborted projects which litter Godard's career even more than they do other directors'. 'There were a lot of projects, an awful lot of projects that never got done.' Godard in interview, 15 December 1979, Colin MacCabe with Laura Mulvey and Mick Eaton *Godard: Images, Sounds, Politics* (London: British Film Institute MacMillan, 1980) p.26. For the abandoned projects of this period see Michel Marie, *A Bout de souffle* (Paris: Nathan, 1999), pp. 33–34.

21. For the back story of Truffaut and Godard's collaboration, see T:210–211 and 300–301.

22. A studio production has to be analysed very differently from an independent production.

23. February 1958, no.80 inside cover. Preminger was a priviled reference for Godard from 'Defence and Illustration of Classical Construction'.

24. See David Richards, *Played Out: The Jean Seberg Story* (New York: Random House, 1981), pp.84–85.

25. ibid.

26. Philippe Durant, *Belmondo* (Paris: Robert Laffont, 1993), p.139.

27. Interview, Pierre Rissient, January 2002.

28. Godard talks of their relationship both in terms of 'an old family servant' but also as a relationship between Napoleon and one of his generals. The reference to the Napoleonic generals is all the more striking in that Godard, to my knowledge, talks almost not at all of Bonaparte.

29. The Japanese had left Indo-China in the hands of the Vichy French.

30. The function of the cameraman can be divided into two – there is the task of lighting the scene (lighting cameraman) and the task of framing the picture (camera operator). Coutard usually combined both functions.

31. In fact Latouche had little to do on this film although he feels Godard took some comfort from his presence as they both returned in silence to their rooms in the rue de Rennes. Latouche also worked as an assistant on *Le Petit soldat* but then went on

to a long career, mainly as an editor, in French television. When in 1963 Godard finally sold the shorts they had made together he sent Latouche, who had worked for free, the money he had promised him.

32. Quoted in *Chambre 12, Hôtel de Suède* (dir. Claude Ventura and Xavier Villetard, 1993).

33. 'I'm trying to make music in the country. If I go to the woods to make good music, a music inspired by the wood or the animals and then shoot every animal and chop down every tree so that I was sure I was making my own music . . . well it's the same with film.' Colin MacCabe et al, op.cit., p.133.

34. Coutard's account quoted in Michel Marie op. cit., pp.55–56 is misleading as it does not mention that the stock used for day shooting was Gevaert 36.

35. Michel Marie, op.cit., pp.12–13.

36. Interview, Roland Tolmatchoff, June 2002.

37. Jean-Luc Godard, op.cit., p.30: 'I had made a film which was two and a quarter, two and a half hours long and it couldn't be more than an hour and a half long contractually. I remember very well . . . how we invented this famous editing – that people now use in commercials.'

38. Michel Marie, op.cit., pp.41–48.

39. Ibid: 'un film magistralement promotionné' pp.115–118. There are two stories that circulate constantly about Godard's youth: that he held up a garage at gunpoint and that he broke into and stole from his father's clinic. I suspect that both stories originate with the campaign to promote *Breathless*.

40. Godard had imaginatively cast Balducci as Tolmatchoff. Balducci in promoting the film was promoting his own image.

41. Jean-Pierre Jeancolas, *Histoire du cinéma français* (Paris: Nathan, 1995), p.117.

42. Andi Engel recalls that when Jean-Marie Straub was asked at the Locarno festival about Godard's use of music, he exclaimed, 'Oh la la, Jean-Luc avec sa discothèque.'

43. Michel Marie, op.cit., p.36.

44. David Richards, op.cit., p.85.

45. Or as Joyce elegantly puts it in *Finnegans Wake*: 'Where do thots come from?' where the pun not only links children (tots) and thinking (thoughts) but makes reference to the Egyptian god of writing, the figure of Thoth. It is writing (and the term should be understood in the sense that will apply to any creative articulation) that allows us perhaps the surest way to rework our imaginary identifications.

46. In a posthumously published interview, Gégauff describes the whole phenomenon of the New Wave from the ciné-clubs to the films as the activities of 'obsédés sexuels'. The whole interview has to be taken with a large pinch of salt and Gégauff sounds like someone who prepared for the interview by getting completely drunk, but his comments provide a welcome counterpoint to those histories that limit themselves to theories of *mise-en-scène*. Gégauff, op.cit.

47. 'En marge de "L'Erotisme au cinéma"' *Cahiers du cinéma* 70 (April 1957), pp.27–31. This issue also contains Bazin's luminous thoughts on the *politique des auteurs*.

48. All the information about Karina comes from long interviews conducted in the period February–April 2002. In talking with Karina one cannot but be aware that one is in the presence of a great actress. There are differences between what Karina told me and some other interviews e.g. 'Anna Karina & Jean-Luc Godard Les Enfants Terribles' *Studio* no.67 November 1992, pp.122–126. I have preferred to follow what I was told directly. This part of the book is Karina's story – at least as she told it to me in Paris in the winter/spring of 2002. Pierre Rissient is certain that the role Anna was being offered was the model in the photographer's studio at the end of the film. Karina is adamant that Godard told her repeatedly when they saw the film later that she was destined to be Michel Poiccard's old girlfriend. Godard himself questions whether he insisted on a church wedding in the terms Karina describes, doubts that his father was at the wedding, or that he accompanied her to Deville's set every day.

49. Her mother ran three dress shops in Copenhagen and was to do the costumes for Dreyer's last film *Gertrud* (1964).

50. *La Cinématographe français*, no.1847, 19 December 1959.

51. Every Godard shoot is full of such stories but *Le Petit soldat* is the only example where the evidence seems incontrovertible that Godard cancelled whole day shoots repeatedly.

52. Michel Marie, *La Nouvelle Vague* (Paris: Nathan, 1997), p.44.

53. 'Table-ronde sur *Hiroshima mon amour* d'Alain Resnais', in *La Nouvelle Vague*, eds. Antoine de Baecque and Charles Tesson (Paris: Cahiers du cinéma, 1999), pp.36–62.

54. Godard defines his own generation in terms of their knowledge of cinema, the first generation of directors to have this culture: 'There's the group (along with Uncle Astruc, Kast and – a little apart – Leenhardt) to which should be added what one might call the Left Bank group: Resnais, Varda, Marker. And there is Demy. They had their own cultural background. But that's about the lot' (G:172/1:216). To trace the links between these various film-makers, particularly between Marker and Godard, would be another book.

55. *Le Film Français*, 10 November 1961, no.910, records only 56, 323 spectators in its five-week run.

56. Hélène Frappat, *Jacques Rivette, secret compris* (Paris: Cahiers du cinéma, 2001), p.129.

57. ibid.

58. Marc Cerisuelo, *Jean-Luc Godard* (Paris: Editions des Quatre Vents, 1989), p.77.

59. The brothers Hakim had provided a financial lifeline to Godard and Karina when, in 1961, Karina had been shocked to find the bailiffs at the door for unpaid taxes. Godard's appreciation of the centrality of taxes to the life of the modern state did not extend to filling in his own tax returns and the problem of unpaid taxes is a refrain throughout the early sixties. See Michel Vianey, *En attendant Godard* (Paris: Bernard Grasset, 1966): 'He has never made a tax return. He didn't know how to.' 'I didn't know how to. At the moment I'm working to pay off all the years I owe,'

p.20. The immediate problem in 1961 was solved by Karina taking a role in the brothers Hakim's *La Ronde*, with the proviso that her entire fee was payable on signature to keep the wolf of the taxman from the door.

60. Jean-Luc Godard, op.cit., pp.78–79.

61. Jean–Pierre Jeancolas, *Histoire du cinéma français* (Paris: Nathan, 1995), p.62.

62. *Paparazzi* (dir. Jacques Rozier, 1963).

63. Though Godard's editor Agnès Guillemot still regrets that the film doesn't open directly on to the scene in Cinecittà: 'Everybody says that the tracking shot on the body is very beautiful but I am still very unhappy to have lost the extraordinary effect that cut from the tracking credits shot directly to Palance at Cinecittà.' 'Special Godard – Trente Ans depuis', *Cahiers du cinéma* 437 (November 1990), p.62.

64. The full story of Lang and the Nazis is in fact more complicated than this simple legend. See Patrick McGilligan *Fritz Lang: The Nature of the Beast, A Biography* (New York: St Martin's Press, 1997), pp.176–179.

65. For more detailed discussion of Brecht see Isaac Julien and Colin MacCabe *Diary of a Young Soul Rebel* (London: British Film Institute, 1991) pp.232–236.

66. The only other examples of films that I know of which use many languages are war films like *The Longest Day*.

67. For full details on Rossellini, see Tag Gallagher's magnificent *The Adventures of Roberto Rossellini: His Life and Films* (New York: Di Capo Press, 1998). For a specimen of *Cahiers*'s veneration for Rossellini see Jacques Rivette 'Lettre sur Rossellini' *Cahiers du cinéma* 46 (April 1955), pp.14–24. It is quite possible that more important for Godard than the commercial failures of the New Wave or the collapse of classic Hollywood was Rossellini's renunciation of the cinema in a 1962 press conference: 'there is a crisis today not just in film but in culture as a whole. Film, which is the instrument par excellence for spreading ideas, has had the merit of making the crisis evident, almost palpably so. For this reason I intend to retire from film and dedicate myself to television.' Gallagher, op.cit., p.554.

68. It is this sybil who provides the epigraph to Eliot's *The Waste Land* in the story taken from Peronius's *Satyricon*: 'Yes, and I myself with my own eyes even saw the Sybil hanging in a cage; and when the boys cried at her: "Sybil, Sybil, What do you Want?" "I would that I were dead," she caused to answer.'

69. Interestingly, Gorin remembers that at the time of the Dziga Vertov Group, Rossellini's *Viaggio in Italia* functioned as the example of how you could take the flimsiest of narrative threads and make a film with layers upon layers of meaning – about human relationship, about the history of civilisation.

70. Bitsch claims that the reason that the scene was so long was that the movie was coming in under length and Godard needed to ensure that he honoured his contract.

71. Interview, Anna Karina, March 2002.

72. In her autobiography *Initiales BB* (Paris: Bernard Grasset, 1996) Bardot says that the only direction that Godard gave her was 'to be more like Karina', pp.327–328.

Godard denies this. Bardot's account of the shoot makes no mention of the film whatsoever apart from this comment.

73. Godard had in fact tried to film *Pour Lucrèce* eighteen months previously and it had been abandoned only at the very last minute. Bourseiller's memory, however, is that his own production of *Pour Lucrèce* was without reference to Godard's previous interest in the play.

74. Philippe Durant, op.cit., pp.232–233.

75. In conversation at the Cannes Film Festival, 1999.

76. Jean-Luc Godard, *Introduction à une véritable histoire du cinéma*, p.94.

77. Barbet Schroeder remembers Godard being accused of plagiarism at an early screening of *Alphaville*. 'Of course', Godard replied. 'When one of my characters says "I love you", the "I" is taken from one context, the "love" from another and the "you" from a third.'

78. Godard, op.cit., p.94.

79. Michel Vianey, *En attendant Godard* (Paris: Bernard Grasset, 1966), p.44.

80. Anne Wiazemsky's marriage certificate shows the date of Karina and Godard's divorce as 21 December 1964, thus before the shooting of *Alphaville*. Reynal's memory would suggest that Godard and Karina's relationship continued for six months after their formal divorce.

81. Jacob wrote a series of articles on *Alphaville, Pierrot le fou* and *Made in USA* in the pages of the journal *Cinéma* which attempted to move beyond the more sterile features of the debates on Godard which accompanied every new film. The articles are a sustained attempt to demonstrate the range and subtlety of Godard's cinema.

82. Gilles Jacob, '*Pierrot le fou*', *Cinéma 65* no.101, October 1965, pp.100–101.

83. Jean Rosset, interview, September 2001. There are several rumours of Godard attempting suicide, including one during the fifties when he was working at Fox and one at the end of the sixties after his break-up with Anne Wiazemsky.

84. Dossier Godard, Fonds Truffaut. Bibliothèque du Film.

85. *Les Lettres Françaises*, 21 June 1966.

86. Pauline Kael, *The New Republic*, 19 November 1966. Reprinted in *Kiss Kiss Bang Bang* (New York: Atlantic Little Brown., 1966), p.127.

87. Colin MacCabe et al., op.cit., p.160.

88. 'I was vaguely in love with Marina Vlady . . . and I went to see her at St Paul de Vence without much success' (G:1:17).

4   Student Revolution: Wiazemsky and Gorin

1. My attention was first drawn to this comment by the late Piers Gray. It is used by Simon Schama to open his history of the French Revolution, *Citizens* (London: Penguin, 1989) p.xiii.

2. So shocking was the speech that some dozen delegates had to be carried incapa-

citated from the hall and the following days saw several deaths. See Slavoj Zizek, ed., *Selected Writings of Lenin from 1917* (London: Verso, 2002), p.241.

3. Hervé Hamon and Patrick Rotman, *Génération* (Paris: Seuil, 1987) vol.1. pp.400–401

4. See Karl, Marx, *Capital: A Critique of Political Economy*. 3 Vols. (London: Penguin, 1991). For example 'It is [the rate of profit] that determines the expansion and contraction of production, instead of the proportion between production and social needs, the needs of socially developed human beings.' *Capital* vol.3, (London: Penguin, 1991), p.367.

5. As this was the most prescient of Lenin's analyses, it is worth stressing that Lenin himself was as astonished as anybody else at the speed with which the social democratic parties, far from impotently opposing the war, rallied to the nationalist flag. Famously, Lenin was at first convinced that the edition of the German SPD newspaper *Vorwarts* that carried the news that the German Social Democrats had voted war credits was a forgery. See Colin MacCabe *James Joyce and the Revolution of the Word* (London: Palgrave 2002, 2nd ed.) pp.165–166.

6. It is this dual allegiance to the philosophy of science and the Communist Party which explains Althusser's lack of publications in the fifties. In the late forties a Soviet, Lyssenko, challenged Darwinism by arguing for the inheritance of acquired characteristics. Stalin backed the fraudulent scientist and argued for a distinction between proletarian and bourgeois science so that science itself became a function of the class struggle. Communist philosophers and scientists were pressurised to back both Lyssenko and the philosophical distinction in a campaign which effectively severed any serious links between scientists and the Communist movement.

7. In the autumn of 1980, Althusser's own life was to end tragically with the murder of his wife in his apartment in the Ecole Normale Supérieure and his being deemed too insane to plead in a court case. He did indeed enter a plea, published in a posthumous autobiography *L'Avenir dure longtemps* (Paris: Stock/IMEC, 1992), but the book bears terrible witness to the psychic formation which made him a loyal member of the French Communist Party through four decades.

8. For full details of this see Hervé Hamon and Patrick Rotman, op.cit., pp.255–288.

9. Its unorthodoxy stretches to the inclusion of anarchist texts from Cohn-Bendit's group at Nanterre. But if Godard makes bedfellows of two completely opposed positions, they were the two positions that were to be most evident in May 1968.

10. The cell take their name from the Paul Nizan text which begins with the famous line 'I refuse to allow anyone to say that twenty is the most beautiful age.'

11. Some of the curious features of this dialogue are explained by the fact that while Godard was feeding Wiazemsky her lines through an earpiece, Godard himself could not hear Jeanson's replies.

12. *Journal du Sud Ouest*, 30 July 1967.

13. See Jean-Pierre Jeancolas, 'Cinéma, Censure, Contrôle, Classement' in *La Censure en France à l'ère démocratique*, ed. Pascal Ory (Paris: Editions Complexe, 1997). See

also Jean Pivasset, *Essai sur la signification politique du cinéma: l'exemple français, de la Libération aux évènements du mai 1968* (Paris: Editions Cujas, 1971).

14. And Godard signals the importance of the visa number granted by the minister to allow a film to be released by giving it an unusual prominence amongst his normally sparse credits.

15. For an account of the banning of *La Religieuse* and its long-term political effects see Jean Pivasset, op.cit., pp.213–229.

16. For full accounts of 'l'Affaire Langlois' see Patrick Olmeta, *La Cinémathèque de 1936 à nos jours* (Paris: Editions CNRS, 2000), pp.119–148, G. Langlois et G. Myrent, *Henri Langlois: premier citoyen du cinéma* (Paris: Denoël, 1986), pp.319–357), Richard Roud op.cit., pp.148–160, Antoine de Baecque et Serge Toubiana op.cit., pp.461–472.

17. Richard Roud, op.cit., p.154.

18. Bernardo Bertolucci in conversation, July 2002.

19. It is interesting to think how different *La Chinoise* would have been with Sollers, a representative of the new intellectual wave, rather than Jeanson, a long-time collaborator of Sartre and *Les Temps Modernes*. It is also a striking example of how Godard has always made his films with whatever material is to hand. And if there is nothing 'improvised' about them, there is an enormous amount left to chance.

20. 'You know I can't read' (G1:311). Jean-Pierre Gorin emphasises that Godard's reading often stopped at the table of contents. When Peter Sellars was working on *Vivre sa vie* at Harvard he was struck by how many of Godard's references came right at the beginning or right at the end of books. Véronique Godard recalls her elder brother often telling both her and Claude that you needed to read only the first and the last page of any book.

21. It is not that Godard did not remain in close contact. Both Karina and Wiazemsky stress a closeness with Truffaut and Rivette. But there was no shared project of the kind that united them in the fifties.

22. For an account of Cannes 1968 see de Baecque and Toubiana op.cit., pp.472–477.

23. At least one of the film-tracts was made with the artist Gérard Fromanger. Mo Teitelbaum also remembers attending a demonstration-cum-happening with Fromanger and Godard in early June at Alesia in the south of Paris where passers-by were encouraged to take little statues that the demonstrators distributed on the streets. The demonstration ended with Godard being bundled into a police car.

24. It seems that Godard shot no footage of the riots. There is one famous image of him brandishing a super-8 camera but he told Chris Marker that it had no film inside.

25. Interview, Anne Wiazemsky, August 2002. The following year, 1969, Tolmatchoff asked Godard if, according to a long-standing promise, he could use his name to help get a film off the ground. Godard said that he would have to ask his political group for permission and reported back that permission had been refused.

26. At this parting Bourseiller told Godard that 'there will always be a bowl of soup for

you here' and indeed about a year later, there was a knock on the door and Godard asked, 'Where is the soup?', but having eaten, he departed never to return.

27. Interview, Jean-Pierre Gorin, April 2002.

28. Hercules Bellville and Adil Jussawalla, 'Eye Witness Reports of the Godard Explosion at the NFT', *Listener* 12 December 1968.

29. Wiazemsky says that at this time Godard had 'an extraordinary capacity for hate'.

30. See Michael Goodwin, Tom Luddy, Naomi Wise, 'The Dziga Vertov Film Group in America: An Interview with Jean-Luc Godard and Jean-Pierre Gorin,' *Take One* vol.2. no.10 (March–April 1970).

31. *Cahiers du cinéma*, Supplement to no.437 special Godard (November 1990), p.60.

32. Interview, Claude Nedjar, July 2002.

33. Truffaut had originally been interested in the project but had to pass when the financing for *Fahrenheit 451* was in place. In a letter which had thrilled the writers, Robert Benton and David Newman, Truffaut said that he had 'taken the liberty of passing it on to Jean-Luc Godard'. 'For our producers, however, the idea of Godard didn't sit quite as comfortably as Truffaut. We attempted to quiet their fears, even bully them into our enthusiasm. By the time Godard showed, they were willing to see what happened, if (understandably) nervous about a director who had the reputation of (a) making movies in three weeks and (b) never having worked from a script in his entire career.

'Once again the ever-helpful Helen Scott was present, but the meeting between all of us – producers, writers and Godard – remains more risible in her memory than in ours. Godard was everything we had heard – mercurial, impulsive, rash, brilliant. What it boiled down to was this: he had been supposed to start another film in Paris next month, but he didn't feel much like doing it. He liked the script of *Bonnie and Clyde* very much and thought he would do that. In three weeks from now.

'Our producers went white. But, they said, we were not ready, that is, there was no deal, no financing, no studio. Godard said it didn't matter; we immediately agreed with him. Why not? He said, that day, two things which are forever writ upon our memories: "If it happens in life, it can happen in a movie." This to the producer's objection that the key elements might not be perfectly pulled together in three weeks time. And, "We can make this film anywhere; we can make it in Tokyo." This in response to the producers' objection that weather conditions were not right in Texas for shooting at this time of year. A call to the weather bureau in Dallas was made. Strong possibilities of precipitation were predicted. "You see?" said the producer.

' "I am speaking cinema and you are speaking meteorology," said Godard.

'Whatever the problems, we two were ready to commit anything to him under any conditions to go ahead. Make it in Tokyo, so what, it'll be great. And in its own way, it surely would have been. But there was no moving the producers, who were understandably caught short, especially in the area of financing, and there was no *détente* that could be made between them and Godard, in spite of our pleas. The next day we met him for a drink at his hotel. "Call me when the script reverts to your ownership," said he. An hour later he was on the plane back to Paris and the pre-production of *Alphaville*.' *Bonnie and Clyde*, compiled and edited by Sandra Wake and Nicola Hayden (London: Lorrimer, 1972), pp.23–24.

34. Leacock and Pennebaker's method was often called 'direct cinema'. In his article Godard uses the more general term of 'cinéma vérité'.

35. Interview Tom Luddy, April 2002.

36. Almost all the material used in this film was shot by Pennebaker himself. His own explanation for this was that Godard's interest was entirely in what Leacock was shooting. Left to his own devices, Pennebaker spent a lot of time shooting the filming itself.

37. Jean-Luc Godard, op.cit., p.239.

38. In addition to Godard and Roger, there were various visitors from Paris including Daniel Cohn-Bendit and his girlfriend.

39. Roger himself says that the situation was more complicated, and that he and Wiazemsky often shared jokes at the expense of Pépé (Grandad) Godard. There can be no doubting the strength of the attachment that had linked the turbulent young Maoist to the middle-aged film-maker. Roger married Juliet Berto who was to die tragically young in 1990. Grief-stricken, Roger decided to abandon both France and film-making for the West Indies. Godard rang him and invited him down to Rolle in an effort to dissuade him. Roger spent two days in Switzerland during which Godard didn't say a word. When Godard dropped Roger at the train station, he told him, 'You see – you can't go to the West Indies because that will leave me with no one to talk to.'

40. Godard says that he never used this phrase.

41. Sheila Rowbotham, *Promise of a Dream: Remembering the Sixties* (London: Penguin, 2000), pp.220–221.

42. Godard and Gorin give a similar description in an American interview. Gorin – 'What happened was that the two Marxists really willing to do the film took power, and . . .' Godard – 'All the anarchists went to the beach.' Michael Goodwin, Tom Luddy and Naomi Wise, op. cit.

43. For Wiazemsky, Godard's obsessive jealousy was the major cause of the marriage's breakdown.

44. See Georges Sadoul, préface de Jean Rouch, *Dziga Vertov* (Paris: Editions Champs Libres, 1971) Annette Michelson ed. *Kino-eye: The Writings of Dziga Vertov* (Berkeley and Los Angeles: University of California Press: 1984). Vlada Petric *Constructivism in Film: The Man with a Movie Camera* (Cambridge: Cambridge University Press, 1987).

45. Christine Aya, who worked as editor on all the Dziga Vertov material stresses the joyful nature of the collaborative work.

46. For a more extended analysis of *Lotte in Italia* and the other Dziga Vertov films see Colin MacCabe et al., op.cit., chs.3–5.

47. 'Ideology and Ideological State Apparatuses (Notes Towards an Investigation)' in *Lenin and Philosophy and Other Essays*, translated Ben Brewster (London: New Left Books, 1971), pp.121–173. The essay was written at the beginning of 1969 and first published in French in April 1970. Gorin read it soon after it was written and before shooting *Lotte in Italy* in December 1969. The great majority of the film was shot in Godard and Wiazemsky's rue Saint-Jacques flat, although there were some shots of Rome and Milan picked up on a wind-up Bolex.

48. Godard was immediately fascinated by the Black Panthers. Almost all his letters and telegrams to Luddy over the next two years include requests for Panther material and this material is immediately reflected in *One Plus One*.

49. This was not mere paranoia. Their Palestinian contact in Paris, the PLO representative for France, Mahmuid El Hamshari, had been assassinated by Mossad.

50. Interview, Jean-Luc Godard, December 1988.

51. The Dziga Vertov Group did not issue membership cards, but the following names are associated with it at one time or another: Paul Bourron, Jean-Pierre Gorin, Armand Marco, Gérard Martin, Isabelle Pons, Jean-Henri Roger, Raphaël Sorin, Anne Wiazemsky. Bourron and Marco were cameramen. Whether the women really participated in the group is debatable. Claude Nedjar often acted as producer for the group.

52. She was to win an Oscar in the following year (1972) for *Klute* (dir. Alan Pakula).

53. Louis Althusser, *L'Avenir dure longtemps* (Paris: Stock/IMEC, 1992), p.225. In *Le fond de l'air est rouge*, Chris Marker describes Overney's funeral as 'the last parade'.

54. Colin MacCabe, op.cit., p.75. Although there are no accounts of Godard or Gorin actively contemplating terrorism, Sorin tells a hilarious and frightening story of Bourron wanting to make a bomb during the shooting of *Vent d'est*. Sorin suggested that he make a 'very small one'. It was still enough to destroy the hotel bathroom where they were staying. Godard regards the story as a legend.

55. Michael Goodwin, Tom Luddy and Naomi Wise, op.cit.

56. Isabelle Pons, interview March 2002.

57. Zhisui Li, *The Private Life of Chairman Mao* (New York: Random House, 1996).

58. Linhart suffered a collapse in May, unable to reconcile the theoretical primacy of the working class with the student revolution happening in the streets outside the Ecole. Gorin attended the meeting at the Ecole at which Linhart ordered his Marxist-Leninist troops to steer clear of this diversionary battle. Gorin, like many others, ignored Linhart. See Hervé Hamon and Patrick Rotman, op.cit., pp.464–81.

59. Miller married Jacques Lacan's daughter and has become 'the guardian of the flame' of the Lacanian heritage.

5 The Arrière-Boutique: Anne-Marie Miéville and Rolle

1. 'Il faut avoir femmes, enfants, biens, et sur tout de la santé, qui peut; mais non pas s'y attacher en manière que nostre heur en depende. Il se faut reserver une arrière boutique toute nostre, toute franche, en laquelle nous establissons nostre vraye

liberte et principale retraicte et solitude.' Montaigne, *Essais* 1,39 *'De la Solitude'*. Book I. chap. xxxix.

2. The best general introduction to Bataille's thought is his *Eroticism* (London: Penguin 2001). For Kojève on Hegel, see *Introduction à la lecture de Hegel* (Paris: Gallimard, 1979).

3. Anne Wiazemsky told Bernardo Bertolucci in 1967 that she wished to undertake an analysis, but that Godard was convinced that psychoanalysts sexually abused their patients.

4. There are letters in the Zoëtrope files which suggest that at one point Godard was thinking of approaching Paul Newman to play Freud.

5. Godard's contradictory interest in analysis is well captured by his claim to 'occasionally' consult a psychoanalyst (G:2:25). Analysis is not an occasional therapy.

6. See Christophe Bourseiller, *Vie et mort de Guy Debord 1931–1994* (Paris: Plon, 1999), and Vincent Kaufman *Guy Debord: la révolution au service de la poésie* (Paris: Fayard, 2001).

7. Jean-Jacques Schuhl, *Ingrid Caven* (Paris: Gallimard, 2000), p.144.

8. There is a very mannered television programme made in 2000 by Michel Royer entitled *Godard à la télé* which shows just how present Godard has been on French television screens in the past two decades.

9. The Anti-Oedipus refused all terms of interiority and identity in favour of a continuous circulation of energies. The child was not formed within the limited play of the parents' desire, but by the continuous machinery of desire offered by the society. Godard had been deeply influenced by the Anti-Oedipus – the treatment for *Moi, Je* would seem to have been written with Deleuze and Guattari beside the typewriter. However, the influence seems to have been short-lived. *Numéro deux*, while concentrating on the relation between family and society, uses none of the key terms of the Anti-Oedipus in its investigation.

10. Gilles Deleuze, 'On "Sur et sous la communication"' Three questions about *Six Fois Deux* in *Jean-Luc Godard Son + Image 1974–1991*, ed. Raymond Bellour with Mary Lea Bandy (New York: Museum of Modern Art, 1992), p.35. First published in *Cahiers du cinéma* 271 (November 1976).

11. Some of the materials that Godard produced for the Mozambique government can be found in the special issue of *Cahiers*, no. 300. For more on Godard's television see Colin MacCabe et al., op.cit., ch.6.

12. Peter Cowie, *Coppola* (London: Faber and Faber, 1998), p.151–153.

13. Miéville has the primary script-writing credit on *Sauve qui peut*. In all the interviews at the time of its release, Godard stressed that it was Miéville who had urged him to return to the cinema.

14. In an interview with Margot Kernan in the *Washington Post* on 14 September 1980, Godard was even more explicit. 'Anne-Marie asked me how I can invent things like that, and I was obliged to say, because I experienced it.' That is, Godard says, he was once under the desk. 'Yes, and on top of the desk saying the same things to the girls.

There is no difference between my own inside life and my outside life which is there in the picture, with the help of what I see, for I'm not capable of inventing anything.'

15. Godard's sardonic humour is a constant counterpoint to the seriousness of his purpose. Pierre Edelman, a maverick of the French cinema, tells a story which 'si non è vero, è ben trovato'. While shooting *Nouvelle Vague* Godard asked Alain Delon to get into a Mercedes. Delon objected to the nationality of the car and returned to his room in the villa. Some time later he heard the crew turning over, and looking out of his window he saw the camera filming a rather bedraggled donkey beside the car. Godard was speaking to the donkey, 'Alain Delon, get in the car.' Delon approached Godard and asked him what the hell was going on. Godard replied that he had noticed the donkey as he was coming to the shoot. He'd discovered that the donkey was called Alain Delon, and as the star had absented himself, he was shooting the scene with his namesake. Delon said that the donkey was no longer required and got into the car.

16. Belmondo op.cit., p.346–349

17. According to his biography, Truffaut did make some kind of contact at the time of Godard's accident in 1971 (T:585). Truffaut himself refers to 'a couple of moments when we softened (you when I was unhappy in love, me when you were in hospital)' François Truffaut, *Correspondence* edited by Gilles Jacob and Claude de Givray (Rennes: 5 Continents/Hatier, 1988), p.430. English translation Gilbert Adair (London: Faber and Faber, 1988), p.389.

18. François Truffaut, op.cit., p.424/p.384.

19. ibid p.430–431/p.390.

20. If the collaboration with Beauviala in Grenoble had not lived up to expectations – see the long discussion (G1:519–557) – the desire to control the means of production had not wavered at all. The fantasy hatched in the editing room rented for him by Nedjar in 1970 – to fulfil the paternal ambition of living and working in the same place – has been all but realised in Rolle.

21. After seeing *One from the Heart* Godard sent the following note to Coppola: 'Congratulations on "One from the Heart". I am proud to be associated with your way of moviemaking stop JLG'.

22. Isabelle Huppert recalled her initial discussion with Godard about the part: 'We stopped for lunch and I asked him to talk to me a little about the character. He thought for a moment and then replied "It is the face of suffering." That was it. Afterwards he also talked to me of Anna Karina in *Vivre sa vie* which I hadn't seen then. Many years after, when I did see it, I understood why he had said that to me.' 'Isabelle Huppert: Ma vie d'actrice', propos recueillis par Thierry Klifa, *Studio Magazine* 181, September 2002, p.66.

23. James Joyce, *A Portrait of the Artist as a Young Man* (London: Penguin, 1992), p.222. Stephen's theory is placed in montage with student obscenity and the sounds of the city.

24. Colin MacCabe, 'Every Man for Himself', *American Film* June 1984, vol. 9, No.8, p.34.

25. Two exceptions to this general rule were *Allemagne 90 neuf zéro* and *Les Enfants jouent à la Russie*. In both cases Godard relied more heavily than usual on his collaborators – Goupil in Germany, Champetier in Russia.

26. From an economic point of view, it is probably pointless to use models from cinema production to capture Godard's economic being. Much more profitable would be an analysis in terms of Swiss industry: see Jonathan Steinberg *Why Switzerland?*, 2nd edition (Cambridge: Cambridge University Press, 1996) pp. 163–205. I give the example of *Aria* to counter one of the prevalent myths about Godard. This should not be taken to mean that Godard does not have rows over money; but on all the occasions where I am aware of the details money has served only as the medium of the row, it has never been the cause of the basic disagreement. The one exception to this is the film that he was commissioned to make about Mexico during the Grenoble period, for which he certainly received the money. When a new Mexican administration audited the Ministry it was discovered that although the money had been spent, no film had been delivered. Godard told Tom Luddy that he had indeed delivered a film to Mexico City but the Mexicans had never retrieved the film from the airport because they didn't want to make their final payment. Rumour suggests that a film was made: ninety minutes of tourist posters of Mexico. Rumour also says that much of this money funded *Comment ça va?* Commenting on these rumours, Godard referred to the unicorn.

27. See Peter Wollen, 'L'eternel retour' in *Jean-Luc Godard: Son + Image, 1974–1991* eds. Raymond Bellour with Mary Lea Bandy (New York: The Museum of Modern Art, 1992), pp.187–195.

28. Synopsis attached to the dialogues of the finished film.

29. *Art Press*, Special Godard, Hors Serie no.4 (December 1984–February 1985) p.40.

30. For much of the crucial period I was teaching my first term in the Department of English at the University of Pittsburgh. From 1985 on Pittsburgh provided the essential material and intellectual support for my decision to link my academic work to a real engagement with film production.

31. Alain Bergala *Nul mieux que Godard* (Paris: Editions Cahiers du cinéma, 1999), pp.221–249.

32. *Soft and Hard* is perhaps the first finished work in which one can begin to see the method at work, for there are glimpses of *Broken Blossoms*, *Contempt*, *Gone with the Wind*, *Frankenstein* and *Rear Window*, all of which reappear in the *Histoire(s)*. Peter Sellars, who plays William Shakespeare the Fifth in *King Lear*, also thinks that the opaque final sequence in the cinema in that film can be read as another form of preparation. Both Freddy Buache and Alain Bergala have talked of early versions in 1985 and 1986: see Michael Temple and James S. Williams 'Introduction to the Mysteries of the Cinema 1985–2000' in *The Cinema Alone: Essays on the Work of Jean-Luc Godard 1985–2000*. ed Michael Temple and James S. Williams (Amsterdam: Amsterdam University Press 2000), pp.14–15.

33. As Michael Witt makes clear in his fine essay, 'Montage, My Beautiful Care or

Histories of the Cinematograph' in *The Cinema Alone* op. cit., pp.33–50, Godard uses the term 'montage' with such a range of reference that it runs the risk of losing all meaning. The very simple idea that cinema discovered that the juxtaposition of two meanings could create a third and that this form of juxtaposition is not, nevertheless, limited to the cinema, remains a relatively specific claim.

34. Godard's final list of programme titles was different. The titles of the eight episodes are 1a *All the Histories*, 1b *A Solitary History*, 2a *The Cinema Alone*, 2b *Fatal Beauty*, 3a *The Currency of the Absolute*, 3b *The Answer of Darkness*, 4a *The Control of the Universe*, 4b *The Signs Amongst Us*.

35. See *Baadasssss Cinema* (Dir. Isaac Julien, Prod: Minerva Pictures).

36. Jacques Aumont: *Amnésies: fictions du cinéma d'après Jean-Luc Godard* (Paris: POL, 1999). One of the chapters from Aumont's book has been translated into English as part of an impressive volume which is largely focused on the histories: *The Cinema Alone: Essays on the Work of Jean-Luc Godard 1985–2000* eds. Michael Temple and James S. Williams (Amsterdam: Amsterdam University Press, 2000).

37. John Milton, *Complete Prose Works* (New Haven: Yale University Press, 1959), vol.2, p.491.

38. Indeed it was only much later, in an interview at the London Film Festival when he explained that the film was made up of three different films, that I could make any sense of it at all. Even with this explanation it still seems a montage too far, an attempt to resolve by juxtaposition ideas that have not yet been understood in themselves. As always, however, there are shots and scenes that rob one of breath: the tanks breasting the slope down to the Villa Anthy or the actress Bérangère Allaux trying vainly to find the 'Yes' that will satisfy the director. Godard claims that the biographical is irrelevant in understanding this film, but his own account of it seems largely biographical (G 2:375).

39. The phrase 'We are still all here' is used by Godard in the *Histoire(s) du cinéma*. It is taken from the Acts of the Apostles 16:28. The phrase is used after Paul and Timothy have been released from prison by an earthquake. The prison governor is about to commit suicide when Paul stops him with the words 'We are all still here.' The episode is fascinating for offering us one of those moments when we glimpse that conjunction of the Greek mystery cults and Judaism from which Christianity was woven – see Richard Seaford 'Thunder, Lightning and Earthquake in *The Bacchae* and 'The Acts of the Apostes' in *What is a God?*, ed. A.B. Lloyd (London: Duckworth, 1997), pp. 139–151. Within the Christian tradition itself the text is used as part of the teaching which forbids suicide.

40. Gilles Jacob, who critically championed Godard's work in the sixties and who has made Godard a constant visitor to Cannes since he became director of the festival in the late seventies, emphasised to me in conversation that 'Godard est un très bon joueur.'

41. See Gregory Vlastos, *Socrates, Ironist and Moral Philosopher* (Cornell: Cornell University Press, 1991).

42. The slogan is used again by Godard most importantly in *Histoire(s) du cinéma*.

43. Pierre Reverdy, *Le Gant de crin* (1927) (Paris: Flammarion, 1968), p.30.

44. Godard has repeatedly said that all the young *Cahiers* critics shared the post-war adolescent dream of bringing out a volume at Gallimard, the publisher of Camus and Sartre. The old dream still had some force. According to Sollers, Godard insisted that the four volumes come out in the traditional orange covers that Gallimard itself had abandoned.

45. Gaumont had once again become a patron of Godard in the eighties and it was Gaumont who took on the massive task of clearing all the rights so that the series could be commercially released. There can be no doubting the commitment of Gaumont's chairman Nicolas Seydoux to Godard's mammoth enterprise. Seydoux, a member of the immensely rich, powerful and Protestant Schlumberger clan, had been part of the bloc that had prevented Rassam gaining control of Gaumont in the early seventies. By the early eighties Gaumont was in tremendous trouble, losing more than $100,000,000 in the period between 1983 and 1985. Rumour has it that in this period Godard wrote to Seydoux asking if there was anything he could do to help. Rumour also relates that when Seydoux was taxed within the company as to why he was spending so much of the company's resources on the *Histoire(s) du cinéma*, Seydoux recalled those dark days and Godard's letter, adding 'he was the only one who wrote'.

46. Jacques Aubert *Joyce avec Lacan* (Paris: Navarin, 1987), p.46.

47. For one of the clearest expositions of the role of incest, see Georges Bataille, *Eroticism* (London: Penguin, 2001), pp.197–200.

48. Richard Brody, 'An Exile in Paradise', *New Yorker* (20 November 2000), pp.62–76.

49. It is of course a consequence of this analysis that we have to consider Godard as a holy man, a Lacanian saint. Anybody bought up like me within the Catholic Church, which stresses the redemption of the fallen soul by grace and whose saints are as such redeemed fallible creatures, saints brimming over with the milk of human kindness, may find that the ascription of sainthood to Godard beggars belief. If, however, we think of those Protestant 'saints' of the Reformation, those independent men so confident of their own relation to God, so secure in their own rectitude that, like Milton, they could conceive of a church with only one member, then it is easy to see Godard as such a saint.

50. The quotation is a riff on Coleridge via Borges: 'Se um homem, em sonhos, atravessasse o Paraiso, e Ihe oferecessem uma flor como provo da sua estade ai, e se, ao despertar, encontrasse essa flor na mao . . . que pensar, nesse caso?' Jorge Luis Borges, 'A flor de Coleridge', *Novas Inquiricoes* (Lisbon: Editorial Querco, 1983), p.17. 'If a man could pass thro' Paradise in a Dream, & have a flower presented to him as a pledge that his Soul had really been there, & found that flower in his hand when he awoke – Aye? and what then?" Samuel Taylor Coleridge, Notebook entry *c.* 1815–1816, *Coleridge's Notebooks*, a selection edited by Seamus Perry (Oxford: Oxford University Press, 2002), p.127. Perry notes that Coleridge himself is adapting a quotation from the German writer Jean Paul: 'Oh, if a mortal

man were to wander in a dream through Elysium, if vast unfamiliar flowers were to
close above him; if one of the blessed were to offer him one of these flowers, saying:
"Let this remind you when you awake that you have not been dream" – how he
would yearn for that Elysian land, whenever he looked at the flower.'

Envoi

1. To what extent the attempt to place film at the centre of a state education system was
a doomed enterprise, to what extent it failed because of those who were in charge of
the Institute when New Labour came to power and to what extent it was deliberately
destroyed by a New Labour determined to eradicate all independent centres of
thought through the use of pliant placemen, must be for others to judge. See Colin
MacCabe, 'Cultural Vandalism,' *Screen International* (4 May 2001).

2. All these matters are discussed in the long interview with Alain Bergala published at
the beginning of the second volume of *Jean-Luc Godard par Jean-Luc Godard* in
1998. In the same interview Godard talks of his relationship with the actress
Bérangère Allaux who plays the actress in *For Ever Mozart*. For Godard the
relationship in which 'nothing happened' was part of a desire to find another
family as a way of finding a different access to his own history. This was the
determining factor, not his 'episodic taste for too young women' (G2:22–23).

3. Since 1996 Godard has published *JLG/JLG, For Ever Mozart, 2 × 50 ans du
cinéma français, Allemagne 90 neuf zéro, Les Enfants jouent à la Russie* at POL. In
each case the title adds the word 'phrases'.

4. Godard had tried, particularly on *Passion*, to mix film and video, but in the end there
was a strict division of medium used – the features on film, the scenarios on video.

5. There is a suggestion that Godard experienced this flight in 1940 in terms of a
recently published children's book Edouard Paisson's *Le Voyage d'Edgar* (Paris:
Grasset, 1938), whose cover is prominent in the film.

6. Freud's fundamental insight into our bisexual being is the insight that we imaginatively identify with both parents.

7. Maria Torok and Nicholas Abraham *The Shell and the Kernel: Renewals of
Psychoanalysis*, edited, translated and with an introduction by Nichola T. Rand
(Chicago: University of Chicago Press, 1994).

8. If one really wished to chart the decline of Hollywood, one could do no better than
to compare two films on mental illness, Samuel Fuller's *Shock Corridor* (1963) and
Ron Howard's *A Beautiful Mind* (2001). Fuller's grasp of the torque of the

individual and the social is brilliantly analysed in Adam Simon's *The Typewriter, the Rifle and the Movie Camera* (1995). It is difficult to find words to describe Howard's mendacious travesty of one of the great American lives, but it is a perfect example of the school of Spielberg. David Thompson understates well in his introduction to *The New Biographical Dictionary of Film* (New York: Knopf, 2002): 'When a thing called *A Beautiful Mind* is so well received, I wonder why so few observe that film (or *that* film, anyway) doesn't know how to get into the mind.'

9. There can be no denying, however, that Hollywood cinema is to all artistic intents and purposes dead. This should not surprise. If we look at the vital lifetimes of the Elizabethan stage or Attic tragedy they hardly stretch two decades while Hollywood had nearly eight. Even in the nineties occasional flickers like *Groundhog Day* or *A Perfect World* recalled former greatness.

10. Richard Brody provides a great deal of detail on Mailer's unwillingness to explore the theme of incest with his own daughter on screen, 'An Exile in Paradise' *New Yorker*, 20 November 2000, pp.62–76.

11. Jesus himself uses the word 'image' only in reference to the question of separation of spirit and state – it is the image of Caesar on the coin which justifies 'Render unto Caesar that which is Caesar's and unto God that which is God's.' Paul uses the Greek word *eikon* on eight occasions but always in the context of the relation between man and God or Christ and God. Rhetorically Godard's words recall the most famous passage of Paul in Corinthians (I, 15: 12–57) in which he promises triumph over death – probably the single most concise statement of Christian hatred of this mortal and corrupt body.

12. There is some evidence that Shakespeare emphasised this in the Folio text, where it is Cordelia rather than her husband, the French King, who is at the head of the French army – see William Shakespeare, *King Lear* ed. R.A. Foakes (London: Arden Shakespeare, 1997), pp.140–142.

Filmography

1. The members of the Dziga Vertov Group varied from film to film. See credits for each individual film.

2. For example, the technical list submitted to the CNC for *Charlotte et son Jules* (1958) credits Charles Bitsch as the director of photography, with Michel Latouche as his assistant. In reality, Latouche was entirely responsible for the photography of the film. Since Latouche, however, did not yet have his professional card as d.p. from the CNC, the producer was obliged to list Bitsch (who did already have his card). Charles Bitsch recalls that Pierre Braunberger regularly submitted his name to the CNC on films Bitsch never worked on, in order to meet the demands of the CNC.

3. Godard in an interview with Henry Chapier, 'Jean-Luc Godard à bâtons rompus,' *Combat*, 17 August 1967, p.9. My translation.

4. It is worth noting that for the release of *Sauve qui peut (la vie)* in France, Godard

insisted that Goupil's short film *Le Père Goupil* precede all screenings of his film (just as Godard would later do with Miéville's short *Le Livre de Marie* and '*Je vous salue, Marie*'), another indication of Godard's recognition of Goupil's contribution to *Sauve qui peut (la vie)*. For more on Goupil's collaboration with Godard, see the credits for *Allemagne 90 neuf zéro*.

5. According to Daniela Giuffrida's filmography, the music was added by Pierre Braunberger, borrowing from other films he produced.

6. Godard shot *Charlotte et son Jules* with the leftover footage from Chabrol's *Le Beau Serge*. See Michel Vianey, *En attendant Godard* (Paris: Bernard Grasset, 1966), p.49.

7. Cécile Décugis is frequently listed as editor or assistant editor for this film. In a conversation on 1 November 2002, Cécile Décugis acknowledged that her name was listed as editor on the credits submitted to the CNC, but that in fact it was Godard who edited it. Given the strict regulations of the CNC, this practice of lending one's name for the technical credits of a film submitted to the CNC was apparently widespread. Similarly, William Lubtchansky would act as a 'prête-nom' for Gérard Martin on *Numéro deux*. See the credits for that film.

8. On a traditional film crew, a Director of Photography usually has three assistants: the cameraman, the focus-puller, and the second assistant. Coutard worked with two assistants at most, and although Claude Beausoleil or Georges Liron are frequently credited as cameraman, it is Coutard himself who framed the shots. With Coutard a new trend was begun, and subsequent directors of photography, including Alain Levent, William Lubtchansky and Armand Marco, all of whom worked with Godard, did likewise. In order to move up in the ranks, a second assistant needed a minimum of three feature films to graduate to the position of first assistant, at which point a first assistant could acquire the much needed professional working card from the CNC.

9. One of the first feature films shot with a portable camera. Presumably, Coutard had used the Cameflex Eclair while serving as a reporter for the French army during the war in Indo-China. The Cameflex had one major drawback: a fairly noisy camera, it necessitated the post-synchronisation of the soundtrack. The post-synchronisation of *A Breathless* took longer than the shoot.

10. Claude Chabrol and Alain Resnais were previous recipients of the Jean Vigo Prize.

11. While preparing *Le Petit soldat*, Godard indicated that its topic would be a new one for a New Wave film: a political thriller addressing a contemporary situation. As Godard began to prepare his second film, the situation in Algeria was reaching a climax. Within the film-maker's circle, his editor Cécile Décugis was directly implicated in the Algerian struggle, and possibly provided a direct inspiration for the film. Questioned by the police in August 1958, Décugis was sentenced, on 13 March 1960, to five years in prison for her involvement with the FLN. See: Hervé Hamon and Patrick Rotman, *Les Porteurs de valises: La Résistance française à la guerre d'Algérie* (Paris: Albin Michel, 1979).

Décugis was thus unavailable to edit *Le Petit soldat,* and the edit was begun by Nadine Marquand. For personal reasons, however, Marquand quickly abandoned the job. Godard asked assistant editor Lila Herman to recommend someone, and she suggested Agnès Guillemot, one of her professors at l'IDHEC.

12. It is no accident that there are no travelling shots in *Les Carabiniers.* Charles Bitsch recalls that Godard wanted to shoot the film completely in the manner of the reportages that Coutard shot for the French army in Indo-China. Interview, Charles Bitsch, 10 December 2002.

13. Charles Bitsch remembers that there was also an Italian assistant director on the set of *Contempt,* but no longer remembers his name. Similarly, the name of William R. Sivel's boom operator is not known.

14. Scheduled to screen in September 1963 at the Venice Film Festival, *Contempt* was withdrawn by its American producer Joseph E. Levine. Levine demanded that Godard add more shots of Bardot in the buff. Godard responded by drawing up a budget for an additional week of shooting at an exorbitant cost, thinking that it would never be accepted. But the budget was OK by Levine and shortly thereafter in the Studios Jean Mineur, Godard directed several additional scenes. Coutard was unavailable, and Godard hired the young cameraman Alain Levent for the additional work. Thus, Levent shot the the famous scene, following the opening credits, of Bardot and Piccoli on a bed. In addition, inserted within the long scene between Bardot and Piccoli in their Rome apartment, are several shots filmed by Levent: a shot of Bardot running by a lake, and three different shots of Bardot nude against a white, blue and red background. Finally, Jack Palance was also specially flown in from Hollywood to shoot a brief scene with Bardot, to make clear their physical relation. That scene (Palance holds up Bardot's panties) existed briefly, but was subsequently cut from the film. Alain Levent recalls that Godard kept the negative for these additional scenes until payment was effected. Interview with Alain Levent, 23 November 2002.

15. Bardot brought with her several technicians on the set of *Contempt*: Ghislain Dussart, her personal photographer, Tanine Autré, the costumer designer, Laurence Clairval, the wardrobe person, and William R. Sivel, the sound engineer.

16. In the pre-credits submitted to the CNC, Godard envisioned using a Cameflex and a Mitchell for *Bande à part.* Ultimately, Coutard used an Arriflex instead of a Cameflex. The Arriflex, with a blimp, had the distinct advantage over the Cameflex of allowing for synch sound to be recorded with the image.

17. Georges Liron, Jean Garcenot and the gaffer Fernand Coquet all served in the French army in Indo-China with Raoul Coutard. Raymond Cauchetier, who was the set photographer on *Breathless* and *Une Femme est une femme,* served in the French air force in Indo-China. Coutard and his assistants were often referred to as 'Coutard et ses anciens d'Indo'. Occasionally, Godard's collaborators have appeared in small roles or as extras in his films. In *Une Femme mariée,* Georges Liron plays the role of Charlotte's doctor.

18. The credits submitted to the CNC list Nogaret as 'décorateur' (set designer).

19. In the 1960s, Antoine Bonfanti was one of the only sound engineers to work both in recording direct sound and in sound mixing. For Godard, Bonfanti often collaborated with René Levert who recorded the direct sound, while he did the post-production mixing. On *Une Femme mariée* and *Caméra-Œil*, Bonfanti exceptionally recorded the direct sound and did the post-production mixing. Bonfanti was one of the few technicians who made the transition to Godard's militant period, no doubt because he had no *parti pris* against working in 16 mm and because he believed in a politically engaged cinema.

20. Collin's first film for Godard as chief editor; Guillemot supervised. Collin, like Lila (Lakshmanan) Herman, had studied under Agnès Guillemot at l'IDHEC.

21. In the technical credits for the film submitted to the CNC, Eric Simon is listed as the 'ensemblier', (in English: set decorator) that is, the person who, on a traditional film set, works in close collaboration with the 'chef décorateur' (art director) and 'décorateur' (set designer). On *Pierrot le fou*, as in most of Godard's work, there was neither an art director nor a set designer. (Pierre Guffroy is, however, often listed as art director on *Pierrot le fou*. Godard originally wanted to blow up the house at the end of the film, and Guffroy was to be responsible for that. In the end, because of lack of funds, Godard settled for blowing up Belmondo, and Guffroy did not do the film. Interview, Pierre Guffroy, 1999.)

22. The film-within-film was shot in Stockholm.

23. Not to be confused with Jacques Baratier, the film-maker.

24. Nephew of the director of photography Curt Courant. Kurant remembers meeting Godard when the director visited the set of Agnès Varda's *Les Créatures*, shot in the autumn of 1965. According to Kurant, Kodak had recently brought its 4X out on the market, and he recommended using it, instead of Ilford, for *Masculin Féminin*. Kurant did some tests with the 4X (which appear at the end of the film) and Godard accepted Kurant's suggestion. Godard did not ask Kurant to assist with the timing or grading (in French 'étalonnage') of the film but instead did it himself with the timer. Interview, Willy Kurant, 7 December 2002.

25. A graduate of the Vaugirard school (Ecole Nationale de la Photographie et de la Cinématographie), William Lubtchansky began his career as assistant then cameraman to Andreas Winding and Willy Kurant. He became a director of photography in 1968, and has worked in that capacity on several films for Godard. Three of Lubtchansky's assistants went on to become directors of photography for Godard: Caroline Champetier, Dominique Chapuis, and Christophe Pollock.

26. This film was worked on in the lab.

27. This filmography has not included interns on Godard's film crews. An exception has been made for Christine Marsollier, an editing intern on *La Chinoise* and *Week-end*, since she went on to edit most of the Dziga Vertov films under the name of Christine Aya.

28. Godard filmed these two shorts back to back, the way he had done the previous summer with *Deux ou trois choses que je sais d'elle* and *Made in USA*.

29. Marker did the final edit.

30. This list is not necessarily exhaustive.

31. Lubtchansky recalls filming two or three film tracts in Godard's apartment on the rue Saint-Jacques.

32. In the technical credits submitted to the CNC, Godard is listed as director, screenwriter, and director of photography.

33. Lubtchansky filmed outside the Renault Factory at Flins and a few scenes in Paris. He recalls filming in 35 mm. The footage of the events of May was possibly shot by Godard himself with the Beaulieu camera he had recently purchased.

34. Agnès Guillemot, with the help of Christine Aya, assisted minimally on the edit.

35. In the US, Grove Press circulated *British Sounds* under the title *See You at Mao*. This version is signed by 'Jean-Luc Godard and the comrades of the Dziga Vertov Group', and dated March 1969.

36. Lesage lists Elizabeth Kozmian as the editor of *British Sounds*. Christine Aya, who edited the film at Anouchka Films in Neuilly, suggests that Kozmian's name was added because English technicians were needed for the credits.

37. The film was ultimately refused by LWT.

38. According to *Cahiers*, the film was shot in Czechoslovakia at the end of 1968 (*Cahiers du cinéma* 238–239, May–June 1972, p.34). In an article in *Le Nouvel Observateur* entitled 'Jean-Luc ex-Godard', Michel Cournot says the film was made between March and August 1969. The film itself is dated June 1969.

39. In the credits submitted to the CNC, Godard is listed as the screenwriter, director, producer, and director of photography. The only other person mentioned contributing to the film is Jean-Henri Roger, as the assistant director.

40. Lesage incorrectly attributes the voice of Vladimir Lenin to Godard.

41. The technical credits submitted to the CNC on 2 April 1971 list Godard, Cohn-Bendit, and Bazzini as screenwriters, and Godard as the film-maker.

42. The title means 'Struggles in Italy'.

43. In the technical credits submitted to the CNC, Godard is listed as the producer of *Lotte en Italie*; Jean-Pierre Gorin is listed as the director (assisted by Godard) and as screenwriter.

44. Armand Marco recalls that the Debrie was bought for this shoot.

45. The film was ultimately rejected by RAI.

46. Christine Aya recalls that she was working on the edit of this film at Auditel (Avenue du Maine), when she and Godard were involved in a traffic accident on 9 June 1971. Interview with Christine Aya, 19 October 2002.

47. Between November 1969 and the following summer, Godard and Gorin, frequently travelling without a director of photography, made at least six trips to Jordan for this film. See: François Nourissier, 'Godard chez les Feddayin', *L'Express*, 27 July–2 August 1970, p.44.

48. Aya did the initial edit on *Vladimir et Rosa*; the final edit was done by Chantal Colomer.

49. In the credits submitted to the CNC, Godard is listed as screenwriter, director and producer of *Vladimir et Rosa*, and Armand Marco as the director of photography.
50. The film was ultimately refused by German TV.
51. Anne-Marie Miéville.
52. Lesage, p.119.
53. In the technical credits submitted to the CNC on 9 July 1975 (and signed by Anne-Marie Miéville) Godard is listed as the sole author and director of *Numéro deux*. Miéville and Godard are listed as producers with the Sonimage Co. The voice-over of *Numéro deux* likewise identifies Godard and Miéville as producers.
54. Gérard Martin recalls attending a meeting with Godard and several hundred persons at the Cinémathèque Française in 1968. Attempting to break once and for all with the rules of the French film-making establishment, Godard encouraged everyone present to follow his example of tearing up their professional cards. Martin was one of the many who did so. The CNC was aware of this event, and for about ten years refused to replace the professional cards of those who had destroyed theirs. As a result, Martin was officially unable to take credit for the photography of *Numéro deux*, and William Lubtchansky served as a 'prêt-nom'. In the technical credits submitted to the CNC, William Lubtchansky is listed as the director of photography, and Gérard Martin as the video engineer. In the film itself, Martin is credited as technical adviser.
    Martin and his wife Milka Assaf were founding partners with Godard and Anne-Marie Miéville in the Sonimage company. Their little girl Marine Martin plays the role of Vanessa in *Numéro Deux*. Martin remembers that the conversation between the two children in the film (Vanessa and Nicolas) was conducted by himself and Godard, with the children as intermediaries. He whispered to Vanessa/Marine her dialogue via an earphone while Godard did the same for the little boy. Interview, Gérard Martin, 23 May 2002.
55. According to Lubtchansky himself, his contribution to *Numéro deux* was very limited: he was responsible for the 'kinescopage' that is the refilming in 35 mm of the television screen. Interview, William Lubtchansky, 10 November 2002.
56. The 'ici' part of the film was filmed by Lubtchansky in his house in Paris, and the two girls in the film are his daughters.
57. While it is not uncommon on a feature-film shoot to have a second unit, Godard for *Sauve qui peut (la vie)* had the unorthodox idea of asking William Lubtchansky and Renato Berta, two directors of photography with very different styles, to collaborate. See: Michel Ciment and Yann Tobin, 'Entretien: William Lubtchansky', *Positif*, no. 475, September 2000, p.80.
58. In *France tour détour deux enfants* there is no authorial credit and no screenwriting credit (aside from the mention that the work is adapted from G. Bruno's textbook).
59. Miéville is listed in the credits under production.
60. *Jean-Luc Godard par Jean-Luc Godard*, vol. 2, lists these ads as '1988 pubs Girbaud', while Farassino refers to the Girbaud ads 'Closed'.

61. Anne-Marie Miéville.

62. A shoot of eight weeks was anticipated. See *Le Film français* no. 2261.

63. Then President of Canal Plus.

64. *Jean-Luc Godard par Jean-Luc Godard* vol. 2 lists Goupil and Zischler as 'directeurs artistiques', and the technical credits of the film submitted to the CNC on 29 July 1996 also list them with this title, a title signifying their creative contribution to the film (see the remarks on Art Director in the list of crew positions). The credits of the film, however, list them under the heading 'producktionleitung'. This change is perhaps due to the fact that on *Allemagne 90 neuf zéro*, Goupil's various duties this time included financial responsibilities, and he served as the film's production manager. Zischler's position was slightly different (he had, for instance, no budgetary responsibilities) but like Goupil, worked in close collaboration with Godard on the film. Interview, Romain Goupil, 2002.

65. The shoot, according to *Le Film français*, was to have begun in June, but was pushed back. Johanna Ter Steege was originally cast in the film.

66. See Charles Tesson, 'Gall/Godard. Autour d'une métamorphose,' *Cahiers du cinéma* 581 (July–August, 2003): pp.60–69.

67. *Le Film français* 2549.

68. *Eloge de l'amour* was in post-production from February 2000 to January 2001.

Acknowledgements

My first and most important acknowledgement is to the University of Pittsburgh and its Department of English. Dean John Cooper, Vice-Provost George Klinzing and English Chair David Bartholomae all enabled me to take an early sabbatical to write this book and provided me with the necessary support. I am grateful to the British Academy which awarded me grants in both 1993 and 2001 to carry out research in Paris. I must also thank my colleagues and students at the London Consortium and the University of Exeter for putting up with me in the Michaelmas term of 2002 as I finished writing the book.

This book is the product of other people's labour as well as my own. In Sally Shafto I was fortunate enough to have had the assistance of a first-rate Godard scholar who not only provided research and contacts throughout the writing of the book and support in the final editing process, but who also did almost all the crucial picture research and, most important of all, furnished the exemplary filmography. Heather Keenleyside, my colleague at Minerva Pictures, did much of the initial transcription of interviews and also provided bibliographical and editorial assistance. Marie-Pierre Hauville, a good friend since the screening of the 'Century of Cinema' at Cannes, was a constant source of information and encouragement. Frédérique Berthet was the most informed of guides to the economic history of French cinema. In addition I am grateful to Jean Bruno Mukanya, who checked certain records in Geneva for me.

Sally Shafto would like to thank the following: Sylvie Astric (Centre Georges Pompidou); Michelle Aubert, Eric Leroy, Noëlle Huard de Jorna, Aude Vejus-Riellan (Archives Françaises du Film); Christine Barbier-Bouvet (Institut National de l'Audiovisual), Frédéric Boyer (Vidéosphère), Pierre Chaintreul (Centre National de la Cinématogra-

ACKNOWLEDGEMENTS

417

phie), Michael Chaiken, John Gianvito, Michel Marie (Paris III), Roland Rasolofomanjakony (Vidéothèque of Paris III).

This book would have been inconceivable without the resources of two great libraries: the Bibliothèque du Film in Paris and the British Film Institute library in London. Thanks to their very helpful staff and their head librarians, Marc Vernet and Ray Templeton. Much of the background research on French history and culture used the resources of the Ecole Normale Supérieure, rue d'Ulm in Paris. Nancy Goldman at the Pacific Film Archive was most obliging in making their Godard collection available to me.

My agent Andrew Wylie provided me with the most patient and understanding of editors in Liz Calder of Bloomsbury and Jonathan Galassi of Farrar, Straus and Giroux. Bill Swainson provided invaluable editorial advice throughout the writing of the book, and Jonathan Galassi and Pascal Cariss provided the most sharp and acute of editorial comments.

The following read the manuscript in whole or in part and I owe them my thanks: David Bartholomae, Frédérique Berthet, Claude Godard, Jean-Luc Godard, Véronique Godard, Stephen Heath, Margaretta Jolly, Marcia Landy, Heather Keenleyside, Chris Marker, Anne-Marie Miéville, Zoe Pagnamenta, Sally Shafto, Brenda Whitney. I owe a special thanks to Michel Marie for his generosity in directing my studies.

The following provided important help and encouragement: Dudley Andrew, Antoine de Baecque, Mary Lea Bandy, Paul Bove, Isabelle Clerc, Caroline Kaplan, Michael Eaton, Yves Citton, Antoine Compagnon, Lee Grievson, Paula Jalfon, Michal Jarrety, Jean-Pierre Jeancolas, Isaac Julien, Laura Kipnis, Patrizia Lombardo, Rob Mitchell, Laura Mulvey, Keith Reader, Jonathan Sehring, Gerard Vaugeois. Throughout my stay in Paris Moustapha Safouan proved the firmest of friends.

I owe a deep debt of gratitude to Claude and Véronique Godard and to their late sister Rachel. The help and friendship that they extended to me was genuine and generous. I hope this book repays some of their kindness.

Finally, if this book has any merit it is in large part due to conversations with Chris Marker, *il maestro di color che sanno*.

Picture Credits

3. *Match* 29 December 1960: 'Oui, c'est BB'. *Photo: Ghislain Dussart/Rapho.*

4. *Ciné Révélation* no. 196, 1957: 'Brigitte Bardot que l'on voit sur les écrans dans *Une Parisienne*, termine *Les Bijoutiers au clair de lune*.' *All rights reserved.*

5. *Jours de France* 20 June 1959: 'Brigitte Bardot, la plus jolie et la plus célèbre aviatrice du cinéma français.' *Photo: Manuel Litran.*

6. *Match* 14– 21 May 1955: 'Brigitte Bardot à Cannes'. *Photo: Philippe Halsman/ Magnum.*

7. *Match* 23 January 1960: 'B.B. Maman'. *Photo: Walter Carone.*

8. *Jours de France* 17 October 1964: 'Brigitte, son plus bel anniversaire'. *Photo: Ghislain Dussart/Rapho.*

9. *Match* 4 June 1960: 'Une Nouvelle Affaire Bardot'. *Photo: Sam Levin.*© *Ministère de la Culture – France.*

149 Brigitte Bardot. *Photo Jacques Harvey. All rights reserved. Collection la Bibliothèque du Film.*

152 Godard demonstrating for Jacques Doniol-Valcroze the handstand he performed for Brigitte Bardot during the filming of *Contempt*, from Doniol-Valcroze's documentary on Godard, 1965. *Photo: Georges Pierre. All rights reserved. Collection Cahiers du cinema.*

153 Jack Palance, Brigitte Bardot and Michel Piccoli in *Contempt*, 1963. *Collection la Bibliothèque du Film.*

154 Five frame stills from *Contempt*, 1963: Brigitte Bardot; Raoul Coutard; Michel Piccoli and Fritz Lang; Jack Palance; Brigitte Bardot, Michel Piccoli and Fritz Lang.

156 Brigitte Bardot and Michel Piccoli in *Contempt*, 1963. *Collection la Bibliothèque du Film.*

164 Anna Karina in *Bande à part*, 1964.

166 Godard on the set of Jacques Doniol-Valcroze's documentary about him, 1965. *Photo: Georges Pierre. All rights reserved. Collection Cahiers du cinéma.*

167 Anna Karina and Eddie Constantine in *Alphaville*, 1965.

168 Anna Karina and Laszlo Szabo in *Alphaville*, 1965.

171 Anna Karina in *Pierrot le fou*, 1965.

171 Jean-Paul Belmondo and Anna Karina in *Pierrot le fou*, 1965.

171 Jean-Paul Belmondo in *Pierrot le fou*, 1965.

173 Chantal Goya in *Masculin Féminin*, 1966.

173 Jean-Pierre Léaud in *Masculin Féminin*, 1966.

174 Intertitles from *Masculin Féminin*, 1966.

176 Laszlo Szabo as Richard Widmark shows his police card while Paula Nelson (Anna Karina) looks on in *Made in USA*, 1966. *Photo: Marilu Parolini. Collection Laszlo Szabo.*

177 Richard Widmark's police card in *Made in USA*, 1966. *Collection Laszlo Szabo.*

177 Anna Karina in a bar in *Made in USA*, 1966.

178 Donald Siegal (Jean-Pierre Léaud) dies in *Made in USA*, 1966.

186 Article announcing Anne Wiazemsky as the lead in Bresson's new film *Au hasard,*

Balthazar in the 'Loisir' section of *Arts,* 3–9 November 1965. *Collection Bibliothèque Mazarine.*

188 Anne Wiazemsky as Marie in *Au hasard, Balthazar,* 1966. *Collection Cahiers du cinéma.*

198 Anne Wiazemsky. *Paris Match,* 5 August 1967. *Reportage Pierre Domenech/Roger Picherie.*

199 Article on the Godard-Wiazemsky wedding in *Paris Match,* 5 August 1967. *Reportage Pierre Domenech/Roger Picherie.*

200 Two frame stills from *Week-end,* 1967.

207 *From right to left:* Godard, Alain Jouffroy, Jacques Roubaud, and Eugène Guillevic (third from left) marching with members of the Syndicat des acteurs, 29 May 1968. *Photo: Jacques Marie, AFP.*

208 Images of Daniel Cohn-Bendit, including the celebrated slogans 'We are all German Jews' and 'We are all undesirable', from silk-screen posters. *Photos: François Fernandez. All rights reserved.*

209 Godard, Paris, May 1968. *All rights reserved.*

210 Godard, Paris, May 1968. *All rights reserved.*

211 Godard and Mick Jagger during the filming of *One Plus One,* 1968. *All rights reserved. Collection Cahiers du cinéma.*

213 Godard and Agnès Guillemot in editing room, 3, rue Washington. *Photo: Yvon Beaugier. Courtesy Télérama. All rights reserved. Collection Agnès Guillemot.*

222 The preparatory class of Lycée Louis-le-Grand '60–'61. Jean Pierre Gorin is seated third from the left in the front row. Robert Linhart is in the second row, standing third from the right. Raphaël Sorin is to his left, Jacques-Alain Miller to his right. *Collection Raphaël Sorin.*

223 Raphaël Sorin and Jean-Pierre Gorin (left) with unknown friend. *Collection Raphaël Sorin.*

226 Raphaël Sorin holds up a book on Dziga Vertov on the set of *Vent d'est* in Rome, 1969. *Collection Raphaël Sorin.*

230 Godard and Jean-Pierre Gorin in Palestine for the shooting of *Jusqu'à la victoire,* 1970. *Collection Isabelle Pons.*

234 Godard looks through the latest issue of the Maoist journal *La Cause du peuple* at the printer's before it goes on sale, Paris, November 1970. *AFP.*

236 Jean-Paul Sartre and Godard at a press conference in Paris, February 1971. *AFP.*

239 Anne-Marie Miéville and Godard in *Après la réconciliation,* 2000. *Collection Cahiers du cinéma.*

242 Anne-Marie Miéville in *Après la réconciliation,* 2000. *Collection Cahiers du cinéma.*

246 'Here' – a family watches the television, from *Ici et ailleurs,* 1976.

246 'Elsewhere' – a young Palestinian prepares for death, from *Ici et ailleurs,* 1976.

252 Pierre Oudry and Sandrine Battistella in promotional cards from *Numéro deux,* 1975.

Index

Films appear under title, with director's name in brackets. JLG signifies Jean-Luc Godard

Eloge de l'amour (JLG film), 50, 62, 187, 320, 322–8, 331–2, 333
Eluard, Paul: *Capital of Pain* (poems), 168
Erlanger, Philip, 104
Esposito, Gianni, 100
Esprit (journal), 59–61, 70
Essex university, 217–18
Estates General of Cinema, 249–50
Et Dieu créa la femme (Vadim film), 147
Eustache, Jean, 239
Existentialism, 56, 205
Express, L' (magazine), 107
Expressionism, 78

Faithfull, Marianne, 266
Fantômas (Feuillade serial), 43, 48
Fascism, 183
Faye, Suzanne, 121
Fellini, Federico, 170
Fémis, La (National Film School), 321
Femme coquette, Une (JLG film), 84
Femme est une femme, Une (JLG film), 110, 133–6, 141, 149, 169
Femme mariée, Une (JLG film), 59, 164–6, 175, 201
Fénélon, François de Salignac de la Mothe, 79
Ferreri, Marco, 250
festival du film maudit *see* Biarritz
Feuillade, Louis, 48
Film comme les autres, Un (JLG film), 209, 248
Film français, Le (trade paper), 108–9
Film-tracts (JLG film), 209, 255–6
films: archiving, 46–7; sound, 59, 78–80; distribution, 60
First World War *see* World War I (1914–18)
Flaubert, Gustave: *Bouvard et Pécuchet*, 93
Flaud, Jacques, 104, 106
Fonda, Jane, 232–4
Fontanets, Hugues, 84
For Ever Mozart (JLG film), 7, 294, 304. 307
Foucault, Michel, 64, 76, 191, 227, 235, 238
Fox film company, 52, 81, 87–8
France: Protestantism in, 18–21; defeat (1940), 25, 50, 60; post-1945 military conflicts, 83; laws on French cinema, 105–7, 201–3; and Algerian war, 132–3; May 1968

events, 180, 200–1, 209–10; Communist Party in, 184–5, 196
France, Anatole, 42, 57
France Soir (newspaper), 128
France tour détour deux enfants (JLG film), 254, 259–60
Franck, Bernard, 102
Franju, Georges, 46
Franju, Jacques, 46–7
French Revolution, 245
Freud, Sigmund, 124–5, 289, 315
Frey, Sami, 149
Froeschel, F.-C., 55
Fromanger, Gérard, 218
Fuller, Sam, 176

Gai savoir, Le (Joyful Knowledge; JLG film), 204, 207, 216, 254, 258
Gaille, Raymond, 32
Galéa, Geneviève, 143
Gallimard (publishers), 70–1, 315
Gance, Abel, 42
Garnett, Tony, 217
Gaulle, Charles de: on Sartre, 56; return to power (1958), 104, 106, 132; and film censorship, 201–3; and May 1968 events, 209–10; and JLG's *Eloge de l'amour*, 331
Gaumont (film corporation), 232, 253, 260–1, 288, 315
Gazette du cinéma, La, 55, 57–8, 63, 70, 72–3, 76
Gégauff, Paul, 55, 87–8
Generale della Rovere (Rossellini film), 120
Genet, Jean: Truffaut and, 69; *Un Chant d'amour*, 55
Geneva: JLG moves to (1952/3), 82–4
Gerig, Hélène (*née* Godard; JLG's aunt), 11, 39
Gerig, Willy, 39
German Social Democratic party, 194
Germany, Year Zero (Rossellini film), 73, 103
Giap, General Vo Nguyen, 115
Gide, André, 7, 52, 83
Giraudoux, Jean: *Pour Lucrèce*, 162
Girl in Every Port, A (Hawks film), 49
Girl with Shoes, The (Schedes film), 126
Giroud, Françoise, 107–8
Giscard d'Estaing, Valéry, 253
Gish, Lillian, 124
Glass, Philip, 330
Godard family: JLG's relations with, 1; in Switzerland, 22
Godard, Claude (JLG's brother):

appearance, 2; birth, 17; sports, 23; piano playing, 24; in Boy Scouts, 30; on parents' marriage breakdown, 30; at Montriant with JLG, 35; and JLG's painting, 36; on JLG's early film scripts, 38; meets JLG on return from South America, 39; and JLG's neurosis, 40; on *Le Petit soldat*, 133
Godard, Georges (JLG's grandfather), 10–12, 35
Godard, Hélène (JLG's aunt) *see* Gerig, Hélène
Godard, Jean-Luc: relations with family, 1–2, 4, 17–18; appearance and manner, 2, 267; use of language, 2; childhood and upbringing in Switzerland, 4–5, 18, 23–6; and religion, 5, 18–19, 23, 317; birth, 17; sports, 23, 28; trapped in France in 1940–1, 25–6, 50; school education, 28–30; attends Lycée Buffon in Paris, 30–2; in Boy Scouts, 30; differences with father, 30, 40; and parents' marriage breakdown, 30; produces pamphlet for Nyon relatives (1947), 32–4; thefts, 32, 34, 40, 70, 82, 84, 150; moves to school in Lausanne, 34–5; writes early film scripts, 35–6, 38; painting, 36; registers at Sorbonne to study anthropology, 36; praises Rouch, 37; trip to South America, 39; separation from family, 40–1; treated in mental hospital, 40; disregard of legal niceties over film rights, 51; in Paris, 52–3; works for Fox, 52, 88; full-time devotion to cinema, 54; reviews in *Gazette du cinéma*, 55; Bazin's influence on, 62–3; at Biarritz festival, 67–8, 70; friendship with Truffaut, 67–8, 70; early film criticism, 72–4, 76–7, 92–4; aesthetic of realism, 76–9, 241; uses pseudonym 'Hans Lucas', 76; writing style, 76; leaves Paris for Switzerland (1952/3), 82; takes Swiss nationality, 83; works as construction site telephonist, 83–4; plays in film, 84; meets Chabrol, 88; works for Braunberger, 88; early fictional shorts, 89–92; provides voice for Belmondo in *Charlotte et son Jules*, 91, 113; contributes to *Arts*, 92,